D1606129

Critical Essays on Washington Irving

Critical Essays on Washington Irving

Ralph M. Aderman

G. K. Hall & Co. • Boston, Massachusetts

Copyright 1990 by Ralph M. Aderman
All rights reserved.

First published 1990.

10   9   8   7   6   5   4   3   2   1

Library of Congress Cataloging-in-Publication Data

Critical essays on Washington Irving : [edited by] Ralph M. Aderman.
   p. cm.—(Critical essays on American literature)
   Includes bibliographical references.
   ISBN 0–8161–8896–3
   1. Irving, Washington, 1783–1859 — Criticism and interpretation.
   I. Aderman, Ralph M. II. Series.
PS2088.C75   1990
818'.209—dc20   90–35739
                                       CIP

The paper used in this publication meets the minimum requirements
of American National Standard for Information Sciences—Permanence of Paper for Printed Library Materials, ANSI Z39.48–1984.
♾™

Printed and bound in the United States of America

CRITICAL ESSAYS ON AMERICAN LITERATURE

This series seeks to anthologize the most important criticism on a wide variety of topics and writers in American Literature. Our readers will find in various volumes not only a generous selection of reprinted articles and reviews but original essays, bibliographies, manuscript sections, and other materials brought to public attention for the first time.

Critical Essays on Washington Irving is a comprehensive collection of scholarship on one of the most important American writers. The book contains both a sizable gathering of early reviews and a broad selection of modern scholarship, including reprinted essays by some of the most distinguished writers and scholars of the century. Among the authors of reprinted reviews and articles are John Lambert, Henry Brevoort, Jr., Henry D. Gilpin, Edgar Allan Poe, Henry A. Pochmann, Walter A. Reichart, Donna Hagensick, Lewis Leary, Donald A. Ringe, and Jeffrey Rubin-Dorsky. In addition to an extensive introduction by Ralph M. Aderman, which provides an overview of Irving's career and the reaction to his work, there are also two original essays commissioned specifically for publication in this volume, new studies by Wayne R. Kime and Jenifer S. Banks. We are confident that this book will make a permanent and significant contribution to American literary study.

James Nagel, GENERAL EDITOR

Northeastern University

For Alice

CONTENTS

INTRODUCTION

The commentary on Washington Irving and his writings is voluminous, as an examination of the scholarly studies and bibliographies will reveal. Irving was subjected to extensive critical scrutiny and enthusiastic appreciation during his lifetime, and interest still runs high as the new scholarly edition of his writings nears completion.[1] Part of the ongoing attention stems from the historical fact that Irving was the first American writer to be extensively praised in England, and part to the fact that his polished style, delicate humor, and attractive subject matter appealed to a wide spectrum of discerning readers. Moreover, in his lifetime Irving was a congenial, accessible gentleman who moved easily among common people and nobility, equally at home in the drawing room, the library, or the counting house, in the stagecoach, the sailing vessel or steamship, or the railroad car. Wherever Irving went after he attained literary success, he was welcomed and feted, often to his discomfort and embarrassment. The public attention and adulation were not of his choosing; they were part of the price he had to pay for his success as a man of letters during the first six decades of the nineteenth century.

The reader approaching Irving needs assistance in making his way through the density of the text. Haskell Springer's reference guide of more than a decade ago,[2] although by no means exhaustive, is a useful starting point for examining the scholarship, criticism, and commentary relating to the work and ideas of America's first successful professional author. Another important source of information about Irving scholarship is the chapter in *Fifteen American Authors Before 1900*, edited by Robert A. Rees and Earl N. Harbert.[3] The author in the original edition was Henry A. Pochmann, the general editor of the Irving edition. In the revised edition James W. Tuttleton updated and expanded Pochmann's essay. In 1936, as a supplement to his two-volume biography, Stanley T. Williams and Mary Allen Edge prepared a bibliography that listed the various editions of Irving's writings, together with selected items of criticism.[4] Three years earlier William R. Langfeld and Philip C. Blackburn issued a descriptive bibliography useful for collectors of Irving's books and anyone else interested in their physical makeup.[5] Their descriptions have been extended by Jacob Blanck in the fifth volume of his *Bibliography of American Literature*.[6] Other lists and guides also include Irving, but they overlap with the sources mentioned above.

Washington Irving's public writing career began in 1802, when he contributed nine essays under the name of Jonathan Oldstyle to his brother Peter's newspaper, the *Morning Chronicle*. For the next fifty-seven years Irving continued to write, and the outpourings from his pen attracted widespread interest and comment from friends and critics at home and abroad. Born in 1783, the year of the treaty of peace with Great Britain at the close of the Revolution, Irving grew up with the new nation and helped to establish its distinctive national literature. Gifted with an easy style, verbal facility, and ready wit, he soon attracted attention with his contributions to *Salmagundi* and with *Knickerbocker's History of New York*. While these books elicited limited praise, with the appearance of *The Sketch Book*, written while he was living in England, he, like Byron, awoke one morning to find himself famous, the toast of literary critics and connoisseurs of good writing on both sides of the Atlantic. *Bracebridge Hall* and *Tales of a Traveller* followed quickly, and Irving was universally acclaimed as one of the finest living prose writers in English. A sojourn in Spain produced his biographies of Columbus and his companions, the *Conquest of Granada*, and *The Alhambra*, the latter a romantic celebration of the Moorish palace and its legends and traditions. Upon returning to the United States in 1832, Irving turned his attention to his native land, its resources, and its heroes, with *A Tour of the Prairies, Astoria, The Adventures of Captain Bonneville*, and the *Life of George Washington*, interspersed with biographies of Mahomet and Oliver Goldsmith, impressionistic sketches of Abbotsford and Newstead Abbey, legends of Moorish Spain, and descriptions and tales relating to his beloved Hudson River. Irving's wide-ranging interests combined with his skill in organizing and presenting a variety of subjects produced a steady flow of books with exceptional appeal to readers in all levels of society.

His early efforts in *Salmagundi*, written in collaboration with James Kirke Paulding and William Irving, attracted limited attention from local critics who noted the satire and ridicule heaped upon human behavior but did not identify the efforts of the individual contributors. A number of the Mustapha letters, which imitated the pattern of the foreign visitor in Goldsmith's *The Citizen of the World*, were reprinted with approval. Negative critical reactions included objections to the occasionally slovenly grammar, inaccurate use of words, and overuse of "God" and "Devil," "expressions which do not add any thing of wit, or force, or dignity, or eloquence, or delicacy, to literary productions."[7] Other reactions were mixed. Thomas Green Fessenden engaged the Salmagundians in a verbal battle in which each side hurled epithets at the other. The splenetic Fessenden was irritated by their jibes, and Irving and company were amused by his testy attacks upon their taste and wit.[8] A more positive response came from an English traveler, John Lambert, who took the book home with him and brought out an edition of it in 1811.[9] Lambert recognized the intrinsic artistic merit in the volume and in a long introduction suggested to his countrymen that "they will not only find considerable amusement and instruction, but also be convinced that the contempt in which American literature is generally held in this country is both unjust and groundless." In his analysis of the humorous satire and social criticism, Lambert positively emphasized the kinship of the American book with its English counterparts both in subject matter and style. This volume, the first published work of Irving in England, elicited a favorable response from the *Monthly Review* of London, which welcomed it "as the fore-runner of a species of writing in America, that above all others tends to cultivate the taste and improve the morals of a nation."[10]

Salmagundi was followed by Irving's first solo work, *Knicker-bocker's History of New York* (1809), the writing of which diverted him while he was recovering from the shock of Matilda Hoffman's death. In it he continued the satiric treatment of the behavior and attitudes of early New Yorkers, some of whose descendants were outraged by his irreverent treatment of their ancestors. At the time the book attracted little critical attention. The *Monthly Anthology* called it an "amusing book . . . the wittiest our press has ever produced," filled with "aptness and fertility of allusions."[11] The *Port Folio*, in noticing the second edition in 1812, remarked that the writings of Diedrich Knickerbocker were so well known that further analysis or discussion was unnecessary.[12] Henry Brevoort presented Walter Scott with a copy of that edition, and the novelist was much taken with its style, which he felt resembled that of Swift and Sterne.[13] When Irving visited Abbotsford a few years later, Scott readily associated him with his burlesque history. However, only after the success of *The Sketch Book* did *Knickerbocker's History* attract a significant readership in England. Enterprising publishers pirated the book in 1820, and within a year seven editions had appeared in Great Britain.[14] Then readers and reviewers examined it as a forerunner of *The Sketch Book* where the same witty style was used for purposes of burlesque and satire. Critics seized upon it for extended commentary, with at least thirteen notices in the periodical press by March 1821.[15]

But it is necessary to back up and examine the genesis and reception of *The Sketch Book*, the work which established Irving's literary reputation in England and reaffirmed his distinctive worth in America. After Irving had gone to Liverpool in 1815 and had seen the family importing business go bankrupt in 1818, he found it necessary to look for a means of supporting himself. He had been working intermittently on impressionistic essays, vignettes, and descriptions in the time he could spare from his duties at the counting house, and he hit upon the idea of publishing these sketches in several clusters over an extended period of time, a pattern which had been successful in the *Salmagundi* venture. With brother Ebenezer and Henry Brevoort handling the details of seeing the material through the press in New York, Irving sent a steady stream of miscellaneous pieces to them.[16]

The first number of *The Sketch Book* quickly attracted attention in the *New York Evening Post* on 26 June 1819, three days after its publication, in a notice prepared by a "literary friend," who may have been Henry Brevoort.[17] By September Richard Henry Dana, Sr. had prepared a long critique with generous extracts of the first two numbers for the *North American Review*,[18] in which he hailed Irving's success in his belletristic endeavors. Although he preferred the vigor of Irving's earlier writings to the "feminine, *dressy*, elegant and languid" style of *The Sketch Book*, Dana regarded his compatriot as "a man of genius," "the most popular writer in the country," and "a standard author amongst us."

Irving's new work soon made its way to England, and the editors there were quick to seize the sketches and reprint them. By early October the *Kaleidoscope, or Literary and Scientific Mirror* of Liverpool had printed "The Wife," and William Jerdan's *Literary Gazette* had excerpted everything from the first number except "Rip Van Winkle."[19] When Jerdan learned that an English edition was in preparation, he refrained from reprinting more of the sketches, an action for which Irving was grateful.[20]

That English edition was published at Irving's expense by John Miller, who went bankrupt just as the volume containing the first four numbers appeared. John Murray, who had earlier declined to bring out the work because he could not secure the copyright, thereupon bought Miller's stock and added the second volume.[21] The shrewd English publisher was prepared to cash in on the widespread public interest created by the excerpts printed in the magazines.

Even before the English edition appeared, John Gibson Lockhart praised Irving in the pages of *Blackwood's*[22] and asked ruefully why he had not published his sketches initially in England. In July 1820 Lockhart devoted another notice to *The Sketch Book*, which was followed a month later by a favorable critique in the *Edinburgh Review* by the powerful Francis Jeffrey.[23] They were joined belatedly by Henry Matthews in the *Quarterly Review*;[24] he too was greatly impressed and called it "one of the best samples which we have yet seen of American literature." The three great British critical journals had examined *The Sketch Book* and had given it their approval, though not without some carping remarks about Irving's Americanisms and occasional grammatical lapses. Other English journals echoed the enthusiastic comments of the "Big Three" reviews.[25] Within a year after its publication in England *The Sketch Book* was generally accepted as a significant literary work, one to be used as a touchstone in assessing other American books.

Irving followed his successful miscellany with another collection of essays, tales, and descriptions centered around Master Simon Bracebridge. It was published almost simultaneously in America and London, and thus John Murray was able to secure a clear copyright. As in the case of *The Sketch Book, Bracebridge Hall* was more widely noticed in England than in America; the English recognized and applauded a fresh talent, even though it came from overseas. With a more mature and better established periodical press they were able to examine and assess in much fuller detail the work of the young American writer who had taken the country by storm. Every English editor wanted to pass along his impressions of Irving's writings, and many who had overlooked *The Sketch Book* remarked about it in their reviews of *Bracebridge Hall.* Many critics praised Irving's restrained and conciliatory attitude toward the mother country, and the reviewer for the *London Magazine*[26] summed up the charitable feelings of many of his compatriots: "The author of the Sketch Book has certainly done very much towards cementing the friendship of his own nation and ours. England respects American talent and modesty—and America kindly regards English honour and hospitality." Some critics observed that *Bracebridge Hall* did not measure up to *The Sketch Book*, that it was too bookish and contrived. Francis Jeffrey, however, was favorably disposed toward the work, though he felt that it was "monotonous and languid," with "too little variety of characters for two thick volumes" and too much of "Irving's extraordinary kindliness and disarming gentleness." Nonetheless, he found the reading of it pleasant, and he was charmed by "the singular sweetness of the composition, and the mildness of the sentiments" and "the liquid music of his periods."[27] In general, the critical response was favorable, even enthusiastic, with most of it coming from the English.[28]

During this period of critical activity in England the *Port Folio* of Philadelphia observed that Irving "continues to enjoy the friendship and the munificent patronage of the English people. . . . His varied excellencies have been extolled by all parties:—even the radicals of the Examiner and the whigs of the Edinburg [*sic*], have for once exchanged the whine of complaint for notes of praise."[29] It might be noted that Jeffrey expressed the wish that Irving would be more politically partisan, that he would, of course, support the Whigs of Jeffrey's party and "be rude and surly to our particular opponents."[30] In other words, Irving's aloofness and political neutrality contributed to the blandness and gentility of his writing, an approach which some of the politically charged reviewers held against him.

With the publication of *Tales of a Traveller* the attitude of English readers changed. Conditioned by the literary quality and attractive subject matter of *The Sketch Book* and, to a lesser extent, of *Bracebridge Hall*, they looked for the American writer to provide them with more fresh, nicely executed material in his newest work. Such was not to be the case, however. Reviewers searched in vain for freshness, novelty, and invention; and when they did not find them, they attacked him with a barrage of hostile notices which dwelt upon all his weaknesses and shortcomings. John Gibson Lockhart, who had been laudatory and sympathetic earlier, found *Tales of a Traveller* very disappointing; only in the American stories of the last section did he find anything worthwhile.[31] Peregrine Bingham, writing in the *Westminster Review*, used his notice to extol the virtues of Utilitarianism and to chide Irving for a lack of concern over social and economic issues and for "the poverty of [his] invention, and the absence of all acuteness in observing manners, and sketching characters," for a lack of intellectual courage, and for "a wavering timidity." In Bingham's view Irving failed in his handling of the problems of the human condition in these tales.[32] Other critics also expressed disappointment with Irving for wasting his talents and for introducing vulgarities and risqué scenes into his stories. Occasionally there was sparing praise, but the prevailing tone throughout these English notices was negative.[33]

The *Quarterly Review*[34] used the occasion of the appearance of *Tales of a Traveller* to comment on the status of Irving's literary reputation, which had ebbed somewhat since the appearance of *The Sketch Book*. Nevertheless, his work had considerable merit, and the reviewer appraised it judiciously and candidly, observing that

> he must in future be true to his own reputation throughout, and
> correct the habits of indolence which so considerable a part of the
> "Tales of a Traveller" evince. The indulgence which he so fairly
> deserved at his outset, as an ingenious stranger, intuitively proficient
> in the style and ideas of the mother country, must now cease, and
> he must be considered in future as not only admitted to the full
> freedom and privileges of the English guild of authorship, but
> amenable at the same time, as an experienced craftsman, to its most
> rigorous statutes.

The article concluded by "congratulat[ing] him on the rank, which he has already gained, of which the momentary caprice of the public cannot long deprive him." In the eyes of the *Quarterly Review* Irving had attained the highest pinnacle in literary and critical circles and must, therefore, be subject to the most rigorous critical standards.

American reviews were far fewer in number and more generally sympathetic. While recognizing his literary achievements, they also anticipated an unfavorable response from British critics who, they felt, perhaps unjustifiably, were reluctant to acknowledge anything meritorious from American writers. Even with this hostile reception, Americans were reminded that Irving "has certainly done more than any other to make us respectable abroad, as a *literary* people, but we think he had advanced our national reputation for scholarship and talent chiefly, by directing the attention of others upon us; by persuading them that we may produce something here worth looking after."[35] The *New-York Mirror*[36] tried to undercut the harshly negative criticism of a Mr. Simpson of the *Philadelphia Columbian Observer*, which it quoted in full, by asserting that Irving "is far from a servile copyist, yet his compositions display the same firm fancy, the same rich, pensive, meditative vein of thought, varied by flashes of wit. . . . " Another critic observed that while the British recognized Irving's literary achievements, they also condemned the "overweening nationality" of Americans in general at the same time that they did not oppose it in themselves.[37] After studying English reactions to Irving's writings, American reviewers of *Tales of a Traveller* often turned to general issues of patriotism and nationalism along with their discussions of literary excellence. With his writings Irving, after all, had provided a swift and forceful rebuttal to Sydney Smith's condescending question, "In the four quarters of the globe, who reads an American book? or goes to an American play? or looks at an American picture or statue?"[38] Now Americans could proudly point to Irving as an exemplar of their achievement in the arts.

With the publication of *Tales of a Traveller* the first phase of Irving's writing, characterized by impressionistic sketches, tales, and descriptions, often spiced with humorous touches, gothic or sentimental elements, and satiric or fanciful details, came to an end. With his permanent departure from England and his ultimate removal to Spain, Irving turned to a new area of interest—history and biography—and a new approach grounded on factual data and fresh research. But even here we discover that he could not entirely abandon the imaginative, fanciful qualities which had permeated his earlier sketches. His accounts of Columbus and his companions (1828, 1831) are filled with luminous details that vivify the facts gathered from dusty documents in the moldering archives in Spain. In *The Conquest of Granada* (1829), through the persona of Fra Antonio Agapida, Irving reverted to the more familiar style of Geoffrey Crayon, and in *The Alhambra* (1832) he returned to the style and pattern of

The Sketch Book. His experiences and researches in Spain broadened his outlook and enabled him to present fresh subjects to a host of loyal followers who were captivated by his polished style and easy narrative manner.

Once again the English reviews predominate in critiquing Irving's *Life and Voyages of Columbus.*[39] Some magazines which would not ordinarily have noticed the biography did so because their readers enjoyed Irving's writing, even, it would seem, when it was more serious and factual. Consequently the biography was widely reviewed, with most critics praising it for its careful research and vivid presentation of details. Some found it too prolix, while others felt that the importance of the subject matter justified the detailed treatment. Some reviewers reacted differently to the same aspect of Irving's treatment. For example, the *Monthly Magazine and British Register*[40] suggested that Irving should have dealt more fully with the moral implications of Columbus's behavior, while the *Eclectic Review*[41] approved of Irving's moral neutrality. Perhaps because of the subject matter, more American reviewers examined the book and gave it their vote of approval, often with copious extracts from it.[42] Actually the book's weaknesses—its heavy borrowing from Navarrete and its lack of critical tone—were overlooked by most reviewers.[43]

When Irving learned that an unauthorized American abridgment of *Columbus* was being planned and when he heard that Murray was interested in an abridged version for his Family Library, he decided to prepare the condensation himself and issue it simultaneously on both sides of the Atlantic. The reception of the abridgement was favorable, with the *Athenaeum* asserting that the new lean version was preferable to the diffusiveness of the original volumes.[44] Other reviewers praised the book for its fusion of "the elegancies of the imagination with the sterling solidity of truth," and for its classic writing which "is replete with interest."[45] American critics ignored the abridgement, apparently preferring to limit their comments to the three-volume edition that had appeared earlier.

Irving followed his *Columbus* with *A Chronicle of the Conquest of Granada*, a romanticized version of the defeat of the Moors by Ferdinand and Isabella. Because he wanted to give freer rein to his imagination than a historian was permitted, Irving created the persona of Fra Antonio Agapida, whose manuscript he was purportedly editing. Some reviewers objected to his approach because they could not determine whether Irving was writing history, fiction, or a combination of both, and they felt that he echoed too many of Fra Agapida's prejudices in his narrative and neglected aspects of Moorish history and culture which would have given balance to it.[46] Henry D. Gilpin in the *American Quarterly Review* used Irving's distorted treatment of Moorish history as an excuse to give a brief summary of the activities of the Moors in Spain,[47] and Irving himself wrote an anonymous digest of the book for the *Quarterly Review*, asserting that his object in presenting the material as he did was "to produce a complete and authentic body of facts relative to the war in question, but arranged in such a manner as to be attractive to the reader for mere amusement."[48] Other notices praised the historical details and Irving's manner of presenting them,[49] but the *London Magazine* took him to task for glamorizing war.[50] While some critics expressed reservations about his handling of history, most felt that he performed a useful service with his sprightly, entertaining narrative.

When Irving returned to London in the fall of 1829 to become secretary of the American Legation, he brought with him the unfinished sketches about the Alhambra. Eventually he was able to steal enough time from his diplomatic duties and socializing to finish the work and sell it to Colburn and Bentley, for Murray had decided not to risk further losses with Irving's new book.[51] The volumes on the Moorish palace evoked favorable comments from the critics, with the *Athenaeum* stating that "we know few who can equal him in the art of transferring living and breathing flesh and blood to his canvas."[52] On the basis of the new book the *Literary Guardian* proclaimed Irving "decidedly the first English prose-writer of the day."[53] The *Literary Gazette*, long a champion of Irving's work, praised him for bringing American literature to the forefront and for establishing friendly literary relations between America and Great Britain.[54] Most of the other notices were laudatory, with an occasional objection or quibble that he was not maintaining the level of performance attained in *The Sketch Book*. Numerous American critics added their plaudits, so Irving was riding the crest of critical acclaim when he returned to the United States in the spring of 1832.[55]

For a time Irving sought to acquaint himself with his native land, which had changed considerably during his seventeen-year absence abroad. In the company of friends he traveled up the Hudson, visited New England and upstate New York, and took advantage of an offer to accompany Henry Ellsworth, an Indian commissioner, on a visit to some tribes in Arkansas. He completed his circuit of the country with a swing through the Deep South and ended in Washington, where he remained through the rest of the session of Congress. In his first year at home he thus renewed himself by examining his country geographically, politically, and socially.

After numerous distractions he turned his notes from the western tour into a travel narrative, *A Tour on the Prairies*, which was to be the first of three volumes presented to the public as *The Crayon Miscellany*. The first number was followed by *Abbotsford and Newstead Abbey* and *Legends of the Conquest of Spain*, both of which derived from jottings and sketches in his notebooks. Critics greeted Irving's

Tour with enthusiastic acclaim, praising his style, fresh subject matter, and humorous treatment of the material.[56] Only *Fraser's Magazine* dissented, referring to its tasteless humor, lack of realism, and its inept handling of a barbaric subject.[57] *Abbotsford and Newstead Abbey* attracted little critical attention. Termed too long and too stale by the *Athenaeum*,[58] it was adjudged more favorably by other reviewers, some of whom found the volume more interesting than *A Tour on the Prairies*.[59] The third volume of the *Miscellany, Legends of the Conquest of Spain*, elicited several notices that recognized Irving's artistry in handling romantic episodes relating to the Moorish wars.[60] These critical reactions echoed the general approval Irving had received for his earlier productions, but no overwhelmingly favorable responses are to be noted for these first books appearing after his return to America.

While working on *The Crayon Miscellany*, Irving was approached by John Jacob Astor to prepare a history of his fur-trading activities. To facilitate his own work, Irving proposed that Astor employ Pierre Munroe Irving, Washington's nephew, to organize and digest the materials relating to the company's activities. By mid-February 1836 Irving had completed the manuscript, which dealt with another aspect of the West, the exploitation of its natural resources. Irving, however, portrayed the venture as an example of an enterprising American wresting his fortune from the wilderness through his willingness to take risks and to work hard to attain his goals. Throughout his narrative Irving showed the potential of the West to provide a fortune for a highly motivated individual, and he offered the story of Astor's success as a model for other ambitious Americans. Most reviewers praised Irving's literary skill, one calling it a "finished and exquisite narrative,"[61] and another noting his sympathetic identification with the "heroes of his tale."[62] Edward Everett admired Astor's "commercial courage" but noted that his venture did not immediately lead to great profit or extensive settlement of the trans-Mississippi region. Still this effort was acknowledged as the first of many that would eventually lead to the settling of the continent.[63] As was his custom, Everett filled most of his notice with summaries and direct quotations. In *Astoria* the critics found further evidence of Irving's easy style and flowing narrative.

The sequel to *Astoria* was *Adventures of Captain Bonneville* or *The Rocky Mountains*, as the first American edition was titled. The work, Irving's rewriting of Bonneville's diary and notes during his western explorations, attracted little critical attention. The *Monthly Review* observed that "As a literary production . . . these volumes possess the ease and grace of style which Mr. Irving could not, if he would, throw aside; . . . they at the same time appear to furnish a specimen of a very prevalent practice of later years, viz. of book-making. . . . " The critic further noted that Irving repeated scenes and episodes frequently and that the book could have been reduced by two-thirds without any loss of effectiveness.[64] Another reviewer commented on Irving's felicitous descriptions of western scenery and on his "agreeable narrative" and echoed earlier remarks about Irving's genius.[65]

It seems that Irving's working of western American materials increasingly failed to attract critical notice. While *Astoria* elicited at least six American and three British reviews,[66] *Bonneville* drew only scant notice in the United States and in England.[67] For nearly two decades Irving's writings had regularly provided critics with new materials for analysis, but now the novelty was wearing off. More and more he drew upon earlier notes and drafts of his own or reworked the materials provided by others; and while the polished style and narrative luster were still present, the substance lacked novelty and urgency. Irving, it would seem, had reached a midlife crisis that was reflected in the critical response to his writings.

The practice of using his own literary scraps continued in his contributions to the *Knickerbocker Magazine* between March 1839 and October 1841, when he was committed to provide a sketch or tale for every monthly issue. During this period he managed to revise and expand an earlier sketch of Oliver Goldsmith into a two-volume biography that became part of Harper's Family Library and John Murray's Colonial and Home Library, but these editions evoked no critical responses. His biographical account of the consumptive poetess Margaret Davidson printed with her poems attracted little critical notice. Of three reviews of her work only Edgar Allan Poe's mentions Irving and then to assert that he indulges in hyperbole in attributing divine inspiration to the writing of her poetry.[68] Irving, it should be noted, only rearranged the biographical materials that had been passed on to him. Increasingly his writings were feeble and desultory, showing little of the creative and imaginative vigor of his *Sketch Book* years.

Although Irving had long contemplated a biography of George Washington, his attempts at serious work on it were thwarted by interruptions that diverted his energies into other channels. First, in 1842 he accepted the appointment as United States minister to Spain, which enabled him to return to one of his favorite regions. However, his duties were so distracting and his health so precarious that he had no time for work on the biography. After his return to Tarrytown in 1846 he was soon involved in preparing a revised edition of his writings for George P. Putnam, an enterprising New York publisher who did much to revive Irving's waning reputation. The fourteen titles, issued in fifteen volumes between 1848 and 1851, attracted only moderate critical response, with numerous reiterations of praise for Irving's literary genius, his flawless style, and his narrative skill.[69]

These tendencies, plus his desire to reap as much financial gain as possible, are apparent in the 1855 appearance of *Wolfert's Roost*, a collection of journalistic pieces originally published in *Knickerbocker Magazine* and *The Magnolia*. While the anthology evoked only limited criticism, it elicited the usual laudatory comments[70] and enabled Irving to capitalize on the public interest created by the appearance of his collected works. Ever mindful of public favor and the revenue it generated for him, Irving tried to keep new editions or reprintings on the booksellers' shelves.

With the appearance of the Author's Revised Edition some critics and reviewers took the opportunity to assess Irving's entire literary output. Often by using one of the newly published volumes as a springboard, they appraised the quality and durability of his writings, often concluding that his earliest works had a freshness and vigor that were replaced by increased sentimentality and romantic gentility. The bold, irreverent satire and good-natured raillery of *Salmagundi* and *Knickerbocker's History* were muted, and in their place appeared the sedate expressions of a writer consciously attempting to please his readers as he entertained and diverted them. More evident also was Irving's "book-making" or reworking of borrowed materials into offerings that would appeal to the uncritical reader. Irving the literary artist, astute critics observed, was increasingly replaced by Irving the professional writer who turned out pieces that would have the greatest monetary value. Irving had an almost uncanny ability to anticipate favorable public response to his materials (seen, for example, in the reworking of his biography of Goldsmith); and when he joined forces with George P. Putnam to produce a new collected edition, he changed and revised some of his earlier writings to reflect the attitudes and values of his readers at midcentury. In the numerous critical appraisals at this time Irving came across as a talented stylist with limited originality but great ability to transform his observations and the ideas of others into pleasant, entertaining reading. Such general evaluations reveal that Irving had attained the status of a classical writer, one against whom other aspirants could be measured. Horace Binney Wallace, for example, examined Irving's writing in terms of the Coleridgean distinction between the fancy and the imagination and found it lacking in the exercise of the imagination. Irving's use of fancy is evident in his characterizations and his humor, where everything is superficial and nothing involves any delving beneath the surface or internalizing, no psychological probing.[71] Such analysis goes beyond the commonplace commentary about Irving's felicitous style and attempts to examine his writing in the light of rigorous critical principles.

Irving's last major work was his *Life of George Washington* in five volumes, which were issued between 1855 and 1859. The most searching analysis of the biography appeared before he had completed the work. In a discussion of the first four volumes G.W. Greene appraised Irving as a historian and as a writer, noting particularly his careful organization, his sweeping narrative power, his vivid descriptions, his steady control of materials, his sincerity, his concern with truth and reality, and his sense of style. He "never attempt[s] a style of writing that is not in harmony with his habits of thought; so that his words become the natural expression of his conceptions." Greene concluded that "Mr. Irving has succeeded perfectly in the task which he had set himself,—a history of Washington which should bring him home to every heart by bringing him distinctly before every mind."[72] Such a detailed discussion of Irving's method and artistry was the exception at this time, but it served as a useful assessment of his long career as a writer. By contrast, most of the volumes of the biography received slight notice in the press; the perfunctory comments, however, were generally favorable.[73] In the last years of his life critics were more likely to write appreciative notices about the total corpus of his work, emphasizing his geniality, his "simple, direct, and natural style," and his classic qualities.[74] Irving had become an honored fixture on the American literary scene.

Many of the notices about Irving during the last decade of his life were chatty accounts about visits to Sunnyside, reminiscences of meetings with him, or popular discussions of his career. H. T. Tuckerman,[75] T. A. Richards,[76] N. P. Willis,[77] Charles Lanman,[78] Theodore Tilton,[79] G. P. Putnam,[80] J. Wynne,[81] D. G. Mitchell,[82] J. E. Cooke,[83] J. G. Wilson,[84] Frederick S. Cozzens,[85] and anonymous essayists[86] elaborated on various facets of his hospitality, warmth, and graciousness to visitors. While they contribute little to our understanding of his literary achievements, they add to our knowledge of his friendships and social activities.

Other essays written in the twilight of Irving's life continue the appraisals of his writing career. Shortly after the appearance of the Author's Revised Edition, George Ripley surveyed his activities and spoke of his genius, his literary versatility, his patriotism, the universality of his appeal, "the curious felicity of his style," and his gentility. He noted, "The writings of Mr. Irving are no less distinguished by the truthfulness and purity of their moral tone, than by the delightful humor, and their apt delineations of nature and society."[87] Another discussion called attention to the popular appeal of his writings,[88] and the Reverend R. Allyn, while generally praising his work, found him deficient in originality.[89] Irving's reputation as a literary pioneer in America was safe, especially with older, more conservative readers.

Irving's death on 28 November 1859 prompted a flood of obituaries and eulogies. Many tributes by friends and associates appeared in the waning days of the year and in the early months of 1860. Sermons by the Reverend William Creighton and the Reverend J. Seldon Spencer at Christ Church, Tarrytown, extolled his virtues and his humanity.[90] The New-York Historical Society heard eulogies from George Bancroft and William Cullen Bryant,[91] and the Massachusetts Historical Society, in a special meeting, listened to the remarks of Henry Wadsworth Longfellow, Edward Everett, Thomas Aspinwall, Cornelius C. Felton, and Oliver Wendell Holmes and heard a letter from George Sumner.[92] A special volume entitled *Irvingiana: A Memorial of Washington Irving* brought together eulogies, memorials, essays on various aspects of Irving's career, reminiscences, unpublished letters by Irving, and miscellaneous materials relating to the deceased author.[93] The public mourning for Irving in the press and in special meetings carried on for several months, and it was apparent that affection for the man and admiration for his writings continued after his death.[94] Many of the essays and tributes appearing in the months and years following Irving's death were reminiscences filled with anecdotes and impressions based on personal encounters. A number of the writers were deeply moved by their intercourse with Irving, and they enlivened their accounts with details of his gracious kindness and his self-effacing modesty.[95]

The publication of Pierre M. Irving's *Life and Letters of Washington Irving* in four volumes between 1862 and 1864 stirred up some interest in Irving's writings and filled in from letters and journal excerpts many details in his life. Some other details had been provided in Charles R. Leslie's *Autobiographical Recollections*[96] so the public's curiosity for more facts was satisfied for the time. If published comments are a valid indicator, it is evident that public interest in him was flagging. Putnam continued to issue collected editions, but they probably remained unread on the purchasers' shelves.

Little critical notice of Irving appeared in the decade after the publication of the *Life and Letters,* but the approach of the centenary of his birth created a renewed interest in him. In 1879 David J. Hill brought out a biography that praised Irving as a pioneering American writer. The following year essays by C. D. Warner, W. C. Bryant, and G. P. Putnam were issued as *Studies in Irving.*[97] The essays by Bryant and Putnam had first been presented to the public in the months following Irving's death, while Warner's was prepared as a preface to the Geoffrey Crayon Edition of Irving's works, published in the *Atlantic Monthly* in rewritten form,[98] and incorporated into his life of Irving (1881). The articles outline the high points of Irving's career and emphasize his gentleness and sensitivity and his lack of intellectual and critical power.

To commemorate the one-hundredth anniversary of Irving's birth, *The Critic* commissioned a number of brief statements by prominent

writers and critics on various aspects of Irving's life and career.[99]
These remarks were uniformly favorable and provided a suitable
eulogy for the man who, more than any other, made American
literature respectable in the first half of the nineteenth century.
Another centennial tribute, probably by George William Curtis, appeared in the "Editor's Easy Chair" in *Harper's New Monthly Magazine*. It noted that "Irving's exquisite literary art, the freshness and
gaiety and originality of *Knickerbocker*, the charming legends of the
Hudson, the idyllic England of the *Sketch-Book* and *Bracebridge Hall*,
the picturesque and poetic narrative of the *Columbus*, all touched by
the nameless grace of a gentle, humane, refined, and healthy genius,
secure to him as to Goldsmith a long and affectionate remembrance."[100]

Another observance, held at Christ Episcopal Church in Tarry-
town on 3 April 1883, resulted in the publication of *Washington
Irving: Commemoration of the 100th Birthday by the Washington Irving
Association*.[101] The memorial volume included the texts of talks by
D. G. Mitchell, C. D. Warner, Judge Noah Davis, the Reverend J.
Seldon Spencer, and Dr. W. C. Wilkinson, which reminisced about
and eulogized the man who had lived at Sunnyside. The adulatory
tone of the remarks was appropriate for the commemorative occasion.

The decades following this meeting added very little of significance to our understanding of Irving. Critical currents were shifting,
and Irving's romanticism and sentimentality no longer engrossed readers. While they admired his style, they were put off by his genteel
evasions of reality. People who had known Irving in his declining
years set down their reminiscences or produced admiring biographical
sketches. Among these were Frederick Saunders, Donald Grant Mitchell, Charles Hemstreet, and George William Curtis.[102] Other writers,
including a number of academics, presented many of the same familiar
details in the later years of the nineteenth century and the first two
decades of the twentieth century.[103] Their perfunctory comments,
often included in historical surveys of American literature, throw no
new light on Irving the man and add few fresh critical insights, but
they do help to keep his name and writings before the eyes of readers
nurtured on the current doctrines and examples of literary realism
and naturalism. Some new details about Irving's relations with his
English publisher appear in Samuel Smile's biography of John Murray,[104] and T. T. P. Luquer's edition of Irving's letters to John Howard
Payne[105] documents the close working relationship between the two
men in London in the 1820s. Other letters from Irving to Mrs. Jane
Renwick and her son James appeared in 1915,[106] along with George
S. Hellman's editions of Irving's letters to Henry Brevoort and Brevoort's letters to Irving.[107] Irving's letters to John Pendleton Kennedy,
which were also printed about the same time, provide illuminating

insights into his relations with a southern friend and admirer.[108] The publication of these letters and some of Irving's journals[109] provides the impetus for a fresh, serious study of Irving's life, writings, and ideas in the period between the two world wars.

During the period of World War I several studies dealing with Irving's overseas reputation appeared. In his *American Literature in Spain* (1916), J. DeLancey Ferguson studied Irving's critical reception and found that his work received superficial treatment from Spanish critics. G. D. Morris[110] examined his reception in France in 1916, and the following year H. E. Mantz included Irving in his *French Criticism of American Literature Before 1850.*[111] Both studies consider Irving's treatment by French critics and reviewers. In 1918 William B. Cairns in *British Criticisms of American Writings, 1783–1815* noted one review of *Salmagundi.* Four years later he brought out a sequel covering the period from 1815 to 1833, with a long chapter devoted to the critical responses to Irving's writings.[112] Cairn's careful analyses with generous quotations from the reviews provide us with a full statement of British reactions to Irving's writings through *The Alhambra* (1832). Other studies relating Irving to other European cultures appeared in the following decade and in general outlined both the critical response to Irving and his use of literature, history, folklore, and traditions from western Europe.[113]

These background materials, coupled with the publication of various journals, notebooks, and letters, provided the substance for a new, more realistic look at Irving's life and times. In the sixty years following P. M. Irving's *Life and Letters,* biographers had to depend on that adulatory account by an overprotective nephew for their information, information which was carefully orchestrated to preserve the image of a genial, genteel gentleman who epitomized the positive values of home and family. Irving, as Pierre portrayed him, was a gracious, decorous man whose actions reflected the national ideals that most Americans adored. With the appearance of George S. Hellman's *Washington Irving Esquire, Ambassador at Large from the New World to the Old* (1925), the idealized image of Irving began to change. He was pictured as being disorganized, indifferent, erratic, and moody, traits that made him more human and credible. Hellman challenged Pierre's conception of Irving as a man whose enduring love for Matilda Hoffman prevented him from ever marrying by suggesting that he proposed to Emily Foster in Dresden and was rejected by her.[114] Irving's public role as diplomat in London as secretary of the American Legation and in Madrid as minister is emphasized, as is his role as advisor and confidant of Martin Van Buren during his terms as vice-president and president. Hellman shows Irving to be more involved in public affairs and to be a man sufficiently attracted to a young woman to propose marriage to her. In discussing these episodes, Hellman distorts his presentation, so that his biography, with its revisions of Pierre's treatment, tips the balance in another direction. The book represents the start of a reconsideration of Irving that culminated in the monumental study of Stanley T. Williams a decade later.

Williams set as a goal for himself the collection and study of every scrap of Irving's writing he could locate. In the process he turned up long-forgotten journals and notebooks, caches of letters to relatives and friends, drafts and manuscripts of books and essays, and unpublished materials.[115] With these materials at hand he prepared a long, meticulously documented two-volume biography and notes for a study of Irving's critical reception that incorporated the fruits of his exhaustive search in the libraries of Europe for reviews, critical analyses, and translations of Irving's work. These materials bulked so large that Williams added a third volume covering the bibliographical items.

The ten years that Williams devoted to the study of Irving resulted in a biography, which critics hailed as definitive and complete. In it Williams recreated the life of a gifted but unoriginal writer who seemed to lack a driving purpose in life, a man who was willing to react to crises and external circumstances and to recast the ideas of others into pleasing prose and well-turned periods. *Salmagundi,* for example, was social satire in the manner of Goldsmith; *Knickerbocker's History of New York* was a spoof on a popular guidebook by Dr. Samuel L. Mitchill and on the dubious backgrounds of the proud Dutch patricians of New York; *The Sketch Book* and its sequels were written to provide Irving with funds to live abroad; the Spanish books grew out of an invitation to come to Spain to translate documents relating to Columbus; *A Tour on the Prairies, Astoria,* and the biography of Captain Bonneville represent his fortuitous use of American materials at a time when his countrymen were clamoring for a serious literary treatment of the West; his biographies of Goldsmith and Mahomet were potboilers that utilized materials he had accumulated and not thoroughly exploited. Irving, then, was a literary opportunist, not a serious writer who had developed an artistic vision that he set out to fulfill during his lifetime. Rather, according to Williams, Irving moved by chance from project to project and succeeded because he was able to appeal to readers with his pleasant style, his expert handling of sentiment and feeling, his vivid descriptions, and his interesting, gripping narratives. Having more literary talent than most of his contemporaries, Irving succeeded at a time when the United States was trying to create a positive position in the eyes of British and Continental critics. Irving, in the right place at the right time, took advantage of his opportunities and established himself as one of America's first professional men of letters. Thus for

Williams, Irving proved to be a challenging and interesting subject for investigation but a somewhat less rewarding topic for biographical study.

Attempts at writing a life of Irving since Williams have been more limited and focused. Claude G. Bowers treated Irving's activities in Spain during his two extended stays in a popular fashion in *The Spanish Adventures of Washington Irving*.[116] Like Irving, Bowers was an American minister to Spain, and he wrote about his predecessor with an understanding and appreciation of the vexing diplomatic and social problems that Irving faced. Edward Wagenknecht in *Washington Irving: Moderation Displayed*[117] approaches his subject from three angles—"The Life," "The Man," and "The Work"—and makes a persuasive case for Irving as a man who generally espoused a middle-of-the-road course in life. Wagenknecht sympathetically treats Irving's life and career topically and especially in the second part of his study offers perceptive insights into the influences and associations that helped to shape his life and literary career. A slight biography by Johanna Johnston, *The Heart That Would Not Hold*,[118] sentimentalizes Irving and offers nothing new for the serious reader. A more illuminating study, Philip McFarland's *Sojourners*,[119] juxtaposes Irving against some of his contemporaries and provides a cultural and intellectual background for discussing his ideas and attitudes. Other biographical details can be found in Ben Harris McClary's *Washington Irving and the House of Murray: Geoffrey Crayon Charms the British, 1817–1857*,[120] an exhaustive study of Irving's relationship with his English publisher, based on the letters and records in the Murray archives.

A biography fully utilizing the fruits of the research that went into the production of the recent volumes of the collected writings, letters, journals, and notebooks of Irving has not yet appeared. Andrew B. Myers, a scholar involved in the Irving edition and in the activities of Sleepy Hollow Restorations and the Washington Irving Society, is at work on a new life, but the rich array of materials for such a work inevitably lengthens and complicates the project. His study should provide a definitive statement about Irving in the context of his times, incorporating much new information unavailable to Williams more than fifty years ago.

Other aspects of Irving criticism and scholarship have grown markedly in the last half century. With the expansion of academic teaching and research, more scholars and critics have turned their attention to problems relating to Irving and his work. An attempt will be made to sketch only some of the main areas of concern, and as suggested earlier, the reader is advised to turn for the specific details to the bibliographies and essays on Irving scholarship mentioned at the start of this introduction.

Much of the recent critical analysis of Irving's work is to be found in essays which are too numerous to discuss here. Only three significant book-length studies of his writings have appeared in the last fifty years—William L. Hedges's *Washington Irving: An American Study, 1802–1832*,[121] Martin Roth's *Comedy in America: The Lost World of Washington Irving*,[122] and Jeffrey Rubin-Dorsky's *Adrift in the Old World: The Psychological Pilgrimage of Washington Irving*.[123] Hedges deals with the literary and cultural influences upon Irving, and he points out that Irving had a negative, moody, insecure side to his nature that counterbalanced his mellow, genial, sociable side. Roth focuses on Irving's earlier satiric writings, especially *Knickerbocker's History*, and argues that his use of burlesque and comedy through the persona of Diedrich Knickerbocker was important in the early development of a distinctive American literature. Rubin-Dorsky concentrates on Irving's fiction between 1815 and 1832 and attempts to show that "it was his story of dispossession, told in various fictional forms and through different personae, that affected (and I would maintain, still touches) the hearts and minds of his countrymen" (p. xiv). Irving's psychological pilgrimage, as Rubin-Dorsky presents it, is concerned with the personal and cultural pressures upon him during his stay abroad. All these studies touch upon the influences that shaped Irving's writing, and all three illuminate various facets of that development.

Two new essays written for this volume add further perspectives to our understanding of Irving. Wayne R. Kime's "The Author as Professional: Washington Irving's 'Rambling Anecdotes' of the West" examines *A Tour on the Prairies, Astoria,* and *The Adventures of Captain Bonneville* in light of his work as a professional writer. Kime concludes that "Each book draws upon skills Irving had developed at earlier stages in his career, so that together they constitute a reprise or recombination of his several styles" that reflect the mature professionalism of the author in his early fifties. In "Washington Irving, the Nineteenth-Century Bachelor" Jenifer S. Banks considers Irving's relationships with women during his lifetime. Using the insights and theories of feminist criticism, she concludes that his conservative nature and his ambivalent attitude toward women, plus the tragic loss of his first love and the uncertainty of his finances, prevented him from marrying and accepting traditional domestic responsibilities.

Another area—studies of foreign influence and reception—continued in the post-World War II period the investigations noted earlier. Stanley T. Williams, who devotes a long chapter to Irving in *The Spanish Background of American Literature*,[124] updates the earlier work of J. D. Ferguson. Irving and Germany have been dealt with by Walter A. Reichart in *Washington Irving in Germany*,[125] by Henry A. Pochmann in a chapter in *German Culture in America*,[126] by Harvey

W. Hewett-Thayer in *American Literature as Viewed in Germany, 1818–1861*,[127] and by Morton Nirenberg, *The Reception of American Literature in German Periodicals*.[128] Their studies indicate that the American writer was popular in Germany, and the first two scholars also discuss Irving's debt to German literature and folklore.

Bibliographical and textual problems relating to Irving's writing have been analyzed in great detail in the various volumes of the new edition of his works issued by Twayne Publishers. The editors have tried to resolve the problems resulting from the discrepancies between surviving manuscripts and printed texts and between the texts of different editions of the same work, always taking into account the author's intention and trying to preserve it in their edition. The problem of physical format and printed textual variants has been addressed by William R. Langfeld and Philip C. Blackburn[129] and by Jacob Blanck in volume five of the *Bibliography of American Literature*,[130] but their work is not as exhaustive as that of the Irving editors.

The volumes of essays devoted specifically to Irving are useful tools for the student of his work. These provide, in handy form, materials gathered from printed sources or compiled from symposiums. A selection of new perspectives, *Washington Irving Reconsidered*, was edited by Ralph M. Aderman,[131] and another collection of seven essays, *Washington Irving: A Tribute*, was compiled by Andrew B. Myers.[132] Myers also gathered forty-five selections and issued them under the title of *A Century of Commentary on the Works of Washington Irving, 1860–1974*.[133] These articles and excerpts include appreciations and critiques from contemporaries like William Cullen Bryant, W. M. Thackeray, D. G. Mitchell, and G. W. Curtis; from literary historians like Barrett Wendell, William B. Cairns, Fred Lewis Pattee, and Vernon Louis Parrington; from biographers like George S. Hellman and Stanley T. Williams; and from scholars and critics like Marcus F. Cunliffe, Terence Martin, Nathalia Wright, and William L. Hedges. The selections provide a rich sampling of the critical responses to America's first successful professional man of letters in the century after his death. In 1983 a conference on Romanticism at Hofstra University brought together a number of Irving scholars who read papers that were subsequently published as *The Old and New World Romanticism of Washington Irving*.[134] The volume, edited by Stanley Brodwin, consists of fourteen essays that deal with the nature of Irving's romantic impulses and analyze their manifestations in his writings. By using the new Irving edition the participants in the conference were able to draw upon the most reliable texts and utilize the latest developments in Irving scholarship.

The study of Irving continues with undiminished vigor, with new interpretations incorporating new critical and cultural perspectives.

As the following commentaries suggest, Irving and his writings have survived since 1807 the exhaustive scrutiny of serious readers who have brought a variety of critical views to bear upon him and his work. These reactions, ranging from high praise to carping negativism, suggest that even as he evokes differing responses to his ideas and attitudes, Irving's work contains enduring elements that will engage readers and critics as long as his work survives.

RALPH M. ADERMAN

University of Wisconsin

Notes

1. This thirty-volume edition, published by G. K. Hall and now nearing completion, includes his published and unpublished writings, journals and notebooks, letters, and a comprehensive bibliography.

2. Haskell Springer, *Washington Irving: A Reference Guide* (Boston: G.K. Hall & Co., 1976). This work can be updated with the annual listings in *American Literary Scholarship* (Duke University Press) and the annual bibliographies of the Modern Language Association of America, and with Haskell Springer and Raylene Penner, "Washington Irving: A Reference Guide Updated," *Resources for American Literary Study* 11 (Autumn 1981): 257–79.

3. *Fifteen American Authors Before 1900*, ed. Robert A. Rees and Earl N. Harbert (Madison: University of Wisconsin Press, 1971). The revised edition was published in 1984.

4. Stanley T. Williams and Mary Allen Edge, *A Bibliography of the Writings of Washington Irving: A Checklist* (New York: Oxford University Press, 1936).

5. William R. Langfeld and Philip C. Blackburn, *Washington Irving: A Bibliography* (New York: New York Public Library, 1933). See also Edwin T. Bowden, *Washington Irving: Bibliography* (Boston: Twayne Publishers, 1989).

6. Jacob Blanck, *Bibliography of American Literature*, vol. 5 (New Haven: Yale University Press, 1970).

7. *Port Folio* 3 (16 May 1807): 307–8; *Monthly Register, Magazine and Review of the United States* 3 (August 1807): 148–54.

8. *Weekly Inspector* 1 (7, 21 February 1807): 275–76, 299–300; 2 (6 March 1807): 30–31; *Salmagundi*, ed. Bruce Granger and Martha Hartzog, *The Complete Works of Washington Irving*, vol. 6 (Boston: G. K. Hall & Co., 1977), 97–98, 103–15, 345–46.

9. *Travels through Canada, and the United States of North America, in the Years 1806, 1807, and 1808* (London: R. Phillips, 1810), 2:98; *Salmagundi*. With an introductory essay and explanatory notes by John Lambert (London: Printed for J. M. Richardson, 1811).

10. *Monthly Review* 65 (August 1811): 418–24.

11. *Monthly Anthology and Boston Review* 8 (February 1810): 123–28.

12. *Port Folio* 3rd Ser., 8 (October 1812): 344–45.

13. *Letters of Henry Brevoort to Washington Irving*, ed. George S. Hellman (New York: G. P. Putnam's Sons, 1918), 1: 99; *The Letters of Sir Walter Scott, 1811–1814*, ed. H. J. C. Grierson (London: Constable & Co., 1932), 3: 259.

14. Williams and Edge, *Bibliography*, 62.

15. *Literary Chronicle and Weekly Review* 2 (7, 14, 21 October 1820): 641–44, 659–61, 678–81; *Literary Gazette* 4 (21, 28 October, 4 November 1820): 674–76, 695–96, 707–9; *New Monthly Magazine* 14 (December 1820): 686; *Edinburgh Magazine and Literary Miscellany* 7 (December 1820): 543–48; *Gold's London Magazine, and Theatrical Inquisitor* 2 (December 1820): 577–88; *London Magazine and Monthly Critical and Dramatic Review* 2 (December 1820): 577; *Monthly Review* 94 (January 1821): 67–74; *Edinburgh Monthly Magazine* 5 (February 1821): 232–48; *British Critic* N. S. 15 (March 1821): 261–72. In addition, John Gibson Lockhart, before the appearance of any English edition of *Knickerbocker's History* had reviewed it with generous extracts, declaring that "Mr Washington Irving is one of our favourites among English writers of this age—and he is not a bit the less for having been born in America." *Blackwood's Edinburgh Magazine* 7 (July 1820): 360–69.

16. Details concerning its genesis are given in Stanley T. Williams, *The Life of Washington Irving* (New York: Oxford University Press, 1935), 1: 173–76.

17. A notice of Part 2 appearing in the *Evening Post* on 3 August echoes a statement which Irving had made in a letter to Brevoort five months earlier: ". . . if they [Irving's writings] possess merit in the class of literature to which they belong it is all to which I aspire in the work. I seek only to blow a flute accompaniment in the national concert, and leave others to play the fiddle & frenchhorn." Washington Irving, *Letters*, vol. 1, 1802–1823, ed. Ralph M. Aderman, Herbert L. Kleinfield, and Jenifer S. Banks (Boston: Twayne Publishers, 1978), 543. It seems quite likely that Brevoort helped to promote the work in addition to carrying out editorial duties.

18. *North American Review* 9 (September 1819): 322–56.

19. *Kaleidoscope* 2 (24 August 1819): 25; *Literary Gazette* 3 (25 September, 2, 9 October 1819): 617–20, 634–35, 648–50. During the course of the next year the *Kaleidoscope* was to reprint virtually all the pieces in *The Sketch Book*. William B. Cairns, *British Criticisms of American Writings, 1815–1833*. University of Wisconsin Studies in Language and Literature, no. 14 (Madison: University of Wisconsin, 1922), 60–62.

20. About *The Sketch Book* Jerdan later observed, "I had the pleasure and honour to launch it at once, fill the sails, and send it on its prosperous voyage." *The Autobiography of William Jerdan* (London: Arthur Hall, Virtue, & Co., 1852) 2: 290. In gratitude Irving presented Jerdan with the printed volumes of the work. This set, now in the Special Collections of the Golda Meir Library of the University of Wisconsin–Milwaukee, has the imprint of John Miller in vol. 1 and John Murray in vol. 2.

21. For a detailed account of the English publication see David W. Pancoast, "How Washington Irving Published *The Sketch Book* in England," *Studies in American Fiction* 14 (Spring 1986): 77–83.

22. *Blackwood's Edinburgh Magazine* 6 (February 1820): 554–61.

23. *Blackwood's Edinburgh Magazine* 7 (July 1820): 360–69; *Edinburgh Review* 34 (August 1820): 160–76.

24. *Quarterly Review* 25 (April 1821): 50–67.

25. See the notices in *New Monthly Magazine* 13 (March 1820): 303–8; *Literary Chronicle and Weekly Review* 2 (18 March, 26 August 1820): 177–80, 546–49; *Literary Gazette* 4 (8 April 1820): 228–29; *Investigator* 1 (May 1820): 156–63; *British Critic* 13 (June 1820): 645–54; 14 (November 1820): 514–25; *Edinburgh Monthly Review* 4 (September 1820): 303–34; *Monthly Review* 2 ser., 93 (October 1820): 198–207; *Monthly Magazine or British Register* 50 (1 November 1820): 304, 362–63.

26. *London Magazine* 6 (November 1822): 436–39, reprinted in *Port Folio* 15 (February 1823): 156–60.

27. *Edinburgh Review* 37 (November 1822): 337–50.

28. See *Literary and Scientific Repository* 4 (May 1822): 422–32; *Literary Chronicle and Weekly Review* 4 (25 May 1822): 321–24; *Blackwood's Edinburgh Magazine* 11 (June 1822): 688–92; *Literary Gazette* 6 (1 June 1822): 339–41; *London Museum; or Record of Literature, Fine Arts, Science, Antiquities, the Drama, etc.* 1 (1 June 1822): 83–85; *Kaleidoscope* n. s., 2 (11 June 1822): 385; *Edinburgh Magazine and Literary Miscellany* 11 (July 1822): 91–96; *European Magazine* 82 (July 1822): 55–57; *Gentleman's Magazine* 92 (July 1822): 54–56; *Ladies' Monthly Museum* 16 (July 1822): 40; *Leeds Correspondent* 4 (July 1822): 185–95; *Literary Speculum* 2 (July 1822): 118; *Monthly Literary Register* 1 (July 1822): 192; *New Edinburgh Review* 2 (July 1822): 151–77; *Monthly Magazine or British Register* 53 (1 July 1822): 548; *Literary Melange, or Weekly Register of Literature and the Arts* (Glasgow) (10 July 1822): 54; *Monthly Censor, or General Review of Domestic and Foreign Literature* 1 (August 1822): 353–56; *Monthly Review* 2 ser., 98 (August 1822): 400–14; *British Critic* n. s., 18 (September 1822): 299–311; *Scottish Episcopal Review and Magazine* 2 (September 1822): 429–36; *London Magazine* 6 (November 1822): 436–49; *London Examiner* (15 December 1822): 792–93.

29. *Port Folio* 2 (November 1822): 447.

30. *Edinburgh Review* 37 (November 1822): 340.

31. *Blackwood's Edinburgh Magazine* 16 (September 1824): 291–304.

32. *Westminster Review* 2 (October 1824): 334–46.

33. See *Literary Chronicle and Weekly Review* 6 (28 August, 4 September 1824): 545–49, 563–67; *Literary Gazette* 8 (8 August, 4 September 1824): 545–46, 565–68; *Edinburgh Magazine and Literary Miscellany* 15 (September 1824): 325–36; *European Magazine* 86 (September 1824): 251–54; *Lady's Magazine and Museum of Belles-Lettres* n. s. 5 (September 1824): 484–91; *Kaleidoscope* 5 (14 September 1824): 85–86; *Ladies' Monthly Museum* 20 (October 1824): 222; *Metropolitan Literary Journal and General Magazine of Literature, Science and the Arts* (October 1824): 538–45; *Monthly Critical Gazette* 1 (October 1824): 465–68; *Monthly Magazine* 58 (October 1824): 260; *London Magazine* 10 (October 1824): 401–6; *Universal Review* 2 (November 1824): 259–72; *London Examiner* (5 September 1824): 563–65; *Imperial Magazine* 7 (January 1825): 82–85; *Eclectic Review* 42 (July 1825): 65–74.

34. *Quarterly Review* 31 (March 1825): 473–89.

35. *United States Literary Gazette* 1 (15 September 1824): 61.

36. *New-York Mirror* 2 (25 September 1824): 70–71.

37. *Atlantic Magazine* 2 (November 1824): 60.

38. *Edinburgh Review* 33 (January 1820): 79.

39. See *Literary Gazette* 12 (2 February 1828): 65–67; *Kaleidoscope* 8 (12 February 1828): 265–67; *Athenaeum* no. 7 (12 February 1828): 102–3; no. 9 (22 February 1828): 131–33; no. 10 (26 February 1828): 150–51; *London Weekly Review* 2 (16, 23 February 1828): 97–99, 115–17; *Literary Chronicle and Weekly Review* 10 (23 February, 22 March 1828): 118–20, 184–85; *New Monthly Magazine* 22 (March 1828): 288–96; *Ladies' Monthly Museum* 27 (March 1828): 170–71; *Lady's Magazine* n. s., 9 (March 1828): 145–49; *London Magazine* 2 ser., 10 (March 1828): 281–325; *Monthly Review* n. s., 7 (April 1828): 419–34; *Edinburgh Review* 48 (September 1828): 1–32.

40. *Monthly Magazine or British Register* n. s., 5 (April 1828): 407–10.

41. *Eclectic Review* n. s., 29 (March 1828): 224–32.

42. See *American Quarterly Review* 3 (March 1828): 173–90; *New-York Mirror* 5 (22 March 1828): 295; *Southern Review* 3 (August 1828): 1–31; *Western Monthly*

Review 2 (September 1828): 227–36; *Philadelphia Album* 3 (14 September 1828): 134–35; *North American Review* 28 (January 1829): 103–34.

43. Williams, *Life of Irving*, 2: 307.

44. No. 115 (13 March 1830): 148–49. The critic for the *Electric Review* (3rd ser., 4 [August 1830]: 97–98) also praised the abridgement.

45. *Dublin Literary Gazette* 1 (13 March 1830): 162–63; *Edinburgh Literary Journal* 3 (13 March 1830): 161.

46. *Edinburgh Literary Journal* 2 (6 June 1829): 1–4; W. H. Prescott, *North American Review* 29 (October 1829): 293–314.

47. Vol. 5 (March 1829): 190–221.

48. Vol. 43 (May 1830): 55–80.

49. *London Literary Gazette* (23 May 1829): 329–31; *Monthly Review* 3rd ser., 11 (July 1829): 430–35.

50. 3rd ser., 3 (June 1829): 529–56.

51. See Ben Harris McClary, *Washington Irving and the House of Murray: Geoffrey Crayon Charms the British, 1817–1856* (Knoxville: University of Tennessee Press, 1969), 133, 155–56, 167.

52. No. 236 (5 May 1832): 283–84.

53. Vol. 2 (5 May 1832): 65–68.

54. Vol. 16 (28 April, 5 May 1832): 257–60, 278–80.

55. *Monthly Review* n. s., 2 (June 1832): 221–47; *New Monthly Magazine* 36 (June 1832): 242; *Eclectic Review* 8 (July 1832): 1–8; *Westminster Review* 17 (July 1832): 132–45; *Royal Lady's Magazine* 5 (January 1833): 30–32; *New-York Mirror* 9 (23 June 1832): 401–3; *New England Magazine* 3 (July 1832): 81–82; *American Monthly Review* 2 (September 1832): 177–89; *North American Review* 35 (October 1832): 265–82.

56. See *Knickerbocker Magazine* 5 (April 1835): 352–55; *Monthly Review* 4th ser., 1 (April 1835): 467–79; *Southern Literary Messenger* 1 (April 1835): 456–57; *New England Magazine* 8 (May 1835): 409–10; *Dublin University Magazine* 5 (May 1835): 554–72; *Portland Magazine* 1 (May 1835): 255–56; *American Quarterly Review* 17 (June 1835): 532–33; *Western Monthly Magazine* 3 (June 1835): 329–37; *North American Review* 41 (July 1835): 1–28; and *Southern Literary Messenger* 1 (September 1835): 8–12. For a comprehensive analysis of the critical reactions to *A Tour on the Prairies,* see Martha Dula, "Audience Response to *A Tour on the Prairies,*" *Western American Literature* 7 (Spring and Summer 1973): 67–74.

57. *Fraser's Magazine* 12 (October 1835): 409–15.

58. No. 393 (9 May 1835): 345–46.

59. *Knickerbocker Magazine* 5 (June 1835): 559; *Southern Literary Messenger* 1 (July 1835): 646–48.

60. *Southern Literary Messenger* 2 (December 1835): 64–65; *Fraser's Literary Chronicle* 1 (23 January 1836): 117–18; *Metropolitan Magazine* 15 (February 1836): 34; *New-York Mirror* 13 (6 February 1836): 251; and *Monthly Repository* n.s., 10 (February 1836): 81–89.

61. *Westminster Review* 26 (January 1837): 318–48.

62. *American Quarterly Review* 21 (March 1837): 60–74.

63. *North American Review* 44 (January 1837): 200–37.

64. *Monthly Review* 4th ser., 2 (June 1837): 279–90.

65. *New-York Review* 1 (October 1837): 439–40.

66. In addition to the ones previously cited, they include *Western Monthly*

Magazine 5 (November 1836): 685–87; *Monthly Review* 4th ser., 2 (December 1836): 487–98; *Knickerbocker Magazine* 9 (January 1837): 88–90; *Dublin University Magazine* 9 (February 1837): 167–76; *Southern Literary Journal* 3 (March 1837): 30–41; and *Southern Literary Messenger* 3 (January 1837): 59–68.

67. The two notices are cited above.

68. *Graham's Magazine* 19 (August 1841): 93–94. The other reviews appeared in *Knickerbocker Magazine* 18 (July 1841): 71–72; and A. S. Hillard in *North American Review* 53 (July 1841): 139–46.

69. See, for example, the review of *A History of New York* in *Literary World* 3 (2 September 1848): 604–7; *The Sketch Book*, *Literary World* 3 (7 October 1848): 703–4; *Holden's Dollar Magazine* 3 (April 1849): 206–9; *Adventures of Captain Bonneville*, *Literary World* 4 (16 June 1849): 515; *The Life of Oliver Goldsmith*, *Literary World* 5 (1 September 1849): 173–74; *Holden's Dollar Magazine* 4 (October 1849): 633; *Knickerbocker Magazine* 34 (October 1849): 348–51; *North American Review* 70 (April 1850): 265–89; *Mahomet and His Successors*, *Literary World* 5 (22, 29 December 1849): 537–39, 560–61; *New Englander* 8 (February, August 1850): 153, 481; *North British Review* 13 (February 1850): 189–224; *Southern Quarterly Review* 17 (April, July 1850): 248, 529; 20 (July 1851): 173–206; *Literary World* 6 (27 April 1850): 415–16; *North American Review* 71 (October 1850): 273–307; *Christian Observer* 162 (June 1851): 378; *Astoria* and *The Crayon Miscellany*, *North American Review* 69 (July 1849): 175–96; *Conquest of Granada*, *Holden's Dollar Magazine* 6 (October 1850): 630; *The Alhambra*, *Literary World* 8 (3 May 1851): 356. Notices of the Author's Revised Edition are to be found in *Christian Review* 15 (April 1850): 203–14; *American Whig Review* 12 (December 1850): 602–16; *Methodist Quarterly Review* 16 (October 1856): 537–49.

70. See A. Stevens, *National Magazine* 6 (May 1855): 385–94; *New Monthly Magazine* 2nd ser., 104 (July 1855): 297–99.

71. *Sartain's Magazine* 7 (November 1858): 288–98. This essay was reprinted in Wallace's *Literary Criticisms and Other Papers* (Philadelphia: Parry & McMillan, 1856): 67–91.

72. George Washington Greene in *North American Review* 86 (April 1858): 330–58.

73. See *Knickerbocker Magazine* 46 (July 1855): 74–76; 47 (March 1856): 304–6; *North American Review* 83 (July 1856): 1–30; *Littell's Living Age* 55 (17 October 1857): 177–81.

74. See *Harper's Monthly Magazine* 2 (April 1851): 577–80; *New Monthly Magazine* 97 (April 1853): 424–33; *Dublin University Magazine* 45 (March 1855): 369–78.

75. "Washington Irving" in *Homes of American Authors* (New York: D. Appleton & Co., 1864), [35]–61.

76. "Sunnyside, the Home of Washington Irving," *Harper's Monthly Magazine* 14 (December 1856): 1–21.

77. "Willis at Sunnyside," *Littell's Living Age* 54 (12 September 1857): 699–702; "Willis at Sunnyside. No. 2," *Littell's Living Age* 55 (24 October 1857): 241–43.

78. "A Day With Washington Irving," *Once a Week* (31 December 1859): 5–8.

79. "Half an Hour at Sunnyside," *Independent* 11 (24 November 1859): 1.

80. "Recollections of Irving. By His Publisher," *Atlantic Monthly* 6 (November 1860): 601–12.

81. "Washington Irving," *Harper's New Monthly Magazine* 24 (February 1862): 349–56.

82. "Preface," *Dream Life: A Fable of the Seasons* (New York: Charles Scribner's Sons, 1863), v–xiii.

83. "Irving at Sunnyside in 1858," *Hours at Home* 1 (October 1865): 507–12; "A Morning at Sunnyside with Washington Irving," *Southern Magazine* 12 (June 1873): 710–16.

84. "Washington Irving" in *Bryant and His Friends: Some Reminiscences of the Knickerbocker Writers* (New York: Fords, Howard, and Hulbert, 1886), 157–78.

85. A. D. F. Randolph, "Leaves from the Journal of Frederick S. Cozzens, " *Lippincott's Monthly Magazine* 45 (May 1890): 739–48.

86. "Washington Irving: His Home and His Works," *New York Quarterly* 4 (April 1855): 66–83; "Recollections of Washington Irving," *Continental Monthly* 1 (June 1862): 689–700; "A Visit to Sunnyside, on the Banks of the Hudson: The Residence of the Late Washington Irving," *Eclectic Magazine* 64 (n. s. 1) (April 1865): 497–501; "One of Irving's Old Cronies," *Critic* 3 (31 March 1883): 142.

87. *Harper's New Monthly Magazine* 2 (April 1851): 577–80.

88. Sir Nathaniel in *New Monthly Magazine* 97 (April 1853): 424–33.

89. *Methodist Quarterly Review* 16 (October 1856): 537–49.

90. *Sermons on the Occasion of the Death of the Late Washington Irving* (New York: Pudney & Russell, 1859).

91. See George Bancroft's remarks in *Littell's Living Age* 65 (9 June 1860): 620–21; and William Cullen Bryant's *Discourse on the Life, Character and Genius of Washington Irving* (New York: G. P. Putnam, 1860).

92. *Proceedings of the Massachusetts Historical Society* 4 (December 1859): 393–423.

93. *Irvingiana* (New York: C. B. Richardson, 1860).

94. See notices of Irving's death in *Eclectic Magazine* 49 (January 1860): 139; *Southern Literary Messenger* 30 (January 1860): 73–74; *Knickerbocker Magazine* 55 (January 1860): 96–99, 113–28; *New Monthly Magazine* 118 (February 1860): 213–21. W. M. Thackeray's eulogy, "Nil Nisi Bonum," appeared in *Cornhill Magazine* 1 (February 1860): 129–34.

95. Among these accounts, in addition to others mentioned earlier, D. G. Mitchell, "Washington Irving," *Atlantic Monthly* 13 (June 1864): 694–701; Evert A. Duyckinck, "Washington Irving" in *National Portrait Gallery of Eminent Americans* (New York: Johnson, Fry & Co., 1862), 2: 99–109.

96. London: John Murray, 1860.

97. New York: G. P. Putnam's Sons, 1880.

98. "Washington Irving," *Atlantic Monthly* 45 (March 1880): 396–408.

99. James H. Morse, "Washington Irving"; C. D. Warner, "Irving's Humor"; O. W. Holmes, "Irving's Power of Idealization"; G. W. Curtis, "Irving's 'Knickerbocker' "; Edmund Gosse, "Irving's 'Sketch-book' "; and S. H. Gay, "Irving the Historian," *The Critic* 3 (31 March 1883): 137–42.

100. *Harper's New Monthly Magazine* 66 (April 1883): 790–91.

101. Published in New York by G. P. Putnam's Sons in 1884.

102. See Saunders, *Character Studies, With Some Personal Recollections* (New York: Thomas Whitaker, 1894); Mitchell, *American Lands and Letters: The Mayflower to Rip Van Winkle* (New York: Charles Scribner's Sons, 1897); Hemstreet, *Literary New York: Its Landmarks and Associations* (New York: G. P. Putnam's Sons, 1904); and Curtis, *Washington Irving: A Sketch* (New York: The Grolier Club, 1891).

103. See, for example, Henry A. Beers, *An Outline Sketch of American Literature*

(New York: Phillips & Hunt, 1886), 92–101; Charles F. Richardson, *American Literature, 1607–1885* (New York: G. P. Putnam's Sons, 1889), 258–80; F. H. Underwood, *Washington Irving* (Philadelphia: J. B. Lippincott, 1890); Robert H. Nichols, "Washington Irving," *Yale Literary Magazine* 58 (February 1893): 178–86; W. W. Gist, "Washington Irving," *The Chautauquan* 18 (October 1893): 48–52; William Dean Howells, *My Literary Passions* (New York: Harper & Brothers, 1895), 23–27; Barrett Wendell, *A Literary History of America* (New York: Charles Scribner's Sons, 1900), 169–80; William Peterfield Trent, *A History of American Literature* (New York: D. Appleton & Co., 1903), 221–33; H. W. Boynton, *Washington Irving* (Boston: Houghton Mifflin & Co., 1901); Richard Burton, *Literary Leaders of America* (New York: The Chautauqua Press, 1903), 12–41; Leon H. Vincent, *American Literary Masters* (Boston: Houghton Mifflin & Co., 1906), 3–32; William B. Cairns, *A History of American Literature* (New York: Oxford University Press, 1912), 162–74; William P. Trent and John Erskine, *Great American Writers* (New York: Henry Holt & Co., 1911), 20–27.

104. *A Publisher and His Friends: Memoir and Correspondence of the Late John Murray*, 2 vols. (London: John Murray, 1891).

105. "Correspondence of Washington Irving and John Howard Payne," *Scribner's Magazine* 48 (October, November 1910): 461–82, 597–616.

106. *Letters from Washington Irving to Mrs. William Renwick, and to Her Son, James Renwick, Written between September 10th, 1811 and April 5th, 1816* ([New York: Columbia University, 1915]).

107. *Letters of Washington Irving to Henry Brevoort*, 2 vols. (New York: G. P. Putnam's Sons, 1915); *Letters of Henry Brevoort to Washington Irving Together with Other Unpublished Brevoort Papers*, 2 vols. (New York: G. P. Putnam's Sons, 1916).

108. Killis Campbell, ed., "The Kennedy Letters: A Sheaf of Unpublished Letters from Washington Irving," *Sewanee Review* 25 (January 1917): 1–19.

109. *The Journals of Washington Irving*, ed. William P. Trent and George S. Hellman, 3 vols. (Boston: The Bibliophile Society, 1919); *Notes and Journal of Travel in Europe, 1804–1805*, ed. William P. Trent, 3 vols. (New York: The Grolier Club, 1921).

110. *Washington Irving's Fiction in the Light of French Criticism*, Indiana University Studies, no. 30 (Bloomington, Ind.: Indiana University, 1916).

111. New York: Columbia University Press, 1917.

112. *British Criticisms of American Writing, 1815–1833*, University of Wisconsin Studies in Language and Literature, no. 14 (Madison: University of Wisconsin Press, 1922.

113. See E. Arens, "*Washington Irving im Rheinland (1822). Ein Beitrag zur Geschichte der Rhein-Romantik*," *Eichendorff-Kalendar, 1927/28. Ein Romantisches Jahrbuch* (1927): 93–120; Adolph B. Benson, "Scandinavians in the Works of Washington Irving," *Scandinavian Studies and Notes* 9 (1927): 207–23; Emilio Goggio, "Washington Irving and Italy," *Romanic Review* 21 (January–March 1930): 26–33, and "Washington Irving's Works in Italy," *Romanic Review* 22 (October–December 1931): 301–3; Henry A. Pochmann, "Irving's German Sources in *The Sketch Book*," *Studies in Philology* 27 (July 1930): 477–507, and "Irving's German Tour and Its Influence on His Tales," *PMLA* 45 (December 1930): 1150–87; Stanley T. Williams, "The First Version of the Writings of Washington Irving in Spanish," *Modern Philology* 28 (November 1930): 185–201, and "Washington Irving and Fernán Caballero," *Journal of English and Germanic Philology* 29 (1930): 352–66.

114. More recently, Mary Weatherspoon Bowden has suggested that Irving was also seriously interested in Serena Livingston. See "1815–1819: Prelude to Irving's *Sketch Book*," *American Literature* 41 (January 1970): 566–71.

115. "Washington Irving and Matilda Hoffman," *American Speech* 1 (June 1926): 463–69; "Washington Irving's Religion," *Yale Review* 15 (January 1926): 414–16; *Notes While Preparing Sketch Book, etc., 1817* (New Haven: Yale University Press, 1927); *Tour of Scotland, 1817, and Other Manuscript Notes* (New Haven: Yale University Press, 1927); "Unpublished Letters of Washington Irving: Sunnyside and New York Chronicles," *Yale Review* 16 (April 1927): 459–84; "Letters of Washington Irving: Spanish Fetes and Ceremonies," *Yale Review* 17 (October 1927) 99–117; *Letters from Sunnyside and Spain* (New Haven: Yale University Press, 1928); "Washington Irving's First Stay in Paris," *American Literature* 2 (March 1930): 15–20; *The Journal of Washington Irving (1823–1824)* (Cambridge Mass.: Harvard University Press, 1931); *Washington Irving and the Storrows: Letters from England and the Continent, 1821–1828* (Cambridge, Mass.: Harvard University Press, 1933); "Washington Irving, Matilda Hoffman, and Emily Foster," *Modern Language Notes* 48 (March 1933): 182–86; *Journal, 1803* (London: Oxford University Press, 1934); *Journal of Washington Irving, and Miscellaneous Notes on Moorish Legend and History* (New York: American Book Co., 1937); "Introduction" to *Letters of Jonathan Oldstyle*, Facsimile Text Society, no. 52 (New York: Columbia University Press, 1941). Williams also collaborated on the editing of some Irving manuscripts: with E. Herman Hespelt, "Two Unpublished Anecdotes by Fernán Caballero Preserved by Washington Irving," *Modern Language Notes* 49 (January 1934): 25–31; with E. Herman Hespelt, "Washington Irving's Notes on Fernán Caballero's Stories," *PMLA* 49 (1934): 1129–39; with Ernest E. Leisy, "Polly Holman's Wedding: Notes by Washington Irving," *Southwest Review* 19 (July 1934): 449–54; with Leonard B. Beach, "Washington Irving's Letters to Mary Kennedy," *American Literature* 6 (March 1934): 54–65. Williams and Beach also edited *The Journal of Emily Foster* (New York: Oxford University Press) in 1938. Clara Louise Penney edited Irving's *Spanish Diary of 1828–29*, which was published by the Hispanic Society of America in 1926. Numerous other letters and journals were published after World War II, and they have all been incorporated into the recently published *Complete Writings of Washington Irving*.

116. Boston: Houghton Mifflin Co., 1940.

117. New York: Oxford University Press, 1962.

118. New York: M. Evans & Co., 1981.

119. New York: Atheneum, 1979.

120. Knoxville: University of Tennessee Press, 1969.

121. Baltimore: Johns Hopkins University Press, 1965.

122. Port Washington, N. Y.: Kennikat Press, 1976.

123. Chicago: University of Chicago Press, 1988.

124. New Haven: Yale University Press, 1955, 2: 3–45.

125. Ann Arbor: University of Michigan Press, 1957.

126. Madison: University of Wisconsin Press, 1957, 367–81, 696–705. In this study Pochmann broadened the scope of his earlier treatment of Irving mentioned in note 113.

127. Chapel Hill: University of North Carolina Press, 1958, 18–37.

128. Heidelberg: C. Winter, 1970, 42–53.

129. *Washington Irving: A Bibliography* (New York: New York Public Library, 1933).

130. Pp.1–96.

131. Hartford: Transcendental Books, 1969. These essays also appeared in *American Transcendental Quarterly*, no. 5 (First Quarter 1970).

132. Tarrytown: Sleepy Hollow Restorations, 1972.

133. Tarrytown: Sleepy Hollow Restorations, 1976.

134. New York: Greenwood Press, 1986.

CONTEMPORANEOUS
REVIEWS AND ESSAYS

[Review of *Salmagundi*, Volume 1]

Anonymous[*]

The design of this publication is to ridicule the follies, and laugh at the prevailing fashionable absurdities, literary, political, and personal, of our good citizens, and their worthy wives, daughters, sisters, mothers, and grand-mothers. This design is executed with so much spirit, wit, genius, elegance, and humour, as to place the Salmagundi on the same height of excellence with the effusions of Rabelais, of Swift, of Addison, and Voltaire. It seems superfluous to transcribe any passages from a book, which is undoubtedly, in the hands of every lover of merriment and gaiety; neither is it an easy task, to select from such an abundant assemblage of sportive excellence those periods, which might be deemed to stand pre-eminent for their keenness and brilliancy. One specimen however of the Salmagundi's talent at covering the impotent exertions of stupid absurdity with ridicule, we shall insert, although we do, in our most serious and solemn apprehension, think that the measures of *political idiocy*, at which our author laughs, are calculated to raise *no light* emotions in the bosom of any one, who feels for the best interests of America, for *those interests*, which a knavish and cowardly system has laid prostrate in the dust, and polluted with infamy and degradation. . . .

It is necessary to note, that occasional inaccuracies in the language, and sins against grammar, occur in the Salmagundi, as the use of the verb *"set"* for *"sit"*—the word *"who"* for *"whom,"* and some other negligencies of the same sort; which the gentlemen, who produce this work, are more especially bound to correct, and avoid because, as there is now a conspiracy of all the dunces in the Union, with N. G. Dufief at their head, to wage perpetual war against *sense* and *grammar*, there is no other help for the cause of sound learning, than that those, who eminently excel in genius, wit, and taste, should always, both by precept and example, enforce the necessity of *gram-*

[*] Reprinted from *Monthly Register, Magazine, and Review of the United States* 3 (August 1807): 148–54.

matical accuracy, as the only sure foundation, upon which good writing can rest.

There is yet another objection, which truth and justice compel us to make against the writers of the Salmagundi, namely, their frequent use of the words—"*God*,"—"*Devil*,"—expressions which do not add any thing of wit, or force, or dignity, or eloquence, or delicacy, to literary productions. . . .

Let the Salmagundi, therefore continue to pour out its sportive effusions of wit and merriment upon the passing follies of the day; but let its authors also remember, that to minds, *such as theirs*, the effusions of merriment and wit are but the relaxations of a leisure hour, are but the unbending of the higher powers of the intellect; powers which, if directed by an elevated and honourable ambition, must enable them to bind round their brows the never-fading wreath of moral, political, and literary excellence. Let the *graver* hours of these men, who in their moments of gaiety, can give birth to a production which the wits of London and of Paris might be proud to own; a production, which often united the broader banter of Swift with the more chastened and delicate humour of Addison, be devoted to exertions worthy of their more serious and more laborious study, and America might at no distant day, hail as the brightest ornaments of her senate and her bar, those striplings, whose wit has compelled her to laugh at the folly of her own children.

The Salmagundi itself cannot help, occasionally shewing to us, that its authors possess far higher powers, than the mere faculty of a rapid and ludicrous association of ideas; it contains instances of the tender and the pathetic, which prove that our wits can exercise as sovereign a sway over the softer and the better feelings of the heart, as they do over the risible muscles. . . .

[Review of *Knickerbocker's History of New York*]

Anonymous°

Captain Hudson, an Englishman, commanding a ship belonging to the Dutch East India Company, while prosecuting a voyage for the discovery of a northwest passage to China, entered the bay of New York in the year 1609. He advanced up the majestick river Mohegan, as it was called by the Indians, but which now bears his name. After his return to Holland, the Dutch government sent out

° Reprinted from *Monthly Anthology and Boston Review* 8 (February 1810): 123–28.

a ship with a few colonists who took possession of the country, called it Nieuw Netherlands, and began to build the present city of New York, under the name of New Amsterdam. The Dutch retained possession of this fine, and from its situation very important country, till 1664, when an English expedition, commanded by colonel Nicholls, arrived before the city, which was surrendered to him by capitulation. It was immediately erected into an English province, which, as well as its capital, took the name of New York.

The meagre annals of this short-lived Dutch colony have afforded the ground work for this amusing book, which is certainly the wittiest our press has ever produced. To examine it seriously in a historical point of view, would be ridiculous; though the few important events of the period to which it relates are, we presume, recorded with accuracy as to their dates and consequences.

These materials, which would hardly have sufficed to fill a dry journal of a few pages, are here extended to two volumes. They only compose the coarse net-work texture of the cloth, on which the author has embroidered a rich collection of wit and humour. The account of these honest Dutch governours has been made subservient to a lively flow of good natured satire on the follies and blunders of the present day, and the perplexities they have caused. This writer, wisely enough perhaps, laughs at what makes others groan; and if anything can be hoped from ridicule, the rash imbecility of those ignorant *plagiarists*, who have been for some years past carrying on war by proclamations and resolutions, might by this work be shamed into a retreat and concealment.

The great merit, and indeed almost the only one, which the varied labours of former times have left to the literature of the present day, aptness and fertility of allusion, will be found almost to satiety in these pages. Those who have a relish for light humour, and are pleased with that ridicule which is caused by trifling, and, to the mass of the world, unobserved relations and accidents of persons and situations will be often gratified. They will soon perceive that the writer is one of those privileged beings, who, in his pilgrimage through the lanes and streets, the roads and avenues of this uneven world, refreshes himself with many a secret smile at occurrences that excite no observation from the dull, trudging mass of mortals. "The little Frenchmen, skipping from the battery to avoid a shower with their hats covered with their handkerchiefs;" the distress of "the worthy Dutch family" annoyed by the vicinage of "a French boarding house," with all its attendant circumstances, even down to "the little pug-nose dogs that penetrated into their best room," are examples among many others of this disposition. The people of New England are the subject of many humorous remarks, but we are glad to observe made with so much good-nature and mingled compliment and satire, that they themselves must laugh.

It is vain to attempt to analyse a work of this kind. . . .

[Introductory Essay to Salmagundi]
John Lambert°

So little is really known of the United States of America, on this side of the Atlantic, that it is not a matter of much surprise to find the most absurd and ridiculous prejudices existing with regard to every thing belonging to that country. The unfortunate revolution, which terminated in the emancipation of our colonies, is certainly the ostensible cause of the jealousy which exists between the two nations; and, of the two, I think our prejudices against the Americans are stronger than their animosity towards us.—I believe it is more difficult for a parent to pardon the undutiful behaviour of a child than for a child to forget the ill-treatment of a parent. The same reasoning may, perhaps, apply to nations as well as to individuals; for the conduct of men, in their public capacity, is guided very often by the same feelings and passions as influence them in private life.

From what source, however, such antipathy may flow, it is, at all events, to be regretted, for it not only tends to prevent that friendship and cordiality which ought ever to exist between England and America, but will, if not timely checked, burst into a flame that may hereafter be difficult to quench. I do not here mean to cast any reflection on our government, who, it must be confessed, have exhibited, in repeated instances, a considerable degree of conciliation and forbearance. The Americans themselves are, in many respects, equally culpable; for, by their open encouragement of European traitors and emissaries, they have occasioned much of that rancour which has contributed both to retard the settlement of the differences between the two nations and to sow discord and enmity among themselves.

The animosity, however, of the Americans is chiefly of a political nature, whereas our prejudices extend to every thing American, whether it be the politics of the democrats, the manners of the people, or the ladies' teeth!—it is thus the Americans have the advantage of us. They are intemperate in politics, but their intemperance extends no farther; they are noisy and blustering, like our-

° Reprinted from *Salmagundi; or, The Whim-whams and Opinions of Launcelot Langstaff, Esq., and Others* . . . (London: Printed for L. M. Richardson, 1811), [v]–liv.

selves, in their complaints of other nations; they are jealous of all encroachments on their liberties, and tenacious of their political opinions even to a fault.—But view them in private life; in their hours of relaxation; in the circle of friendship; and it will be found that they do not deserve the opprobrium that has been cast on their character. . . .

In introducing to the patronage of the British public a literary production of the United States, it is my first care to remove those prejudices which exist in the minds of too many of my countrymen against every thing of American origin; many, I dare say, already begin to prick up their ears at the very name of *American* literature, and, perhaps, suspect that I have an intention of palming upon them, for American genius, the sterling wit of some English author, driven to that country by his grinding creditors. Now, though I will not undertake to deny that many a poor author may really have made his escape to that land of freedom, yet I positively assure my *gentle*, as well as genteel, readers, that the *Salmagundi* is, bona fide, a *dish* of real American cookery; and, if they will only allow me first to disperse those little acrimonious crudities that prevent digestion, I will present them with such an excellent ragout of wit, humour, and genius, that they may feast on for ever without the least apprehension of a surfeit. A SALMAGUNDI is, indeed, a dish that may at first alarm some of delicate appetites, especially those who have no great partiality to the country in which it was cooked; but if they can only be prevailed on to taste it, I promise them it will act like the stimulating curry of India, without which the poor half-stewed nabob would die for want of an appetite! But, metaphor apart, I am confident that, if these essays are favoured with an attentive perusal, and the mind of the reader divested of the prejudices in favour of our own eminent writers in that department, they will not only find considerable amusement and instruction, but also be convinced that the contempt in which American literature is generally held in this country is both unjust and groundless. As it is my intention, in this introductory essay, to notice the most striking passages and characters in the Salmagundi, I shall, in order to prepare the reader for such observations, preface them with a hasty review of the origin of the American union, and of the present state of the manners, customs, and dispositions, of the people in that country. This will, I hope, serve both to elucidate a considerable portion of the work in question, and to remove many of those false impressions which now prejudice the minds of Englishmen; if I am instrumental, even in the smallest degree, to the removal of one such impression, I shall feel myself amply compensated for any feeble aid which I may have lent towards the attainment of so desirable an object. . . .

The distinguishing feature of the Salmagundian Essays is humourous satire, which runs through the whole work like veins of rich ore in the bowels of the earth. These essays partake more of the broad humour and satirical wit of Rabelais and Swift than the refined morality of Addison and Johnson; their chief aim is to raise a laugh at the expense of folly and absurdity, and to lash the vices of society with the rod of satire:—they do not pretend to improve mankind by a code of ethics and morals, and, therefore, should not be tried by the same critical laws as the British Essays. The American Salmagundi bears much the same relation to the Spectator and Rambler as Roderic Random does to Sir Charles Grandison and Pamela.—The authors, however, have, in several instances, proved that they can speak to the heart as well as the mind; it is only to be regretted that they have not oftener written in a style that seems by no means a stranger to their pen, and which might have contributed to give their work a more classical and instructive tone than it at present bears; nevertheless, it possesses a rich fund of information for those who are desirous of becoming acquainted with the manners of the American people; for, though it naturally partakes of caricature, yet the features of society are rather heightened than distorted. A very favourable trait in the character of this work, and of which few humourous productions can boast, is the chastity of idea as well as diction which pervades the whole. Though wit, humour, and satire, are its principal ingredients, yet the thoughts and language are clothed in the most chaste and modest habiliments. It is also as free from dulness, pedantry, and affectation, as it is from indecency and immorality; and the best proof of the good sense and abilities of its authors is, that they have avoided that quaint and ridiculous phraseology, so common among the generality of writers in their country. The Salmagundi has afforded much entertainment to the Americans, who have bestowed on it the utmost applause; and, as the whole of the Essays abound in applications to the manners, customs, and constitution, of England, it will therefore, I think, be read with almost as much interest by us as if it had been written expressly for this country. The characters are, for the most part, "representatives of their species," and apply equally to an Englishman as an American. It is thus that they become interesting to us in a double capacity;—First, in their general application to society at large, and, secondly, in the picture they present of American manners, hitherto so imperfectly known on this side of the Atlantic.

From an observation in No. 1, on the character of Anthony Evergreen, it appears that the hours for meals must have undergone as great a change in America as in Europe. "When the ladies paid tea visits at three in the afternoon"—they must have dined at eleven or twelve, breakfasted at six, and rose at four or five. It was then that that glorious luminary, the sun, was more honoured than the tallow-chandler: Now, the reverse is the case; and the votaries of pleasure and dissipation seem to dread the light of day, with as much horror as they dread the examination of their own hearts. How little we estimate the benefits we possess, and covet those beyond our reach, is strikingly exemplified in our disregard of one of the greatest enjoyments of this life,—*day-light*. . . .

Our dramatic authors and performers will, no doubt, agree with Launcelot Langstaff, that the critics, who so often unmercifully castigate their labours, "frequently create the fault they find, in order to yield an opening for their criticisms, and censure an actor for a gesture he never made, or an emphasis he never gave."—From the ire of Launcelot, against "neighbour Town," it would appear that New York can boast of as *sound* newspaper critics on the drama as London. As theatrical performances on the other side of the Atlantic are but of modern date, the Americans of course are acquainted only by name with the old English practice of pit-criticism, in vogue a century ago, consequently they cannot estimate the loss we have sustained, and the miserable exchange we have made from that open and manly decision on dramatic merits, to the anonymous criticism of concealed friends or foes. . . .

When we complain that the taste of the age, for dramatic spectacles, is vitiated and depraved, we may, in a great measure, attribute it to the change which has taken place in the mode of criticism, by which bad comedies, miserable farces, and despicable pantomimes, are puffed up, much oftener than good plays are written down. We are, now-a-days, so attentive to *costume* and *propriety*, that the more important parts of the drama are neglected; and the attention of the people diverted from the instructive lessons and delightful sentiments elicited in the many admirable dramatic pieces, of which our country can boast, to the gaudy display of pantomimical pageantry, and the exhibition of real dogs and horses. If former times were marked by errors in theatrical costume, they were, however, distinguished by a greater attention to the real worth and intrinsic merits of the drama. The sight of the critic in the pit was sufficient to check the least impropriety in the actor, and to rouse him to all the exertion of which he was master. The performer, a century ago, had the dread before him of having his talents investigated at "Button's," and other coffee-houses, by the first wits of the age;—and, if he regarded his credit, he always took care how he passed through such an ordeal.

The observation of Will Wizard, that because he had "never seen Kemble in Macbeth, he was utterly at a loss to say whether Mr. Cooper performed well or ill," is an excellent piece of satire on those critics, whose only criterion of judgement is comparison; and who, being completely at a loss what to say respecting an actor's powers, are compelled to drag forward another, in order to *measure* the talents or defects of the one by the other. The suggestion that, if Lady Macbeth had stuck the candle in her night-cap, it would have had a greater effect than the setting it down on the table, or holding it in her hand, (as censured by other critics,) inasmuch as it would have marked more strongly the derangement of her mind, is highly ludicrous, as well as severe on those who are so apt to carp at trifles. So likewise are the observations on errors of costume, and not dipping the daggers so deep in blood by an inch or two, as formerly. The new reading of *"Sorry Sight,"* is no bad hint to the commentators on Shakespeare, and not inapplicable to Mr. Kemble's *"Aitches."*

Frequent mention is made in these Essays of the word *Cockney.* This phrase is not meant merely for a Londoner, but is intended to designate those consequential gentlemen from England, who cross the Atlantic on the strength of a consignment from Birmingham or Liverpool. These gentry are too apt to estimate the genius of the Americans by the standard of their own intellects, and flatter themselves how much they will "astonish the natives" on their arrival. Disappointed, however, at not attracting that notice, and causing that degree of astonishment which they fondly expected, they speak with contempt of every thing that is American. The men are brutes;—the women have bad teeth;—the towns are paltry;—the plays are wretched;—the performers miserable;—in short, there is nothing in America as there is in England: and comparisons are hourly drawn between things which bear not the slightest resemblance to each other. Thus it is that the vender of hardware, and broad cloth becomes a critic out of mere spite: He dashes away while his consignment lasts, (too often indeed at the cost of his employers;) and, though he may fail to attract the notice of the *natives* by his merits, he generally contrives to appropriate to himself a tolerable share of their contempt. A most admirable portrait of a Birmingham hero is given in these Essays in the character of Tom Straddle: It abounds with comic touches, and displays a wit and humour, that would do honour to the productions of any of our essayists.

The allusions to the French people, in various passages of the Salmagundian Essays, prove that the writers entertained no very favourable opinion of those who have settled in the United States; and that they thought a little wholesome castigation from their pens might be of service to them. The numerous bands of Frenchmen, who have flocked to that country since the French revolution, have, by no means, tended to the improvement of American manners or morals, or the removal of any of those prejudices which existed between England and America; on the contrary, both domestic dissipation and foreign rancour have considerably increased. The lightness and frivolity of the French character is neatly touched off in several of the Essays; and the deleterious influence of their example on the grave disposition of the Americans successfully exposed. They have inundated America, as they have this country, and may well be said to "hop about the town in swarms, like little toads after a shower." It would have been happy for both parties, had their conduct been as exemplary as the reception they met with was liberal; but many are the melancholy instances to the contrary, both in the privacy of domestic retirement as well as in the public walk of politics. They have debauched the wives and daughters of their benefactors,— corrupted the manners of society,—and sowed dissention and rebellion throughout the country. Even their own countryman, the Duke de Rochefoucault Liancourt, in his travels through the United States, can find no excuse for them; and, unreservedly, consigns them to the merited execrations of the Americans. It would, however, be uncharitable to include all Frenchmen in this accusation; it is the dregs of the revolution only who have acted in this manner. There are many who have deserved the hospitality they met with; yet, I fear their number is not equal to those who have abused it.

In contrast to this feeling, with regard to the French, it must afford Englishmen much satisfaction to find the sentiments of a great portion of the American people highly favourable towards them, from a variety of causes. In various parts of these Essays, these favourable sentiments are repeatedly displayed,—particularly in the character of Christopher Cockloft—and the rest of his family. Their antipathy to the French,—partiality to every thing English,—Christopher's voyage to Halifax, to hear our king prayed for in church as he was before the revolution,—giving a dinner on the king's birth-day,— and a variety of other traits, which, though they may be nothing more than the eccentric features of a fictitious character, are, I think, intended as delineations of real traits existing among a considerable portion of the people. Several instances are also mentioned in these Essays of the attention and partiality displayed towards our countrymen arriving in the United States: even an insignificant fellow is represented as having worked himself into the good graces of the citizens, merely because he was an *Englishman.* The claim of consanguinity as well as individual interest is, no doubt, a strong motive of their attachment to Great Britain, which they often denominate *home,* especially those who once lived under the British government, and whose sentiments have been but little changed since the revolution. Others who were children when that event took place, have imbibed from their cradle, as it were, the true republican spirit. Hence though they may prefer British to French interests, are yet tenacious of their independence almost to a fault, and equally jealous of British usurpation as of French intrigue. As to those who are styled Democrats, Jacobins, and Tories, I look upon the violent among them more as a mixture of factious Europeans than real Americans. They have unfortunately from the nature of the government too much influence in political matters; but I think it extremely unfair to judge of the character of the Americans by the scum of the country.

The writers of Salmagundi have happily enough availed themselves of the opportunity which the Tripolitan prisoners gave them, to introduce a very humourous character into their work. *Mustapha Rub-a-dub Keli Khan* is one of the most diverting personages in the whole groupe; and his opinion of the Americans, formed on the prejudices of his own nation, open an extensive field for satire. This character has also the merit of being well supported, for he seldom exceeds the bounds of his supposed knowledge of American manners; and, where he has occasion to go farther, the information is generally conveyed to him through the medium of some acquaintance or bystander, by which means he is not a mere *American* observer, tricked out in a *shawl* and *turban.* He really possesses as much the semblance of a Mahomedan as it is possible for fiction to give. The Citizen of the World is more of an Englishman in a Chinese dress than Mustapha an American in masquerade. When a foreign character is brought forward for our amusement, he ought to reason as well as speak agreeable to his own ideas, formed on the manners, customs, and prejudices, of his nation; unless indeed we are to consider him as gifted with a cosmopolitan spirit, and general knowledge of the world,—a foundation on which Goldsmith most likely formed his Chinese Letters. . . .

A considerable portion of Salmagundi is appropriated to the exposure and ridicule of certain travellers who have visited the United States; and whose illiberal aspersions and ridiculous prejudices have drawn upon them the censure of every candid and impartial person. Nor have others, who never crossed the Atlantic, altogether escaped the satirical lash of these witty writers, as the names of Carr and Kotzebue evidently prove. That the Irish knight should be so unfortunate as to excite the ridicule of the Americans as well as his own countrymen is rather singular; and if it had not been satisfactorily proved to the contrary, I should have condemned the "Stranger in New Jersey," as a plagiarism on "My Pocket Book!" That this was also the opinion of those American critics who endeavoured to write down the Salmagundi may be seen from the note attached to No. 13. From that declaration it however appears, that the "Stranger in New Jersey" is an original production, and made its appearance in these Essays at New York one month before "My Pocket Book" was published in London. This circumstance is peculiarly unfortunate for the knight's literary reputation, as it tends to confirm the opinion which the author of "My Pocket Book" had formed of his "Stranger in Ireland." He has also unluckily the double misfortune of suffering under American and English satire, as it were, of one accord, without the possibility of any previous understanding between the writers to that effect. Weld, Moore, Parkinson, and Priest, who have been particularly severe in their strictures on the American character, also come in for their share of the rod.—Indeed they merit it much more than poor Sir John, who was hardly a fair object of correction: but it might perhaps be done with a view to prevent his visiting the country, though from the general style of his writings I should conceive they would have found him perfectly harmless.

The Essay on Style may put in its claim for as large a portion of merit as any one in the whole work. The portrait which is there drawn of the manners of fashionable upstarts is an admirable picture from life, not only as it exists in New York, but also in London. How many families of "Giblets" have we seen in this metropolis, whose sudden elevation from the counter to the chariot has astonished the vulgar and alarmed the great. Never was style, as it is understood in fashionable language, better defined, nor its ridiculous absurdities better pourtrayed, than in that Essay. The humourous contrast of style as it is found in different countries, and the innovations which it occasions in domestic families, are agreeably depicted. But the preposterous whim of Bellbrazen, the Haytian beauty, and the sudden elevation of the Giblets, from the manners of their grub-worm father to the dashing career of fashionable folly, are most happily hit off, and display a rich fund of satirical wit and humour. Who is there that will not immediately recognize in the following passage the manners of our vulgar fashionables, and of those *ci-devant* citizens, who in their migration from Pudding-lane to Portman-square, have bewildered themselves with *style?*—

> Then commenced the hurry and bustle and mighty nothingness of fashionable life;—such rattling in coaches! such flaunting in the streets! such slamming of box-doors at the theatre! such a tempest of bustle and unmeaning noise wherever they appeared! the Giblets were seen here, there, and every where;—they visited every body they knew, and every body they did not know; and there was no getting along for the Giblets. Their plan at length succeeded: by dint of dinners, of feeding and frolicking the town, the Giblet family worked themselves into notice, and enjoyed the ineffable pleasure of being for ever pestered by visitors, who cared nothing about them; of being squeezed, and smothered, and par-boiled, at nightly balls and evening tea-parties. They were allowed the privilege of forgetting the few old friends they once possessed; they turned their noses up in the wind at every thing that was not genteel; and their superb manners and sublime affectation at length left it no longer a matter of doubt that the Giblets were perfectly in *style*.

Another admirable picture from life is presented to us in the character of "My good aunt Charity,"—a simple, curious, old maid, who unfortunately "died of a Frenchman!" This portrait is drawn with all that warmth of colouring which heightens without disfiguring the features; and though highly ludicrous, is yet a true delineation of human nature. Hogarth never painted with more animation and satirical truth than the authors of Salmagundi have written. Many an antiquated old maid, and many a female gossip, may contemplate the several features of their dispositions in that mirror of formality and curiosity. The buckram delicacy of "My aunt" in the hey-dey of youth,—and the religious turn she took when that period was past, are highly humorous; the latter is also an excellent satire on those who in their old age make up at "*love-feasts*" for the disappointments they have sustained in *real love*. The other peculiarities of aunt Charity's character are equally appropriate; and even that one, viz. *curiosity*, which unluckily caused her "to die of a Frenchman" was an innocent foible with her. It would be happy for society were it always so with others; but the invincible desire which some females at a certain age,—married as well as single,—widows as well as old maids,—have of knowing every body's character,—business,—and mode of living, and looking after every one's affairs but their own, is too frequently the offspring of pride, envy, and jealousy. There cannot be a more dangerous character in a small society than the *envious gossip*, who makes it her business to "get at the bottom of a thing," be it good or bad.—Under the specious mask of friendship and kindness a woman of this description will work herself into the favour of her unsuspecting acquaintance, and, when possessed of the information she sought for, will never fail to sow discord among them;—like poor aunt Charity, but with less innocent motives, "she will not sleep a wink all night" for fear another Mrs. Sipkins should get the start of her in the morning, and tell her story first. This endeavour "to give currency to the *good-natured* things said about every body" is not the only peculiarity of the *envious gossip*, for, so anxious does she pretend to be for the truth of what she asserts (as is the case with all notorious liars), that, if her word is doubted, her neighbours must be brought face to face; away, then, she hobbles from house to house, and never closes her eyes until she has set her little community together by the ears.

Women of this description are the pests of small towns and villages, and will, over their tea and cards, consign more reputations to infamy than even their tongues can repeat; for a shrug and a sneer are, if possible, more dangerous. By such arts married people have been made miserable, and friends and acquaintance been rendered implacable enemies. But what makes a character of this description the more detestable is, that every thing is done out of *pure loving kindness;* for instance, she shall be so mightily afraid lest you, or any of your family, should be contaminated, by acquainting with such and such a character, that she immediately discharges her whole budget of lies, scandal, and malignity, to the utter annihilation, perhaps, of the reputation of some worthy family or innocent girl; this is what she terms friendly advice, and a proof of the interest she takes in your welfare! Such is the true character of an *envious gossip,* whose impertinent interference in her neighbours' affairs, while it destroys their happiness, does but render herself miserable, and, sooner or later, makes her the object of universal hatred and disgust:—— "Take warning, therefore, my fair country-women, and you, oh, ye excellent ladies! whether married or single, who pry into other people's affairs, and neglect those of your own household, who are so busily employed in observing the faults of others that you have no time to correct your own, remember the fate of my dear aunt Charity, and eschew the evil spirit of curiosity."

A considerable part of these essays are appropriated to the fair sex, and a tolerable portion of satirical correction and wholesome advice dealt out to them; their injurious experiments of tight-lacing, to render themselves fine figures, are frequently noticed, and some humourous animadversions passed thereon, which cannot, I should think, be unpalatable to them, even if they are not inclined to alter their proceedings. It is a pity that the American ladies, who are by nature elegantly made, should resort to experiments which injure their constitutions and put them in torture. The practice of tight-lacing, the eating of pickles and chalk, and the smoking of tobacco, are, I believe, no strangers to European females; but, whatever necessity the daughter of a Dutch burgomaster, or English farmer, might have for such arts to reduce their size, I do not think those who are naturally slim have any occasion to adopt them. . . .

Another subject of animadversion, on which the writers of Salmagundi have dwelt in some of their essays, is the folly of what is called style, and the present fashionable mode of "murdering time." Modern life is admirably displayed in the essay on style, and in some of the passages of Mustapha's letter on the assembly. After contemplating such scenes of folly, bustle, and dissipation, one cannot help being struck with the insensibility of the people who live in the vortex of fashionable life, and who pursue their career of daring extravagance and vapid nothingness to the very grave, without resting on their journey for one moment to contemplate the awfulness of their situation.—The old and the young are alike engaged in the same senseless routine of folly and absurdity. What man of sense, wishing to marry, would chuse a woman whose days and nights are engrossed with the preparations for, and participations in, continual routs, balls, and card-parties? What satisfaction can be derived from a woman thus educated? Surely such an incessant exposure of female youth and beauty to the gaiety and dissipation of public parties must be as detrimental to the morals as to the health. . . .

The observations which I have made in the course of these essays have arisen out of the various subjects contained therein, and if I have not done my authors all the justice they merit, it is because they have not had an editor of equal talent with themselves. I cannot do better than conclude this Introductory Essay in their own language, and hope my fair countrywomen will be as ready to comply with their request as the American ladies were:—"We recommend to all *mothers* to purchase our essays for their daughters, who will be taught the true line of propriety, and the most adviseable method of managing their beaux. We advise all *daughters* to purchase them for the sake of their mothers, who shall be initiated into the arcana of the bon ton, and cured of all those rusty old notions which they acquired during the last century.—Parents shall be taught how to govern their children; girls how to get husbands; and old maids how to do without them."

[Review of *The Sketch Book*, No. 1]

Henry Brevoort, Jr.°

This is a new production said to be from the elegant and racy pen of Washington Irving, Esq. The first number contains five distinct sketches, viz: a sketch of Mr. Crayon; a sketch of a sea voyage; a sketch of Roscoe, the historian; a sketch of a wife; and a sketch of low life in an inland Low-Dutch village, as it appeared some sixty or eighty years ago, and which is thrown into the form of a story, entitled Rip Van Winkle. The graces of style; the rich, warm tone of benevolent feeling; the freely-flowing vein of hearty and happy humour, and the fine-eyed spirit of observation, sustained by an enlightened understanding and regulated by a perception of fitness— a tact—wonderfully quick and sure, for which Mr. Irving has been heretofore so much distinguished, are all exhibited anew in the Sketch Book, with freshened beauty and added charms. There are few pieces of composition in the language, of similar design, equal to the account of Roscoe: it is a just and noble-spirited eulogium, united with a well discriminated, rapid, sketchy delineation of the character of that elegant historian, that does equal honor to the subject and the writer. The "Wife" is beautifully pathetic, and in these times of commercial disasters will be read with interest, and, it is to be hoped, with *benefit*,

° Reprinted in part from *New-York Evening Post*, 26 June 1819.

by many. But Rip Van Winkle is the master-piece. For that comic spirit which is without any infusion of gall, which delights in what is ludicrous rather than ridiculous, (for its laughter is not mixed with contempt,) which seeks its gratification in the eccentricities of a simple, unrefined state of society, rather than in the vicious follies of artificial life; for the vividness and truth, with which Rip's character is drawn, and the state of society in the village where he lived, is depicted; and for the graceful ease with which it is told, the story of Rip Van Winkle has few competitors. There appears, also, to be a design to exhibit the contrast between the old provincial times, and the state of things subsequent to the American revolution.

Possibly the man, who after reading Paradise Lost, said, with a look and tone of the most skeptical sagacity, that he did not believe half of it, might look over these sketches with indifference; but all those who are not yet sublimed with pure intellect, nor become inveterately wise; who still retain a feeling of human infirmities, and a relish for nature, will be well-pleased with them; and will probably wait, with pleasant anticipations, for the remaining contents of Mr. Crayon's port-folio.

Addition

The above is furnished by a literary friend, whose judgment on such subjects, generally speaking, I respect—therefore I have given it a place as it stands. But after perusing the work myself, I am compelled to say that I cannot concur in opinion with him as to the last sketch, that of Rip Van Winkle. With much elegance of manner, we think probability however, should not be wholly overlooked. The tale of the Wife is undoubtedly the author's happiest effort. We wish the work every possible success.

As an elegant and accurate piece of typography, (with the single exception, *lay* for *lie*,) it reflects great credit on the American press; and we hope the publication will meet with the encouragement it merits.

[Review of *The Sketch Book*, No. 2]
Henry Brevoort, Jr.°

The Sketch Book of Geoffrey Crayon, gentleman, No. 2.—A short time since, we had the pleasure of briefly announcing to the public

---

° Reprinted from *New-York Evening Post,* 3 August 1819.

the appearance of the first number of this work; we have now particular gratification in being enabled to state, that its reception has fully realised our anticipations. The second number has just been published: it contains sketches of "English writers on America,"— "Rural life in England,"—"The Broken Heart,"—and, "The Art of Book-making."

In the first article, the subject of our social relations with England is dispassionately stated, and exhibited in many original and conciliating points of view. The author exposes the impolicy of England in repressing our kindred sympathies by her haughty tone of superiority; nor has he overlooked the undue importance that we attach to the refuted calumnies and paltry insults of her angry writers. England, with all her faults, is still the country that we regard with feelings of deepest interest: in her, we trace the original features of our national and individual character: from her centuries of experience, we have derived the deep foundations of our civil liberty, and social institutions; by contemplating the perfection to which she has advanced all the arts of civilization, we catch a glimpse of what we are destined to become—But these affinities, instead of binding us in a friendly alliance of kind offices, seem destined to engender an eternal collision in all the objects and pursuits that constitute the pride and ambition of two powerful and high-spirited nations—It is the leading object of our author, to soften the bitter spirit of contempt and recrimination, which has so frequently sullied the literature of both countries, and nearly destroyed those courtesies that would otherwise have existed between them.

"Rural life in England," is an exquisitely finished sketch. The sensibilities of the author appear to have been fully awakened by those picturesque aspects of moral and external beauty peculiar to old and highly-cultivated countries. His delineations breathe the freshness and the fragrance of a summer's shower. The characteristic features of rural life in England rise distinctly to our view, with nearly the force and reality of the scene itself.

The sketches entitled, "The Broken Heart," and "The Art of Book-making," are specimens of that happy facility of the writer, in varying the subject and the style of his compositions—But we turn from their obvious merits, to say a word in relation to the author and his immediate designs. We think Mr. Irving has conceived the plan of his work, with the happiest adaptation to his peculiar turn of mind, which is thus left at liberty, to act upon a wide range of subjects, "sometimes treating of scenes before him, sometimes of others purely imaginary, and sometimes wandering back with his recollections to his native country." For ourselves, we would cheerfully participate in all his wanderings, either abroad or at home, throughout every varying scene of human existence, which shall call forth the richness of his humour, or excite the deep pathos of his feelings. In these dispositions, we believe his admirers heartily concur; and he may take our assurance, that he has already accomplished his designs beyond the diffidence of his hopes. His countrymen hail his reappearance as a writer, with the endearing cordiality of one, who had been too long absent, but has unexpectedly returned, with sympathies still tenderly linked to his native land.

The literary ambition of Mr. I. aims simply at a flute accompaniment, in our national concert of authors, leaving to the more aspiring the management of the louder instruments. We gladly perceive that he never suffers himself to be allured from his natural character, by a pompous display of his subject, or by an attempt to plunge his readers into the unfathomable depths of learning and research. We wish to mark this integrity of design, exclusively for the benefit of certain Linnean critics, who have been puzzled in defining the object of his Sketches, and of classing them with any of the popular elegies of the day. Tradition affirms, that one of the notable tragedies of Sophocles, was returned by a geometer, with the appalling demand of what it was intended to demonstrate?—Mr. I. stands somewhat in this awkward predicament, although his friends might plead the examples of Addison, Goldsmith and Mackenzie, to countenance the humility of his ambition.—But truly we live in an age which has brought down science from her sublime heights, to dwell in highways and market places. Amidst the solemn fopperies of the would be wise, it is indeed a refreshing indulgence to follow an author in his careless rambles through the lower regions of Parnassus. We reverence the cause of true science; nor would we be understood to scoff at its unaffected votaries; but no one knows, who has not essayed the task, how cheaply an author may decorate his pages with the scattered fragments of learning, lying so invitingly at his mercy, in the multitudinous transactions and encyclopedias of our times. Our author has found out the art of book-making; he has traced to their fountain head, those muddy rills of knowledge that sometimes spread themselves even in America. It is not impossible, therefore, that in the future numbers of his work, he may avoid the labor of writing from the resources of his own mind, by compiling the present state of the Catholic question—the vast results of polar expeditions; or, peradventure, strike out some new geological hypothesis which shall reject the vulgar agency of fire or water. In such ambitious speculations, we fear, the admirers of his fine genius, might seek in vain for his sportive humor; his nice discrimination of character; his romantic associations of thought and language; his pure and affecting morality, and all the nameless graces of a style, so appropriate to the captivating path of literature he has chosen to pursue.

[Review of *Knickerbocker's History of New York, Second Edition*]

John G. Lockhart°

Mr. Washington Irving is one of our first favourites among the English writers of this age—and he is not a bit the less for having been born in America. He is not one of those Americans who practise, what may be called, a treason of the heart, in perpetual scoffs and sneers against the land of their forefathers. He well knows that his "thews and sinews" are not all, for which he is indebted to his English ancestry. All the noblest food of his heart and soul have been derived to him, he well knows, from the same fountain—and he is as grateful for his obligations as he is conscious of their magnitude. . . .

The great superiority, over too many of his countrymen, evinced by Mr. Irving on every occasion, when he speaks of the manners, the spirit, the faith of England, has, without doubt, done much to gain for him our affection. But had he never expressed one sentiment favourable to us or to our country, we should still have been compelled to confess that we regard him as by far the greatest genius that has arisen on the literary horizon of the new world. The Sketch Book has already proved, to our readers, that he possesses exquisite powers of pathos and description; but we recur, with pleasure, to this much earlier publication, of which, we suspect, but a few copies have ever crossed the Atlantic, to shew that we did right when we ascribed to him, in a former paper, the possession of a true old English vein of humour and satire—of keen and lively wit—and of great knowledge and discrimination of human nature.

The whole book is a *jeu-d'esprit,* and, perhaps, its only fault is, that no *jeu-d'esprit* ought to be quite so long as to fill two closely printed volumes. Under the mask of an historian of his native city, he has embodied, very successfully, the results of his own early observation in regard to the formation and constitution of several regular divisions of American society; and in this point of view his work will preserve its character of value, long after the lapse of time shall have blunted the edge of these personal allusions which, no doubt, contributed most powerfully to its popularity over the water. . . .

We shall return to the volumes again, for we suppose we may consider them as in regard to almost all that read this Magazine, "as good as manuscript." Enough, however, has been quoted to shew of what sort of stuff Mr. Irving's comic pencil is composed—and enough to make all our readers go along with us in a request which we have

° Reprinted from *Blackwood's Edinburgh Magazine* 7 (July 1820): 360–69.

long meditated, viz. that this author would favour us with a series of novels, on the plan of those of Miss Edgeworth, or, if he likes that better, of the author of Waverley, illustrative of the present state of manners in the United States of America. When we think, for a moment, on the variety of elements whereof that society is every where composed—the picturesque mixtures of manners derived from German, Dutch, English, Scottish, Swedish, Gothic, and Celtic settlers, which must be observable in almost every town of the republican territories—the immense interfusion of different ranks of society from all these quarters, and their endless varieties of action upon each other—the fermentation that must every where prevail among these yet unsettled and unarranged atoms—above all, on the singularities inseparable from the condition of the only half-young, half-old people in the world—simply as such—we cannot doubt that could a Smollet, a Fielding, or a Le Sage have seen America as she is, he would at once have abandoned every other field, and blessed himself on having obtained access to the true *terra fortunata* of the novelist. Happily for Mr. Irving that *terra fortunata* is also to this hour a *terra incognita;* for in spite of the shoals of bad books of travels that have inundated us from time to time, no European reader has ever had the smallest opportunity of being introduced to any thing like one vivid portraiture of American life. Mr. Irving has, as every good man must have, a strong affection for his country; and he is, therefore, fitted to draw her character *con amore* as well as *con gentilezza.* The largeness of his views, in regard to politics, will secure him from staining his pages with any repulsive air of bigotry— and the humane and liberal nature of his opinions in regard to subjects of a still higher order, will equally secure him from still more offensive errors.

To frame the plots of twenty novels can be no very heavy task to the person who wrote the passages we have quoted above—and to fill them up with characteristic details of incidents and manners, would be nothing but an amusement to him. He has sufficiently tried and shewn his strength in sketches—it is time that we should look for full and glowing pictures at his hands. Let him not be discouraged by the common-place cant about the impossibility of good novels being written by young men. Smollet wrote Roderick Random before he was five-and-twenty, and assuredly he had not seen half so much of the world as Mr. Irving has done. We hope we are mistaken in this point—but it strikes us that he writes, of late, in a less merry mood than in the days of Knickerbocker and the Salmagundi. If the possession of intellectual power and resources ought to make any man happy, that man is Washington Irving; and people may talk as they please about the "inspiration of melancholy," but it is our firm belief that no man ever wrote any thing greatly worth the writing, unless under the influence of buoyant spirits. "A cheerful mind is what the muses love," says the author of *Ruth* and *Michael,* and *the Brothers;* and in the teeth of all asseverations to the contrary, we take leave to believe that my Lord Byron was never in higher glee than when composing the darkest soliloquies of his Childe Harold. The capacity of achieving immortality, when called into vivid consciousness by the very act of composition and passion of inspiration, must be enough, we should think, to make any man happy. Under such influences he may, for a time, we doubt not, be deaf even to the voice of self-reproach, and hardened against the memory of guilt. The amiable and accomplished Mr. Irving has no evil thoughts or stinging recollections to fly from—but it is very possible that he may have been indulging in a cast of melancholy, capable of damping the wing even of *his* genius. *That,* like every other demon, must be wrestled with, in order to its being overcome. And if he will set boldly about *An American Tale, in three volumes duodecimo,* we think there is no rashness in promising him an easy, a speedy, and a glorious victory. Perhaps all this may look very like impertinence, but Mr. Irving will excuse us, for it is, at least, well meant.

[Review of *The Sketch Book* by Geoffrey Crayon]

Francis Jeffrey°

Though this is a very pleasing book in itself, and displays no ordinary reach of thought and elegance of fancy, it is not exactly on that account that we are now tempted to notice it as a very remarkable publication,—and to predict that it will form an era in the literature of the nation to which it belongs. It is the work of an American, entirely bred and trained in that country—originally published within its territory—and, as we understand, very extensively circulated, and very much admired among its natives. Now, the most remarkable thing in a work so circumstanced certainly is, that it should be written throughout with the greatest care and accuracy, and worked up to great purity and beauty of diction, on the model of the most elegant and polished of our native writers. It is the first American work, we rather think, of any description, but certainly the first purely literary production, to which we could give this praise; and we hope and trust that we may hail it as the harbinger of a purer and juster taste—the foundation of a chaster and better school, for the writers of that great and intelligent country. Its genius, as we have frequently

° Reprinted from *Edinburgh Review* 34 (August 1820): 160–76.

observed, has not hitherto been much turned to letters; and, what it has produced in that department, has been defective in taste certainly rather than in talent. The appearance of a few such works as the present will go far to wipe off this reproach also; and we cordially hope that this author's merited success, both at home and abroad, will stimulate his countrymen to copy the methods by which he has attained it; and that they will submit to receive, from the example of their ingenious compatriot, that lesson which the precepts of strangers do not seem hitherto to have effectually inculcated.

But though it is primarily for its style and composition that we are induced to notice this book, it would be quite unjust to the author not to add, that he deserves very high commendation for its more substantial qualities; and that we have seldom seen a work that gave us a more pleasing impression of the writer's character, or a more favourable one of his judgment and taste. There is a tone of fairness and indulgence—and of gentleness and philanthropy so un-affectedly diffused through the whole work, and tempering and har-monizing so gracefully, both with its pensive and its gayer humours, as to disarm all ordinarily good-natured critics of their asperity, and to secure to the author, from all worthy readers, the same candour and kindness of which he sets so laudable an example. The want is of force and originality in the reasoning and speculative parts, and of boldness and incident in the inventive:—though the place of these more commanding qualities is not ill supplied by great liberality and sound sense, and by a very considerable vein of humour, and no ordinary grace and tenderness of fancy. The manner perhaps through-out is more attended to than the matter; and the care necessary to maintain the rythm [sic] and polish of the sentences, has sometimes interfered with the force of the reasoning, or limited and impoverished the illustrations they might otherwise have supplied.

We have forgotten all this time to inform our readers, that the publication consists of a series or collection of detached essays and tales of various descriptions—originally published apart, in the form of a periodical miscellany, for the instruction and delight of America—and now collected into two volumes for the refreshment of the English public. The English writers whom the author has chiefly copied, are Addison and Goldsmith, in the humorous and discursive parts—and our own excellent Mackenzie, in the more soft and pathetic. In their highest and most characteristic merits, we do not mean to say that he has equalled any of his originals, or even to deny that he has occasionally caricatured their defects. But the resemblance is near enough to be highly creditable to any living author; and there is sometimes a compass of reasoning which his originals have rarely attained. . . .

It is consolatory to the genuine friends of mankind—to the friends of peace and liberty and reason—to find such sentiments [as those expressed in "English Writers on America"] gaining ground in the world; and, above all, to find them inculcated with so much warmth and ability by a writer of that country which has had the strongest provocation to disown them, and whose support of them is, at the present moment, by far the most important. We have already pledged ourselves to do what in us lies to promote the same good cause;— and if our labours are only seconded in America with a portion of the zeal and eloquence which is here employed in their behalf, we have little doubt of seeing them ultimately crowned with success. It is impossible, however, in the mean time, to disguise that much more depends upon the efforts of the American writers, than upon ours; both because they have naturally the most weight with the party who is chiefly to be conciliated, and because their reasonings are not repelled by that outrageous spirit of party which leads no small numbers among us at the present moment, to reject and vilify whatever is recommended by those who are generally opposed to their plans of domestic policy. . . .

In justice to the work before us, however, we should say, that a very small proportion of its contents relates either to politics, or to subjects at all connected with America. There is a "Legend of Sleepy Hollow," which is an excellent *pendant* to Rip Van Winkle; and there are two or three other papers, the localities of which are Transatlantic. But out of the thirty-five pieces which the book contains, there are not more than six or seven that have this character. The rest relate entirely to England; and consist of sketches of its manners, its scenery, and its characters, drawn with a fine and friendly hand— and remarks on its literature and peculiarities, at which it would be difficult for any rational creature to be offended. . . .

We believe that we have now done enough for the courteous and ingenious stranger whom we are ambitious of introducing to the notice of our readers. It is probable, indeed, that many of them have become acquainted with him already; as we have found the book in the hands of most of those to whom we have thought of mentioning it, and observe that the author, in the close of his last volume, speaks in very grateful terms of the encouragement he has received. We are heartily glad of it, both for his sake and for that of literature in general. There is a great deal too much contention and acrimony in most modern publications; and because it has unfortunately been found impossible to discuss practical questions of great interest without some degree of heat and personality, it has become too much the prevailing opinion, that these are necessary accompaniments to all powerful or energetic discussion, and that no work is likely to be well received by the public, or to make a strong impression, which does not abound in them. The success of such a work as this before us, may tend to correct this prejudice, and teach our authors that gentleness and amenity are qualities quite as attractive as violence and impertinence; and that truth is not less weighty, nor reason less persuasive, although not ushered in by exaggerations, and backed by defiance.

[Review of *Bracebridge Hall*]   Anonymous°

We commenced the perusal of this work with no ordinary anticipations. We recollected that the author was not only an American, but a citizen of our own state. Our national pride, therefore, and our local partialities, were alike enlisted in his favour. We recollected too, that he had already been admired for the beauty and grace of his compositions, his humorous delineations of character, and the general simplicity of his style—and what was still more, that he had found favour in the eyes of the English literati, and had been tolerated, if not praised, by the Scotch Reviewers.

We confess, also, that the appearance of the volumes, (two handsomely printed octavos,) and the price the author is said to have received for the manuscript, (to say nothing of the price of the volumes themselves,) had no little agency in exciting our imagination as to the merits of the work. We took up the book, therefore, predisposed to admire, and almost predetermined to applaud. But a perusal, we are compelled to say, has in some measure shaken our faith, and abated the ardour of our feelings. But, let us not be misunderstood. The book has, indeed, fallen short of our expectations, but is nevertheless a very considerable book; and we doubt not, will be read by many with eagerness, if not delight: For fashion is as arbitrary and as capricious in the library, as she is at the toilet, and often influences the mind, while she disfigures the body. If, however, we did not consider the work before us, as possessing a merit independent of fashion; as containing something to admire as well as to censure, we should suffer it to pass without the labour of a comment.

There was an error, we think, in not giving it the name of its predecessor; for it is formed of the same sort of materials, and is in shape and character and substance the same. Bracebridge Hall is, indeed, nothing more nor less than a continuation of the Sketch Book. Its title, therefore, is injudicious. It leads the reader to anticipate something new; and, to the votaries of fashion at least, a disappointment, in that particular, is apt to be fatal. . . .

° Reprinted from *Literary and Scientific Repository* 4 (May 1822): 422–32.

It is impossible, we find, to give any thing like an abridgement, or summary of the work before us. It is neither a history, nor a tale, nor a poem; but possesses advantages unknown to either. It is, for instance, immaterial with which volume you commence, or at which end of the volume. It is a sort of series, or rather a given number, of sketches and descriptions of squires and maids and matrons and bachelors and lovesick girls and schoolmasters and priests and apothecaries and doctors and dogs; intermingled with stories, both long and short, having no other connexion than that of contiguity, and no other order than that of succession. . . .

From the number and variety of the characters introduced, and the acknowledged taste and humour of our author, the reader will naturally anticipate many fine heads and spirited sketches. And he will not be altogether disappointed: there is some good painting, and many quaint, as well as humourous delineations. But we do think the author has, in a few instances, rather overstepped the modesty of nature, and passed from the ludicrous to the absurd. He has certainly embellished his Hall with a number of coarse, if not fantastical portraits, the originals of which, if we mistake not, are much oftener to be met with in the decorations of a barber's shop, than in the walks of real life. They are, indeed, mere caricatures, and if as such they can please, we have no sort of objection. . . .

The character of the Squire, is natural, and well sustained. Master Simon and General Harbottle make no inconsiderable figure, and are sufficiently whimsical and amusing. "The fair Julia," though the acknowledged heroine of the Hall, is rather an insipid article. She seems to be but of little use, and is consequently but little used. She is occasionally seen, "sauntering along, leaning on her lover's arm, with a soft blush on her cheek, and a quiet smile on her lips, and a bunch of flowers in her hand, hanging negligently by her side." For the sake of variety, she is, indeed, once mounted on horseback; and for the sake of effect, is, of course, thrown off and killed, and brought back to life again,—according to the established practice, and most approved recipes. Indeed, all the love scenes of our author, are puerile and mawkish; characterized by a morbid sensibility, and by a fastidious and artificial arrangement of common place details, language, and scenery. The story of Annette, may be taken as a fair sample of his taste and genius, in organizing and developing these delicate matters. . . .

The story of "The Stout Gentleman" is told with cleverness, it displays a good deal of minute observation, and a very happy talent of picturing with cleverness and fidelity the fleeting objects and incidents of the day. But it is too long; a fault applicable to almost every story in the book, and indeed to the book itself. It has, however, another fault, which, considering the class of readers to whom our author must mainly look, as well for the profit, as the fame of his production, (we mean the fair and the fashionable,) is still more objectionable. There is a half hidden looseness, an indelicacy of allusion in the story, which should have found no place in a book destined, if not designed, as an ornament to the sopha, and as a modest companion at the parlour window. . . .

It is impossible not to admire the prudence and delicacy, with which our author has touched upon the interesting, but dangerous subject of politics. While he proudly, and no doubt sincerely, declares his increasing attachment to the republican principles, he eulogises the aristocracy of Great Britain; descants upon the dignity of descent, and the generous pride of illustrious ancestry! The glorious freedom of the British constitution, is prudently admired, and the great body of the English people are timely and judiciously praised. A light and careless shaft is indeed occasionally, but playfully thrown at radicalism; and now and then a good humoured squib, at that patriotic spirit which is inspired by Port, and that loyalty which is the offspring of Burgundy. But these are evidently intended to exhibit the impartiality of the author, and wisely calculated to amuse, rather than to wound. . . .

It was our intention to have said something in relation to the language and style of the work before us, and with this view, we had noted many exceptionable passages: we shall, however, content ourselves by simply remarking, that the merit of the composition, consists in its *grace* rather than in its *purity*. Such words as *rejuvenate*, and such phrases as "perilous to discussion," "champion his country," "champion the rights of the people," "to qualify the *damp* of the night air," "implicit confiding," &c. &c. are certainly as remote from purity, as they are from good taste. Upon the whole we are apprehensive, that these volumes will add but little to the reputation of their author. They embrace, indeed, a variety of subjects, and contain many sensible observations and just reflections; but the subjects want importance, the observations novelty, and the reflections force. The stories that are introduced, are composed of the ordinary romance materials, and not very skilfully combined. They excite but little interest, and make but a faint impression. The work, however, contains much genuine humour;—many picturesque discriptions [*sic*], and is recommended by a style, remarkable for its simplicity and graceful ease.

[Review of *Bracebridge Hall*]   Francis Jeffrey[°]

We have received so much pleasure from this book, that we think ourselves bound in gratitude, as well as justice, to make a public acknowledgment of it,—and seek to repay, by a little kind notice, the great obligations we shall ever feel to the author. These amiable sentiments, however, we fear, will scarcely furnish us with materials for an interesting article;—and we suspect we have not much else to say, that has not already occurred to most of our readers, or, indeed, been said by ourselves with reference to his former publication. For nothing in the world can be so complete as the identity of the author in these two productions—identity not only of style merely and character, but of merit also, both in kind and degree, and in the sort and extent of popularity which that merit has created—not merely the same good sense and the same good humour, directed to the same good ends, and with the same happy selection and limited variety, but the same proportion of things that seem scarcely to depend on the individual—the same *luck*, as well as the same labour, and an equal share of felicities to enhance the fair returns of judicious industry. There are few things, we imagine, so rare as this sustained level of excellence in the works of a popular writer—or, at least, if it does exist now and then in *rerum natura*, there is scarcely any thing that is so seldom allowed. When an author has once gained a large share of public attention,—when his name is once up among a herd of idle readers, they can never be brought to believe that one who has risen so far can ever remain stationary. He must either rise farther, or begin immediately to descend; so that, when he ventures before these intoxicated judges with a new work, it is always discovered, either that he has infinitely surpassed himself, or, in the far greater number of cases, that there is a sad falling off, and that he is hastening the end of his career. In this way it may in general be presumed, that an author who is admitted by the public not to have fallen off in a second work, has in reality improved upon his first, and has truly deserved a higher place by merely maintaining that which he had formerly earned. We would not have Mr. Crayon, however, plume himself too much upon this sage observation; for, though *we*, and other great lights of public judgment, have decided that his former level has been maintained in this work with the most marvellous precision, we must whisper in his ear that the million are not exactly of that opinion; and that the common buz [sic] among the idle and impatient critics of the drawing-room is that, in comparison with the Sketch Book, it is rather monotonous and languid;

[°] Reprinted from *Edinburgh Review* 37 (November 1822): 337–50.

that there is too little variety of characters for two thick volumes; and that the said few characters come on so often, and stay so long, that the gentlest reader at least detects himself in rejoicing at being done with them. The premises of this enthymem [sic] we do not much dispute; but the conclusion, for all that, is wrong. For, in spite of these defects, Bracebridge Hall is quite as good as the Sketch Book; and Mr. C. may take comfort,—if he is humble enough to be comforted with such an assurance—and trust to us, that it will be quite as popular, and that he still holds his own with the efficient body of English readers.

The great charm and peculiarity of his work consists now, as on former occasions, in the singular sweetness of the composition, and the mildness of the sentiments,—sicklied over perhaps a little, now and then, with that cloying heaviness into which unvaried sweetness is so apt to subside. The rythm [sic] and melody of the sentences is certainly excessive: As it not only gives an air of mannerism from its uniformity, but raises too strong an impression of the labour that must have been bestowed, and the importance which must have been attached to that which is, after all, but a secondary attribute to good writing. It is very ill-natured in us, however, to object to what has given us so much pleasure; for we happen to be very intense and sensitive admirers of those soft harmonies of studied speech in which this author is so apt to indulge himself; and have caught ourselves, oftener than we shall confess, neglecting his excellent matter, to lap ourselves in the liquid music of his periods—and letting ourselves float passively down the mellow falls and windings of his soft-flowing sentences, with a delight not inferior to that which we derive from fine versification.

We should reproach ourselves still more, however, and with better reason, if we were to persist in the objection which we were at first inclined to make to the extraordinary kindliness and disarming gentleness of all this author's views and suggestions; and we only refer to it now, for the purpose of answering and discrediting it, with any of our readers to whom also it may happen to have occurred.

It first struck us as an objection to the author's courage and sincerity. It was quite unnatural, we said to ourselves, for any body to be always on such very amiable terms with his fellow-creatures; and this air of eternal philanthropy was nothing but a pretence, put on to bring himself into favour; and then we proceeded to assimilate him to those silken parasites who are in raptures with every body they meet, and ingratiate themselves in general society by an unmanly suppression of all honest indignation, and a timid avoidance of all subjects of disagreement. Upon due consideration, however, we are now satisfied that this was an unjust and unworthy interpretation. An author who comes deliberately before the public with select monologues of doctrine and discussion, is not at all in the condition of a man in common society, on whom various overtures of baseness and folly are daily obtruded, and to those whose sense and honour appeals are perpetually made, which must be manfully answered, as honour and conscience suggest. The author, on the other hand, has no questions to answer, and no society to select: his professed object is to instruct and improve the world—and his real one, if he is tolerably honest, is nothing worse than to promote his own fame and fortune by succeeding in what he professes. Now, there are but two ways that we have ever heard of by which men may be improved— either by cultivating and encouraging their amiable propensities, or by shaming and frightening them out of those that are vicious; and there can be but little doubt, we should imagine, which of the two offices is the highest and most eligible—since the one is left in a great measure to Hell and the hangman,—and for the other, we are taught chiefly to look to Heaven, and all that is angelic upon earth. The most perfect moral discipline would be that, no doubt, in which both were combined; but one is generally as much as human energy is equal to; and, in fact, they have commonly been divided in practice, without surmise of blame. And truly, if men have been hailed as public benefactors, merely for having beat tyrants into moderation, or coxcombs into good manners, we must be permitted to think, that one whose vocation is different may be allowed to have deserved well of his kind, although he should have confined his efforts to teaching them mutual charity and forbearance, and only sought to repress their evil passions by strengthening the springs and enlarging the sphere of those that are generous and kindly.

The objection in this general form, therefore, we soon found could not be maintained;—but, as we still felt a little secret spite lingering within us at our author's universal affability, we set about questioning ourselves more strictly as to its true nature and tendency; and think we at last succeeded in tracing it to an eager desire to see so powerful a pen and such great popularity employed in demolishing those errors and abuses to which we had been accustomed to refer most of the unhappiness of our country. Though we love his gentleness and urbanity, on the whole, we should have been very well pleased to see him rude and surly to our particular opponents; and could not but think it showed a want of spirit and discrimination that he did not mark his sense of their demerits, by making them an exception to his general system of toleration and indulgence. Being Whigs ourselves, for example, we could not but take it a little amiss, that one born and bred a republican, and writing largely on the present condition of England, should make so little distinction between that party and its opponents—and should even choose to attach himself to a Tory family, as the proper type and emblem of the old English character. Nor could we well acquit him of being "pigeon-livered—and lacking gall," when we found that nothing could provoke him to give a palpable hit to the Ministry, or even to employ his pure and powerful eloquence in reproving the shameful scurrilities of the ministerial press. We were also a little sore, we believe, on discovering that he took no notice of Scotland, and said absolutely nothing about our Highlanders, our schools, and our poetry.

Now, though we have magnanimously chosen to illustrate this grudge at his neutrality in our persons, it is obvious that a dissatisfaction of the same kind must have been felt by all the other great contending parties into which this and all free countries are necessarily divided. Mr. Crayon has rejected the alliance of any one of these, and resolutely refused to take part with them in the struggles to which they attach so much importance; and consequently has, to a certain extent, offended and disappointed them all. But we must carry our magnanimity a step farther, and confess, for ourselves, and for others, that, upon reflection, the offence and disappointment seem to us altogether unreasonable and unjust. . . . A good part of Mr. C.'s reputation, and certainly a very large share of his influence and popularity with all parties, has been acquired by the indulgence with which he has treated all, and his abstinence from all sorts of virulence and hostility; and it is no doubt chiefly on account of this influence and favour that we and others are rashly desirous to see him take part against our adversaries—forgetting those very qualities which render his assistance valuable, would infallibly desert him the moment that he complied with our desire, and vanish in the very act of his compliance. . . .

To Mr. C. especially, who is not a citizen of this country, it can scarcely be proposed as a duty to take a share in our internal contentions; and though the picture which he professes to give of our country may be more imperfect, and the estimate he makes of our character less complete, from the omission of this less tractable element, the value of the parts that he has executed will not be lessened, and the beneficial effect of the representation will in all probability be increased. . . .

We consider, therefore, the writers who seek to soften and improve our social affections, not only as aiming *directly* at the same great end which politicians more circuitously pursue, but as preparing those elements out of which alone a generous and enlightened political liberty can ever be formed—and without which it could neither be safely trusted in the hands of individuals, not prove fruitful of individual enjoyment. We conclude, therefore, that Mr. Crayon is in reality a better friend to Whig principles than if he had openly attacked the Tories—and end this long, and perhaps needless apology for his neutrality, by discovering, that such neutrality is in effect the best nursery for partisans of all that can be shown to be clearly and unquestionably right. And now we must say a word or two more of the book before us.

There are not many of our readers to whom it can be necessary to mention, that it is in substance, and almost in form, a continuation of the Sketch Book; and consists of a series of little descriptions and essays on matters principally touching the national character and old habits of England. The author is supposed to be resident at Brace-bridge Hall, the Christmas festivals of which he has commemorated in his former publication, and among the inmates of which, most of the familiar incidents occur which he turns to account in his lucu-brations. These incidents can scarcely be said to make a story in any sense, and certainly not one which would admit of being ab-stracted. . . .

We can scarcely afford room even to allude to the rest of this elegant miscellany. "Ready money Jack" is admirable throughout—and the old General very good. The lovers are, as usual, the most insipid. The Gypsies are sketched with infinite elegance as well as spirit—and Master Simon is quite delightful, in all the varieties of his ever versatile character. Perhaps the most pleasing thing about all these personages, is the perfect innocence and singleness of pur-pose which seems to belong to them—and which even when it raises a gentle smile at their expense, breathes over the whole scene they inhabit an air of abstraction and respect—like that which reigns in the De Coverley pictures of Addison. Of the Tales which serve to fill up the volumes, that of "Dolph Heyliger" is incomparably the best—and is more characteristic, perhaps, both of the author's turn of imagination and cast of humour, than any thing else in the work. "The Student of Salamanca" is too long, and deals rather largely in the commonplaces of romantic adventure:—while "Annette de la Barbe" [sic], though pretty and pathetic in some passages, is, on the whole, rather *fade* and finical—and too much in the style of the sentimental afterpieces which we have lately borrowed from the Parisian theatres.

On the whole, we are very sorry to receive Mr. Crayon's fare-well—and we return it with the utmost cordiality. We thank him most sincerely for the pleasure he has given us—for the kindness he has shown our country—and for the lessons he has taught, both here and in his native land, of good taste, good nature, and national liberality. We hope he will come back among us soon—and remember us while he is away; and can assure him, that he is in no danger of being speedily forgotten.

[Review of *Tales of a Traveller*]   John G. Lockhart°

In the next Number of the Quarterly, there will be, *inter alia,* a fine puff of Washington Irving's "Tales of a Traveller," because Mr. Irving's publisher is Mr. Murray,—and there will also be a puff of it in the Edinburgh;—first, because Mr. Irving is an American, and, secondly, because his book is not of the kind to interfere at all with any of Mr. Constable's own publications. But I am really sick of exposing all this nonsensical stuff.—So turn we to Mr. Washington himself, and see what is to be said of these volumes by a plain impartial man, who has nothing to do either with Murray or Constable, and who thinks neither the better nor the worse of a man for being born in New York.

I have been miserably disappointed in the "Tales of a Traveller." Three years have elapsed since the publication of Bracebridge Hall, and it had been generally given out that the author was travelling about the Continent at a great rate, collecting the materials for a work of greater and more serious importance. Above all, it was known that Mr. Irving had gone, *for the first time,* to Italy and to Germany; and high expectations were avowed as to the treasures he would bring back from these chosen seats of the classical and the romantic, the beautiful and the picturesque. With the exception of a very few detached pieces, such as the description of the Stage-coachman, and the story of the Stout Gentleman, Mr. Irving's sketches of English life and manners had certainly made no lasting impression on the public mind. Everybody recognized the pen of a practised writer, the feelings of an honourable and kind-hearted man, and occasional flashes of a gently-pleasing humour in the tournure of a sentence, but, on the whole, they were but insipid diet. There was no reality about his Yorkshire halls, squires, parsons, gipsies, and generals; and his pathos was not only very poor, but very affected; in point of fact, mawkish and unmeaning were the only epithets anybody thought of applying to such matters as his Essay on Windsor Castle, and James I. of Scotland, his "Broken Heart," his Student of Salamanca, &c. &c. These affairs were universally voted Washington Irving's balaam, and the balaam unquestionably bore in Bracebridge Hall a proportion of altogether insufferable preponderance. But all this was kindly put up with. It was said that the author had been too hasty, in his anxiety to keep up the effect he had produced in his Sketch Book; and that, having dressed up all his best English materials in that work, he had, *ex necessitate,* served up a hash in the successor. But give him time, allow him to think of matters calmly and quietly, open new fields of

° Reprinted from *Blackwood's Edinburgh Magazine* 16 (September 1824): 291–304.

observation to him, and you shall see once more the pen of Knickerbocker in its pristine glory. This was the general *say*, and when Germany was mentioned, everybody was certain that the third *Sketch-book* would not only rival, but far surpass the first.

The more benign the disposition, the worse for Mr. Irving now. He has been not only all over Germany, but all over Italy too; and he has produced a book, which, for aught I see, might have been written, not in three years, but in three months, without stirring out of a garret in London, and this not by Mr. Irving alone, but by any one of several dozens of ready penmen about town, with whose names, if it were worth while, I could easily enliven your pages. The ghost stories, with which the greater part of the first volume is occupied, are, with one exception, old, and familiar to everybody conversant in that sort of line. The story of the Beheaded Lady, in particular, has not only been told in print ere now, but much better told than it is in Mr. Irving's edition. To say the truth, a gentleman like this, who goes about gaping for stories to make up books withal, should be excessively scrupulous indeed, ere he sets to work upon anything he hears. A new story is a thing not to be met with above once or twice in the ten years; and the better a story is, the more are the chances always against its being new to other people, whatever it may be to one's self. Mr. Irving, being evidently a man of limited reading, ought to have consulted some more erudite friend, ere he put most of these things to press. My own dear D'Israeli alone could, I venture to say, have shewn him printed and reprinted editions of three-fourths of them, in one half hour's *sederunt* over a sea-coal fire in the British Museum. It is becoming daily a more dangerous thing to pillage the Germans, and I strongly advise Mr. Irving to be more on his guard the next time.

The matter of these ghost stories of his, however, is not the only, nor even the chief thing, I have to find fault with. They are old stories, and I am sorry to add, they are not improved by their new dress. The tone in which Mr. Irving does them up, is quite wrong. A ghost story *ought* to be a ghost story. Something like seriousness is absolutely necessary, in order to its producing any effect at all upon the mind—and the sort of half-witty vein, the little dancing quirks, &c. &c. with which these are set forth, entirely destroy the whole matter. [I speak of his management of European superstitions, be it noticed, and not at all of the American.] There were some ghost stories in the Album, well worth half a ton of these. The Fox-hunters are *crambe recocta*, and bad *crambe* too; for Mr. Irving no more understands an English fox-hunter, than I do an American judge. The same thing may be said of the whole most hackneyed story of Buckthorne, which is a miserable attempt at an English Wilhelm Meister; and yet one can with difficulty imagine a man of Mr. Irving's sense producing this lame thing at all, if he had read *recently* either that work or the *Roman Comique*. Buckthorne is really a bad thing—*nulla virtute redemptum*. A boarding-school miss might have written it.

But the German part of the adventure has turned out exactly nothing, and this will perhaps be the greatest mortification to those who open Mr. Irving's new book. Anybody, at least, who had read Knickerbocker, and who knew Deutchland, either the upper or the nether, *must* have expected a rich repast indeed, of Meinherren and Mynheers. All this expectation is met with a mere cipher. There is nothing German here at all, except that the preface is dated *Mentz*, and that the author has cribbed from the German books he has been dabbling in, some fables which have not the merit either of being originally or characteristically German.

The Italy, too, is a sad failure—very sad, indeed! Here is an American, a man of letters, a man of observation, a man of feeling, a man of taste. He goes, with a very considerable literary reputation, as his passport at once and his stimulus, to the most interesting region, perhaps, in the old world, and he brings from it absolutely nothing except a few very hackneyed tales of the Abruzzi Bandits, not a bit better than Mrs. Maria Graham's trash, and the narrative of a grand robbery perpetrated on the carriage of Mr. Alderman Popkins! The story of the Inn at Terracina is, perhaps, as pure a specimen of Leadenhall-street common-place, as has appeared for some time past. Why a man of education and talent should have ventured to put forth such poor secondhand, second-rate manufactures, at this time of day, it entirely passes my imagination to conceive.—Good Heavens! are we come to this, that men of this rank cannot even make a robbery terrific, or a love-story tolerable? But, seriously, the use Mr. Irving has made of his Italian travels, must sink his character very wofully. It proves him to be devoid not only of all classical recollections, but of all genuine enthusiasm of any kind; and I believe you will go along with me when I say, that without enthusiasm of some sort, not even a humourist can be really successful. If Mr. Irving had no eyes for tower, temple, and tree, he should at least have shewn one for peasants and pageants. But there is nothing whatever in his Italian Sketches that might not have been produced very easily by a person (and not a very clever person neither) who had merely read a few books of travels, or *talked* with a few travellers. Rome, Venice, Florence, Naples—this gentleman has been over them all, crayon in hand, and his Sketch-book is, whereever it is not a blank, a blunder.

Mr. Irving, after writing, perhaps after printing one volume, and three-fourths of another, seems to have been suddenly struck with a conviction of the worthlessness of the materials that had thus been passing through his hands, and in a happy day, and a happy hour, he determined to fill up the remaining fifty or sixty pages, not with milk-and-waterstuff about ghosts and banditti, but with some of his own old genuine stuff—the quaintnesses of the ancient Dutch heers and frows of the delicious land of the Manhattoes. The result is, that this small section of his book is not only worth the bulk of it five hundred times over, but really, and in every respect, worthy of himself and his fame. This will live, the rest will die in three months.

I do most sincerely hope this elegant person will no longer refuse to believe what has been told him very often, that all real judges are quite agreed as to the enormous, the infinite, and immeasurable superiority of his American Sketches over *all* his European ones. If he does not, he may go on publishing pretty octavos with John Murray for several years to come; and he may maintain a very pretty rank among the Mayfair bluestockings, and their half-emasculated hangers on; but he must infallibly *sink* altogether in the eyes of really intelligent and manly readers—whose judgment, moreover, is always sure, at no very distant period to silence and overpower the mere "commenta opinionum."

It is, indeed, high time that Mr. Irving should begin to ask of himself a serious question,—"What is it that I am to be known by hereafter?" He is now a man towards fifty—nearly twenty years have passed since his first and as yet his best production, "the History of New York," made its appearance. He has most certainly made no progress in any one literary qualification since then. There is far keener and readier wit in that book,—far, far richer humour, far more ingenious satire, than in all that have come after it put together; and, however reluctant he may be to hear it said, the style of that book is by miles and miles superior to that in which he now, almost always writes.

Long ere now, Mr. Irving must, I should think, have made considerable discoveries as to the nature and extent of his own powers. In the first place, he must be quite aware that he has no inventive faculties at all, taking that phrase in its proper and more elevated sense. He has never invented an incident—unless, which I much doubt, the *idea* of the Stout Gentleman's story was his own;—and as for inventing characters, why, he has not even made an attempt at that.

Secondly, the poverty and bareness of his European Sketches alone, when compared with the warmth and richness of his old American ones, furnishes the clearest evidence that he is not a man of much liveliness of imagination; nothing has, it seems, excited him profoundly since he was a stripling roaming about the wild woods of his province, and enjoying the queer *fat* goings-on of the Dutch-descended burghers of New York. This is not the man that should call himself, as if *par excellence*, a *traveller—caelum non animum mutat,*—he is never at home, to any purpose at least, except among the Yankees.

Thirdly, Mr. Irving must be aware that he cannot write anything serious to much effect. This argues a considerable lack of pith in the whole foundations of his mind, for the world has never seen a great humourist who was nothing but a humourist. Cervantes was a poet of poets—and Swift was Swift. A mere joker's jokes go for little. One wishes to consider the best of these things as an amusement for one's self, and as having been an exertion of the *unbending* powers only of their creator. Now Mr. Irving being, which he certainly is, aware of these great and signal deficiencies, is surely acting in a foolish fashion, when he publishes such books as The Tales of a Traveller. If he wishes to make for himself a really enduring reputation, he must surpass considerably his previous works—I mean he must produce works of more uniform and entire merit than any of them, for he never can do anything better than some fragments he has done already. He must, for this purpose, take time, for it is obvious that he is by no means a rapid collector of materials, whatever the facility of his penmanship may be. Further, he must at once cut all ideas of writing about European matters. He can never be anything but an imitator of our Goldsmiths here,—on his own soil he *may* rear a name and a monument, *are perennius,* for himself. No, he must allow his mind to dwell upon the only images which it ever can give back with embellished and strengthened hues. He must riot in pumpkin pies, grinning negroes, smoking skippers, plump jolly little Dutch maidens, and their grizzly-periwigged papas. This is his world, and he must stick to it. Out of it, it is but too apparent *now,* he never can make the name of Washington Irving what that name ought to be.

Perhaps there would be no harm if Mr. Irving gave rather more scope to his own real feelings in his writings. A man of his power and mind must have opinions of one kind or another, in regard to the great questions which have in every age and country had the greatest interest for the greatest minds. Does he suppose that any popularity really worthy a *man's* ambition, is to be gained by a determined course of smooth speaking? Does he really imagine that *he* can be "all things to all men," in the Albemarle Street sense of the phrase, without emasculating his genius, and destroying its chances of perpetuating fame? I confess, there is to me something not unlike impertinence, in the wondrous caution with which this gentleman avoids speaking his mind. Does he suppose that we should be either sorry or angry, if he spoke out now and then like a Republican, about matters of political interest? He may relieve himself from this humane anxiety as to our peace of mind. There is no occasion for lugging in politics direct in works of fiction, but I must say, that I cannot think it natural for any man to write in these days so many volumes as Mr. Irving has written, without in some way or other expressing his opinions and feelings. He is, indeed, "A gentle sailor, and for summer seas." But he may depend on it, that nobody has ever taken a strong hold of the *English* mind, whose own mind has not had for one of its first characteristics, *manliness*, and I have far too great a respect for the American mind, to have any doubts that the same thing will be said of it by any one, who, two or three hundred years hence, casts his eye over that American literature, which, I hope, will, ere then, be the glorious rival of our own.

But enough for this time. Few people have admired Mr. Irving more than myself—few have praised him more—and certainly few wish him and his career better than I do at this moment. . . .

[Review of *Tales of a Traveller*]   Anonymous°

We are frequently unreasonable in our demands upon the writers who administer to our amusement. It is unfair, upon the appearance of a new production from a favourite author, to try it by the standard of our own expectations, rather than by the plan and the intention which he himself had in view when he undertook it. If the Tales of a Traveller have not the same delightful variety, nor so many of those happy transitions from grave to gay, that are the peculiar charm of this ingenious Writer's former productions, they will not, or, at least, ought not to abate one jot of the well-earned reputation of Mr. Irving,—of that reputation, we mean, which is weighed fairly with the merit by which it has been acquired, and in scales undisturbed by those capricious and fitful judgements to which all kinds of popularity are exposed.

Indeed, the Tales of a Traveller may be considered as a continuation of the Sketch Book. The same facility of touch, the same elegance, sustained without labour, and polished without art, may be traced in each. No author writes better English; and he is the solitary instance in which an American may read a salutary, though mortifying lesson to many of our native writers, in whose eyes Transatlantic literature is not likely to find much favour. The reason is, that he has courted and pursued our language in those haunts where it is alone to be found in full strength and perfection—the writings of our elder authors. Add to this, there is scarcely one (among those at least who write for our lighter hours) who is gifted with a more

° Reprinted from *Eclectic Review* N. S. 24 (July 1825): 65–74.

playful imagination; while, in the grave, insinuated humour which, in his hands, never loses its effect by being too ostentatiously displayed, but takes us constantly by surprise, and on occasions when it was least expected,—in this respect he has not often been surpassed.

Yet, if we have been amused by the Tales of a Traveller, it is not because they are highly finished or skilfully contrived. With one or two exceptions, they seem all wanting in those satisfactory conclusions for which we pant so ardently, when our curiosity has been put to the rack, and our sympathies worked to a considerable fermentation. They often break off suddenly, like those broken skeins of incident, of which our dreams are composed. They have a beginning, a middle, but no end. Such, however, is the power of our friend Crayon, that we are pleased even while we are disappointed, and follow him with delight through the different avenues of his story, though they "lead to nothing." It is, moreover, that he has conferred upon sketches comparatively so light and unfinished, the full interest of more complete and systematic pictures. In this, the hand of a master stands revealed. "Thus painters write their names at Co." Natural feelings expressed in the language of nature, good sense imparted in the manner and tone of good sense, will always fascinate. . . .

The stories are many of them told by the guests of a fox-hunting Baronet, who kept bachelor's hall in jovial style in an ancient rook-haunted mansion. The dinner was prolonged, as is usual, after a hard day's sport, till a late hour; and a heavy winter-storm which set in towards the evening, rendered it necessary for them to take up their quarters, for the night, in the same house. The conversation turns upon ghosts. Of these, the adventure of My Uncle is one, and it provokingly breaks off just where it ought to have gone on. Our Author is, apparently, much enamoured of these experiments upon our love for the marvellous; for he seems to have had no other end in raising our curiosity, than suddenly to let it down to disappoint us. In the story of My Aunt, which follows, he practises the same joke.

We like "the Bold Dragoon or the Adventure of My Grandfather," much better. The genuine, quiet humour of the Author breaks forth in this "rigmarole Irish romance," as he justly calls it, amidst the wildest and absurdest of all incidents. . . .

The adventure of the German student is an interesting, though not altogether an original story. It is a case of intellectual disease produced by a secluded life and misdirected reading. . . .

The Mysterious Stranger and the Young Italian are powerfully written; but we were better pleased with Buckthorn and his friends, in the second part of the first volume. The Author exhibits some singular pictures of literary life; and here we must be allowed to remark, that although some of the caricatures may have had prototypes in real nature, yet, the finish of the pictures, and the grouping of the figures, must be the product of pure imagination. "The club of queer fellows" is a misnomer. It should have been the club of dull fellows. In this sketch, the wonted powers of the Author evidently slumbered. Buckthorn is an entertaining companion. He is a true practical philosopher, who sees every thing on the right side, and "takes the buffets and rewards" of the fickle goddess "with equal thanks."

The strolling Manager in the second volume, is broad, good-humoured caricature; but the pictures of the Italian banditti who infest the road from Rome to Naples, in the third part, are from life. The incidents, we are convinced, are for the chief part authentic. The Painter's adventure is founded upon an incident that happened to an abbè in the family of Lucien Bonaparte, at a villa near Rome, and, if we mistake not, the Author took it from the interesting and able work of a female writer, called "Rome in the Nineteenth Century.". . .

There is some excellent Dutch painting in the fourth part of the work. The Money-diggers is quite in the Teniers style, a style in which the Author is singularly happy. On the whole, these volumes have yielded us considerable entertainment; and those who take no pleasure in invidious comparisons between the last and the former productions of the writer, and who will consent to be carried along without cheating themselves of a great portion of rational amusement, by mingling with the sensations excited by the Tales of a Traveller, the recollections of what they felt on the perusal of the earlier productions of Geoffrey Crayon,—by those, in fact, who have not sate down to the perusal with unreasonable expectations, which it is no sin in him not to have gratified; they will be welcomed as an agreeable accession to the stock of light reading. Mr. Crayon's great excellence lies in serving up a variety of dishes to please a variety of tastes. There is tenderness for the sentimental, and (for humour and sensibility are seldom far distant from each other in the human bosom) force and caricature for those who are inclined to be inno-cently merry. Sometimes, indeed, the Writer stoops to cater for grosser palates. If, as a writer of Tales, Mr. Irving is surpassed by the great Northern Enchanter, it is in a department to which he does not affect to belong. Yet, he sometimes reminds us of the style and manner of that artist; particularly in local and sentimental description, and in that lively transmission of sensations and impressions, which not only brings before us a picturesque and faithful picture of the scene described, but raises at the same moment, the feelings which it is calculated to inspire. We regret that we cannot dismiss these volumes, however, with an unqualified sentence of commendation.

In his former works, Mr. Irving was apparently studious to avoid any thing bordering on either coarseness or profaneness. We know not whether it is because he thinks worse of the public, or because he is *worsened* by his travels, that, in the present volumes, he displays a levity, and sometimes stoops to a vulgarity, which must pain a serious, and disgust a delicate mind. If Mr. Irving believes in the existence of Tom Walker's master, we can scarcely conceive how he can so earnestly jest about him: at all events, we would counsel him to beware how he conjures in that name, lest his own spells should prove fatal to him.

[Review of *Life and Voyages of Christopher Columbus*]   Alexander Hill Everett°

This is one of those works, which are at the same time the delight of readers and the despair of critics. It is as nearly perfect in its kind, as any work well can be; and there is therefore little or nothing left for the reviewer, but to write at the bottom of every page, as Voltaire said he should be obliged to do, if he published a commentary on Racine, *Pulchrè! bene! optimè!* And as the reputation of the author is so well established, that he does not stand in need of our recommendation as a passport to the public favor, it may appear, and in fact is, almost superfluous to pretend to give a formal review of his book. Nevertheless, we cannot refuse ourselves the satisfaction of adding the mite of our poor applause to the ample and well deserved harvest of fame, that has already rewarded the labors of our ingenious, excellent, and amiable fellow citizen; nor would it, as we conceive, be proper to omit noticing in this journal a work, however well known to the public, which we consider as being, on the whole, more honorable to the literature of the country, than any one that has hitherto appeared among us. Before we proceed to give our opinion in detail of the "History of the Life and Voyages of Columbus" we shall offer a few remarks on the character and merit of Mr. Irving's other works, premising that we write under the influence of the feelings that naturally result from a good deal of friendly personal intercourse with this gentleman. If any reader shall suspect, that we judge Mr. Irving too favorably because we know him too well, he is quite at liberty to make any deductions from the sum total of our commendation, that he may on this account deem in candor to be necessary.

° Reprinted from *North American Review* 28 (January 1829): 103–34.

Mr. Irving shares, in some degree, the merit and the glory that belong to the illustrious hero of his present work, that of leading the way in a previously unexplored and untrodden path of intellectual labor. He is the first writer of purely Cisatlantic origin and education, who succeeded in establishing a high and undisputed reputation, founded entirely on literary talent and success. This was the opinion expressed by a very judicious and discerning writer in the Edinburgh Review, upon the first publication of the "Sketch Book"; and it is, as we conceive, a substantially correct one. In saying this, we are perfectly aware that there have been found among us, at every period during the two centuries of our history, individuals highly distinguished, both at home and abroad, by important and useful labors in various branches of art and science. We mean not to detract, in the least, from their well-earned fame, which we cherish, on the contrary, as the richest treasure that belongs to their posterity, and would do everything in our power to establish and enlarge. We say not that Mr. Irving is the first or the greatest man that ever handled a pen in the United States. . . .

In the rapid progress of our population, wealth, and literary advantages, the period arrived, when the calls of business no longer absorbed all the cultivated intellect existing in the country; when, after these were fully satisfied, there remained a portion of taste, zeal, and talent to be employed in purely literary and scientific pursuits; when the public mind was prepared to acknowledge and appreciate any really superior merit, that might present itself, in those departments; when in fact the nation, having been somewhat galled by the continual sneers of a set of heartless and senseless foreigners upon our want of literary talent, was rather anxious to possess some positive facts, which could be offered as evidence to the contrary, and was prepared of course to hail the appearance of a writer of undoubted talent, with a kind of patriotic enthusiasm; when finally, for all these reasons, the first example of success, that should be given in this way, would naturally be followed by an extensive development of the same sort of activity, throughout the country, in the persons of a host of literary aspirants, sometimes directly imitating their prototype, and always inspired and encouraged by his good fortune, who would make up together the front rank of what is commonly called a school of polite literature. To set this example was the brilliant part reserved, in the course of our literary history, for Mr. Washington Irving. His universal popularity among readers of all classes, on both sides of the Atlantic, resting exclusively on the purely literary merit of his productions, wholly independent of extraneous or interested motives, attested by repeated successes, in various forms of composition, and stamped by the concurrence and approbation of the most acute, judicious, and unsparing critics, justifies, beyond a shadow of doubt, his pretension to be viewed as the valorous knight, who was called, in the order of destiny, to break the spell, which appeared, at least to our good natured European brethren, to be thrown over us in this respect; to achieve the great and hitherto unaccomplished adventure of establishing a purely American literary reputation of the first order; and demonstrate the capacity of his countrymen to excel in the elegant, as they had before done in all the useful and solid branches of learning. To have done this is a singular title of honor, and will always remain such, whatever laurels of a different kind may hereafter be won by other pretenders. Thoroughly labored and highly finished as they all are, Mr. Irving's works will hardly be surpassed in their way. . . . it can never be disputed that the mild and beautiful genius of Mr. Irving was the Morning-Star, that led up the march of our heavenly host; and that he has a fair right, much fairer certainly than the great Mantuan, to assume the proud device, *Primus ego in patriam.* To have done this, we repeat, is a singular triumph, far higher than that of merely adding another name to a long list of illustrious predecessors, who flourished in the same country. It implies not merely taste and talent, but *originality,* the quality which forms the real distinction, if there be one, between what we call *genius* and every other degree of intellectual power; the quality, in comparison with which, as Sir Walter Scott justly observes, all other literary accomplishments are as dust in the balance. It implies moreover the possession of high and honorable moral qualities; the bold and daring resolution, that plans with vigor and decision; the unyielding firmness of purpose, that never tires or falters in the task of execution. These qualities, which are obviously necessary to such success as that of Mr. Irving, have also, as exemplified in his writings, been carefully kept within bounds, and have not only been prevented from running into their kindred excesses, but, on the contrary, have been judiciously and gracefully veiled from the public eye, by the outward forms that rather belong to a character of an opposite cast; a modesty, that has never deserted him under all his popularity, and a scrupulous regard for decorum and propriety as well as the higher principles of morals, from which the dazzling success, that has unfortunately attended a different line of conduct in some contemporary writers, has never for a moment induced him to deviate. This combination of estimable and in some respects almost contradictory moral qualities, with a high intellectual power and fine taste, tends to render the influence of Mr. Irving's example not less favorable to the country, in a moral point of view, than it is in a purely literary one.

The great effect which it has produced, in this latter respect, is sufficiently evident already, in the number of good writers, in various forms of elegant literature, who have sprung up among us within the few years which have elapsed since the appearance of Mr. Irving, and who justify our preceding remark, that he may fairly be considered as the founder of a school. . . . We only intend to intimate, that he has the peculiar merit and fortune of having taken the lead, under the influence of these causes, in a course, in which he could not but be followed and sustained by numerous successors, who would of necessity be more or less affected by the form and character of his productions. The fact that several of the more distinguished writers, who have since appeared, are from his own state,—while it is partly accounted for by the vast extent, population, wealth, and generally thriving situation of that "empire in embryo," New York; circumstances which all tend very strongly to stimulate every form of intellectual activity,—must nevertheless be regarded in part, as a proof of the direct operation of the success of Mr. Irving.

Having thus noticed the circumstances, that attended the appearance of this writer in the literary career, we shall now offer a few observations on the character and value of his works. We trust that, in treating this subject somewhat fully, we shall not be considered, by our readers, as giving it a disproportionate importance. . . .

If we examine the works of Mr. Irving, with reference to the usual division of manner and substance, we may remark, in the first place, that his style is undoubtedly one of the most finished and agreeable forms, in which the English language has ever been presented. Lord Byron has somewhere spoken of him, as the second prose writer of the day, considering Sir Walter Scott as the first; but with due deference to his lordship's judgment, which was far from being infallible in criticism or anything else, we cannot but consider Mr. Irving, as respects mere style, decidedly superior to Sir Walter. The latter, no doubt, has exhibited a greater vigor and fertility of imagination, which, with his talent for versification, entitle him to a higher rank in the world of letters; but viewing him merely as a prose writer, his style, when not sustained by the interest of a connected narrative, will be found to possess no particular merit, and in some of his later writings is negligent and incorrect to an extent, that places it below mediocrity. That of Mr. Irving, on the contrary, is, in all his works, uniformly of the first order. Its peculiar characteristic is a continual and sustained elegance, the result of the union of a naturally fine taste, with conscientious and unwearied industry. His language is not remarkable for energy, nor have we often noticed in it any extraordinary happiness or brilliancy of mere expression. Though generally pure and correct, it is not uniformly so; and there are one or two unauthorized forms, which will be found by a nice observer to recur pretty often. Its attraction lies, as we have said, in the charm of finished elegance, which it never loses. The most harmonious and poetical words are carefully selected. Every period is measured and harmonized with nice precision. The length of the sentences is judiciously varied; and the *tout ensemble* produces on the ear an effect very little, if at all, inferior to that of the finest versification. Indeed such prose, while it is from the nature of the topics substantially poetry, does not appear to us, when viewed merely as a form of language, to differ essentially from verse. . . .

If the elegant prose of Mr. Irving be, as we think it is, but little inferior in beauty to the finest verse, and at all events one of the most finished forms of the English language, the character and the substance of his writings is also entirely and exclusively poetical. It is evident enough that "divine Philosophy" has no part nor lot in his affections. Shakespeare, though he was willing to "hang up philosophy," out of compliment to the charming Juliet, when he chose to take it down again, could put the Seven Sages of Greece to the blush. But such is not the taste of Mr. Irving. His aim is always to please; and never to instruct, at least by general truths. If he ever teaches, he confines himself to plain matter of fact. He even goes farther, and with the partiality of a true lover, who can see no beauty except in the eyes of his own mistress, he at times deals rather rudely with philosophy, and more than insinuates that she is a sort of prosing mad-cap, who babbles eternally without ever knowing what she is talking of. . . . But though we think Mr. Irving heretical on this head, we can hardly say that we like him the less for it, being always pleased to see a man put his heart and soul into his business, whatever it may be, even though he may, by so doing, (as often happens) generate in himself a sort of hatred and contempt for every other. Within the domain of poetry, taking this word in its large sense, to which he religiously confines himself, Mr. Irving's range is somewhat extensive. He does not attempt the sublime, but he is often successful in the tender, and disports himself, at his ease, in the comic. Humor is obviously his *forte*, and his best touches of pathos are those, which are thrown in casually, to break the continuity of a train of melancholy thoughts, when they sparkle in part by the effect of contrast, like diamonds on a black mantle. But it is when employed on humorous subjects, that he puts forth the vigor of a really inventive genius, and proves himself substantially a poet. "Knickerbocker," for example, is a true original creation. His purely pathetic essays, though occasionally pleasing, are more generally somewhat tame and spiritless. As a writer of serious biography and history he possesses the merit of plain and elegant narrative, but does not aspire to the higher palm of just and deep thought in the investigation of causes and effects, that constitutes the distinction of the real historian, and supposes the taste for philosophical research, which, as we have said before, is foreign to the temper of our author.

Such, as we conceive, are the general characteristics of the style and substance of the works of Mr. Irving. We notice their deficiencies and beauties with equal freedom, for such is our duty as public critics, and we have too much respect for our friend to suppose, that his appetite for fame requires to be gratified by unqualified praise. This can never, in any case, be merited, and is therefore always worthless; while the favorable effect of just and candid criticism is heightened, by a discriminating notice of the weak points, that are of course to be found in all productions. We shall now proceed to offer a few more particular observations upon the separate works, dividing them, for this purpose, into the two classes of those that were written before and after the author's departure for Europe. Although the general characteristics, which we have pointed out, are common to both these classes, there are some differences of manner between them, that are worth attention. The "Life of Columbus," again, varies materially from any of the preceding publications, and will naturally be considered by itself, as the immediate subject of this article.

The former class comprehends *Salmagundi* and the *History of New York*, besides some smaller and less important productions. These exhibit the talent of the author, in the full perfection of its power, developing itself with a freshness and freedom, that have not perhaps been surpassed, or even equalled, in any of his subsequent writings, but directed, on the other hand, by a somewhat less sure and cultivated taste. There is a good deal of inequality in "Salmagundi," owing probably in part to a mixture of contributions by other hands; but the better pieces are written in Mr. Irving's best manner. Take it altogether, it was certainly a production of extraordinary merit, and was instantaneously and universally recognised as such by the public. It wants of course the graver merits of the modern British collections of Essays; but for spirit, effect, and actual literary value, we doubt whether any publication of the class since "The Spectator," upon which it is directly modelled, can fairly be put in competition with it. We well remember the eagerness, with which the periodical return of the merry little yellow dwarf was anticipated by all classes of readers, and the hearty good will, with which he was welcomed. "Sport that wrinkled care derides, / And Laughter holding both his sides," uniformly followed in his train. So irresistibly attractive and amusing were the quips and cranks of the odd group of mummers that moved under his management, that our grave, business-loving, and somewhat disputatious citizens were taken, like Silence in the play, ere they were aware; and when the show was over, were surprised, and in some cases rather chagrined, to find that they had been diverted from their habitual meditations on the Orders in Council and the New England Platform, by the unprofitable fooleries of the Cockloft family and the Little Man in Black, the state of the Tunisian Ambassador's wardrobe, and the tragical fate of poor Aunt Charity, who died of a Frenchman. Mr. Irving appears to have had no other object in view, but that of making a sprightly book and laughing at everything laughable; but the work necessarily assumed, to a certain extent, the shape of a satire on the abuses of popular government; since the administration of the public affairs is the great scene of action, upon which the attention of the community is always fixed, and which must be treated, in jest or earnest, by all who mean to have an audience. The vices and follies, that most easily beset our practical statesmen, their endless prolixity in debate, their rage for the bloodless glory of heading the militia in a sham fight, their habitual waste of dollars in attempting to economize cents, are hit off in a very happy manner; but as the satire is always general, and the malice at bottom good-natured and harmless, nobody took offence and we all laughed honestly and heartily; each, as he supposed, at the expense of his neighbor. Nor are we to conclude that because Mr. Irving has made the abuses of popular government, and the weaknesses incident to those who administer such a system, the objects of his satire, that he is a political heretic and a secret foe to liberty. The best human institutions are of course imperfect, and there is quite as much advantage to be derived from a just and good-humored exposition of the weak points of our own government, as from a continued fulsome and exaggerated panegyric on its merits. Mr. Irving, we may add, was probably directed in the choice of the subjects on which to exercise his pleasantry, by the mere force of the circumstances under which he wrote, and not by any general views of the theory of government.

The decided success and universal popularity of his first attempt naturally encouraged him to repeat it, and "Salmagundi" was pretty soon followed by the *History of New York.* This we consider as equal to the best, and in some respects perhaps superior to any other of our author's productions. It is the one, which exhibits most distinctly the stamp of real inventive power, the true test, as we have hinted, of genius. The plan, though simple enough, and when hit upon sufficiently obvious, is entirely original. In most other works of the same general class of political satire, such as those of Rabelais and Swift, the object of the work is effected by presenting real events and characters of dignity and importance in low and ludicrous shapes. "Knickerbocker" reverses this plan, and produces effect by dressing up a mean and trifling fund of real history, in a garb of fictitious and burlesque gravity. The conception is akin, no doubt, to the general notion of the mock heroic, as exemplified, for instance, in Pope's "Rape of the Lock," but the particular form, in which it is applied by the learned and ingenious Diedrich, is not only unusually happy, but wholly new; and the work possesses of course a character of complete originality, which does not belong to any of the others. *The*

Stout Gentleman is a second application of the same principle, still more exquisitely wrought up and only inferior in the comparative smallness of the canvass. The execution of "Knickerbocker" corresponds in felicity with the merit of the plan. The graphic distinctness, with which the three Dutch governors, whom nobody ever heard of before, are made to pass before us, each endowed with his appropriate intellectual, moral, and personal habits and qualities, is quite admirable; and the political satire is conveyed with great effect, and at the same time in a very fine and delicate manner, through the medium of these remote characters of the old world. There are some ineffectual attempts at wit in particular passages, and here and there a little indelicacy, which is the more objectionable, as it is inconsistent with the plan of the mock heroic, and in place, if admitted at all, only in the *travestie.* There is also a somewhat uncouth display of commonplace historical learning in the first book, where the author, while in the act of ridiculing pedantry, as he supposes it to be exemplified in the person of the worthy "Diedrich," betrays, we fear, a slight shade of the same quality in himself. But notwithstanding these blemishes, which are indeed so trifling, that we are almost ashamed to have mentioned them, the execution of the "History of New York" is in the main completely successful. If we were called on to give a preference to any one of our author's productions over all the rest, we should with little hesitation assign the palm to this.

These, with some smaller pieces to which we shall briefly advert hereafter, are all the works, which were published by Mr. Irving before his departure for Europe, and which belong to what may be called his first manner. Soon after their appearance, he visited England, where, and in other parts of Europe, he has resided ever since; and we heard nothing of him for several years, until at length he brought out the *Sketch Book,* which first made him known to the literary world abroad. In the long interval which had elapsed, since the appearance of his former productions, a "change had come over the spirit of his dream." Advancing years had probably a little moderated the exuberant flow of his youthful spirits, and the natural effect of time had, we fear, been increased by other causes; if it be true, as we have reason to suppose, that our amiable countryman had in the interim taken some lessons in the school of that "rugged nurse of virtue," so beautifully celebrated by Gray, who has in all ages been but too much accustomed to extend the benefit of her tuition to the votaries of polite learning. Whether under the influence of these causes, aided perhaps by the wholesome terror, which an American candidate for European favor might be expected to feel of the iron rod of the ruling critics, or for whatever other reason, certain it is, that the genius of Mr. Irving appeared to be a little rebuked at this his second apparition, and spoke in a partially subdued tone.

The characteristics of the "Sketch Book" are essentially the same with those of the preceding works; but, with somewhat more polish and elegance, it has somewhat less vivacity, freshness, and power. This difference constitutes the distinction between Mr. Irving's first and second manner, the latter of which is preserved in all his subsequent publications, excepting the one now immediately before us. Of these two manners the one or the other may perhaps be preferred by different readers, according to their different tastes. We incline ourselves to the former, conceiving that spirit and vigor are the highest qualities of style, and that the loss of any merit of this description is but poorly compensated by a little additional finish. The change would have been however of less importance, had it appeared only in the language, but it is also displayed in the substance of the second series of publications; and it is here particularly, that we discover what we deem the unpropitious influence of a residence abroad on our author's talent. Not only is his language less free and sparkling, but the reach of his inventive power seems to be reduced. The Crayons and Bracebridges, including Master Simon, are Sketches indeed, and in water colors, compared with the living roaring group of Cockloft Hall; and although we find occasional returns of the author's best manner in "The Stout Gentleman," "Rip Van Winkle," "Sleepy Hollow," "The Money-diggers," and so forth, the rich material employed in these pieces is not, as before, the staple of the work, but a passing refreshment, that serves excellently well to remind us of what we wanted, but from the smallness of its quantity rather awakens than satisfies the appetite.

As it is difficult or rather impossible to suppose any actual diminution of power in the author, we must take for granted, that the difference in question is owing to the change in the general character of his subject. Humor and satire are, as we said before, evidently his *forte* and these compose the substance of the preceding works. There is but little attempt at the pathos in "Salmagundi," and none in "Knickerbocker." The subjects of satire are principally the abuses of government and the follies of leading characters and classes; and hence these works, though light in form, have an elevated object, which gives them dignity and solid value. Looking at them in a literary point of view, the circumstance of writing upon subjects actually before his eyes gives his pictures the truth to nature, which is the chief element of all excellence in art. Had the author proceeded on the same plan in his latter publications, he would have taken for his subject the abuses of government and the follies of leading classes and characters, as exemplified in the old countries. This again would have opened a field for the exercise of his peculiar talent, still more rich and various than the former one. Into this, however, whether from a terror of criticism, a wish to conciliate all parties alike, a natural modesty, a want of acquaintance with foreign manners and institutions, or for whatever reason, he did not choose to enter. Indeed the task of satirizing the manners and institutions of a country, in which one is at the time residing as a guest, is so ungracious, that we can neither wonder nor regret, that Mr. Irving should have shrunk from it with instinctive disgust. It is nevertheless certain, that the subjects alluded to are the best, indeed almost the only good ones, for lively and pungent satire; and that in voluntarily resigning them, our author was compelled to deprive himself almost wholly of the use of his favorite and most efficient instrument. He still, it is true, exercises it with no little skill and success, upon subjects afforded by the fund of vice and folly common to all nations, as in the story of the Lambs and the Trotters, but we think with less effect, than when following his original instinct, and laughing *con amore* at the peculiar foibles of his own dear countrymen. Conscious probably that the field for satire, which he felt himself at liberty to explore, was less rich and productive than he could have wished, he calls in the aid of the pathetic and sentimental; in which departments, though, as we have said before, occasionally successful, he is seldom eminently so,—seldom exhibits the bright, sharp, true expression of nature, which we see in his best comic pictures. In other portions of these works, such as the whole description of Bracebridge Hall, as it appears in the "Sketch Book," and the work of that name, the tone wavers between the sentimental and the comic, and we hardly know whether the author meant to ridicule or eulogize the manners he describes; which, however, are in either case evidently manners of his own creation, having no prototype in this or any other period of English history. Bracebridge Hall with its Christmas sports and its Rookery, its antiquarian Squire, and its Master Simon, is as much a castle of fairy land, as the one in which the Fata Morgana held entranced for six hundred years the redoubtable champion of Denmark. The British country squire is now, as he ever was, and probably ever will be, either a fox-hunter or a politician. Western and Allworthy are the only two varieties of the species; and the squire of Mr. Irving, with his indifference to politics, and his taste for black-letter lore, is as completely a fancy-piece, as the Centaurs and Harpies of the ancient poets. These castles in Spain occupy a considerable portion of the second series of works; and we really cannot but wonder how Mr. Irving, generally so just and acute an observer of nature, should have failed so completely in seizing the true aspect of rural life in England, or why, if he saw it as it is, he should have given us an unreal mockery of it instead of a correct picture. It is refreshing and delightful to find how, under all the disadvantages of writing on domestic subjects in a foreign land, he recovers his wonted power, and disports himself with his pristine grace and sprightliness, the moment that he lays the scene of his fable at home. No sooner does he catch a glimpse of the venerable Kaatskill, lifting his shaggy head over his white ruff of ambient clouds, and frowning on the glorious Hudson as it rolls below; no sooner do the antique gable-roofed domes of the Man-hattoes, and Albany, and the classic shades of Communipaw rise upon his fancy, than "his foot is on his native heath and his name is M'Gregor." When we think of this, although we rejoice that Mr. Irving has been able, as he might not otherwise have been, to levy a large and liberal golden contribution from the superfluity of the mother country, this being, as it were, a spoiling of the Egyptians, we sometimes regret, for his own fame, that he ever left America. There was a fund of truth, as well as ill nature, in the remark of one of the paltry, scandal-mongering novelists of the day, that Mr. Irving would have done better to stay at home, and pass his life among the beavers.

We have stated above, that the sentiment, which probably in-duced Mr. Irving to refrain from exercising his satirical talent upon the institutions and public characters of Great Britain, was a natural and highly laudable one; but we cannot conscientiously speak with the same approbation of his apparent disposition to represent the British aristocracy under a favorable point of view, as compared with the other classes of the people. If this representation were true, we should not object to it, although the sort of complacency, with which it is put forward, would still, in a foreigner and a republican, be somewhat ungraceful. But the worst of it is, that it is obviously and notoriously the reverse of the truth. Let us take as an example the account given in the "Sketch Book" of the author's attendance on public worship at a village church, where he met with the family of a nobleman and that of a wealthy merchant. The former, especially the young men and women, were all attention, candor, simplicity, and true moral dignity; the latter all bad taste, affectation, and vulgarity. Now every one, who has seen anything of Europe, knows perfectly well, and Mr. Irving certainly by this time, whatever he may have done when he wrote the "Sketch Book," better than any body, that if there be a class of persons in that part of the world, who as a class may be said to be more deficient than any other in simplicity, candor, and a correct notion of true moral dignity, it is precisely this very British aristocracy, especially in its younger branches, to which our author attributes these virtues. . . .

While we have felt it a duty to point out this error in the tone and spirit of Mr. Irving's later works, we must add, that we do not, as some have done, attribute it to any hankering in him after the aristocratic institutions and habits of Europe. We acquit him entirely, as we have said before, of political heresy; and without supposing him to be deeply versed in the theory of government, we have no doubt that he is strongly and sincerely attached to the republican institutions and forms established in his country. Neither do we believe, that he was influenced in making this representation, by an interested wish to conciliate the British aristocracy, for the purpose of obtaining their patronage as a writer, or admission into their circles as a gentleman. We have too high an opinion of Mr. Irving's independence, delicacy, and elevation of mind, to suspect him for a moment of such baseness. We think it probable, that he wrote the parts of his work to which we now allude, under the influence of an illusion, resulting naturally from his former situation and literary habits. Without having studied the subject of government very deeply in the abstract, or possessing probably any very precise general notions respecting it, he was led by the original bent of his mind and his local and social position, to employ himself, for several years, in ridiculing the abuses of popular institutions, and the peculiar follies and weaknesses of republican statesman. Thus far he kept himself within the line of truth and nature; for popular governments, however valuable, certainly have their defects, and republican statesmen, like all other mortals, their besetting sins and characteristic foibles. Now, although it does by no means follow from this, that monarchy is a perfect system, or an established aristocracy *ex officio* a corps of Lord Orvilles and Sir Charles Grandisons, it was perhaps not unnatural, that Mr. Irving, habitually gathering his impressions more from impulse and feeling than argument, should, by constantly looking at the ridiculous features of one form, be led to take up a too flattering idea of the other. Some such mental operation as this appears to have been the source of the illusion under which, as we conceive, he was at one time laboring; and when he wrote the "Sketch Book," where the error in question is most apparent, he probably had not had much opportunity to bring his ideal picture to the test of comparison with real life, for it was not, we believe, until he had acquired a high reputation in England, by the publication of this work, that he frequented very intimately the circles of the British aristocracy. We have reason to suppose that he has since reformed his theory on this subject, and we mention the fact with pleasure, as a proof that the opportunities he has had for actual observation, have not been lost upon his naturally acute and sagacious, as well as sensitive mind.

Having thus cleared our consciences (we trust without doing injustice to our author) by pointing out certain particulars, in which we consider his European manner inferior to his American one, we return with pleasure to the remark we made before, that the former has somewhat more of elegance and polish than the latter; that the characteristics of both are (with the deductions we have specified) substantially the same; that all his productions are among the most agreeable and attractive, as they certainly have been among the most popular of the time; that they do the highest honor to himself and through him to his country; and that he has already secured and will permanently maintain, in our literary annals, the brilliant position of the harbinger and founder of the American school of polite learning.

We come now to the "History of the Life and Voyages of Columbus," which has furnished the immediate subject and occasion of the present article. This work differs essentially in manner, as we have already said, from any of the preceding. It exemplifies on a larger scale, and in a more complete and finished way, the plan of the short biographical sketches, which the author published before his departure for Europe, principally of contemporary officers of the navy. We shall first endeavor to ascertain the class of historical writing to which it belongs, and then make a few remarks upon the merit of the execution and the general value of the work.

The great division of this department of literature, is into the two classes of philosophical and purely narrative history. They are not, it is true, separated by a very strict line, but on the contrary run into each other, each possessing to a certain extent the peculiar characteristics of both; but the distinction is nevertheless real, and whenever a writer has talent enough to give his work a marked character, it is evident at once, to which of the two classes it belongs. The object of philosophical history is to set forth by a record of real events, the general principles, which regulate the march of political affairs; that of purely narrative history, to give a correct and lively picture of the same events, as they pass before the eye of the world, but with little or no reference to their causes or effects. . . .

Mr. Irving's present work, if technically classed according to the general principles just stated, belongs to the lower species of history, and is so described by himself in his preface. "In the execution of this work," he remarks, "I have avoided indulging in mere specu-lations or general reflections, excepting such as naturally arose out of the subject, preferring to give a minute and circumstantial narrative, omitting no particular that appeared characteristic of the persons, the events, or the times; and endeavoring to place every fact under such a point of view, that the reader might perceive its merits, and draw his own maxims and conclusions." The omission of all general speculation is indeed a good deal more complete than this preliminary declaration would have necessarily led us to suppose it, since the exception of "such reflections as naturally arise out of the subject" would admit almost any degree of latitude in this respect. In point of fact, there is no political speculation whatever, the very few reflections that are interspersed being on matters of ordinary private morality. In giving this color to his work, Mr. Irving doubtless followed instinctively the natural bent of his genius, which does not incline him, as we have repeatedly observed, to philosophical researches;

but he has thereby produced a much more valuable literary monument, than with his peculiar taste and talent, he could have done in a different way. In estimating the positive worth of particular works, we must take into view the merit of the execution, as well as the dignity of the class to which they belong; and if the latter be, in the present instance, of a secondary order (though still secondary only as compared with the very highest and most glorious exercises of intellect), yet such have been the good taste and felicity of our author, in the selection of his subject; such his diligence, research, and perseverance in collecting and employing his materials; and such his care in giving the highest finish and perfection to the style; that he has been able to bring out a work, which will rank with the very best histories of any age or nation, which will take a permanent place in the classical literature of the language, which is, in fact, one of the most agreeable, instructive, and really valuable productions to be met with any where, and one that, as we remarked above, does, on the whole, more honor to the learning of our country, than any previous work written on this side of the Atlantic.

For the particular kind of historical writing, in which Mr. Irving is fitted to labor and to excel, the "Life of Columbus" is undoubtedly one of the best, perhaps we might say without the fear of mistake, the very best subject afforded by the annals of the world. While his discoveries possess the importance belonging to political events of the first magnitude, the generous elevation of his mind, the various fortunes that chequered his course, and the singularity, the *uniquity* rather, if we may be allowed to coin a word, of his achievements, throw a sort of poetical and romantic coloring over his adventures, and render him of all others the fittest hero for a work of this description; which, as we have shown above, is essentially a poem. The only objection, that could possibly be made to the choice of the subject, would be, that it was before exhausted; and this has in fact been said, by some of the newspaper critics of the mother country. The assertion is however quite groundless. Before the publication of the work before us, there was no satisfactory account of Columbus in any language. The one given by his son is, as is well known, merely a brief and imperfect sketch; and the portion of Robertson's "America" which is devoted to him, though as large as it could be with propriety, considering the author's plan, did not allow a detailed and accurate investigation of the events of his life. Into this and other general histories, Columbus enters partially as one of the leading personages of the age, and is treated in connexion with the rest; but the singular splendor and prodigious permanent importance of his actions, as well as the moral grandeur and sublimity of his character, entitled him fully to the honor of a separate and detailed biography. How much finer and loftier a subject is he, than his contemporary

Charles the Fifth, who has yet furnished a theme for one of the best histories in the language! The materials, printed and manuscript, were ample, but not accessible in their full extent, excepting to a person resident, for the time, in the capital of Spain. We consider it therefore as a singularly fortunate circumstance, that Mr. Irving should have been led, in the course of his pilgrimage abroad, to visit this, on some accounts, unattractive part of Europe. Thus favorably situated, and possessed of all the talent and industry necessary for the purpose, he has at length filled up the void, that before existed, in this respect, in the literature of the world, and produced a work, which will fully satisfy the public, and supersede the necessity of any future labors in the same field. While we venture to predict that the adventures of Columbus will hereafter be read only in the work of Mr. Irving, we cannot but think it a beautiful coincidence, that the task of duly celebrating the achievements of the discoverer of our continent, should have been reserved for one of its inhabitants; and that the earliest professed author of first-rate talent, who appeared among us, should have devoted one of his most important and finished works to this pious purpose. "Such honors Ilion to her hero paid, / And peaceful slept the mighty Hector's shade."

In treating this happy and splendid subject, Mr. Irving has brought out the full force of his genius as far as a just regard for the principles of historical writing would admit. This kind of history, although it belongs essentially to the department of poetry, does not of course afford any room for the display of the creative power in the invention of facts or characters; but, in this case, the real facts and characters far surpass in brilliancy any possible creation of mere fancy, and in the other requisites of fine poetry, a judicious selection and disposition of the materials, a correct, striking, and discriminating picture of the different personages, a just and elevated tone of moral feeling, and above all, the charm of an elegant, perspicuous, and flowing style, Mr. Irving leaves us nothing to desire, and with all, who can look beyond mere forms and names into the substance of things, sustains his right, which he had before established, to the fame of a real poet. To say that this work is superior to any professed poem, that has yet been published, on the life of Columbus, would be giving it but poor praise; since the subject, although attempted by bards of no slight pretensions, has not yet been treated in verse with eminent success. We would go farther than this, and express the opinion, that Mr. Irving's production may be justly ranked with the fine narrative or epic poems of the highest reputation. A polished and civilized age may well be supposed to prefer, especially in a long composition, the delicate melody of flowing prose, setting forth a spirited and elegant picture of actual life, to the "specious wonders" of Olympus or fairy land, expressed in artificial measures, strains and subjects that seem more naturally adapted to a yet unformed, than to a mature and perfect taste. Hence a fine history and a fine novel may perhaps with propriety be viewed as the greater and lesser epic (to use the technical terms) of a cultivated period, when verse is better reserved for short poems accompanied by music. But however this may be, and with whatever class of compositions we may rank the work before us, its execution entirely corresponds, as we have said before, with the beauty of the subject, and leaves of course but little room for the labor of the critic. The interest of the narrative is completely sustained from the beginning to the conclusion, and is equal through-out, for any mature mind, to that of the best romance. Instinctively pursuing the bent of his genius, the author has everywhere brought out into full relief the most poetical features of the story. He dwells, for instance, with peculiar pleasure on the golden age of innocence and happiness, that reigned among the natives of Haiti before the arrival of the Spaniards. The careless and luxurious indulgence, in which they passed their peaceful hours beneath "the odorous shade of their boundless forests," under the amiable sway of a beautiful Queen, who is represented as charming their leisure with her own sweet poetry, seems to realize the notion of an earthly elysium; and if there be, as there probably is, some little exaggeration in the coloring of the picture, it must be viewed as a natural effect of the just indignation and horror, with which we contemplate the devilish malice which afterwards carried death and destruction through these bowers of simple bliss. The two leading personages are happily con-trasted, not by labored parallels, but indirectly by the mere progress of the story. The towering sublimity and bold creative genius of the Admiral; the sagacity, activity, and dauntless courage of the Adelan-tado; the faithful and tender attachment with which they stood by each other, through a long life of labor, danger, and suffering; these are moral traits, that furnish out another picture, not less beautiful and even more edifying, than that of the Indian Paradise.

We are grateful to Mr. Irving, for bringing particularly into view the high religious feeling, which uniformly governed the mind of Columbus, which led him to consider himself as an agent, expressly selected by Providence for the accomplishment of great and glorious objects,—and how, but by a poor quibble upon words, can we refuse him that character?—which induced him finally to look forward to the recovery of the Holy Sepulchre, as the last labor of his life, to be undertaken after the complete accomplishment of all his projects in the New World. If there be any error in the passages, which treat of this particular, it consists in underrating the merit of this conception of Columbus, which appears to be viewed by Mr. Irving as the effect of an amiable, but somewhat visionary and mistaken enthusiasm. . . .

It would give us pleasure to expatiate at greater length upon the

merit of the beautiful and valuable work before us; but we perceive
that we have reached the proper limit of an article, and must here
close our remarks. We cannot however refrain from expressing our
satisfaction, at the very favorable manner with which Mr. Irving's
"Life of Columbus" compares with one or two works of a similar
kind, that were published about the same time by the best writers
of the mother country. The "Life of Napoleon" by Sir Walter Scott,
and the "Life of Sheridan" by Moore, particularly the former, resemble it so nearly in plan and form, that, coming out, as they all
did, about the same time, they exhibit in a manner a trial of skill
between three of the most elegant writers of the day. We feel a
good deal of pride as Americans in adding, that our countryman
appears to have retired from this dangerous contest with a very
decided advantage, we think we might say a complete victory, over
both his competitors. We mean not to deprive these illustrious transatlantic bards of any fame, to which they may be justly entitled, by
the productions in question; nor do we mean to represent Mr. Irving's
general reputation as at present superior or equal to theirs. We simply
state the fact as it is, considering it to be one highly honorable to
our countryman and our country. We shall even go farther, being in
a patriotic vein, and while we freely admit that Mr. Irving's fame is
and ought to be at present inferior to that of the two British poets
abovementioned, we shall take the liberty of adding, that we are not
quite sure whether it will always remain so. Moore and Scott have
already done their best, and from the character of their productions
for some years past, as compared with those of earlier date, it is
evident that they will not hereafter excel or perhaps equal their past
efforts. Mr. Irving's talent seems to us, on the contrary, to be in a
state of progress; for although his second manner be, as we think,
inferior, on the whole, to his first, the difference is not, as we have
already expressly stated, owing to any decay of genius, but to an
unfavorable change of scene and subject; and in this first specimen
of a *third* series of publications, we recognise, though under a somewhat grayer form, a developement of power superior to that which
is displayed by any of the preceding ones, even should the "History
of New York" as a bold original creation, be considered as belonging
to a higher class of writings. We also recognise in the selection of
the subject, the persevering industry with which the work has been
executed, and the high tone of moral feeling that runs through the
whole of it, the symptoms of a noble spirit, on which the intoxicating
cup of public applause acts as a stimulant rather than an opiate. Mr.
Irving is still in the vigor of life and health; and when we see him
advancing in his course in this way, with renovated courage and
redoubled talent at an age when too many hearts begin to wax
prematurely faint, we are induced to anticipate the happiest results

from his future labors; and are far from being certain, as we said above, that he may not in the end eclipse the most illustrious of his present contemporaries and rivals. We rejoice to find, from the selection of the subject of the work now before us, that though long a wanderer, his thoughts are still bent on the land of his birth. Although we wish not to hasten his return before the period when he shall himself deem it expedient, we indulge the hope that he will sooner or later fix his residence among us, and can assure him that whenever he may think proper to do so, he will be welcomed by his countrymen as a well deserving citizen and a public benefactor. When he shall be seated again upon his native soil, among his beavers, if Mr. D'Israeli pleases, when he shall again apply to those subjects of strictly native origin, in which his genius seems to take most delight, the force of his mature talent, and the lights of his long and varied experience, we think we may expect with reason a *fourth* series of publications, that shall surpass in value all the preceding ones, including even that, which he has now so honorably opened with the work before us.

[Review of *A Chronicle of the Conquest of Granada*]   Anonymous*

Washington Irving's reputation in this country depends on his "Sketch Book." Neither his "Tales of a Traveller," nor his "Life of Columbus," have met with nearly so much success. There is a great deal of merit, however, though of different kinds, in both these works. Irving is not a very powerful or original thinker; but he possesses, to perfection, the art of expressing winning sentiments in graceful and elegant language. He has cultivated his taste in composition with almost Addisonian nicety; and he sails over the summer sea of prose rejoicing in the soft breezes that follow his track. Like his prototype, he perhaps sacrifices too much to the Graces; yet he is so full of refinement and polish, that it is not difficult to forgive him for being less masculine and nervous.

"A Chronicle of the Conquest of Granada," is a title which very imperfectly explains the nature of the exceedingly handsome book before us. On seeing it announced, we were unable to make out whether we were to expect a piece of fiction, a history, or a mixture of both. The mixture of both comes nearest the truth. Taking for the basis of his work certain voluminous manuscripts left scattered, through

* Reprinted from *Edinburgh Literary Journal* 2 (6 June 1829): 1–4.

different convent libraries in Spain, by a monk of the name of Antonio Agapida, (for the existence and authenticity of whose writings, we are, of course, willing to take Mr. Irving's word,) he contrives to present us with a well-connected and glowing narrative of the ten years' war, which commencing in 1478, terminated with the extinction of the Moorish dynasty in Spain. As we have a great deal to say in favour of this production, it may be as well to pave the way for our praise, by pointing out in the first place, what we feel to be its defects, although these, we are glad to say, are not numerous.

We have to remark, *primo loco*, that the "Chronicle" commences too abruptly. Had Mr. Irving favoured us with a brief historical introduction for the purpose of tracing rapidly the leading events which had characterized the dominion of the Moors in Spain, beginning with their memorable victory over Roderick, on the banks of the Guadalete, nearly eight hundred years before their final overthrow, and including some short notices of the Ommeyades, the Almoravides, and other illustrious houses, and of the wars they had so frequently carried on against the Christians, he would have invested his subsequent details with greater interest than they are at present likely to possess for the general reader, who is plunged at once *in medias res*, though in all probability sufficiently ignorant of the political and civil relations which had previously subsisted between the two people. In like manner, our author errs towards the conclusion of his Chronicle, which ends nearly as abruptly as it begins, leaving the reader's curiosity only imperfectly satisfied. Another fault we have to find is, that Mr. Irving has too easily fallen into the tone of the old Monk Agapida, with regard to the comparative merit of the Moors and Christians, whom the Catholic chronicler of course viewed in very different lights, invariably undervaluing the Moors, and servilely extolling the worshippers of the cross. Mr. Irving, who affects to be indebted to Agapida only for his facts, ought to have been cautious of introducing into his own narrative, the prejudices of a party writer. In the war, whose incidents he describes, the Moors were, in point of fact, the injured people, for a kingdom and country were wrested from them, to which conquest originally, and subsequent possession for many generations, had confirmed their title. They were, besides, an heroic and noble-minded race; and it is well known that their progress in civilization, aided as that had been by the reminiscences of their Eastern descent, was more rapid and efficient than that of their Spanish neighbours. We do not therefore like to think that a "Chronicle of Granada" should deny to its most distinguished possessors, the praise so justly due to them. One other objection, and we have done. There is a little too much monotony especially in the first volume, in the perpetual succession of forays, and rencounters, and petty engagements, and small military expeditions, which it describes. Some of these are highly interesting and full of romance, and as the work proceeds the operations become more important; but we cannot help regretting that the narrative is not more frequently relieved by incidents which would have broken in upon the interminable series of skirmishes, sieges, and battles, and which, in the glimpses they might have presented of the domestic manners of the times, would have afforded a profitable and agreeable variety. Mr. Irving might easily have availed himself of the facilities afforded by his present residence in Spain, to achieve this additional object.

As a whole, however, we have been very much charmed with this work. The subject is a remarkably happy one; and its execution is worthy of the best days of chivalry. The Moors, who, in the time of their greatest glory, reigned masters over all Spain, had, in the decay of their power, gradually been deprived of territory after territory, till the kingdom of Granada alone remained. It remained, however, powerful and flourishing, and there was not a Moor who did not feel towards it as a father who has lost all his children save one, and who heaps upon the survivor the whole affections of his heart. And Granada was worthy of a patriot's love, with the tideless Mediterranean on its shores, with its green hills and majestic sierras, with its deep, rich, and verdant valleys, with its cities and their alhambras, and with an air so pure, and sky so serene, that the Moors believed the paradise of their prophet to be situated in that part of the heaven which overhung their kingdom. When, therefore, the ambition of Ferdinand and Isabella, who had united under one sceptre, the kingdoms of Castile, Leon, and Arragon, directed its attention to the conquest of Granada, it was no marvel that one of the fiercest and most anxiously contested wars took place that ever depopulated a country;—it was no marvel that every inch of ground was disputed, and that the Spaniards, animated by a desire to drive the infidels finally and for ever out of Spain, and the Mahometans, no less desirous of preserving a country and a name in Europe, should perform such prodigies of valour as had rarely been equalled, and have never been surpassed. These are the deeds which Mr. Irving undertakes to recount, and he does so in a style such as becomes the author of the "Sketch Book,"—flowing, graceful, and picturesque. . . .

[Review of *Voyages and Discoveries of the Companions of Columbus*]

Henry D. Gilpin°

When we noticed, three years since, a former production of Mr. Irving, we took occasion to express an opinion of its merits, which has been fully confirmed. No work of the present era appears to have afforded more general and unmingled gratification to its readers, than his Life of Columbus; and he has received, in the approbation, not only of his own countrymen, but of Europeans, the most gratifying reward an author can desire. The fame which he had acquired, and that most justly, by the happy works of fiction in which he was introduced to the public, is now changed into one of higher character; and he becomes entitled to take his stand among those writers who have done more than amuse the fancy, or even gratify the heart. He is to be classed with the historians of great events; for if the period of which he has treated is limited, or the persons whose actions he has described are not numerous, yet the one included within it, short as it was, circumstances that have produced in effect which long ages have not always surpassed in importance or wonderful consequences; and the others embrace individuals whose actions have more deeply affected the human race than many of the revolutions of great and populous nations.

Having these feelings in regard to the former work of Mr. Irving, we open the present volume with mingled apprehension and pleasure. We rejoice that we are to follow again the same guide in adventurous voyages among the clustering Antilles; but we almost fear that the narrative may want much of that interest, novelty, and beauty, which make the story of Columbus among the most attractive ever recorded.

. . .

Our readers will, themselves, be able to form a just estimate of the power and skill of the writer, and of the pleasure to be derived from the story he has recorded. We venture to say, that by none will that estimate be otherwise than favourable.

The style of Mr. Irving has been objected to as somewhat elaborate, as sacrificing strength and force of expression, to harmony of periods and extreme correctness of language. We cannot say that we have been inclined to censure him for this. If he assumed a style more than usually refined, it was in those works of fiction, those short but agreeable narratives, in which he desired to win the fond attention of the reader, but in which he never endeavoured to call up violent emotions, to engage in the wild speculations of a discursive

° Reprinted from *American Quarterly Review* 9 (March 1831): 163–86.

fancy, or to treat topics requiring logical or historical correctness. For such works as the Sketch Book, we believe the style adopted by Mr. Irving to be eminently well fitted, and we do not hesitate to attribute much of the success of these charming tales to this very circumstance. We believe so the more readily, because we find him adopting in the Life of Columbus, and in the volume before us, a different manner, but one equally well suited to the different nature of the subject he treats. Without losing the elegance and general purity by which it has always been characterized, it seems to us to have acquired more freshness, more vivacity; to flow on more easily with the course of the spirited narrative; to convey to the reader that exquisite charm in historical writing—an unconsciousness of any elaboration on the part of the writer, yet a quick and entire understanding of every sentiment he desires to convey.

But connected with this, the writing of Mr. Irving possesses another characteristic, which has never been more strongly and beautifully exhibited than in the present volume. We mean that lively perception of all those sentiments and incidents, which excite the finest and pleasantest emotions of the human breast. As he leads us from one savage tribe to another—as he paints successive scenes of heroism, perseverance, and self-denial—as he wanders among the magnificent scenes of nature—as he relates with scrupulous fidelity the errors, and the crimes, even of those whose lives are for the most part marked with traits to command admiration, and perhaps esteem—every where we find him the same undeviating, but beautiful moralist, gathering from all lessons to present, in striking language, to the reason and the heart. Where his story leads him to some individual, or presents some incident which raises our smiles, it is recorded with a naive humour, the more effective from its simplicity; where he finds himself called on to tell some tale of misfortune or two—and how often must he do so when the history of the gentle and peaceful natives of the Antilles is his subject—the reader is at a loss whether most to admire the beauty of the picture he paints, or the deep pathos which he imperceptibly excites.

Nor has he shown less judgment in the selection of his subject. To all persons the discovery of this continent is one which cannot fail to engage and reward attention—to him who loves to speculate on the changes and progress of society, to him who loves to trace the paths of science and knowledge, to him who loves to dwell on bold adventures and singular accidents, to him who loves carefully to ascertain historical truth. We scarcely know any topics at the present day, explored and exhausted as so many fields have been, that afford a richer harvest than those which Mr. Irving has now selected. We trust that many more works are yet to be the fruits of his most fortunate visit to the peninsula. The sources of information so liberally opened to him, and already so judiciously used—and which have contributed to add new reputation to so many names honourable to Spain—must yet furnish ample materials to illustrate other men, to disclose the incidents attending other adventures; and we trust that three years more may not elapse, before we again sail with our author over the newly discovered billows of the Pacific, or explore the plains of Mexico and Peru, or wander with some of the hardy adventurers who first dared to penetrate the defiles of the Andes.

We have already mentioned, in the notice of Columbus, the circumstances which led Mr. Irving to the investigation of this period of Spanish history, and the facilities afforded him in the prosecution of his labours. The materials for this volume were procured during the same visit. In addition to the historical collections of Navarrete, Las Casas, Herrera, and Peter Martyr, he profited by the second volume of Oviedo's history, of which he was shown a manuscript copy in the Columbian library of the cathedral of Seville, and by the legal documents of the law case between Diego Columbus and the crown, which are deposited in the Archives of the Indies.

[Review of *The Alhambra*]   Anonymous*

In the works of Washington Irving there is more polished elegance than rough strength: he is always graceful and neat, flowing and harmonious; he has few errors either in language or in sentiment; his art in blending the humorous with the pathetic is not little, nor is he deficient in knowledge of human nature, nor unskilful in the delineation of human character. He has, however, less of simplicity and vigour than we wish; his imagination cannot exercise much power over the past: his American characters far surpass his other delineations. The present work dawned on his fancy as he mused amid the magnificent ruins of the Alhambra; it has been his wish to recall the days when the Moors ruled in the fairest provinces of Spain, and when the deeds of arms were frequent between them and their Spanish neighbours. To recall the dead to life, to make them move and act in character, requires a genius of high order; nor can we withhold the praise from the author, of having in several of his stories succeeded in this difficult art. We are, however, of opinion that his success in delineating from the living is at least equal to his drawings from the dead,—and were proof of this required, the present volumes

* Reprinted from *Athenaeum*, no. 236 (5 May 1832): 283–84.

would supply it at once. Indeed, we know of few who can equal him in the art of transferring living and breathing flesh and blood to his canvas. . . .

[Review of *The Alhambra*]   Anonymous°

All greatness, and beauty, and skill of every description, which have been long previously talked of, produce . . . inadequate impressions on many people. If Demosthenes could be brought among us by a miracle, he would not come up to our pre-existing opinion. If Venus herself were once more to rise from the deep, she would, ten chances to one, be eclipsed by some Broadway belle, with bishop sleeves, and a jewel on her forehead. In the same way, a popular writer has a serious disadvantage to contend against in those unmeaning and vague expectations elicited by a brilliant fame; and we should not be surprised to learn, that many individuals have perused the volumes now under consideration, without that glow of delight—those bursts of laughter—that soft tenderness, into which one is surprised by a sudden gleam of wit, or an unexpected touch of pathos. He who writes with chasteness and simplicity, will fail to arrest the admiration of many a reader. Some pass over his unobtrusive charms, either from carelessness, or want of taste, as they would over the modest, but exquisitely beautiful flowers which gem the meadow, eclipsed by the glare of others more gaudy, but less fragrant and lovely. How many prefer the striking powers of Mrs. Radcliff to the simple nature, wit, and wisdom of Addison. Such will find little to admire in these pages. The world in this, as well as in many other respects, is unreasonable. It is, in a measure, injurious to a literary reputation, for a writer to produce a very perfect and popular composition. The "Pleasures of Hope" was the death of Mr. Campbell, and Mr. Moore was never thoroughly convalescent from the effects of Lallah Rookh. Walter Scott survived his superb poetry only by energetically entering upon an entirely new and uncultivated field where he got along tolerably well, till he had the misfortune to produce Ivanhoe, from which he survived only to lead a lingering and unequal career. Even Geoffrey Crayon, is something of a valetudinarian in these respects. His Sketch Book, and Bracebridge Hall, are the greatest enemies his future productions will probably ever meet; and we have every reason to fear that his Columbus has put

° Reprinted from *New-York Mirror* 9 (23 June, 1832): 401–3.

an end to hopes of his succeeding hereafter in the department of
history.

Yet the tales of the Alhambra are brilliant and striking, told with
the most delightful grace of language, and addressed to the imagination of all classes. The preliminary sketches, relating the author's
ramblings over Spain, his approach to the palace, from which the
volumes derive their title, his drawings of character, his minute
household observations, his moonlight thoughts on that interesting
scene, his reveries from the various points of prospect, are, in our
estimation, really delicious. Their very familiar and easy simplicity
makes them so. They are impressed in every page, every line, every
word, with the reality of truth and the glow of nature. They are
evidently no inventions, but transcripts. His scenes stretch away before
you; his people move, look, and walk, with an individuality and a
force only to be produced by the hand of a master. Indeed, the
opening pages are full of those delightfully graphic and pleasing
delineations, peculiar to this author, and worthy of the best parts of
the Sketch Book. The want of nationality is balanced by the richness
of their historical associations; some of these will make the heart of
the student beat, as he sits in his narrow and obscure chamber, tied
down, peradventure, forever, to one single spot of the globe. Nothing
can exceed the pleasure with which we accompany the author in his
peregrinations. We are no half-way admirer of the former writings
of *Crayon*, Knickerbocker, and Jonathan Old Style. We have been
led by the same warm and gentle heart, the same refined and cultivated mind, the same soft and melting, yet disciplined imagination
for many a year long gone by. We have been with him in the pit of
our theatre, through the crooked lanes and antiquated Dutch houses
of our town, along the windings of the blue Hudson, and among the
luxuriant valleys and heaving hills, which deepen and swell up from
her emerald banks. We have followed, delighted observers, in the
train of his Dutch heroes, on their sublime and warlike expeditions;
and we have been ushered, by his welcome and potent rod, into
many a rich and mellow and melancholy scene in "merrie England;"
by her ancient piles, her meandering rivers, her magnificent palaces,
and gardens: now, indeed it is pleasant to keep still onward with
such a companion, over distant and more strange scenes, to the banks
of the streams of Spain; by her mountains, topped with silver; to her
old cities and romantic towers. We are *there* actually, while reading
the Alhambra. We see the summit of the Sierra Nivada [*sic*]; we hear
the rills and fountains playing through the palace; we see the moon,
pouring her floods of light into every court and hall and ruined
decoration; and we are surprised to perceive what strong impressions
are made on us, and by how few words. We are charmed, completely,
to follow him in his quiet observations through those lofty and

dilapidated towers and to be so well beguiled by the flowing fancies which gleam along his pages; and by that continual and sweet play of all the most delicate and beautiful lights and shades of pathos and humor. He is as fresh as ever in his feelings. He looks upon the wonders around him with the enthusiastic ardor of a glowing boy.

There is not a string in his soul but is tuned for the true harmony of poetry. It still vibrates responsive to every passing impression, to every moral or natural beauty. Indeed his perceptions of nature and the world, which we were prepared to find blunted by travel and years, are yet alive in all their pristine vigor, and are exercised with a grace and a discrimination peculiar to himself, upon every golden sunset—every dim mountain-top—every light incident of real life. Who but he could have so wrought up the trifle of the pigeon. There is another remark to be made, *en passant*, on our author. One cannot help smiling at the right hearty enthusiasm with which he rouses himself to paint every pretty woman he meets. It is positively delightful to come suddenly, (as we continually do, by the way,) upon one of his "plump little black-eyed Andalusian damsels," with her "bright looks and cheerful disposition;" or some other rosy cheeked maiden, with dark eyes, and round and pleasant form. When he lays hold of such an one, he does it with a downright sincerity, and an outbreaking of gladness and spirit, which actually do our heart good, and he never lets her loose without bestowing upon her such a list of sweet adjectives as refresh our ideas most wonderfully. . . .

[Review of *The Alhambra*]   Anonymous*

Mr. Irving has the rare fortune of wide present fame with the promise of at least equal favor and distinction hereafter. His faults may be noted as minutely as if he belonged to a remote age, and they will be commented upon with the same kind of fairness and good humor that we extend to an ancient; so that no strife of vindication is raised, and his popularity suffers no diminution. He does not receive the strained and vehement praises of an idolatrous few who are occupied in detecting latent beauties, and whose very manner of extolling an author is full of indirect pity or contempt for the less discerning reader; but he hears a general and hearty acknowledgment of properties that are fitted to delight all. He writes of his countrymen and of foreigners; he enters their dwellings, describes their classes, amusements, and occupations, relates their ex-

* Reprinted from *American Monthly Review* 2 (September 1832): 177–89.

ploits seriously or gravely, paints their habits, usages, and follies; he
tells the truth on all sides, and all are instructed and entertained; no
prejudices are shocked and no pride is wounded. The satirist, the
painter, the chronicler, the foreigner, is always a friend. He spends
a large and it may be the best part of life in other countries, and
mixes with the people as one who has made his home among them,
rather than as a mere observer of outlandish character and modes;
as one who loves to study familiarly what there is alike and various
in different countries, and not as one driven abroad "to seek new
haunt for prey," because he had devoured the little there was at
home. He returns to his own land after many years, and finds he
was expected and desired, that his own people have watched him
with pride and affection through all his rambles and sojourns, and
that every word he has sent them of others was also pleasing news
of himself. We cannot then in any way regard him as a book-maker,
however the case may be. We are reminded rather of a man of
genius, of nice fact, and a liberal, even temper, taking noiseless survey
of life and nature and events with relish and single-heartedness, and
finding as much pleasure in talking things over as he ever felt in
looking at them. Though he is our countryman he calls forth nothing
but what is generous in nationality. For once, we are allowed to
forget that we are but of yesterday and have yet a character to gain
in literature; we forget that Englishmen sneered before and praise
now; we think only of an eminent American writer who has borrowed
largely from many countries and made all his debtors.

And as we are here strongly impressed with it, we might speak
of that most delightful of all critical offices, the giving of free, fearless
praise, and objecting, if need be, with the same bold frankness. So
annoying is it to feel for ever in doubt lest you are saying too much,
or not discriminating precisely the character of what is good,—so
impoverishing to one's own mind to be always frugal towards another,
and so chilling to be anxiously exact and qualifying in every word
we utter, that a critic is the most grateful of all readers and students
when he is at liberty to surrender himself to an unreserved, luxurious
liking of an author, and to regard his business for the time as little
more than the expression of delight, mingled, it may be, with friendly
differences of opinion and taste. The grave or harsh countenance of
a public literary censor, all the manner of a judge, whether indicating
his sense of authority or responsibleness, disappears, and he becomes
the companion if not the worshipper of some high genius, too high
to be estimated by common rules, and too engrossing or overpowering
to leave the mind coolness or leisure for formal strictures or praise.

Great as Mr. Irving's power is in relating or describing what is
real, it is far greater in the higher walk of invention. Still there is
so much of the same manner in his real narratives and sketches, and

in those which are wholly or mainly of his own creation, that perhaps his distinct merit in each has not been enough considered. A certain character of humor, romance, tenderness, meditation, and dramatic vivacity belongs to the man; and as one or more of these qualities appear in all his writings, we may often confound his facts with his fancies, or else underrate the grave value of the former, when indeed we ought only to wonder at his original resource and truth of invention in the latter. What injury this is to do him as an historian, we cannot say; and we shall feel no concern about it till we find that his ambition is professedly and chiefly directed to giving us precise facts, instead of exhibiting, according to his old practice, such general truth as can be figured in glowing pictures, and in sketches rather adapted to the times or people he writes of, than borrowed from unquestioned records or documents. And this is said without in the least intending to impugn the historical credit of his "Columbus," abounding as it certainly does in romantic and dramatic interest, but for which as for other professed historical works, he prepared himself by researches in foreign libraries that entitle him to a high place among zealous and successful antiquaries. It might be seen as if, in the office of an historian, he had been led by his peculiar temperament to select just such a period and such characters, manners, and incidents as would allow him to indulge his imagination and all his poetical or romantic tendencies to the full, and enable him notwithstanding to preserve the dignity and bear the authority of a grave instructor. But most probably it matters little with him what subject he takes. He could not help bringing the same mind to it, and shaping and coloring it accordingly. The sun, with the never-failing ministry of clouds or shadows, is daily making poetry of all that it shines on.

In speaking of his strictly original writings, we should say that humor is his most striking quality, heightened as it often is by a sentimental or a grotesque air, which it receives from connexion with grand or romantic scenes and incidents, and characters tinged with melancholy. It is no argument against such a union and effect, that Milton has produced the most offensive burlesque, by the punning gibes he puts into the mouths of Angel and Archangel during the pause of the celestial fight and the moment after its renewal. He showed a want of both humor and taste in this. It was surely no time, no place, no company for jesting, and we doubt not that our countryman's genius would have been rebuked in that presence. There must be a harmony in the very contrasts to produce the effect we speak of, and Mr. Irving knows how to bring the wildest spots and most startling superstitions to the aid of what is strictly droll or comic, and they receive from it in turn the more vividness and terror, so that the mere mention of his surpassing power in humor has at once reminded us of his mastery of the grand and even terrific.—His

humor is as unlike as possible a certain ingenious, painstaking collection and assortment of piquant, smart, striking things, each drawing
attention to itself, and all of them failing to produce one entire piece,
or one generous mixture of surprise, mirth, and healthful exhilaration.
Just so it is with a set conversation of professed wits or wags, who
would shun an easy natural continuity of talk as flat prosing, and
labor all the time for the strange and sparkling, abhorring the relief
of any thing simple and unpretending, and content only with a series
of explosions and flashes, each if possible louder and brighter than
the preceding, and finally as wearisome as a jest-book, wearisome
beyond all dullness. Our author is a reveller in humor. He has had
it all to himself, and we must enter fully into his spirit and ways if
we would profit by the communication. It is not the product of sudden
association or a momentary play of fancy, and must not be examined
parcel by parcel. His imagination, and a highly poetical one, is full
of the matter in hand and sees the end from the beginning. There
is a scene, there are persons, there is something going on. The
commonest object, the commonest action, ordinary discourse, every
day people and occupations,—no matter what it is, and we know not
how it is,—they all at once have a strange power over us; they have
all conspired to do something they never did before singly or together.
They are just as truly before us as they ever were, yes, more distinctly
before us, and yet all dispose us to riot, frolic, or temperate mirth.
Every thing is turned into humor, the very atmosphere is loaded with
it; and the charm once upon us, it is never broken. We may have
all this delight in perfect solitude; not a sound of laughter may escape
us, nor a smile gather on the lips. It is inward, salubrious joy. Our
faculties are brightened, our tempers sweetened, our prospects look
clearer, tranquility loses its apathy, the dull moral sense, its morbid-
ness; we have even gained new knowledge and seen better into man's
characters. And the benevolence of his humor is as remarkable as
any thing, and we may add, too, its conscientiousness; for it will not
let the laugher become a scorner. Nothing is dealt unkindly or unjustly
with; nothing respectable or useful is made ridiculous or contemptible,
however it be made to serve a comic purpose. We are pleased to
see things in their new relation, without valuing them the less in
that we have been accustomed to.—Now, that there is at times a
fondness for caricature, and a little forcing of words to droll uses,
and occasional symptoms of a determination to be queer where there
is no call for it, and no impulse to it, is probably very true, and must
pass for what it is worth.

   Next to the author's humor, we may distinguish his power in the
pathetic. The two may belong very well to the same mind in its most
healthy state. Yet, of the two, there is more peril in attempting the
pathetic when not in the mood, or when a man has not the genuine

principles of art or taste always at hand, to guide him as if with instinctive readiness and certainty. There is danger, because it is always so easy and so agreeable to work the mind to a merely artificial sympathy; and sometimes where the object is entitled to sincere sympathy and has actually excited it, yet it may not be delicately exhibited. Perhaps no feeling, generous as it is, needs more the governance of a sound taste, than that of pity, when the artist would produce in another the whole emotion that has spread so spontaneously and apparently with no help at all through his own mind. And the effect of a failure is much more serious than that of a poor jest. If sentiment becomes mawkish, distress, tawdry or theatrical, if there is a protracted deliciousness in sorrow that would not be comforted for worlds, if there is a plaintiveness and languor of tone in grief, that seems to be kept up chiefly because the ear is soothed; we say, that this is not of true feeling, and such exhibitions should only be in ridicule of false woes and self-fabricated misfortunes or perplexities. Something of these faults we have seen or fancied in more than one of Mr. Irving's pathetic tales; and yet it is strange that we should have begun with doubts and censures, when tenderness is one of his greatest beauties; a diffusive influence, a thin, soft vapor that rests upon him and his thoughts almost every where. It is upon his landscapes, upon summer in its heaving, tranquil profusion, and autumn in its coat of many colors as the favored child of the year; upon the river of a new world the first time it is explored by the foreign settler, and upon the approach to the yet undiscovered islands of the West; and it is seen equally in an endless variety of characters, in the submission of a desolate mother, in Langstaff's autumn walk with Evergreen, in the dejection of Columbus, and in the Indian's purity, gentleness, content, and hospitality. Besides that the author's temperament fits him for the contemplation and painting of what is in itself deeply moving, he furnishes also another evidence of the fact, that a strong affection for nature and all that is beautiful, delicate, and lovely, is serious as well as happy, and that the fullness of delight is not without melancholy.

His power of description is the next quality that presents itself, and the difficulty of saying what distinguishes it, is, that it takes so many forms. If, like some masters of our art, we could by a severe analysis ascertain some one element or principle that marks all his descriptive writings, our work would be easily done; we might have the credit of a theory, and tempt others to think that a bold and fortunate epithet had revealed the secret of his beauty and defined its character. Let us see if it will help us to name some of the classes of describers. There is the austere, and the gorgeous; one, all amplitude and glory, the other, rigid and shorn. There is the faithful painter of forms, positions, and colors, of every thing that is external, and another who is not content unless he makes his feelings as visible as the object that affects them, and puts them both together. One is minute, or full of detail; another has fewer facts, and yet is called more picturesque, because he knows better how to stir the imagination. One sets us in the midst of things, and another makes us patient spectators of the canvass. One opens a scene to us by a word, another clouds every thing by amplification. Without swelling the list, we leave the reader to select from it what he approves and give it to Mr. Irving, and add whatever may further define his own idea of the author's admirable talent for description. On this point we shall record only one experience of our own, and that is the feeling newness or freshness that is upon all his pictures;—not a modern air or the dazzling polish of art, but the exhilarating brightness of risen day or of the dreams of boyhood; a splendor and purity that remind us, however strangely, of scenes in "The Arabian Nights," and at the same time of the Eden Isle of Robinson Crusoe. He may be employed upon events and personages of a distant period, upon our own country at the hour of its discovery, or the earliest expedition of a foreigner up his favorite Hudson, and yet there is nothing venerable or worn with age,—all is in primeval youth, and as if touched for the first time by his hand. Nothing is older than the fancies we have preserved of our earliest days; and whether his scenes be true or imaginary, whether we have ever seen them or not, we seem to have once dreamt of them all, and here they are before us again.

We believe, however, that the principal objections to Mr. Irving's style and use of language have been raised from passages in his descriptive and sentimental writings. His manner, to all appearance perfectly effortless, often wants the variety, spirit, and true expression of perfect ease. Its very facility and graceful finish or roundness may have concealed from the writer himself much of vapidness and indefiniteness. The mannerism which grew up most naturally from his cast of mind may have gained a mastery over him of which he is wholly unconscious, and induce him to write always as he always has written, merely in obedience to habit. Then it is that a superfluity of words will be noticed, words, too, that are rich, powerful, and delicious, but lose their force and luxuriousness in the use to which they are put. A vaporous, uncertain, roundabout way of expression may be adopted from a mistaken notion of dignity or elegance.—It seasonably occurs to us in the midst of these objections, that it is hardly safe for any one to say, that this or that thing is unnatural or insincere in another. The critic may have his own poor prejudices; the writer perhaps is heedless, versatile, and prodigal, and less in the humor to do himself justice at one time than at another. Our own idea of the character and destiny of his serious style may be partly shadowed forth by a passage from "The Alhambra," describing the architecture of the Court of Lions: "It is characterized by elegance rather than grandeur, bespeaking a delicate and graceful taste, and a disposition to indolent enjoyment. When we look upon the fairy tracery of the peristyles and the apparently fragile fretwork of the walls, it is difficult to believe that so much has survived the wear and tear of centuries, the shock of earthquakes, the violence of war, and the quiet though no less baneful pilferings of the tasteful traveller. It is almost sufficient to excuse the popular tradition, that the whole is protected by a magic charm."—If we should insist upon one objection to his serious manner more than another, it would be to his frequent avoiding familiar language that would tell the very thing, and preferring a made-up expression which, though some may think it looks more respectable, is yet both less significant, and somewhat ludicrously formal. When Camilla was about to feed a caged bullfinch, Miss Burney no doubt thought it would give proper dignity to the action to say, that "she drew out the receptacle for the bird's nourishment to replenish the machine." Would it be believed that we could match this in passages from our author, from Scott, and another eminent tale-writer of our time? The defect may be of less moment in men of such abundant and varied excellence, but it is an injury even to them, and they are doing still greater harm to others, so far as they have classic authority; and we wish that some fatal word of reprobation could be discovered or invented, that would put down for ever all such foppery or carelessness.

Since the author is chiefly known as a writer of narratives, real or fictitious, it might be proper to dwell a little upon his manner of telling a story. But we must be content with having touched upon it in our rambling recollections of his numerous writings, as it is high time to speak of the work named at the head of this article and the latest from his pen. His "Conquest of Granada," and his notices of Columbus and other discoverers, are the fruit of diligent, responsible research; and the volumes before us appear to be the fruit of some inquiry, some observation, and perhaps more of reveries, in the scenes he describes. They give us a pleasant, airy account of the Alhambra, the ancient Moorish fortress in Granada, with "Tales and Sketches of the Moors and Spaniards," in some way connected with this romantic pile, and a few characteristic details of the author's way of spending his time during a sojourn there of several months. To those of us who know little of the interior of Spain, of the domestic state of things there, and of the speech, habits, and notions of the common people, Mr. Irving's book will give some information, at least as regards a part of the country; though for all that we know, what he says of things there at the present day, may be true of things as they were ages ago. . . .

The description of the Alhambra itself takes several chapters of the first volume. It is not a continued architectural or garden or mountain sketch; the author wanders from place to place, exploring the desolate interior, or examining the outside from different points, and cheering his descriptions with his own little adventures, and with the legends he picks up from his guide, or has found in other quarters. No solitude can be more intense than his at times in the Alhambra, and none more thoroughly happy. The plan of this part of the work is skilfully contrived to make one acquainted with the city, its castellated palace and surrounding country.

Without going further into details, we may add that the "Truant Bird," and the "Tower of Comares," (both a little in Miss Mitford's manner,) Governor Manco with his corporal, the notary, and soldier; the fancies which possessed the author as he looked out from the balcony, and the adventures of the Pilgrim of Love who could talk with the birds, are among the parts of the work that are clearest in our memory, and probably they will be favorite chapters with all readers. To those who in early life knew just enough of the Moorish race to be haunted with images of Oriental splendor in dress and arms and palaces and gardens, of the indolence of a luxurious people and climate, united with the most desperate valor and accomplished chivalry in open or predatory war; to those who are enchanted with their beautiful superstitions, and with the poetry, music, and love, that softened what was barbarian in their habits and tempers; and who are fond of tracing to this old and fallen people much of the charm that hangs over unchanging Spain,—to such this work will be most acceptable, for it is a good deal of a romance after all, and an air of Eastern fiction seems to become the fortunes of this once splendid and formidable race more than the most veritable and informing history.

[Review of *The Crayon Miscellany*, No. 1—*A Tour on the Prairies*]

Anonymous*

The return of Washington Irving to the United States, has been welcomed, not only by the literary circles of our larger cities, but by the acclamations of a whole people, who claim him with pride as their countryman. If fame be his object, he should be satisfied; for no living author is more widely known, or more universally admired. . . .

* Reprinted from*Western Monthly Magazine* 3 (June 1835): 329–37.

We are never thus disappointed with Irving. True to nature, he does not draw exaggerated pictures; faithful to his duty as a moralist, he never shocks the delicacy, nor alarms the moral sense of the reader, by a violation of decorum, or a perversion of any of the great rules of right and wrong. Polished, correct, and elegant in style, we recur to his writings with renewed pleasure, because every perusal discloses some new beauty.

Mr. Irving has produced some things which have never been excelled, and never will become obsolete. Among the early efforts of his pen, when his genius was in its full vigor, and the materials out of which he wove his inimitable sketches were abundant, are productions which combine wit and invention with richness of thought, purity of sentiment, delicacy of feeling, and an exquisite felicity of language. Superior to Addison in genius and taste, we know of no English writer, to whom he can be so properly compared as Goldsmith. It is of course understood, that we do not attempt to compare him with writers out of his own class—with poets, novelists, or meta-physicians. We could draw no parallel between the genius of such a man, and that of Byron, Moore, or Scott. He is, strictly speaking, an essayist, and should be compared with Addison, Steele, Goldsmith, and the periodical writers who have succeeded to them. Tested by this rule, he will be found to stand at the head of his class.

We have not forgotten that our gifted countryman, has written the life of Columbus, and has in the successful execution of that noble task, displayed the research, the patience, the vigor of intellect, the clearness of thought, the accuracy and elevation of style, which marks the accomplished historian. America has not produced another work of history so finished as this; and Great Britain has nothing more elegant. It places Irving by the side of Robertson, and shows that if he had not chosen to be the best essayist of his time, he might have been among the most eminent of modern historians. . . .

Irving's history is not inferior to his other works; it is a noble monument of intellectual vigor and industry: but it will never be half so popular as Knickerbocker or the Sketch Book. The former will be read by the scholar and statesman, the latter, by the great mass of English readers. The name of Columbus is the property of the world, and his history is identified with that of several nations; but Rip Van Winkle, Ichabod Crane, and the Little Gentleman in Black, belong to American literature, and to Washington Irving.

We have not been among those who have railed at Irving for his long residence abroad, or who have supposed that his absence from his own country, was the result of any want of patriotism, or alienation of affection. There was a degree of indelicacy, as well as intolerance, in the spirit of those criticisms. The private concerns of an author should be as sacred from impertinent remark, as those of any other gentleman; and if he chooses to reside in London, rather than New York, no one should inquire into the reasons of an election which he has an undoubted right to make. Mr. Irving's character and history were too well known to his countrymen, to require any explanation or defence, in reference to a residence abroad, from which his country has derived honor and instruction.

Mr. Irving has not been a voluminous writer. He has composed with deliberation, and finished with great care, whatever he attempted. In this respect, he is a benefactor to the literature of his country, and a model for its writers. His purity of diction, his exquisite finish, and his labored accuracy of style, demand the highest commendation. He has had the good taste and independence to write English, when the fashionable compositions of the English themselves, were clothed in a mongrel dialect made up of the shreds and patches of every modern language—when a gibberish, in which all the living tongues of Europe were mingled in inextricable confusion, was the courtly medium of fashionable conversation in London—and when the great mass of polite literature professedly written in our vernacular, was so interlarded with scraps of trashy songs or proverbs, picked up by conceited travelers abroad, as to resemble a decent garment of broadcloth, patched with a variety of flimsy, and gaudy, and party-colored materials. . . .

Mr. Irving has not been ashamed of his country, or of his mother tongue, and has not been seduced by bad models, or deluded by the popularity which his genius gained for him in the fashionable circles of London.

It is long since we have been favored with any thing from the elegant pen of this favorite writer; and the public have been anxiously looking for his reappearance. Since his return to America, and especially since his tour through the western states, it has been currently reported, that his genius was again luxuriating in its native atmosphere, and his pen employed upon a subject, the scene and character of which would be American. But so well was his secret kept, that, in this region at least, not the most distant conjecture could be formed, of the nature of the anticipated work. That it would be shaped out of materials collected in the forests and prairies of the West, seemed to be probable; but whether it would turn out to be a collection of facts, or a work of fiction—the diary of a traveler, the sketches of a Geoffrey Crayon, or a new series from the port folio of Deidrick [sic] Knickerbocker, none could tell, or guess.

The long expected volume has arrived at last, and we have the pleasure of accompanying our favorite author through scenes, which are new to him, and fresh in themselves. Irving on the prairies! Washington Irving among the honey-bees, the wild horses, and Osages of the frontier! The very idea has a novelty about it, which will induce many to read this captivating volume, who might not otherwise be allured either by the writer, or the subject. It is the combined attraction of an old favorite, with a new topic, which induces us to open this book with avidity, and to linger among the delightful periods of Mr. Irving, with a sense of enjoyment scarcely inferior to that with which he beheld the grassy plain, the wild buffalo, and the picturesque Indian horseman.

But many will be disappointed when on first opening the book, they will discover that nothing is said on subjects and scenes most familiar and most interesting in themselves. The return of our long exiled countryman to the United States, and his visit to the West, caused quite a sensation among us. To see Mr. Irving was a high treat to all who admire genius allied with purity of character—but to see the author of the Sketch Book, the biographer of Columbus, veritable editor of the writings of Deidrick [sic] Knickerbocker, on the shores of the "beautiful river"—to behold him hailed with acclamation in the theatre of Cincinnati, a city not older than himself— to greet him in the "dark and bloody ground"—was something so out of the common way, as to be noted among the extraordinary occurrences of the times. Next to seeing and hearing in proper person, the amiable and highly gifted man, who is the most popular of our native writers, was the anticipated pleasure of perusing his forthcoming book. We felt a very natural and laudable curiosity to know what would be said of us and our country, by one who has traveled over many foreign lands, and looked attentively at all that is worthy of observation, in the wealth, the industry, and the arts, of other nations. On these points we were in the dark, for although Mr. Geoffrey Crayon looked pleased, while among us, he said little, but journeyed courteously and quietly along, with a placid air of satisfaction, which only made us the more inquisitive, in reference to the pleasant musings in which his fancy appeared to find enjoyment.

Those who had formed such expectations, will not find them gratified—and it is perhaps well that such is the case—for Mr. Irving's transit was too rapid to enable him to form any just appreciation of the people, the industry, or the institutions of the newly settled states. Passing these in silence, he commences his narrative at "Fort Gibson, a frontier post of the far West, situated on the Neosho, or Grand River, near its confluence with the Arkansas," and after a spirited recital, of the adventures which befel him in a tour of several weeks, through the hunting grounds of the Osages and the Pawnees, closes his tale at the same point.

From the hasty perusal we have been alone able to bestow upon this volume, we should say, that it contains more incident than is customary in the works of this writer, but bears all the features of ease, polish, and elegance, which render his style so exquisitely felicitous. We do not find, nor do we expect, those beautiful touches of quiet thought, and happy illusion, and chastened humor, which distinguish the other writings of our favorite; but in their stead, we have lively narrative, comprising a series of admirable pictures of border life, drawn with a rare fidelity, and finished with inimitable spirit. The writer rises in our estimation as we remark the versatility with which he adapts himself to scenes so foreign from all his former experience, throwing aside the indolence of the scholar, and the associations of the closet, and entering with all his heart into the spirit of the wild scenes, and bold companions, that were grouped around him. When we add that his style, and train of thought, are happily adapted to his subjects, and that among the variety of topics suggested by such a tour, he has judiciously selected those which are least hacknied, and most strikingly picturesque, we have expressed what have occurred to us as the peculiar excellencies of this agreeable volume. It is one of the best of the author's productions, and will be as acceptable to readers in the Atlantic states, on account of its originality and truth, as it will be popular on our side of the mountains, in consideration of the kind and partial tone in which the manners, employments, and diversions of the dwellers of the border are described. We have witnessed much that he has described, and are more familiar with many of the scenes that engaged his attention, than we are with the customs of the city, in which we now reside; and we are sure that we have read this book with a relish, that could be produced only by the fidelity and gracefulness of the author's recital. Nothing can be more natural, for instance, than his description of a bee hunt. . . .

This is by no means the most interesting passage in the book; but is a fair specimen both of the style and matter. Other scenes occurred, which, however, familiar to those who have roamed over the western prairies, were new to him; and these are described with the freshness of language, produced by a glowing first impression.

We hope that this will not be the last of the Crayon Miscellanies, but that the author will continue for many years to enrich the literature of a country of which he is one of the greatest and most cherished ornaments.

[Review of *The Crayon Miscellany*, No. 2—*Abbotsford and Newstead Abbey*]

Edgar Allan Poe°

We hailed with pleasure the appearance of the first number of the Crayon Miscellany, but we knew not what a feast was preparing for us in the second. In Abbotsford and Newstead Abbey, the author of the Sketch Book is at home. By no one could this offering to the memories of Scott and Byron have been more appropriately made. It is the tribute of genius to its kindred spirits, and it breathes a sanctifying influence over the graves of the departed. The kindly feelings of Irving are beautifully developed in his description of the innocent pursuits and cheerful conversation of Sir Walter Scott, while they give a melancholy interest to the early misfortunes of Byron. He luxuriates among the scenes and associations which hallow the walls of Newstead, and warms us into admiration of the wizard of the north, by a matchless description of the man, his habits, and his thoughts. The simplicity and innocence of his heart, his domestic affections, and his warm hospitality, are presented in their most attractive forms. The scenes and the beings with which Sir Walter was surrounded, are drawn with a graphic pencil. All conduce to strengthen impressions formerly made of the goodness and beneficence of Scott's character, and to gratify the thousands who have drawn delight from his works, with the conviction that their author was one of the most amiable of his species. No man knows better than Washington Irving, the value which is placed by the world (and with justice) upon incidents connected with really great men, which seem trifling in themselves, and which borrow importance only from the individuals to whom they have relation. Hence he has given us a familiar (yet how beautiful!) picture of Abbotsford and its presiding genius; but the relics of Newstead, which his pensive muse has collected and thrown together, brightening every fragment by the lustre of his own genius, are perhaps even more attractive. He touches but a few points in Byron's early history, but they are those on which we could have wished the illumination of his researches. The whole of the details respecting Miss Chaworth, and Byron's unfortunate attachment to that lady, are in his best manner. The story of the White Lady is one of deep interest, and suits well with the melancholy thoughts connected with Newstead. An instance of monomania like that of the White Lady, has seldom been recorded; and the author has, without over-coloring the picture, presented to his readers the history of a real being, whose whole character and actions and

° Reprinted from *Southern Literary Messenger* 1 (July 1835): 646.

melancholy fate belong to the regions of romance. In nothing that he has ever written, has his peculiar faculty of imparting to all he touches the coloring of his genius, been more fully displayed than in this work. . . .

[Review of *The Crayon Miscellany*, No. 3—*Legends of the Conquest of Spain*]

Edgar Allan Poe†

We feel it almost an act of supererogation to speak of this book, which is long since in the hands of every American who has leisure for reading at all. The matter itself is deeply interesting, but, as usual, its chief beauty is beauty of style. The Conquest of Spain by the Saracens, an event momentous in the extreme, is yet enveloped, as regards the motives and actions of the principal *dramatis personae* in triple doubt and confusion. To snatch from this uncertainty a few striking and picturesque legends possessing, at the same time, some absolute portion of verity, and to adorn them in his own magical language is all that Mr. Irving has done in the present instance. But that he has done this little well it is needless to say. He does not claim for the Legends the authenticity of history properly so called,— yet all are partially *facts*, and however extravagant some may appear, they will all, to use the words of the author himself, "be found in the works of sage and reverend chroniclers of yore, growing side by side with long acknowledged truths, and might be supported by learned and imposing references in the margin." Were we to instance any one of the narratives as more beautiful than the rest, it would be *The Story of the Marvellous and Portentous Tower.*

[Review of *Astoria*]

J. A. Roebuck‡

Of Mr. Irving's labors in this work the extracts we have given will enable the reader to judge. Out of materials not very favorable to his purpose he has succeeded in weaving a connected and exciting narrative. Great art has been employed, though none appears. The simplicity of style accords well with the whole history; and although

† Reprinted from *Southern Literary Messenger* 2 (December 1835): 64–65.
‡ Reprinted in part from *Westminster Review* (American edition) 26 (January 1837): 188.

a striking effect has been produced, no striving after it is at any time apparent. A more finished and exquisite narrative we have never read; the events recorded are in themselves of intense interest, and the scenes in which they occurred equal any the world contains for beauty and magnificence. Need we, after such an enumeration, state, that our critical labors have seldom brought us so much pleasure as that derived from the perusal of ASTORIA.

[Review of *Astoria*]
Anonymous†

He [Washington Irving] identifies himself so willingly with the heroes of his tale, and sympathizes with them so entirely, he depicts so vividly the scenes through which he makes them pass. . . .

The narrative of all these adventures should be perused in Mr. Irving's words, no pen is so fit as his to exhibit all its various phases. He sympathizes perfectly in the exultation, the hardihood, the sufferings and patient endurance of the hunter; he enters, with spontaneous glee, into all the odd traits and wild originality of the fresh characters he encounters, and he interests himself equally with gossiping inquisitiveness in the domestic relations of Pierre Dorion, or the marriage of Duncan McDougal with the clean princess, the daughter of the one-eyed Comcomly. . . .

[Review of *The Rocky Mountains (The Adventures of Captain Bonneville)*]
Anonymous‡

As a literary production, every one may make himself sure that these volumes possess the ease and grace of style which Mr. Irving could not, if he would, throw aside; that they at the same time appear to furnish a specimen of a very prevalent practice of late years, viz. of book-making, is not less manifest. There is a remarkable similarity in the "Adventures"; they consist, for the most part, of a mere repetition of dangers, escapes, privations, dexterous or courageous conduct, cunning, and cruelty, [*sic*] Some parts certainly possess a separate and novel interest; but the whole might, to better purpose, have been comprised in one third of the space of the publication as

† Reprinted from *American Quarterly Review* 21 (March 1837): 60–67.
‡ Reprinted from *Monthly Review*, New and Improved Ser. 2 (June 1837): 279–90.

it stands. The consequence has been, that the art of the author has frequently been put to its stretch, and that to produce effect, he has had to labour and force many points, so as to confer upon his work the appearance of affectation, and to communicate to it the aspect of feebleness. . . .

[Review of *The Rocky Mountains (The Adventures of Captain Bonneville)*]

Anonymous°

Johnson said of Goldsmith, when he was engaged in his history of Animated Nature, "he has the art of saying every thing he has to say in a pleasing manner—he is now writing a Natural History, and will make it as entertaining as a Persian tale." Irving, too, not less a master of English prose, touches nothing that he does not adorn,— *Nihil tetigit quod non ornavit.* In Astoria and the present work he has created his subject by the force of his happy fancy and humor. Through these scenes of the Far West the graces of his pen have literally made the solitary wilderness blossom like a garden, invested the harsh and rugged features of the desert with the air of sublimity, made its gloomy, discoloured rivers poetical, and tinged its barren mountain tops with the rich sunny hues of fancy. . . .

Irving has thrown a better light on the land for young and old. He has shown us that here, in these worn-out times of the world, there is a last foothold left for a remnant of chivalry in the wild life of the Far West. . . . Society travels westward, and has driven adventure to the shores of the Pacific. The free trapper of the great West yet lingers on these farthest outskirts of society, threading— as he is often painted to our eyes in these volumes—the dark defiles of the Rocky Mountains, venturing (so to speak) beyond the sight of land on the shoreless prairie, starving one day on roots, and feasting the next on the rare niceties of the Buffalo hunt, trapping by solitary streams "unsung by poets," or returning to the world full of braggart health to waste his gains in the profusion of the city. At times, too, the picture has a darker shade, when he struggles for life or death with the merciless Indian tribes of the desert. The present work abounds with these motley scenes, and more—it is a constantly shifting panorama of life in one of its most eccentric and varied forms.

We accompany the pleasant Captain through his adventures in this agreeable narrative with much of the feeling we would experience

° Reprinted from *New York Review* 1 (October 1837): 439–40.

in hearing the story from his own mouth. The book is written by the best English prose writer of the day, containing many passages of description that cannot be surpassed, yet still preserves the simplicity of a tale told by a plain, though observant and humorous narrator. Most fine writers would have obscured the subject and destroyed this great charm, but Irving is something better than a fine writer. Perhaps a fine writer would have passed this subject over as beneath him; but in this, too, Irving is something better than a fine writer. He is a man of genius, and genius shows its power in elevating a common subject to its own height. A man of mere fact might have drawn up a useful table of statistics on the Fur Trade, but would never have written this tour of Captain Bonneville. Whether in fact or fable, may Irving continue to send forth more such delightful volumes, and may we live on to read them.

[Review of *The Works of Washington Irving*, Two Volumes]

Anonymous°

A recent traveller in England tells us that a certain noble lady, speaking to him of American writers, condescendingly inquired whether one Irving Washington, or George Washington, or somebody of a name of some sort, had not written a book? What reply was made to the kind inquiry, we are not informed; but we presume the traveller had good-nature enough to surprise her ignorance with the knowledge that a writer named Washington Irving actually existed, and that he was likely to exist some considerable time after she and her companions had been laid in their graves and forgotten.

In spite of the contrary evidence of this noble lady, we believe that Mr. Irving has no reason, like the petulent quack he once found in Westminster Abbey, to rail about the neglect of the world, or complain that merit is suffered to languish in obscurity. If ever there was a writer who may be said to be popular—whose reputation, not confined to one nation, flourishes greatly in two hemispheres—who has made friends of every class of the people, who is read with as much pleasure by childhood as by age, who has attained the rare felicity of filling the hearts of all his admirers with a feeling of personal interest, who has interwoven his own name with the traditionary history or customs of three different and distinct countries,

° Reprinted from *United States Magazine and Democratic Review* 9 (December 1841): 593–97.

and whose fame has suffered no diminution, from the time he first broke upon the literary world till he has virtually withdrawn from it, that writer is Washington Irving. Spain, England, and America have been equally illustrated by his genius; and, but for the accident of birth, it would be difficult to say in which of them he had found the more enthusiastic friends.

"When I first began to write," says our author, in the introduction to Bracebridge Hall, with a modesty not less than his merit,

> it had been a matter of marvel that a man from the wilds of America should express himself in tolerable English. I was looked upon as something new in literature; a kind of demi-savage, with a feather in his head; and there was a curiosity to hear what such a being had to say about civilized society. This novelty is now at end, and of course the feeling of indulgence which it produced. I must now expect to bear the scrutiny of sterner criticism, and to be measured by the same standard with contemporary writers; and the very favor that has been shown my previous writings will cause them to be treated with the greater rigor; as there is nothing for which the world is apt to punish a man more severely than for having been overpraised.

Mr. Irving has now lived long enough to have learned that his anticipations were unwarranted, and that they reflected more credit upon his diffidence than upon his sagacity. He has stood the test of that severer scrutiny which he dreaded; the illusions of curiosity that attended his advent have passed away; the world has seen that he is neither a prodigious wild-man of the woods, nor a cultivated savage; and his works have been most warmly welcomed where education and taste have most enabled his readers to appreciate their excellences. . . .

Mr. Irving, more, perhaps, than any other, has contributed to the happy revolution which has been effected in the spirit of foreign criticism. His eminence, in all the characteristics of manner and thought, is so apparent, that it would have argued downright stupidity in any critic to bring it into question; and, his superiority once admitted, it was natural that literary research should extend its inquiries over the same soil which had produced and nourished so beautiful a plant. Accordingly it was found that he was not alone in the attainment of all the graces of composition; and that many other minds, kindred to his own, already existed among the people whose history, customs, and scenery had inspired his fancy and moved his heart.

We have said that Mr. Irving's eminence was too obvious to be overlooked: no one who diligently studies his writings, and compares them with the best models left us by the lapse of centuries, will fail to perceive the full force of this remark. He combines more of the qualities of a good manner than any author that our reading just now enables us to recall. Not only has he the negative merit of being free from ordinary faults, but he has the much higher merit of many positive excellences. There are four or five points, which strike every intelligent reader, even upon casually opening any one of his volumes. These are, simplicity, picturesqueness, grace, humor, pathos, and refinement, as well as naturalness of sentiment. His simplicity, however, is not that of unadorned art, for he is not without ornament, but that which springs from clear conceptions, an absence of parade, and the intense love of chastity and ease. What he sees he depicts with a heart full of genial sympathy: He catches at once the striking or touching features, which he presents with the fidelity of a draughts-man, but, at the same time, with the feeling of a poet. Like a gentle stream, his thoughts flow on, in liquid melody and crystal brightness, along banks enamelled with flowers, and through rich pasturages of living verdure. No impurities mingle with the current, no shadows darken its surface, no rough breezes break its limpid waters into turbulence and wildness. The sunny skies, the old graceful trees, the forms of human and created beings, are reflected from its bosom; it invites the musing to delightful revery, and teaches the reflective a lesson of harmony and peace. But let it not be imagined that this stream is perpetually running along one unvarying channel, and through an imprisoned course. Nothing pleases us more in this writer, than his vast variety of topic and illustration. As he has said of Roscoe, he has shut himself up in no garden of thought, in no exclusive Elysium of fancy. He has gone forth in the highway and thoroughfare of life; he has planted bowers by the wayside, for the refreshment of the pilgrim and the sojourner, and has opened pure fountains where the laboring man may turn aside from the dust and heat of the day, and drink of the living springs of knowledge. For the many, he furnishes veins of racy and sparkling wit; for the tender, passages of soft and subduing beauty; the lover of external nature will find in him close and graceful description of her forms and appearances; and the lover of his kind, be delighted with faithful portraits of character, or skilful narratives of human incidents; in short, whether grave or gay, whether learned or simple, we shall find somewhere in his pages that which will enchant, move, or instruct. What writer has ever lived, who has greater power in transporting his reader from one land to another, or from one age to another? The mock-heroic pranks of the smoking and fighting Dutch, the humors and whims of modern politicians and quidnuncs, the sports, festivals, and manners of English country life, the chivalric enthusiasm of Spanish knights, the solitary delights of the student, the wild life of a western prairie, the stolid fortitude of the Indian, the pangs of wounded affection, the frolic of villagers, and the silent agonies of a broken heart, are the themes in which he is equally at home, always pertinent, elegant, and effective.

Compared with preceding writers, Irving more resembles Addison and Goldsmith than any others, and the latter more than the former. He has not Goldsmith's power of versification, nor has he excelled, like him, in the drama; but there is in both the same clearness, the same unaffected ease, the same polished simplicity, the same beauteous refinement and elegance. If Irving has any fault, it is that he sometimes suffers his love of the graceful to lead him into feebleness, and that nervous strength and directness are now and then sacrificed to an effeminate harmony. Yet the instances of even this fault are few, and not many writers have written so voluminously and at the same time so correctly. Indeed, we may say of him, what is said in the "Mutability of Literature" of the true poet: "He gives the choicest thoughts in the choicest language; he illustrates them by every thing he sees striking in nature and art; he enriches them with pictures of life, such as it is passing before him. His writings, therefore, contain the spirit, the aroma, if I may use the phrase, of the age in which he lives. They are caskets which enclose the wealth of language— its family jewels, which are thus transmitted in a portable form to posterity." Is it unreasonable to hope that he to whom we owe so much, will now, in the ripened maturity of his age, increase the debt of our gratitude, by some production filled with a higher philosophy and more earnest tone than any to which he has yet attained?

Washington Irving as a Writer   Anonymous°

The name of Washington Irving will be for ever associated with American literature. He has attained the very highest eminence as a writer. Both in England and the United States his works have been universally read with pleasure. Perhaps they have been more generally admired, than the production of any living author on this side of the Atlantic. They are not confined to any class of readers. To nearly every mental condition, they have proved equally acceptable. Though dealing somewhat in fiction, it is evident that he employs it only as the garb in which he arrays real characters. He gives us lively sketches of human nature, concealing only dates, names, and places. But all these he doubtless has, with more or less distinctness, in his own view while writing. It is for this reason, principally, that the most

° Reprinted from *Ladies' Repository* 8 (July 1848): 217–20.

serious minds have ever been in the habit of perusing even his more playful compositions.

Mr. Irving is not a novelist, as he is regarded by those not personally acquainted with his writings. He has not written a single novel. In this direction, he is merely a writer of stories, the facts for which are taken either from history, or from occurrences within the range of his own experience and observation. His first works were more nearly allied to fiction than his later ones. As his mind became more mature, and his moral feelings more settled, he turned his attention more exclusively to topics of serious import; and his success in sober composition is, after all, his best pledge of immortality.

Washington Irving is one of our very best historians. His Life of Christopher Columbus is equal to any thing of its kind ever written. It was never surpassed by the ablest writers of the classic ages. The celebrated Lives of Plutarch are worthy of no comparison, in my humble judgment, with this luminous biography. The Agricola of Tacitus, perhaps the most finished specimen of the species of composition, which we have received from antiquity, is, in many respects, meagre by the side of it. Large as is the work of Irving, few persons have ever taken it up, and laid it by again, for want of interest in its style and subject. No tasteful reader can lay it down, if he has leisure, without reading every page of it. So admirable is the tact, and so charming the style of the biographer, that, though at about midway of the work you perceive every thing that is coming, you read on with unabated pleasure. It is the only work I have ever seen, in which the notes, even to the last one of them, are equally captivating with the text they illustrate. In every respect, the Life of Columbus is a classical production, and, unless accidentally destroyed, will last as long as the English language.

Had Mr. Irving turned his attention more to historical subjects, he might have made himself a fame perhaps superior to that of Hume and Gibbon. Though not now so learned as the latter, nor so profound as the former, of these historians, in what he has attempted he has manifested equal capacity in every variety of talent. His Conquest of Granada, though evidently the work of his idle hours, and not more than a romantic history at best, exhibits fully enough his diligence in searching records and authorities, and his wonderful powers of historical description. His battle scenes are even more vivid than those of Julius Caesar. Let him have studied as laboriously as the author of the Decline and Fall of the Roman Empire, and he would probably have excelled him in any great work which he might have undertaken. His discrimination was not surpassed by that of the great infidel. His knowledge of human nature is decidedly more perfect. The simplicity of his diction forms a striking contrast to the grandiloquence of Gibbon. But more than all, his heart fits him, in every way, to excel that author in every species of composition. There is something peculiarly impressive in the moral character of Irving. No one need inquire what it is. It is found on almost every one of his pages. The great law of his being is human kindness. His large benevolence is ever conspicuous. He must be one of the most amiable men living. His very satire is merciful. He only shows you what he could do, were he not so unboundedly benevolent. He draws his bow upon you, and you acknowledge him a skillful archer; but when the arrow hits you, you find he was only playing. The point and the barb are nothing but a feather. But the mercy of the satire makes you feel the more humble. If you are really guilty, you have the uncomfortable consciousness of owing your life to his clemency.

Mr. Irving is said to be a very quiet, contemplative man. He spends much of his time in reading and meditation. It is also reported of him, that he makes long rambles through town and country, or did make them in his younger days, for the only purpose of observing men and things, and repeating his thoughts by himself and at his leisure. This love of solitude has given him a fine vein of sentiment. His humanity is one of the most apparent of his mental qualities; and it is derived from the same practice of reflection. Had he been exclusively a historian, he never could have passed over, as others do, the bloody horrors of a battle-field, by simply giving us a description of the carnage. As the finishing stroke to every such bloody picture, he would have made you feel most sensibly "Man's inhumanity to man." He would have forced conviction to the most obdurate mind, that war is the foulest work of mortals.

In his Life of Columbus he shows himself everywhere the poor Indians' friend. When they are mercilessly butchered by the Spaniard, with what pathos he pleads their cause! When the reparminientos, or slavery system, was about to be adopted, and the defenseless native turned loose to the goading ambition of wicked men, with what sincerity and spirit he rebukes the oppressors, though the heroes of his work! But his humanity is equally evident in smaller things. What reader of his can have forgotten the sensibility he manifested in the famous prairie hunting scene? His company had been all day pursuing buffaloes on one of the immense prairies of the west. The real sportsmen had killed several in different parts of the field, while he had been riding more to witness the sport of others, than to derive any for himself. But in the latter part of the day, when, probably, his sensibilities had become rather blunted by fatigue, he resolved to join in earnest in the chase. He singled him out an object worthy of his aim. It was a prime, large buffalo, and of the most perfect form. He put spurs to his horse, and soon came within shooting distance of his game. The fatal ball was fired, and lo! the noble animal, in all his pride and glory, fell a dying victim at his feet. Does the sportsman now swell, and bluster, and call his companions to help him enjoy the glory of his deed? Nay; but, standing there alone, he looks on him—he pities him; and from his own account we might believe that he suffers more pain, than the bleeding animal by his side. When he had seen him breathe his last, he would have given the whole prairies, had it been his property, could he have revived the fallen monarch, and sent him bounding in joyous life and liberty over his native plains.

They mistake the character of Mr. Irving as a writer, who suppose him writing merely for the amusement of his readers. This is not true of him even in his lighter articles. His most comical pieces have always a serious end in view. In these you will find him holding up to ridicule some hurtful or good-for-nothing prejudice in the public mind; he is weeding out the noxious plants, which have been growing for centuries in the human heart. And he has certainly been very successful in this business. But he stops not there. He also sows good seed to supply the place of what he has rooted out; and I must believe that he sometimes, perhaps I should say frequently, feels a warm delight, in the consciousness of having done much to implant the principles of morality and virtue in a soil not so likely to be cultivated by other hands. Where the mere philosopher would not be welcome, where the moralist, or even the devout Christian, would scarcely find entrance, his fascinating style gives him joyful admittance; and he rarely departs without leaving a good influence behind him.

There are two peculiar effects of Mr. Irving's writings, which ought to be particularly stated. The first is the pure philanthropy he breathes into your feelings. His benevolence is really contagious. Wherever you read him, he perfectly imbues you with it. Sit down and read his productions a single hour, especially his pathetic pieces, and you will not only rise up a better man, but think better of your fellow creatures. You will compassionate the weak, sympathize with the oppressed, and pity the sorrows of the poor. The other trait in his works is not less happy in its effects. It is the good tone he imparts to the domestic affections. Whenever he treats upon these subjects, he touches, with almost a magic power, the family ties. Need I name those inimitable pieces in the Sketch Book, the Wife, and the Widow's Son? For the last fifteen years I have never been able to read either of them, without shedding such tears as do one good. It is hardly possible for any person to peruse him frequently, without being a more affectionate member of the domestic circle. Whether a father, or mother, or brother, or sister, the reader acquires a stronger, a purer, a holier attachment to family friends. In this particular, Mr. Irving has spread the sweet influences of his good heart over all the families of the land.

The generosity of Mr. Irving is quite equal to his benevolence. Daily instances of this virtue are seen in his private associations; but there are many, also, related of him in his more public capacity. For a long time he had been intending to write a work on a topic connected with American history. He had spent time and labor, and, doubtless, money, in collecting books, manuscripts, and other sources of information. Subsequently, learning that another gentleman—an unfortunate but gifted American author—had chosen the same subject, Mr. Irving not only relinquished his designs entirely to his competitor, but actually sent him all the books and authorities he himself had collected as a free-will offering of a good and noble heart to one who needed and deserved the kindness.

So far as mere style is concerned, though comparatively a minor consideration, Mr. Irving undeniably occupies the very highest place. It has ever been a dispute among critics, whether he is not the best model of a writer now living. Some have placed him high above every writer in the English language. But it is difficult to compare him, in this respect, with most of his competitors. His diction is peculiar to himself, but only, perhaps, because other persons do not generally write quite so well. There is certainly nothing eccentric or affected in his compositions. He writes naturally, easily, smoothly along, as if it were no effort at all for him to compose. He is not so pompous as Gibbon, and writes less as if it were a trade. Burke is more pithy and sententious, but infinitely less beautiful and flowing. Burke sometimes fatigues his reader by gaudy and superfluous imagery. The sentences of Robert Hall are equally smooth and well turned; they are even more elevated and grand; but also more difficult, or rather less easy, to read. Mr. Hall's sentences are in general very lengthy, and slightly elaborate and complex, but never tangled or obscure. Mr. Irving writes with an easy, though not a readier, pen; and in his longest periods, you flow insensibly and without labor along the current of his thoughts, till he gives you liberty to pause.

Perhaps the best analogy lies between him and Mr. Addison as to style. They resemble each other more than any two writers in our language. Indeed, the question of superiority is, by many, reduced, in the final issue, to these two. It would be difficult for any person to decide which author, taken in all respects, he would prefer. So far as fancy, imagination, good taste, and graphic power are concerned, it would require a nice balance to determine which has the greater merit. There is one quality of a good writer, however, in which Mr. Irving, I think, clearly surpasses his great rival—a profound and critical knowledge of the etymology and definition of words. Mr. Addison has been accused, though I think unjustly, of writing as if he were doubtful precisely what word to employ. This is never so much as suspected in Mr. Irving. He always has the very word, generally the only word, capable of giving full expression to his thoughts, and yet glides along apparently without effort. There is another defect which critics have discovered in Mr. Addison's best works. He is said to have frequently added high-sounding but feeble expletives to his sentences, after the sense had been made complete, merely to give his period a round full close. If this be true, Mr. Irving is decidedly his superior, for I will venture to affirm that no such sentence can be found in the whole compass of his productions. Perhaps this may seem a bold expression of opinion; but I will offer no other amendment to it, than that I have, at different times, sought whole hours for an instance without success.

Thus far I have compared Mr. Irving as a writer only with those of the English school. It would be hazardous to attempt to find a man, on this side of the Atlantic, whose best friends would not readily acknowledge his inferior in the use of a beautiful and graphic pen. Dr. Channing surpassed him in the power of multiplying himself, if I may say so, in his readers; but it was evidently not so natural and easy for that distinguished author to compose. Daniel Webster has no superior in the purity, strength, and transparency of his style; his thoughts are sometimes perfect thunderbolts, and scathe and blast every thing opposed to them, by the mere majesty of their power; but as a writer, the great defender of the Constitution must yield the palm to him, whose amiable humility has perhaps never cast a wish, or carried a reverie, to the height occupied by the statesman. What elevation Mr. Prescott would have reached, had Providence spared the continued use of his sight, no one can tell; but the Conquest of Mexico, notwithstanding it was composed by a man, who could not see well enough to correct his own proof, is, after all, the only American work worthy of contending with the Life of Columbus for the prize.

One of the chief sources of Mr. Irving's superiority is his perfect self-possession while he is writing. Unpracticed writers, and even men who have written much without having improved by their experience, frequently, perhaps I should say generally, manifest an uneasiness of spirit, as if they were not satisfied unless they were doing wonders all the while. They come to their task in a perfect frenzy. They continue to work themselves up to a most unnatural and disgusting excitement, and then pounce upon their paper, as if they would snatch it, like an eagle, to the clouds. They leap through their sentences, like the live thunder, from crag to crag. They gleam, and hiss, and roar, as if an Alpine tempest were about to break over your head. If they happen to think of any Greek or Latin author, while they are suffering under this chaos of passion, they will crowd a dozen classical allusions into a single paragraph, and quote twenty verses of Pagan poetry to a page. Fearful lest they have not done

much in what they have already written, in order to redeem themselves in what remains, they dash, and foam, and thunder, more
extravagantly as they proceed. Like ungifted speakers, from the beginning to the end of their performance, they never get fair possession
of themselves; and, when all is over, they have only added another
specimen to that already too numerous class of productions, whose
single quality is their sound.

How differently from all this does Mr. Irving undertake his work!
Without any effort, he writes his leading sentence. From this he
proceeds naturally and smoothly along, as if it were the easiest thing
in the world to write. As his subject grows in his own mind, he gives
fuller and bolder expression to his thoughts. He seems to be in no
hurry to strike his reader with any thing wonderful or new. He allows
his theme to go on and make the development of itself. If it happen
to touch on classical ground, it finds the writer perfectly at home.
Without stopping to deluge you with quotations, he gives you one—
but that one is a gem. If, in the progress of his work, an emotion is
excited by any thing which his subject makes it necessary to say, he
gives it a single stroke of his gifted pen, and it thrills to your very
soul. He never quotes for the sake of quoting, nor to show off the
extent and variety of his reading. Nor does he attempt to cover you
up with roses; if a few flowers chance to be growing near his path,
he weaves you a modest chaplet—but that blooms on your heart for
ever. Nor is he incessantly making pictures, and pressing every ancient
and modern dialect into service, in order to decorate them with all
the gorgeousness of language. Dealing considerably in description, a
variety of scenes must necessarily be crowded upon him on every
page of his composition. But of these he is far from being prodigal.
Instead of drawing out every one that occurs to him, he makes a
choice selection. When one is chosen, wrought out, and finished, it
throws its lustre all around him. His reader marks it with his pencil,
or transfers it to his own imagination, to which it adds a splendor
ever after.

But, on the other hand, Mr. Irving is not a timid, bashful, fastidious
writer. He wears no straight-jacket on his intellectual faculties. With
all his severity of taste, he is always free and easy. You see in him
none of that finical nervousness, which trammels a writer's genius,
and forbids his saying just what he thinks, and precisely as he thinks
it. This is the natural consequence of his modesty. An ambitious
writer, all the while goaded by the impulse of his ruling passion, is
apt to be too careful—perhaps I should have said anxious—of the
mere manner of his writing. As each sentence is written down, he
looks back upon it to criticize its structure, when he ought to be
pushing onward under the full and unchecked inspiration of his
subject. Ambition, at least in a writer, is always weak and timid. The

man loses his thoughts while he is looking after his periods. He ought to be himself lost, or nearly so, in the matter of which he is treating. His taste should be the only restraint upon him; and that should be reduced to such a habit, as to leave him quite unconscious of its influence. If, writing in this natural way, errors creep into his composition, they may be left for a future and critical recension.

There is a sort of sentimentalism, also, to which Mr. Irving is never subject. This consists, I suppose, in a writer's putting on more feeling than his ideas demand. To feel less than the truths advanced would justify, argues obduracy of mind; to feel more, whether in writing or in speaking, fanaticism, the concomitants of which are generally rant and bombast. When thought and feeling are exactly commensurate, when the one precisely tallies with the other, then you have words spoken fitly; and they are indeed "like apples of gold in pictures of silver." You rise from the perusal of a work thus written, neither hardened by contemplating great truths without emotion, nor softened to effeminacy by a continual conflict of boisterous and unmeaning passion. Sound thoughts have been passing down upon your soul, and they have left their own impression. You are a sounder, wiser, better, truer man yourself, by the influence of what you have been reading.

If the present age has produced the exact counterpart of our author, it is in the example of Mr. Dickens. In all this gentleman's productions, there is a constant tendency to over-drawing. His thoughts and feelings seem to be in a perpetual state of insurrection. Like a rake on the high road, he uses the lash too much; and his animal is in a continual perspiration. If his course happen to lie on a clean path, all goes merrily and smoothly onward; but whenever he falls into a rough passage, the dirt flies all around you. You are knocked, and thumped, and jerked, in this direction and in that, without the slightest mercy; and when the race is over, you need all the water he complained the want of in our taverns, not only to cleanse your person, but to cool your fever.

Such writers, to change the figure, seem to be somewhat suspicious of the bill of fare provided by them; and they are only shaking up their readers a little to favor their digestion. But it would be unjust to deny, that Mr. Dickens has written many pages which will forever form a part of the standard literature of our language; and, what is very much for any man's reputation as a writer, he has received the approbation—at least the qualified approbation—of Dr. Channing. But his style is generally too headlong to be commended.

In all respects Mr. Irving seems to stand first in this country as a writer. He has the singular merit of pleasing all classes equally. Those not prepared to admire the skill manifested in the select order of his language, and in the molding and turning of his periods, read him for the amusement gathered from the story. The fine flow of his sentences, his frequent and beautiful alliteration, the rich simplicity of his pictures, and the delightful splendor and genuineness of his emotions, charm other persons less captivated by his subjects. It seems to me that he surpasses all writers in one quality. His style evinces more real science, with less apparent labor, than that of any modern or ancient author.

Having given much merited praise, I will state almost my only objection to Mr. Irving. In nearly all that he has done, he has shown merely what he could do, had his subjects been better chosen. His Sketch Book and his Columbus are almost the only exceptions to this remark. In nearly all his other works, beautiful, charming, captivating as they are, a serious man feels all the while that he might have selected topics more worthy of his genius. It is true, there is next to nothing in all his writings to find fault with; his style is ever like its fountain, pure and splendid; he nowhere descends to vulgarity, even for a moment; and his morality is such as would become a minister at the altar. But, then, when we read such a man, the soul longs to see him soaring higher. We want to see him ranging in majesty through those fields, where such a spirit might meet with angels. We become almost anxious to witness the power of such a style as his on those sublime topics, which, in all ages, have formed the themes of those gifted minds, who have ever stood nearest to the bright purlieus of heaven. O, could the heart of Mr. Irving be touched by that live coal, which sanctified and hallowed the lips of the evangelical Isaiah, in what sweet and captivating splendor would Christianity appear on his classical and immortal pages!

But Mr. Irving is now advanced in years. The gray of age is sprinkled on the crown of his glory. He must soon descend from his lofty summit, and be buried in the dust with his fathers. Such a mind as his, so characterized by sense, so ripe in reflection, so just in perceptions on all other topics, has, undoubtedly, long since settled life's great question. When he goes, he will go with the blessings of his country upon him. Though his body may perish, and lie low in the sepulchre raised by his friends, his fame will survive; his sweet spirit, we trust, will ascend to its Author; and the sorrow of a nation, or rather of an age, will mingle its laments with the wail of the winds that sweep over his grave.

[Review of *The Life of Oliver Goldsmith*]

Anonymous°

We made a brief allusion last month to the Life of Goldsmith by Geoffrey Crayon, and gave an extract from the work, it being then in sheets. The book has since been published and has, no doubt, been extensively read ere this: for, although nothing now could be anticipated in relation to Goldsmith's history, yet every lover of the poet's works, and every admirer of his new biographer, would be naturally anxious to hear how so genial a subject had been treated by our great prose writer. Those who have read the ponderous and particularizing history by Prior, and the more recent and more ambitious biography by Forster, have nothing to learn of the trials, temptations, successes, follies, failures, and virtues of the author of the Vicar of Wakefield. But every one must have felt that a true portrait was yet wanting, that the features of the subject, if truthfully delineated, did not give a just impression of the original, from a lack of an artistic arrangement of the back ground, and a proper disposition of lights and shadows. The whole truth was there, but so displayed as to convey an untruthful impression. No great artist has before attempted the portraiture of Goldsmith's character. But the work has at last been performed in a manner which leaves nothing more to be done, or desired. Improvement on the picture which our own great literary limner has painted of the English humorist is beyond the reach of any hand that will be likely to make such an attempt.

As to the style of this new work by Irving it is interesting to compare it with his earlier productions, and mark the changes in his manner which have gradually been effected by the loss of the world in which he lives, and yet to mark how nearly it is like his best productions. It is worthy of remark, too, that while it abounds in those genial beams of a tolerant nature that invest with a charm the deformities which it exposes, which have distinguished all the writings of this popular author, the biography contains more renchant [sic] strokes of satire, and more indignant enthusiasm against vice and snobbishness, than any of the productions of his more youthful, if not more vigorous period. It is truly delightful to see how he deals a blow to that poor driveller Boswell whenever the literary caitiff comes in his way, and with what a relish he takes by the leg such cormorant publishers as the Newberys and Griffiths of the last century, while the whole race of literary pretenders and parasites must shake in their shoes at the cuffs given to their representatives of the last age.

° Reprinted from *Holden's Dollar Magazine* 4 (October 1849): 633.

Of all the works that Geoffrey Crayon has yet produced this is the one for which literary men have the most reason to be grateful. It is a vindication of the literary character from the attacks of sophists and worldlings, and we can not but think that the author, while writing it, must have had some other aim than merely depicting a faithful and dignified portraiture of an author whose productions have delighted and instructed the world, while he himself has been laughed at as a simpleton, or at best compassionated for his innocence. All that is essential to be known in relation to the life of Goldsmith has been candidly given, while the absurd tales which have found currency respecting him have been very properly suppressed for lack of authentic evidence of their truth. Although the author confesses that the biography is but an amplification of a sketch published many years since, and now completed, or enlarged, to make a volume suitable to accompany the elegant republication of his entire works now in hand by Mr. Putnam, yet there is sufficient evidence in its pages that it was a labor of pure love and too congenial to the "Warm heart and fine brain" of the writer, to owe its existence solely to the suggestion of a publisher. While expressing our admiration of the biography, we cannot but confess our surprise that Mr. Irving should fall into the popular error of making Horace Walpole the scape goat for all sins of his contemporaries towards the "whelp" Chatterton. We can see neither reason nor excuse for being indignant towards Walpole for his neglect of the "wondrous boy," while not a word of reproach is let fall upon the heads of Gray, Mason, Johnson, and the other poets who knew all his circumstances yet never lifted a finger in his aid; certainly no one ever manifested greater interest in the unfortunate youth, or expressed more sincere regret at his death, than Walpole.

[Review of *Mahomet and His Successors*, Volume 1]   Anonymous*

It was not expected that Geoffrey Crayon would, in his projected Life of Mahomet, enter the lists with the learned oriental commentators, or pursue his subject with the theological zeal of a biblical antiquarian; nor were we to expect from him that show of originality— more of the show than the substance—by which the one-idea'd vigor of the Carlyle school fixes the attention of the public. It was not Mahomet the prophet, or the hero, or the conqueror in either capacity,

* Reprinted from *The Literary World* 5 (22, 29 December 1849): 537–38, 560–61.

probably, who filled the author's mind, but the splendid aggregate of all these qualities—the wonderful historic field on which they were displayed, the fount of Arabic power and grandeur, which must ever excite the imagination. His Spanish studies, the pictures of the Alhambra and Granada, in which Irving seems to us always "lapped in Elysium," led him upwards, he intimates to us in his preface, to the sources of the Moslem dominion—which it is to be presumed he sought, not to determine questions of learned controversy or to plunge himself in the metaphysics of character, but to feed his taste for the picturesque in the survey of that shadowy Orientalism, the mixed history and legend, the fact and fable, the truth and error which are inextricably confounded in Islam.

In this congenial pursuit the author has followed, as he tells us, chiefly Spanish sources, a translation of the Arabian historian Abulfeda, while he has been guided by the later learned researches of Dr. Gustav Weil, "the very intelligent and learned librarian of the University of Heidelberg." The book was originally prepared for John Murray's Family Library, and the author says modestly enough of it:—"It still bears the type of a work intended for a Family Library; in constructing which the whole aim of the author has been to digest into an easy, perspicuous, and flowing narrative, the admitted facts concerning Mahomet, together with such legends and traditions as have been wrought into the whole system of oriental literature; and at the same time to give such a summary of his faith as might be sufficient for the more general reader." . . .

Premising that Irving treats the subject in the picturesque associations rather than its severe moral aspects, we shall not detain the reader longer from his work, but for the present and another paper, accompany him in his narrative along the career of the Prophet. It is Mahomet as he appeared to his times, as well as Mahomet *per se*, who is presented. Irving, though he distinguishes the two views from one another, yet allows a genial indulgence to the wonder-workers and legend-makers of the East. These were the translations of the man to the people, such as European Christianity of later ages, too, it should be remembered, has not disdained to employ. . . .

We hardly know how to characterize Irving's description of these extraordinary scenes. As a chapter of history it falls below the dignity and weight of the subject. It is painted in water colors, while it should be cast in bronze. At times even a humorous cast is given to the story as if the whole were a mere Arabian tale of pleasing character and wonderment. But that Washington Irving should have made it interesting as a Fairy Tale, as Johnson remarked of Goldsmith, is a fault of his genius only, and, our readers will agree, a pardonable one. Still the topic was grave and weighty, and it needed a certain severity of treatment—more of the tragic element. But we are not disposed to press this as a defect upon which a work has given us much pleasure in the perusal, and which in its simple transparent style is the vehicle of so much information gracefully and truthfully conveyed. The general estimate of Mahomet appears to us a just one, distinguished by the good sense which marks all the writings of Irving. It is far removed from the vulgar portraits of the man. It rests upon a liberal view of human nature—a genial observation which, as with its Mahometan recording angels, has ten entries of a virtue to one of a vice.

Washington Irving: His Works, Genius, and Character

Horace Binney Wallace°

In nature, in personal character, and in every department of art, there is a quality of excellence which, even in the degree of its perfection, disappoints the efforts of description, and eludes the analysis of the critic, because it consists, not in the magnitude, energy, or splendor of the separate elements, but in the exquisiteness of the proportion, the harmony of the combination, the fineness of the pervading tone, the gentle animation with which it flatters each sympathy into delighted calmness, and wakes no uncomfortable earnestness of reaction. It absorbs and holds all our sensibilities, yet seems to be below, rather than above, the measure of power, with which our minds are familiar, and to fall within the range of our own ambition, desire, or conception. More admiration would disturb the repose of our satisfaction; a more vigorous address to our intellectual apprehension would change the nature of the enjoyment. The ordinary degrees of this character we call the agreeable; the more poignant exhibitions of it we qualify as charming.

To this class or order belong especially the writings of Mr. Irving. Their effect is uniformly pleasant:—we read with perpetual interest, and with the certainty of delight. Yet are we scarcely inclined to commend anything else than the general and composite impression resultant from the whole. We are impressed with no very vivid respect for the author's mental powers or accomplishments, and carry away no decided impressions of vigorous or dexterous or felicitous effort.

° Reprinted from *Literary Criticisms and Other Papers* (Philadelphia: Parry & McMillan, 1856), 67–91. Originally appeared in *Sartain's Union Magazine* 7 (November 1850): 288–98.

We are a little annoyed at being called upon for the reasons of our exclamations of pleasure. If asked our opinion of him, in the absence of his works, our impulse would perhaps be to speak somewhat depreciatingly. Yet while we read we were fascinated; and the enchantment shall assuredly renew itself so often as we come within the action of the strains that "lap us in Elysium." They are productions which communicate pleasure, rather than excite enthusiasm, and are more enjoyed than eulogized. The mystery of the performer seems to consist, not in creating an extraordinary work, but in pre-disposing us, by some magic touch, to be ravished with that which is not greatly remote from common and moderate. The perusal of Mr. Irving's writings is like walking in some familiar lawn, or ordinary scene of nature, on a fine, soft morning in the early spring. . . .

The acceptableness of Mr. Irving's works—the peculiar attraction which they have for every class of readers—illustrates an important truth in criticism, too much overlooked by writers, that in literature, more depends on manner than on style; and manner is an affair of the character more than of the intellect. Power, however great, if it be turbulent and unchastised, stimulates the passions while it impresses the mind; its moral influence excites more appetency than its mental action satisfies; and it leaves the reader disappointed and discontented in the very measure in which he has been moved. On the other hand, there is a tone of decency, decorum, refined reserve, and intentional restraint in composition, which induces in the reader an answering concentration and restriction in feeling, by which he is in a situation to enjoy quiet and moderate interests with a delight at once earnest and calm. Something akin to this is felt in the company of high-bred people. The temper of moderated animation, the controlled and self-guarding attention, the avoidance of strong efforts, and the care with which each one seems to play below his full power, the subdued key to which everything is pitched, tends to create in each person a certain strenuous repose of the feelings which causes commonplace things in such a sphere to inspire pleasure and respect. That state in which sensibility is excited, and then voluntarily checked and drawn back upon itself, is the one of greatest impressibility to what is beautiful and intellectual. How remarkable and how delightful is the moral charm diffused by the mere personal deportment of a refined and thorough-bred gentleman! Very much like that is the spell of retiring dignity and elegant reserve which fascinates in Mr. Irving's writings. And when this sort of manner is found in conjunction with essential genius and genuine finished art, as in his case it undoubtedly is, the delight becomes as irresistible as it is undefinable.

Mr. Irving possesses but little invention. The attractiveness of his tales does not depend upon their material, upon their construction, upon the novelty, variety, or impressiveness of their incidents, upon an anxious crisis or a brilliant denouement, but upon the illustrative talent of the narrator, upon the innumerable occasional decorations that delight us into a forgetfulness of the purpose or want of purpose of the whole, and the pleasant sketches of costume, scenery, and manners which are hung along the conduct of the piece in such profusion, that it resembles at length a brilliant gallery of pictures, built for the display of its own treasures, and not to lead to some definite end. His conception of beauty is not rich or exquisite. In sentiment he is commonplace, dilute, and superficial. Of earnest, deep feeling, he can scarcely be said to have anything at all. Intellectual force or moral sensibility contribute little to his works. But let us not, therefore, suppose that those works are commonplace productions, or the author of them an ordinary person. Let us not imagine that because we cannot detect the seat of a power, or define its nature, components, or origin,—nay, because we can touch this point, and say it is not here, or knock upon that surface, and find for a response, that it issues not thence,—that any doubt is thrown upon the greatness, genuineness, or elevation of that power. In literature, and especially in that fine region in which the genius of Mr. Irving moves, the more subtle and elusive the interest is, the more exalted and consummate is the art; the more evanescent the charm, the more potent is it, the more certain, and the more enduring. In such a department of pure art, to accomplish the greatest result with the least visible display of exertion, is the highest triumph. To impress, and conceal the source of the impression, is mastery in its utmost. When once we are assured that a work is certainly impressive, the difficulty of detecting the reason of that impressiveness enhances the glory of the production. We may talk of the slightness of Mr. Irving's composition; it is easy to make compositions as slight, but not easy to make slightness so effective.

Beauty is a thing of form and place; it may be detected, and analyzed, and reproduced. But infinitely higher and grander in its range, degree, and order, than beauty, is grace; and that is an unsubstantial and unlocal essence. Beauty resides, definitely, in the work in which it is recognized; grace is an electric light evolved by the action of successive parts of the subject upon the mind. It is experimental, and not demonstrative. Certain and absolute in its action upon refined sensibilities, when searched out by the critical eye it is a nervous, flitting, evasive thing. It is the true Galatea of taste, which strikes us in spite of our will, and when we turn to seize it, has fled from our sight, and becomes visible only as it vanishes. It is on this account that ordinary critics, whose minds are always more active than their sentiments are delicate, generally fail to apprehend and appreciate this exalted quality. It is the source of that fresh, delightful fragrance which always exhales from Irving's writings.

In noting, therefore, the absence of great and commanding intellectual force, it will not be thought that we esteem Mr. Irving lightly; on the contrary, we regard him as an extraordinary and admirable artist, standing quite alone among his countrymen; not likely ever to be neglected, or ever to be rivalled. Of the genius of his pencil we shall speak hereafter, but looking at present only at the style and manner of his works, we find a grace as inherent as that of childhood; a gentle gayety as variable yet as unfailing and as unfatiguing as the breezes of June; an indestructible presence of good taste, simplicity, and ease; qualities which, in their separate conception, seem to be slight, yet, in their conjoint effect, are the splendor of fame and the power of immortality. What renders the merit more singular in Irving is, that successful and inimitable as the charm is, it is obviously not spontaneous or unconscious. In strenuous simplicity he almost equals the poet whose stream of verse reflects forever the dewy lustre of the morning of English civility; but what in the Pilgrim of Canterbury's scenes is the natural dazzle of the hour, is, in Irving, clearly the noonday elaboration of profound and much-taught science. Such composition is, in a great degree, a process of rejection; a labor of excision and exclusion, in which, however, excess is fatal; and the full genius and true art of Irving can never be popularly understood, until we can see the weedings of the exquisite violet banks on which he gives us to repose and be intoxicated with purity of sensual bliss, or can analyze the lees of his cup of enchantment, which alone would disclose how composite is the formation of that liquor which, in its final distillation, is as clear and natural as the crystal gushings of the rock. The *"mille decenter,"* which can be seen only in the general effect, are of infinitely greater value than the *"mille ornatus,"* which the eye recognizes and registers.

The prominent faculties in Mr. Irving's genius are OBSERVATION and FANCY. When they act in conjunction,—when quick and lambent Fancy touches with its quaint, kindling ray the fine particular truths which Observation has noted,—we have the brightest and most characteristic exhibitions of his powers.

The minute delicacy of his observation of outward life is remarkable. The eye has been to him a potent instrument of literary fame; it has played the part of a tireless gleaner in the fields of life, bringing in snatches of beauty and grace, trivial in themselves, but invaluable in their disposed and aggregated effect. Mr. Irving has obviously been through life a quiet yet busy watcher of the shapes, the colors, the changes of the landscape, the figures of trees, the forms, motions, and habits of birds, the looks and ways of animals, the appearances and physical peculiarities of men. So exact and special, in many instances, are the lines of description, that we cannot but suppose that it has been his custom, in viewing objects, to make notes upon the spot, or immediately after, so as to preserve the precise peculiarities of things which were afterwards to be worked up in sketches. As the subjects of the exercise of this faculty in him, however, are usually familiar or domestic, and therefore not especially dignified, the traits of observation are mostly hued by humor, or heightened by sentiment, or grouped in some inventive combination; and we meet few examples of incidents or scenes in nature, rendered with simple accuracy, as by historical portraiture of a real occurrence. Yet some such may be found, which challenge comparison with anything in literature, and which place the author in the highest class of faithful copyists of nature in her noblest simplicities, and of art in its most gorgeous complexity. . . .

Fancy, as we have said, is the principal and most active of the creative powers of Mr. Irving, and to its predominance are due alike his most surpassing excellences and his only defects. To that it is owing that as a picturesque painter of material life in all its familiar phases, he shines without an equal. To that is owing the perpetual charm of unwearying liveliness, which commends him to us as a companion in the longest solitudes, and the best entertainer of brief moments of vacuity or gloom. But to this, also, in the exclusive way in which it exists in him, is owing that his works do little else than amuse; and that, too, only the lower and less intellectual portions of our nature. We wish not to diminish the regard that is due to a writer who has delighted us too often to dispose us to criticism; but in pleasing always he has foregone the possibility of pleasing ever in the highest degree; and in making himself perpetually liked, he has consented never to be enthusiastically admired, nor perhaps deeply respected. For the excess and over-cultivation of fancy has been fatal to the exercise of the far greater faculty of imagination. Without staying to unfold the distinction between these two qualities in their entire nature, as seen in fiction, thought, feeling, and the whole action of intelligent man, we may note their difference, as far as the present purpose requires, in reference to the field where, in this instance, the diversity is chiefly illustrated, namely, in description. In an imaginative view of a scene, the mental consciousness of the person, or the moral character of the occasion, reacts upon the outward scene with such overpowering and transfusing energy, that all things around become but types and symbols,—nay, the very complements and visible parts,—of that which is within. You behold the scene, not as it is, but as it is felt or as it appears,—not in its actual condition, but as it is cast and reproduced in a speculum of thought or passion already warped or colored by the master emotion. Everything is subordinated to one prevailing sentiment. Objects are not viewed in their details, but each part is considered in reference to the whole, and colored by the notion of the whole. The spirit of totality and unity, derived from the singleness and intensity of the intellectual medium of conception, predominates. The action of fancy, however, is the opposite of all this.

The absence of imagination is obvious throughout the whole of Irving's writings. But to illustrate, in a single scene, how entirely humor in him is dependent on fancy, and not imagination, we may take the account of the Wacht-meester of Bearn Island, when the herald who had been sent by Governor Kieft arrived at the rebellious fort of Van Rensellaerstein, in the Knickerbocker annals. "In the fulness of time, the yacht arrived before Bearn Island, and Anthony the Trumpeter, mounting the poop, sounded a parley to the fortress. In a little while, the steeple-crowned hat of Nicholas Koorn, the wacht-meester, rose above the battlements, followed by his iron visage, and ultimately his whole person, armed, as before, to the very teeth; while one by one a whole row of Helderbergers reared their round burly heads above the wall, and beside each pumpkin-head peered the end of a rusty musket."

This separation of the wacht-meester's person into a three-storied automation, and this display of his mimic garrison, as in a mirror which leaves their vital consciousness unreflected, is extremely diverting, but it never could be the suggestion of any but an unimaginative mind.

As a double example of the perfection of a description of natural scenery in itself and wholly apart from imagination, and the failure of an attempt to represent the same scene imaginatively, may be cited the view around Tappan Zee as Ichabod Crane rode towards it in the afternoon, and from it at midnight. The former of the two pictures is as follows:

> As he journeyed along the side of a range of hills which look out upon some of the goodliest scenes of the mighty Hudson, the sun gradually wheeled his broad disk down into the west. The wide bosom of the Tappan Zee lay motionless and glassy, excepting that here and there a gentle undulation waved and prolonged the blue shadow of the distant mountain. A few amber clouds floated in the sky, without a breath of air to move them. The horizon was of a fine golden tint, changing gradually into a pure apple-green, and from that into the deep blue of the mid-heaven. A slanting ray lingered on the woody crests of the precipices that overhung some parts of the river, giving greater depth to the dark-gray and purple of their rocky sides. A sloop was loitering in the distance, dropping slowly down with the tide, her sails hanging uselessly against the mast; and as the reflection of the sky gleamed along the still water, it seemed as if the vessel was suspended in the air.

An exquisite, a faultless piece of cabinet painting! undoubtedly drawn and colored upon the spot. It is a portraiture of the scene as it is—abstractly—without reference to any state of feeling in the observer, or any prevailing sentiment in the narrative. In the *pendant* to this, the endeavor has been to exhibit the same locality in immediate relation with a peculiar condition of mind in the hero of the tale.

> It was the very witching time of night when Ichabod, heavy-hearted and crest-fallen, pursued his travel homewards, along the sides of the lofty hills which rise above Tarry Town, and which he had traversed so cheerily in the afternoon. The hour was as dismal as himself. Far below him the Tappan Zee spread its dusky and indistinct waste of waters, with here and there the tall mast of a sloop, riding quietly at anchor under the land. In the dead hush of midnight he could even hear the barking of the watch-dog from the opposite shore of the Hudson; but it was so vague and faint as only to give an idea of his distance from this faithful companion of man. Now and then, too, the long-drawn crowing of a cock, accidentally awakened, would sound far, far off, from some farm-house away among the hills—but it was like a dreaming sound in his ear. No signs of life occurred near him, but occasionally the melancholy chirp of a cricket, or perhaps the guttural twang of a bull-frog, from a neighboring marsh, as if sleeping uncomfortably, and turning suddenly in his bed.

Not thus would these objects have appeared to one who was in such a sensitive and excited condition of mind as presently to mistake an acquaintance with a cloak over his head and a pumpkin on his saddle-bow, for the Headless Horseman of the Hollow carrying his cranium before him. The design of describing the nocturnal scene by sounds rather than by sights is a good one; but each particular noise, instead of being represented in a manner to react with augmenting terror upon the fear-stricken sense of the traveller, is described in such a way as wholly to explain it away as a source of alarm, and to deprive it of the power of affrighting. The things are described not according to the law of terror within the mind of him on whom they were to operate, but according to the law of their actual state, as coldly viewed by an unexcited observer. The mast, which should have appeared as a strange, gleaming thing, weird and spectral, raising indefinite apprehensions; becomes a familiar and calming sight by being referred to a sloop, "riding quietly at anchor under the land." The distant bay of the watch-dog is well managed; but the drowsy crowing of the cock, which might with great effect have been made to have mysterious relation to the return of wandering ghosts to their sepulchral tenements, is brought back to quotidian unmeaningness by being made to proceed from a bird "accidentally awakened." The chirp which, heard at midnight, should have been an unknown signal, is elaborately portrayed as the soothing voice of the domestic and companionable cricket; and the awful bass from the marshes which, in lonely darkness, would have been an unlocal, bodiless horror, thrilling the nerves like a galvanic shock, is divested of all terror and of all dignity, by being the snort of a frog "sleeping uncomfortably, and turning suddenly in his bed." Compare all this with one of Shakespeare's nights! Mr. Irving's failure in this case is to be ascribed to defect of imagination, and consequent excess of inappropriate and discordant detail.

Moreover, this constant following of the minutiae of a scene to turn them into picturesque effect—this constant subordination of reflective action to outward appearance—damps and enfeebles the intellectual power. The fine, strong, manly thought—the vigorous moral reflection—the commanding tone of rational sense—which form so potent and grand an element in the magic of Scott's creations, are not found in Irving. However, it is a false system to criticise a literary work according to what it has not. So viewed, it is seen erroneously as the complement of some imagined whole, and has all its signs reversed. It is wiser as well as kindlier to consider a production of art under the view of what it is and has, and not of what it lacks.

In ideal pictures of inanimate nature, and of animals, trees, and landscapes, Mr. Irving's microscopic fidelity in limning accomplishes some remarkable effects. He does not bring a scene before you by giving the general expression of it, or the leading characteristics, under the form of a mental conception, here and there rendered definite and particular by certain touches of detail. He paints every object separately and exquisitely, fixing your attention upon each in succession, and making the whole a series of special studies. He is in description what Backhuysen is in painting. So prominent is the perspective, so absolute the verisimility, that you seem to have the thing itself, rather than a representation of it. . . .

These are remarkable illustrations of the completeness and vividness with which an object or a scene can, by mere imitative description, be realized under your eye. This faculty we take to be Mr. Irving's *forte;* and its successful exercise by him has given rise to a school of writers, who, with less taste, but in some cases more power, have carried the style to an unlimited height of popularity, but quite beyond the domain of genuine art. We regard Mr. Irving's works as having furnished the original and model of Dickens's descriptive manner; and, if the former has more delicacy, softness, and grace, the other excels in force, range, and vividness. . . .

There can be no doubt of Mr. Irving's supremacy in this class or school. The only question is as to the comparative dignity and elevation of the school itself. For ourselves, we may as well say at once that we do not regard it as belonging to a high order of art. It implies an extremely nice observation, constantly and painfully engaged upon its task; but it involves no act of true creation, no exercise of veritable poetic power. The pictures have no atmosphere; the objects glare directly upon you without passing through any mental medium. Amused, astonished, and perhaps delighted with the work, you feel little respect or interest for the author. His character is not in his production. This is the style of all recent art. . . . The vice of the art of this day, literary and pictorial, poetical and prose, and infecting authors and readers alike, consists in the excess of fancy, and the deficiency of imagination.

In respect to personal portraiture, Mr. Irving is an exquisite delineator of external manners, but has no power of representing character. He paints, not to the mind, by those intellectual touches which flash a complete subject into existence; nor to the conceptive faculty, by seizing those leading traits which draw all the accessories and dependents after them; but to the eye, by the transcription of every individual peculiarity in succession, each of which adds a modifying influence to those that went before, so that the effect is not complete until each stroke has been noted. He never gives you the interior, living, conscious man. You never get hold of the moral being of the creature. You have the mere *larva* of the person; the filmy shell of dress, carriage, and deportment, according to their pictorial impression. There is a complete absence of materiality from his people. They make no noise in walking. When they cross the mead, the grass is not pressed down under their feet. They seem, like Chinese figures in a landscape, to hang a foot or two up in the air. They are shadows; visionary toys in human shape; moving their limbs according as the author of their being draws the strings upon which they are hung; airy forms, flitting in an airy scene. . . .

Humor, as an adopted tone of style, or a permanent habit of mind, is a striking characteristic of Mr. Irving's writings: it seems, however, to be not an original, inherent, spiritual capacity, but an effect resulting from the odd, grotesque action of the fancy and taste. It will be found, almost invariably, that the humorous character of his productions, is external and visible, arising from queerness of outward form, or combination, or allusion; it is humor to the sight, and not to the soul. Quaint, droll, comic,—what you will, in the line of diverting, laughter-moving conceit,—we can scarcely admit his possession of that grand, deep, pathetic, meditative inspiration, Humor;—a faculty which seems to be the combination and the key of all our nature's sympathies; which measures the highest flights of thought, searches the deepest recesses of feeling, and sits upon the firmest seat of sense: the wisest instinct of our minds, the kindliest impulse of our hearts; a prompting always right, a guidance ever graceful; dignifying and endearing what it touches, and having relation to love rather than contempt. It would be neither fair nor practicable to compare the mirthfulness of Irving, with that of the great Cervantic mind, or with that which was the fullest, strongest, most complex action of the mighty genius of Scott; any more than to liken the simple carolings of a shepherd's reed to the multitudinous, interlinked, and infinitely complicated harmonies of one of Handel's oratorios. But taking lower and smaller parallels, the humor of Addison is intellectual, that of Goldsmith moral, and that of Irving purely fanciful. In the author of *The Spectator*, the humorous seems to be the highest action of the rational; the last, and finest, and surest test of sense and argument of right. In Goldsmith, it grows out of a practical and feeling acquaintance with life, and a keen and shrewd, yet affectionate insight into the peculiarities and weaknesses of individual character, and the foibles, vanities, and innocent absurdities of domestic and social relations. In Irving, it is the humor of the picturesque and quaint. It is a ridiculing humor, founded on distortion and misrepresentation; not a genial, enjoying spirit, arising from seeing into the depths of things. In plain truth, Irving is nothing more nor less than the most delicate, graceful, and exquisite of caricaturists.

As an illustration, that humor with Mr. Irving lies in the exercise of fancy, that it exists in the outward and pictorial, and not mentally, and in ideas, we may refer to the opening chapters of Knickerbocker's History. We are told, in a late prologue, that they were intended to burlesque the pedantic lore displayed in certain American works; and the task is long and laboriously followed out. Yet how dull, vapid, and ineffective is the toil! The whole thing is a failure. It is not until we come to the second book, and the portraits of Hendrick Hudson and his mate Jewit, and the Goede Vrouw, that we feel one genuine emotion of merriment, and recognize the cunning of a master.

A sense of the humorous, morally or intellectually, is a sure preservative against extravagance or bad taste; and the extent to which Mr. Irving's drollery is merely a work of the fancy, and of kin to caricature, may be seen in the numerous instances, especially in his earlier writings, in which bizarre conceptions degenerate into mere witless farce, exciting no amusement whatever. Such, we suppose, to be the account of the escape of Communipaw from the Virginia fleet, by the burghers falling to work and smoking their pipes at such a rate, as wholly to conceal the country, and the account of the origin of the name of Anthony's Nose in the Highlands. The latter story is, that as Anthony, the Governor's trumpeter, whose nose was of a very burly size, was sailing up the Hudson, he leaned over the quarter-railing of the galley, early one morning, to contemplate it in the glassy wave below. "Just at this moment, the illustrious sun, breaking in all his splendor from behind a high bluff of the Highlands, did dart one of his most potent beams full upon the refulgent nose of the sounder of brass, the reflection of which shot straightway down, hissing hot, into the water, and killed a mighty sturgeon that was sporting beside the vessel," &c., &c. . . .

If this is humor, we must confess our incapacity to perceive it. According to our impression, the greater part of Knickerbocker's History consists of the farcical rather than the humorous; we pronounce it infinitely droll, but we do not laugh.

In dealing with the pathetic, it is equally obvious, that Mr. Irving's power is not that of reflection, but of operating by visible images. In "The Sketch Book," under the title of Rural Funerals, there are some meditations upon the influence of death upon the affections, which have become rather famous in Elegant Extracts. They are commonplace, overstrained, affected. But turn to the story of "The Widow and her Son," and you will find that the selection of incidents, to bring out all the tender pathos of the tale, manifests a surpassing and resistless art. The first view which we have of the mother, in church: "A poor, decrepit old woman, bending under the weight of years and infirmities: the lingerings of decent pride were visible in her appearance. Her dress, though humble in the extreme, was scrupulously clean. Some trivial respect, too, had been awarded her, for she did not take her seat among the village poor, but sat alone on the steps of the altar."

Then the burial, when the mother had been assisted to kneel down at the head of the coffin at the grave: "Her withered hands were clasped, as if in prayer, but I could perceive, by a feeble rocking of the body, and a convulsive motion of the lips, that she was gazing on the last relics of her son with the yearnings of a mother's heart."

Then her first appearance in the village on the following Sunday: "She had made an effort to put on something like mourning for her son; and nothing could be more touching than this struggle between pious affection and utter poverty; a black ribbon or so, a faded black handkerchief, and one or two more such humble attempts to express by outward signs that grief which passes show."

These are the matchless strokes of genius, and show us that, however Mr. Irving may disappoint, when he deals with abstract reflections and thoughts, he never wanders when he follows the guidance of a visionary eye, inerrant in its truth, and unrivalable in its simple power.

The qualities which we recognize in Mr. Irving, of a mild yet lively fancy, and a refined taste, render him peculiarly well adapted to excel in narrative; and there he certainly assumes a position of especial and distinctive superiority. Walpole has remarked that simple narrative, in English, is one of the rarest and most difficult enterprises of literary art; and if the reason which he gives for it be not sound, at least the fact is verified by all experience. Gibbon was master of every form of style except this; Robertson, when he shone the most was farthest from it; Hume alone approached tolerably near to the standard, yet even in his pages we find ourselves following the progress of a philosopher's views, rather than a history of national events. Bancroft cannot narrate at all, and Prescott narrates with labor and fatigue. But Irving is always simple, direct, onward, informing, yet elegant, lively, and agreeable. The pleasantness which he diffuses over subjects the most barren or the most uncomfortable, arises chiefly from the instinctive quietness with which he seizes everything that is capable of being turned to picturesque effect, and employs it to shed light and grace upon the scene. The art of this system consists in the gentleness and fineness of the frequent rays which are thus shed abroad, and in the absence of strong, startling, and extraordinary lights. Instead of an occasional blaze diffused from prominent points, each incident, object, and interest is made mildly luminous by the lustre of a fancy almost imperceptible in its separate operation. It is by such a process that we are made to follow a troupe of adventurers across the disgusting sterilities of the north-western territories with the same delighted spirit with which we should tread the flowery vales of Cashmere, radiant with odors and ringing with the voices of birds. The unexhausted vigor, the delicate moderation, the consummate judgment with which in "Astoria" the resources of fiction are exerted to beautify the truth without distorting it, and to improve its tone without disturbing its form, are entitled to all admiration and all imitation. In some instances, in which he has allowed his pencil to leave its more brilliant touches upon the canvas, he has reached, in that work, the finest pictures that ever came from his genius. . . .

"The Life and Voyages of Columbus" however, constitute the most felicitous of the more dignified efforts of Mr. Irving's pen. It is impossible that the story of the sublime old tar can ever be told in a manner more thoroughly delightful. It is a "tale to hold children from play, and old men from the chimney corner." You move upon enchanted ground, and every sight and every sound is framed for charming. But this praise implies some grave defects. The determination to make everything picturesque and entertaining is fatal to the truth of the subject. Delays, disgusts, hardships, oppressions, treacheries, and all the harsh, stern elements of the reality, instead of being exhibited in those rough, strong colors which would have kindled a manly sympathy in the reader's heart to make their rudeness welcome, are enamelled in a style of sketchy delicacy of outline and hue, that wholly betrays the genuine qualities of the subject. The rage for catching the picturesque in external effect frequently causes an utterly false notion of the moral aspect of the occasion to be rendered: the eye is fascinated and misled by the visible, material conception of what, intellectually, may be of a directly opposite nature. Thus the picture of Columbus's long and weary suit at the court of Spain, instead of being fully brought out in its uncomfortable and degrading reality, which might annoy the sensibilities of the reader, is touched up with images of romantic scenery which convert the dulness of the period unto brilliant and poetic interest. These years were passed, it would seem, amid scenes of peril and adventure, following up the court in striking situations of wild, rugged, and mountainous war; attending the sovereigns at sieges of Moorish cities, and fighting himself in the dashing forays that gave a zest to the war; until at length "Columbus beheld Muley Boabdil, the elder of the two rival kings of Granada, surrender in person all his remaining possessions and his right to the crown to the Spanish soverigns." It is indeed a very curious study to a literary artist, to observe with what diligent dexterity the historian has mixed up the figure of Columbus with the persons, scenes, occurrences of the day, with whom we associate sentiments of romantic interest; how the gloom of unsuccessful conferences is relieved by the gorgeous costumes of cardinals, and bishops, and noble dames; how the splendid trappings of royalty flit before the dazzled sight; until, at last, the period of this long attendance fills our thoughts as the most entertaining portion of Columbus's life. To the imagination and feelings of the reader the whole thing is an enchanting falsehood. It is really the feebleness and not the force of art which, unable to manage the strong contrasts that should have brought out the noble harmony of the sublime story, levels all in one insipid melody. Moreover, the dreamy, Arcadian style of the narrative causes a complete want of those definite, sharp particularities which, in a history, are indispensable; and which, after all, give an interest and an effect which all the flakes of sentiment and fancy, however accumulated, cannot supply. For example, in attempting to impress us with a notion of the frailty and slightness of the vessels in which Columbus embarked upon his awful mission of exploration, he describes two of them as "light barks not superior to river and coasting craft of more modern days;" open and without decks, &c.; but he nowhere mentions their tonnage. If he had told us that one of the vessels was of only fifteen tons, which is the fact, we should have had a far more vivid conception of the daring of this enterprise. But Mr. Irving is too nice a gentleman to deal in vulgar statistics. The consequence of this style of dainty selection and exquisite indistinctness is that we cannot determine whether we are reading a professed fiction or an intended history. The pictures lack that individuality and force which tell us that we are looking at a portrait and not at a fancy-piece. While we read we are held as by a wondering spell, but when we close the volume, the *"incredulus odi"* succeeds, and we long for a real history of the times, so that we may know how much of the fairy tale we have read is true. In the history of the siege of Granada this puzzle between truth and fiction becomes absolutely offending. We feel as if the chronicler was trifling with us. The essence of romance is poured out in such profusion as to become sickening. In attempting to throw a perfume on the flowers of natural truth he seems to have split the bottle of attar, and the nosegay is fairly fetid with artificial and excessive odor.

The work upon which Mr. Irving's fame as a literary creator and artist will rest in future times is, no doubt, "The Sketch Book." The variety of its materials, the refinement mingled always with natural and familiar ease, the adaptation of its topics and tone to the general sympathy, the union of Italian brilliance with Flemish fidelity in the sketches, render it justly a favorite with all. Walpole used to say, that an author's genius usually comes into flower at some period of his life. And probably there will be little difference of opinion upon the point that "The Sketch Book" is the perfect flower of all of Irving's faculties. "Bracebridge Hall" falls entirely below it. The design of that work cannot be regarded as a happy one; and objectionable as at best it is, the execution of the scheme is such as to develop new faults. In the first place, the plan or groundwork of the thing is misconceived; and the misconception springs from that want of imagination which we have spoken of. The purpose of the work is to sketch the ancient poetic manners of the English people, especially in their country life; and with a view to add the interest of a present scene to the beauty of old romance, the author supposes a character devotedly attached to all bygone customs, and passing his life in an endeavor to realize the life of the past in all the usages upon his own estate. Now, in order that such moral anachronism as Mr. Irving conceives, should be at all probable or possible, the first requisite is that the person from whom it originates should be represented as a man of ardent poetic genius, identifying himself by force of creative energy with the spirit of long departed institutions, and able, by the enthusiasm and force of his character, to infect all around him with the same illusion. Such is not Mr. Irving's Squire; and it is against all consistency, that the commonplace, feeble, vacant creature whom he introduces to us as the proprietor of the Hall, should develop from his own temper, against all surrounding influences, the beautiful elaboration of ideal existence which is exhibited to our view, and that his dependents, stewards, woodmen, and farmers, should breathe the atmosphere of his mind instead of their own actual and real consciousness. The primary and indispensable conditions of the scene are violated. We feel, therefore, in reading this work, a sense of falsity and difficulty. A vigorous imagination would have kept the author from this failure. But the literary defects of Bracebridge Hall are also striking. To refine the critical perceptions and sentiments by diligent familiarity with older models, and to reproduce the spirit of Addisonian grace, might be a worthy ambition; but to subordinate the mind and character to the local and temporary form of a particular passage,—to labor to observe, think, and speak precisely upon the example of the Spectators—to make not a rational imitation, but a mechanical mimicry—is not a very lofty or a very wise employment of genius. As far even as this design is intentionally carried out, it is not successfully done. While the endeavor to imitate Addison is palpable and displeasing, the constant intervention of phrases and even particular words, which are wholly modern and American, exposes the falsity of the counterfeit, and even gives an air of vulgarity to that which, properly used, might have had the dignity of genuineness. It will be observed that the attempt to impart an Addisonian air to the style, consists chiefly in the frequent use of certain expressions which are the accidental peculiarities of the model:—"I could not help observing"—"I am apt to find or to think"—"A very tolerable scholar," &c. But in the midst of these the constant recurrence of such words as "I noticed," and half a dozen others, which are neither Addisonian nor English, not only breaks the illusion, but converts it into an imposture. A greater difficulty, however, is that the imitation is not kept up, and in the nature of the case, could not be kept up. For, the moment that the author becomes warmed, and his mind gets into vigorous play, such is the sympathy between thought and style, that as the former grows earnest the latter becomes characteristic and genuine. This transition from the falsetto of an affected Addisonianism to the natural tones of individual truth, causes the tales,(?) fine and musical as they are, to displease by inappropriateness. Take, for instance, in the early chapters of "Bracebridge Hall," the paragraphs about family servants, and about the duties of women *after* they are married, where the author gives vent to his own serious and sober feelings and opinions upon interesting subjects. They are beautifully written, but have not a touch of the false antiquity of the rest; and this partial change of the key throws everything into discord. It is like a man who, acting a part under a false-face, thrusts out his own features from the mask whenever he has anything particularly clever to say.

Of Mr. Irving's works, generally, it may be observed, that in a grammatical point of view, the style is delicate rather than pure, and more exquisite than correct. His use of words is not exact; indeed, we constantly meet with expressions which it surprises us that a man of good education should, even in the greatest carelessness, let fall. Such phrases as the following: "the creaking of the cords seemed to *agonize her*," in "The Widow and her Son;" "he *emerged his head* out of his shell," in "Bracebridge Hall;" "whom he thought fully entitled of being classed," &c., in the same place; are among several that struck us upon our recent perusal of one or two volumes.

[Review of *Life of George Washington*, Volumes 1–4]   G. W. Greene°

Many concurring causes seem to have pointed out Mr. Irving as the historian of Washington. He had been the first to tell the story of Columbus fully, and to paint the struggles of that sublime genius in colors which, like those of the frescos on the ruins of old Roman palaces, will preserve their freshness unchanged, in spite of time and decay. He was known to have a rare talent for the study of character, seizing readily upon all those delicate shades and nice distinctions which, though essential to the truth of a portrait, and often the only clew to apparent contradictions, escape the common eye. He was acknowledged to be one of the best of narrators, full of life and movement, carrying you from scene to scene with an interest that never flags, possessing all the warmth of a poet, and yet free from that melodramatic exaggeration which is the worst falsifier of history. He was the master of a pure English style, with its graphic epithets and rich cadences, which, while it addresses itself to the understanding and the heart, fills the ear with a delicious melody that thrills you like music. And with all this he had lived in the world, and that in an age full of great events; had mingled freely in the society of different nations; had met face to face the great men of his time; had seen kings upon their thrones, savage chiefs in their native wilds, generals fresh from the battle-field, statesmen surrounded with the pageantry of office, or mourning in involuntary retirement the loss of a power that had become essential to their happiness. He had lived, too, in delightful intercourse with the monarchs of the mind, the great poets who, from the seclusion of their closets, sent forth words that were repeated with rapture in courts and cottages, on the ocean and by the watch-fire; and he had seen them pass away one by one, repeating the lesson of ages, that he who would live in the hearts of men must live for mankind.

Therefore, when it was known that the first volume was in the hands of the printer, there was a general expression of satisfaction among the friends of American literature. They felt that this wondrous story would be told aright; that Washington would be drawn in all the majesty of his greatness; that the charms of exquisite composition, gracing the record of virtue, would form a work which fathers would transmit to their children as a precious legacy. This expectation has been abundantly fulfilled. Each new volume has been received with a welcome that must have carried a cheering glow to the author's heart. You will meet them in steamboats, you will meet them in the

° Reprinted from *North American Review* 86 (April 1858): 330–58.

cars; they have taken their place at the side of the classics in the library, and lie, in rich bindings, among the ornaments of the centre-table. We have seen them call a brighter flush to the cheek of youth, and heard their harmonious periods flowing with impressive solemnity from the lips of age. Seldom has literature witnessed a more perfect triumph; never, one on which the recorder of her checkered annals can dwell with so serene and unsullied joy. . . .

It is generally understood that Mr. Irving began to collect his materials before his mission to Spain, and that his work has conse-quently been growing in his mind some fourteen or fifteen years. It was not, however, till several years after his return that he entered upon it seriously. Meanwhile the Life of Goldsmith, and the History of Mahomet and his Followers, were written, and the revised edition of his Works carried through the press. It was an interval of active exertion, during which he did enough to have made the reputation of any other man, and in fields remote from that which he was preparing to tread. But this was done without losing sight of his great subject, to which he returned from time to time, gradually extending his researches and enlarging his range of inquiry. He visited many, if not most, of the places connected with Washington's private and public career. From his own garden he could look down upon some of the most interesting localities of the war. And the few who could still speak of it as eyewitnesses were glad to repeat their stories to such a listener. Like Sparks, he studied Washington's letters in the originals, to which he could now add the writings of Hamilton, Adams, and Jefferson, and the vast array of facts so laboriously collected and so judiciously arranged by Mr. Force, in his American Archives, one of the most remarkable monuments of historical industry of any age or country. And when the results of this deliberate and comprehensive preparation had arranged themselves in his mind, in distinct and definite forms, the great drama of the Revolution would seem to have unrolled itself before his eyes, in the full grandeur of its proportions, with Washington for its central and directing spirit. Then it was that he took up his pen, like a spectator fresh from some exciting scene, to pour out his recollections in a continuous flow of picturesque narrative. The first volume was published early in 1855; the second, before the close of the same year; the third, in 1856; and the fourth, in 1857. At first he had expected to bring his story within the compass of three volumes; but as he proceeded, the figures came crowding upon the canvas till he found himself compelled to choose between expansion and mutilation. Fortunately for literature and for his own fame, he chose the former. Each part now fills its appropriate place, without jostling or jarring with the others. The first volume contains a full history of Washington's youth, presents an elaborate picture of the severe ordeal through which he passed in the old French war, gives graphic sketches of his domestic life at Mount Vernon, and, tracing carefully the progress of public sentiment during the opening scenes of the Revolution, closes with his arrival at the camp before Boston. The second opens with the siege of Boston, and brings the story down to the battle of Princeton and the first encampment at Morristown. The third is devoted to the campaigns of 1777–79. The fourth contains the closing scenes of the war, and the melancholy history of the Confederation, and ends with the first inauguration; and a fifth will soon terminate the eventful drama.

The first thing that strikes the reader, on closing these volumes, is the skill with which the work is divided, and the judgment with which the proportions of the different parts of its complex narrative are marked out. This alone would entitle its author to a high rank among historians; for it implies the power of vigorous conception, a quality which holds the same place in historical that invention does in poetical composition. To conceive a complicated subject as one, to detect the principle of unity which binds its scattered and often discordant parts into an harmonious whole, and to feel your pen guided by this instinctive appreciation to put everything into its true place, as the particles of matter are arranged by the force of gravitation at their proper distances from the common centre, is a rare and precious gift. A broken and ill-proportioned narrative is as repulsive to the mind as discord is to a musical ear, and this not merely from an inherent love of order, but because we can never fully understand the spirit and relations of that which we cannot grasp as a whole. It is for this, in a great measure, that history is less read than it ought to be. The events of history are full of variety and novelty, often carrying us so far beyond our conjectures as to have made it a common saying, that truth is stranger than fiction. Yet men of fine talents, of profound thought, of eminent literary powers, are frequently unable to excite our interest in the most eventful periods. They fail to discover the latent principle of unity. They treat history as they study it, not as a living whole, with one great heart sending out the vivifying blood to every part of the system and receiving it back again to purify it and transmit it anew to the remotest extremities, but as an aggregate of parts coherent indeed, but not essentially dependent on one another. . . .

Mr. Irving, too, was aided by the nature of his subject; for as regards unity of narrative, the biographer has a great advantage over the general historian. But the manner in which he has availed himself of this advantage deserves the highest praise. Washington is eminently an historical character. From his youth upwards the larger part of his life was closely interwoven with the history of his country. He never stands alone. He is constantly surrounded by public men. Great events group themselves about him, as if by a natural law. Every movement of his seems to communicate life and energy to thousands. As with the prophet of old, his arms are still raised to insure the triumph of his countrymen. And though the two or three intervals of his retirement from public life appear, at first, like the reigns of good kings, to afford but meagre materials to the historian, on looking closer, you perceive that a great work was still going on, and that he is its best exponent.

Therefore, in tracing his career, the historian must frequently leave the immediate subject of his narrative, in order to follow the progress of events in which he does not appear personally. He must describe the movements of distant armies and battles won by other leaders. And yet, while he metes out to every one his due measure of praise, he must preserve for his own hero his appropriate place as guide and director of all. This Mr. Irving has done with singular skill. Washington is emphatically the hero of his narrative, standing out in bold relief from the group of eminent men that cluster around him, everywhere recognized as an all-pervading spirit, breathing life and energy into every part, and felt in the remotest extremities of the land by his controlling will and sublime example. You turn to him instinctively from every battle-field, to see how he will receive the tidings. You feel a double joy at every victory, in the thought that it will lighten his burden. You judge men by their fidelity to him, and measure their services by the estimate in which he held them. And this effect is obtained without any exaggeration of Washington's actions, without forcing him from his natural position, or bringing him officiously forward out of time and place, by so guiding the flexible thread of the narrative as to make him the point at which you instinctively place yourself to watch the gradual development of the eventful plot. . . .

Of purely literary qualifications, the first in historical composition is narrative power. Something more is implied in this than the art of telling a story well; for historical narrative is a succession of stories requiring a capacity of continuous exertion through a long series of events. In power there is the same difference between this and mere story-telling, that there is between carrying a burden a few paces and carrying it through the whole of a long journey. The very men that would trip off the most briskly in one case, might be the first to sink from exhaustion in the other. In this respect, also, the ancients are far in advance of us. Their histories are eminently narrative. The story begins with the first line, and is carried on to the end of the book with a life and movement that seldom flag. . . .

But he [Irving] is richly endowed with the higher qualities of the narrative historian. He possesses a lively imagination, enabling him to enter readily into the feelings and character of another age; an affluent fancy, suggesting picturesque epithets, and happy trains of thought and expression; an extensive range of observation, giving distinctness and life to his conceptions; genial sympathies, which quicken and glow with the images that rise under his pen; and a power of continuous exertion that sustains him unwearied to the end. Simplicity and grace are among the most obvious characteristics of his narrative,—the simplicity of an earnest nature, and the grace of generous cultivation. There is a fine movement in it, lively, animated, and richly varied. It is as clear as a meadow-brook, but rolls on like his own Hudson, now expanding into silvery lakes, now gently sweeping round some green and wooded promontory, and now gathering its waters into a deep and impetuous current, and pouring the resistless volume through a precipitous and rock-bound gorge. And yet, perhaps, if we were called upon to say in what its peculiar merit consists, we should name its full and equable flow. There is nothing abrupt in it. The sentences follow one another with such a natural sequence, so smooth, so harmonious, and withal so full of life, that you are carried forward without ever pausing to measure your progress.

We have given the first place to narrative power, because we cannot conceive of a good history without it. It is the art of telling a story in such a way as to make the incidents their own interpreters. Description holds the next place, and, by bringing particular objects closer to the eye and investing them with their natural attributes, gives greater definiteness and vivacity to the conception. It demands a different kind of talent, consisting chiefly in the power of conceiving form distinctly, and combining it readily into groups and pictures. In narrative the historian is brought into relation with the poet; in description, with both the poet and the painter. Description, indeed, is painting to the mind's eye, and requires that perfect command of the elements of form and color, that ready perception of appropriate shadows and distances, that rare combination, in short, of intuitions and acquired knowledge, which enables the great artist to bring a group or a landscape before the eye with an effect hardly inferior to that of the real scene.

It has been said that Mr. Irving, in his younger days, gave Allston such an impression of his skill with the pencil, as to lead that great artist, whose noble nature was never disturbed by the fear of raising up a rival, to use all his influence with his friend in order to induce him to take up the profession of an artist. However this may have been, it is very evident from Mr. Irving's descriptions that he might have become a great painter. His figures are full of individuality, and drawn to the life. There is no hardness in the outline, no faltering in the touch; everything is rendered with a free and firm hand. His groups are disposed with an instinctive appreciation of the mutual relations and dependencies of the characters. "The School of Athens" does not present a more admirable example than these volumes, of the art of placing a variety of prominent figures upon the same canvas. There are some exquisite pieces, too, of landscape painting, bits of scenery that fill up the backgrounds with the happiest effect, and give a fine relief to the stern groups of warriors and statesmen.[1] Sometimes he paints in detail, and with a wondrous truth and vivacity of coloring. Sometimes he paints in outline, creating as it were an entire scene by a single touch of the pencil. All of his pictures reveal a careful study of nature, an accurate knowledge of details, fine power of combination, and a happy tact in adapting his style and coloring to the particular subject. . . .

The history of the Revolution affords a fine field for the display of this talent, and Mr. Irving has availed himself of it with distinguished success. As the leading men come upon the stage, their previous history is sketched with a few rapid touches, and their characters are unfolded with a nice appreciation of circumstances and motives. Some are drawn with great attention,—full-lengths, in which all the characteristic features are carefully wrought up into a finished picture. Others are happily hit off by a few bold strokes. That fine discrimination which distinguishes the poet's knowledge of the heart, is everywhere apparent. There is a felicitous conciseness, a happy reserve, which adds greatly to the impression. He seems always to know when the portrait is complete, when the conception has been given, and instantly drops his pencil.

He never indulges in disquisitions, though he often closes a chapter with some apposite reflection that rises naturally from the subject. There are many just, many beautiful, and many noble thoughts interwoven with the narrative. But he would seem to have no ambition of being a maker of aphorisms. He for the most part lets the moral and wisdom of the story flow from the story itself; and appears to feel that the reader may be safely intrusted with the care of drawing his own deductions. In this, he has shown, we think, excellent judgment; for if history be philosophy teaching by example, it is to the vividness with which the example is brought before us, rather than to any ethical elaboration of it, that we should look for the efficacy of the lesson.

The general tone of the work is sober and calm. There is no exaggeration of style or sentiment in it. Mr. Irving has formed too just an idea of his subject to employ any but the simplest and most natural forms of expression. If his own good taste had not been sufficient to guard him against fanciful epithets and melodramatic effects, his excellent sense would have shown him how much they are out of place in speaking of Washington. There is a sobriety in Washington's character which repels all the common artifices of rhetoric. His history is full of great results and simple means. If you would speak of him worthily, you must rely wholly upon the grandeur of the thought. . . .

In this Mr. Irving has caught the true spirit of antiquity. He is natural, simple, and earnest, and some of his finest effects are produced with the least apparent effort. Now and then there is a kindling of the imagination, like the occasional flashings up of the more passionate elements of Washington's own nature; but the pervading tone is that of earnest sobriety. He is evidently full of his subject; believes all that he says; is impressed even to solemnity with the moral grandeur of his hero; and, feeling how closely the events of that period are interwoven with the future destinies of our race, tells his story like one too well convinced of the importance of it to think of adding to its impressiveness by pomp of language or brilliancy of metaphor. This, which in some would be but a negative merit, in Mr. Irving is a positive one. For a man of his imagination, with all the wealth of one of the richest of languages at his command, the temptations to let his pen run freely must have been incessant, and sometimes difficult to resist. Many a brilliant thought must have started to his page, which his calmer judgment deliberately repressed. Many a period must have been cut down, which, in its original conception, glowed with gorgeous colors and flowed with majestic harmony.

We should do Mr. Irving great injustice if we were to pass lightly over this remarkable characteristic of his work. It is a tribute to historic truth, as difficult as it is rare, and which deserves especial commemoration. It has been truly said, that a great poet never receives half the praise he is entitled to, because the world never knows how much he erases. . . . If this sacrifice to the laws of art be entitled to our approbation, what ought we to say of that self-denying spirit which, through four large volumes, can keep a rigorous watch over its own impulses, lest it should be betrayed into something inconsistent with the severity of its subject?

It is in a great measure in consequence of this general reserve, that you feel such confidence in the accuracy and fidelity of this history. A tone of sincerity that cannot be mistaken runs through it. An atmosphere of truth surrounds it on every side. There is an air of reality about it which you trust implicitly and without hesitation. It carries with it a weight of internal evidence which goes farther towards securing your conviction than the most imposing array of citations and references. The general truth of history has seldom been called in question by any but those who have reason to fear its decisions; but discredit has often been thrown upon details by the historian's assuming a greater familiarity with them than any but the actors could have had. . . .

Mr. Irving has taken advantage of every opportunity to introduce appropriate details; seasoning his narrative with characteristic anecdotes, which give a pleasant relief to the general gravity of the subject, and serve to bring out those familiar traits, without which our knowledge of a man is always indefinite and unsatisfactory. But he has displayed superior discretion in the choice of them, accepting nothing which was not trustworthy, and rejecting those idle stories which float loosely in the wake of every great man, without any competent witness to vouch for their authenticity.

It may seem superfluous to speak of Mr. Irving's style; but it is so refreshing to meet with a work written in such good taste, and with so graceful an adherence to the pure traditions of our language, that we cannot resist the temptation of dwelling for a moment upon the grateful theme. Every age has a conventional style of its own, arising from circumstances peculiar to itself, and reflecting, with more or less fidelity, its own characteristics. So long as the influences under which it grew up retain their power, it continues to hold its place as the popular standard. But no sooner do they cease to act, than it begins to lose its distinctive features and gradually to assume those of another period. Still there is an element in it which resists this constant tendency to change, and preserves itself with more or less purity through the entire series of transformations. This element is the genius of the language, a lithe and delicate spirit, assuming with miraculous flexibility a strange variety of forms, bending to the strong will, humoring the playful caprice, diffusing itself with subtle expansion throughout the whole body of literature, and giving to the infinite creations of mind the form and lineaments of national unity. Thus, while there is much in which the writers of different ages differ, there is something in which they agree; and this point of agreement furnishes one of the tests by which individual style should be judged. . . .

In Mr. Irving's style there is less of the nineteenth century than in Mr. Bancroft's, and more than in Mr. Prescott's. The character of his early works brought him into that kind of contact with his contemporaries which necessarily affects the forms of expression by its influence upon the forms of thought. In painting objects that lay under his eye, he naturally employed the language of daily life, and when he came to speak of the manners and arts of other ages, or to indulge in the genial exercise of creation, he had already caught as large a share of the characteristics of his own age as was suited to the nature and bent of his mind. His favorite studies, at the same time, served to moderate the effect of these contemporary influences, and to aid him in forming a style in which the genius of the language is preserved without sacrificing the genius of the age. He had conceived an early passion for the old poets and moralists, and had taken a special delight in those exquisite ballads into which men fresh from the people poured all the poetry of common life. He had made himself familiar with popular traditions, had studied the antique drama, and, living in daily intercourse with men of polite conversation, had gathered around himself an atmosphere of pure literature, in which the best elements of the old and the new were naturally and harmoniously blended.

Mr. Irving's language is genuine English, with few words that Addison or Goldsmith would not have used, and few that would not have been readily understood a hundred years ago in the same sense in which he employs them. The arts and inventions of the age have left just traces enough in his style to show that he belongs to a period in which great changes have been wrought in society by the progress of natural and social science. He is fond of idioms, with which he is copiously supplied by extensive reading, directed and enlivened by the habits of good society. He is usually very happy in the choice both of his words and of his idioms, and it is very seldom that one could change either without jeoparding the thought. He evidently feels the power of a word in its place,[2] and some of his pictures owe half their beauty to a felicitous selection of terms. There is a richness and splendor of diction in his essays and tales, which, in his histories, is sobered down to a calm affluence, always adequate to the occasion, but never overflowing in those brilliant periods which are the legitimate ornament of imaginative composition.

In the structure of his sentences there is a pleasing variety, although, like most moderns, he prefers short sentences. Their rhythm is singularly rich and sweet, free from every taint of monotony, and always gratifying the ear by spontaneous adaptation to the thought. Indeed, they leave upon the mind the same kind of impression which poetry does when it has once become associated with sweet music; one never recalls the verses without fancying that he hears the accompaniment.

All is clear and distinct in his periods, which seem like mirrors to his thoughts, reflecting every idea so truthfully, that you feel, while reading him, as if you were looking directly into his mind. And this arises in a great measure from his never attempting a style of writing that is not in harmony with his habits of thought; so that his words become the natural expression of his conceptions. Without any ambitious endeavors to appear strong, he always leaves strong impressions.[3] The image that has found its way to the mind through the medium of his words is sure to remain there in all its freshness.

We cannot call his style simple; for it is too rich for absolute simplicity. And yet it is so natural, the ornaments are so chaste, the words seem to drop so readily into their places, the epithets seem to rise so spontaneously from the subject, the periods seem to flow so easily into one another, that you never think of pausing to reflect on the labor which it must have cost to learn how to use language so skilfully. There is a fine flavor of culture about it which cannot be mistaken, but which, while it shows how conversant he must have been with the best writers, is free from all tincture of pedantry. He never harangues, though he is often eloquent. One may read his sentences effectively, but cannot declaim them. He has more movement than Mr. Prescott, more fluidity than Mr. Bancroft. If we were called upon to name the leading characteristics of his style, we should say that they were rhythm, artistic conception, and a constant play of fancy. It is to his delicate perception of rhythmical beauty that his sentences owe their just and harmonious proportions. It is by his rare power of artistic conception that he enriches them with pictures full of life and movement. And the vivid play of his fancy gathers for him, from the wide realms of animate and inanimate nature, that store of felicitous epithets which illuminates them as with a perpetual glow of soft and rosy light. You never willingly lay down a volume of his till you have finished it; and when you take it up anew, you still feel the pleasure grow upon you as you read. "Fascinating" is the word that we should most readily apply to him as a writer, so irresistible is the influence which he gains over us, and so serene a sense of secret satisfaction does he diffuse through the mind by the graceful flow of his periods.

We think, therefore, that Mr. Irving has succeeded perfectly in the task which he had set himself—a history of Washington which should bring him home to every heart by bringing him distinctly before every mind. A psychological analysis of character, like Coleridge's Pitt, or a philosophical generalization, like Guizot's Essay, however valuable for a certain class of readers,—and surely their value cannot be rated too highly,—would have failed to meet the wants of the thousands who wish to know what Washington did in order to win for himself the holy title of "Father of his Country." The historian of Washington is the great teacher of the nation, who tells us what sacrifices it cost our fathers to prepare for us the blessings that we enjoy; what heroism was required to overcome the obstacles that beset their path; what self-denial it demanded to forget themselves in their love for posterity; how strong their wills, how firm their hearts, how sound their judgment, how serene their wisdom. We should rise from the volume with the whole of the wondrous history imprinted upon our memories, and with our hearts glowing with fervent gratitude and generous patriotism. We should feel that a great soul has been laid open before us, and that we have been permitted to look into its innermost recesses; that we have been brought nearer to one in the touch of whose garments are healing and strength, and that, henceforth, when trials come upon us, and doubts assail us, and our hearts sicken and grow faint at the contemplation of evils for which we can discover no cure, the image of the great and good man will rise before us like a messenger from heaven, to teach us the power of faith and the beauty of virtue.

We regard the brilliant success of these volumes as an occasion of joyful congratulation to the citizens of our republic. It is eminently a national work, upon which they can all look with unmingled pride. It has not merely enriched our literature with a production of rare beauty, but has given new force to those local associations which bind us as with hallowed ties to the spots where great men lived and great things were done. Few will now cross the Delaware without remembering that Christmas night of tempest and victory. Who can look upon the heights of Brooklyn without fancying that, as he gazes, the spires and streets fade from his view, while in their stead stern and anxious faces rise through the misty air, and amid them the majestic form of Washington, with a smile of triumph just lighting for a moment his care-worn features, at the thought of the prize he has snatched from the grasp of a proud and exulting enemy? And Princeton, and Valley Forge, and Monmouth, and the crowning glory of Yorktown,—how do they live anew for us! With what perennial freshness will their names descend to posterity! And those two noble streams that flow to the sea through alternations of pastoral beauty and rugged grandeur,—the lovely Potomac, the majestic Hudson,— how have they become blended by these magic pages in indissoluble association,—the one the cherished home of Washington, the seat of his domestic joys, his rural delights, looked to with eager yearning from the din of camps and battle-fields, sighed for with weary longing amid the pomp and pageantry of official greatness, to which he returned so gladly when his task had been accomplished, and which, dying with the serenity of Christian resignation, he consecrated by the holiest of all associations, the patriot's grave,—the other the scene of cares and triumphs, on whose banks he had passed slow days of hope deferred, whose waters had borne him to and fro through checkered years of dubious fortune, and had witnessed the touching sublimity of his farewell to his companions in arms, and the simple grandeur of his reception as first President of the country he had saved! How meet was it that, while his ashes repose beside the waters of the Potomac, his life should have been written on the banks of the Hudson!

Notes

1. For he seems to have felt, with the great Roman critic, "Historia. . . . tanto robustior quanto verior."—Quint. Lib. II. cap. 4.

2. That faculty which Boileau justly makes a merit in Malherbe:—"D'un mot mis en sa place enseigna le pouvoir." Art Poétique, Ch. I, 133.

3. Justifying the admirable precept of Seneca,—"Debet enim semper plus esse virium in actore, quam in onere."—De Tranq. an. 5.

TWENTIETH-CENTURY ESSAYS

Washington Irving: Amateur or Professional?

Henry A. Pochmann[*]

In recognition of Washington Irving's becoming the first American man of letters to win a wide international reputation, his grateful countrymen fastened upon him titles such as Inventor of the Modern Short Story, Ambassador of the New World to the Old, and Father of American Literature. Gratulatory admiration of this kind engendered a literary reputation that has suffered little diminution, comparable for example to Longfellow's or Holmes's. His fame and his honors, so the story goes, came unsought—the result of a happy conspiracy between fortuitous circumstances and innate talents; and with becoming modesty, he allowed them to rest lightly and gracefully on his slim shoulders.

Irving himself is as responsible as anyone for creating the atmosphere in which such a legend could grow. In his first writings he pictured himself as one of a knot of carefree young blades, who might have been known a generation earlier, in and about New York City, as bloods or macaroni whose primary concern, after wine-women-and-song, was literary dilettantism. In two series of periodical letters and essays appearing in 1802–1803 and 1807–1808 he represented himself as one of "the Nine Worthies," "the Lads of Kilkenny," or "the Ancient and Honorable Order of New York"—the others being his brothers William, Peter, and Ebenezer, Peter and Gouverneur Kemble, Henry Brevoort, Henry Ogden, and James Kirke Paulding. After exhausting the pleasures of the city, they often resorted to an old family mansion of the Kembles on the Passaic (Cockloft Hall in *Salmagundi*) for frolicsome entertainments befitting young bachelors with literary tastes. Sometimes they met for convivial suppers and literary powwows at a genteel public house known as Dyde's, and when their purse was low, contented themselves with "blackguard

[*] Reprinted by permission from *Essays on American Literature in Honor of Jay B. Hubbell*, ed. Clarence Gohdes (Durham: Duke University Press, 1967), 63–76. © 1967 by Duke University Press, Durham, N.C.

suppers" at a porterhouse on the corner of John and Nassau streets. Always they were in good spirits, and almost always their entertainment took a literary turn and concerned whatever social or political overtones the happenings of the day or the whims of the worthies suggested. So it was that the earlier series of letters by Jonathan Oldstyle, in which Irving masqueraded as a kind of nineteenth-century American reincarnation of Tatler-Spectator (of which he wearied after penning nine short epistles for his brother Peter's *Morning Chronicle*), developed into a joint production setting forth the opinions and whim-whams of the gay wags and making what they properly called a Salmagundi, a mixed dish, a medley, a potpourri of personal essays, poetical effusions, social satire, political innuendo, dramatic criticism, and editorial idiosyncrasy. Alternately grave and facetious, the youthful editors posed as "critics, amateurs, dilettanti, and cognoscenti," and proceeded merrily with cocksure insolence through twenty numbers, satirizing the ways of the fashionable world, inserting squibs on the theater, occasionally mixing a little political bastinade, waging war against "folly and stupidity," and teaching "parents . . . how to govern their children, girls how to get husbands, and old maids how to do without them." It was Addison and Steele transplanted from London to New York. It was all good-natured raillery, and all the more welcome as a change of fare from the heavy bombardment of polemics since the days of 1776. The essays were read in coffee-houses and gentlemen's clubs, and they made their way to many a proper belle's toilet table. Many of the "characters" were recognizable, and while some shunned being identified, others were secretly envied. The "fascinating [Mary] Fairlie" was obviously the original of Sophie Sparkle; there was no lack of young ladies who coveted her notoriety; and the superficial disguises under the names of Ding Dong, Ichabod Fungus, and Dick Paddle provoked no affairs of honor. But fatuous theatrical critics, taking a glance at themselves in the mirror of 'Sbidlikens, found it advisable to hold their peace; fashionable upstarts shrank before the portraits of the Giblets; the small beer of politicians soured at the portrait of Dabble; and the feathers of carpet soldiers wilted when they saw themselves paraded in the regiment of the Fag-Rags. *Salmagundi* made no great fortune for the three editors, but it became the talk and the mild terror of the town.

So it came to pass that Irving became less and less regular in his attendance at No. 3 Wall Street, where he had gingerly hung his shingle underneath that of his brother John. Instead of drawing up legal briefs, he was entertaining vague ideas of turning author. To be sure, the law had never been a serious vocation, but as the youngest of five sons of a substantial merchant (all the others already fairly launched in business, medicine, or the law) it behooved him to prepare for a profession. It was expected of him. So for a number of years he harried his inveterate enemies, the fathers of the law, in several lawyers' offices and was duly admitted to the bar "by the grace of God" and Josiah Ogden, his latest mentor, who also served on his examining committee. It is said that at the conclusion of the examination, the other examiner said to Josiah Ogden, "Well, Jo, I guess he knows a little law." "Make it stronger," said Jo, "damned little." But Irving knew very well that not much was expected of him as an attorney. He might take a turn at representing the brothers' business interests, or lobbying for them in Washington, but neither he nor they regarded his commissions or his returns as very weighty. It had already been decided among them that they could afford to indulge their youngest, favorite, and gifted brother to the extent of making him a nominal but profit-sharing partner and so leave him free to cultivate his talents. He would be a proper ornament, and so he was. He had already considered Washington Allston's advice that he turn painter, only to have "doubts and fears gradually cloud over that prospect"; turning now to the opposite extreme, he took a turn at practical politics by participating in a municipal campaign, but one such assay left him and his "forlorn brethren, the Federalists" intolerably beaten and discomfited. While he labored manfully, "talked handbill-fashion with the demagogues, and shook hands with the mob," "was sworn brother to a leash of drawers," and "drank with any tinker in his own language," in the end he had to conclude: "Truly, this saving one's country is a nauseous piece of business, and if patriotism is such a dirty virtue—prithee, no more of it." This does not mean that Irving foreswore for all time any crumbs that might fall into his hands (and several later did) at the dispensation of loaves and fishes in Albany or Washington. Nor did he forget (long after he had given up all ideas of turning painter) his facility at sketching with his pencil a scene for his notebooks when the descriptive power of his words failed him. Keeping a detailed journal early became a confirmed habit, and eventually an inestimable aid to his writing. Emerson called his own journals his "penny-savings bank"; Irving's diaries were in many cases his entire stock-in-trade.

Relieved of business cares by the largesse of his brothers and unconcerned about politics by his own preference, he was free to indulge his tastes and to meet the right people, for whom he had a natural affinity. In Washington he barely arrived before he put on his "pease blossoms and silk stockings" and sallied forth to one of the levees of Dolly Madison, with whom and "half the people in the assemblage" he was "hand in glove" within ten minutes. For the rest he spent his spare hours hobnobbing as agreeably with a knot of "Frenchmen & Democrats" as with his compatriots, the Federalists; and he conducted the regular seasonal campaigns of "banquetry, revelling, dancing, and carousals" in Baltimore, Philadelphia, and "Gotham."

Of a piece with his dilettante pursuit of the law was what he called "the gentlemanly exercise of the pen." If there had been any considerable returns from David Longworth, the printer of *Salmagundi*, and if there had been among their acquaintances any poor-devil authors, he and his writing fraternity might have emulated Byron who, during his expansive youthful years, showed "the same blind contempt for pecuniary gains" and turned the profits of his writings over to his more impecunious scribbling friends. There persisted among them still something of the Renaissance gentleman's attitude toward the products of the pen as the fruits of idle hours, and their monetary gains as beneath a gentleman's notice. When, therefore, "Duskie Davie" volunteered some unsolicited editorial suggestions and voiced objections to the length of the twentieth number of *Salmagundi*, they summarily took their leave and turned to freer pursuits—Irving to another *jeu d'esprit*, a comic history of New York.

Begun with his brother Peter as an *œuvre de joie*, this first full-length book of Irving's turned out quite otherwise before it was finished. Soon after it was fairly begun, the sudden death of Matilda Hoffman threw a pall over the undertaking and a profound and unrelieved gloom over his spirit; but when Peter departed for England, leaving him to go on alone, he rallied, radically revised the plan, and set to a far more serious and prolonged stint of writing than he had ever dreamed possible. After many delays and unanticipated complications, when the book was finally done and the first printing lined his pockets with the tidy sum of three thousand dollars, the young author of twenty-six had learned some serious lessons regarding literary craftsmanship—including the need for painstaking research, meticulous checking of sources, sticking to the plan in hand before giving way to will-o'-the-wisps and vagaries that beckoned invitingly, reliance upon his own resources, however meager they might be, and above all, the necessity for keeping steadily at it, whatever the distractions. The result was a major contribution to the world's store of wit and humor, and its success caused the erstwhile amateur litterateur to have some serious second thoughts then and later, when the once abundant supply of funds from his family diminished. The success of *Knickerbocker* in 1809 confirmed his wish to embrace a writing career, but ten more years were to elapse before he was fully embarked on the road to professional authorship.

Until the War of 1812 began to cloud the horizon, Irving continued merrily as beau, reporter, essayist, satirist, detached politician, and occasional poet to sidestep every commitment that might have resulted in anything so time- and energy-consuming as another full-length book. He occasionally felt the "itching propensity to scribble which every man has who once appeared with any success in print," but did little for two years beyond editing the poems of Thomas Campbell, who then enjoyed in America a vogue nearly equal with that of Scott and Byron. His adulatory biographical sketch won him the friendship of Campbell but served notice that he was unlikely to win many plaudits as a literary critic or that he had as yet arrived at any firm critical principles of his own. Beyond that, it affords the first indication of a mild interest in romantic modes and motifs, of which his writings hitherto had been virtually innocent—an interest that burgeoned a decade later in *The Sketch Book* and made him henceforth a traveler in search of more romantic and picturesque literary provender.

To supplement his irregular education, he immersed himself for varying periods of time in the well-stocked library of his friend Brevoort, or took a turn at lobbying for his brothers' firm in Washington. Next, he devoted upwards of a year to the "irksome business" of editing the *Analectic Magazine*, did a tour of duty as a colonel during the closing years of the War of 1812, and for the rest dutifully slaved in the Liverpool branch of the Irving business but failed to forestall the inevitable collapse of the firm. So ten years clicked by with monotonous regularity while he did little more than form resolutions to resume his interrupted literary career. In the end it was mainly the stimulation of new alliances formed with the reigning literati of London (during brief periods snatched from the grub and grime of the Liverpool counting house), the encouragement of Sir Walter Scott (whom he visited twice at Abbotsford), and the all-too-evident necessity for relying on his pen as the only remaining means to an independent livelihood that led to that rededication of which *The Sketch Book* was born. Begun haltingly and beset by trials of composition and by complications of publication, it proved a greater success even than *Knickerbocker*, and Irving the professional was fairly launched.

Never a tyro in the art of progress through favor, he still dallied with the idea of accepting "some situation of a moderate, unpretending kind," if his friends could swing it; but increasingly his letters and journals put the emphasis on "adding to my literary reputation by the assiduous operations of my pen," on a determination "to win solid credit with the public," "establishing a stock of copyright property," and amassing "a literary estate." So he put by proffered posts in Washington and consular posts elsewhere; he refused the flattering offer of Scott and his friends to edit, for a handsome salary, an anti-Jacobin journal to be founded. He rightly gauged his talents as wayward and his mind too untractable for any regularly recurring task. Indeed, much of Irving's success henceforth was owing to his properly appraising his capacities, or rather his incapacities, and wisely steering his fitful career away from whatever he had learned he could not do well. He knew by now that the only instrument given him was the lowly lyre—that if he would play at all, he must learn to play well on its few strings; that there was little likelihood of swapping the lyre for the harp, or of learning to play variations on an instrument beyond his capacity.

Irving's turn from a devil-may-care scribbler to a circumspect author took place about the time he wrote the stories and essays that form *The Sketch Book*—his first book written specifically for profit. This conversion was accompanied by a more guarded and decorous selection and handling of materials. Heretofore he had not scrupled to paint what the Dutch of New York denigrated as a coarse and libelous caricature of their forebears, or to relate with evident gusto the free love-life of some of the old Dutch worthies—all without the least compunction or remorse. But about the time he turned to writing for a livelihood, he became cautious. In 1818, while preparing a new edition of *Knickerbocker*, he took care to delete certain earthy Elizabethanisms and to remove both anti-British and anti-Catholic passages. He hoped the new *Knickerbocker* and the forthcoming *Sketch Book* might attract readers in Britain as well as in Catholic countries— as, indeed, they did beyond his expectations. But this did not prevent his continuing to record in his journals, for his own edification, any choice morsels he came upon in his travels. Pretty young women continued to elicit near ribald comments, as when he noticed with evident satisfaction meeting a fresh young Irishwoman whom "a man would feel no compunction in begetting children on" (*Journal*, April 8, 1824). Conversely, he made note of "the fierce virtue" of an ugly older woman "who arrogates great merit in preserving what nobody was ever tempted to steal" (*Journal*, Sept. 13, 1822). At Marseilles he recorded with relish how the bootblacks of the town, who knew no English beyond what they had picked up from American sailors, pursued him and his traveling companion, and in an effort to attract their attention and custom, cried, "Monsieur, monsieurs, God dam, God dam son de bish, son de bish." In Syracuse, where he was shown "no less than five thigh bones of St. John the Baptist, three arms of St. Stephen and four jaw bones of St. Peter," he observed in the privacy of his diary, "these disciples must have been an uncommon bony set of fellows." Two months later he was relieved when in Rome, at the church of St. Paul, he was shown "the preserved body of St. Paul." "I was happy to find his bones at length collected together for I had found them in my travels scattered through all the convents of churches I had visited." On another occasion he calculated that if all known fragments of the Cross were collected, they would form "a tolerably stought [sic] ship of the line." Mark

Twain made literary capital of all such tidbits. Not Washington Irving!
The sense of accommodation which prompted him to regard discretion
as the better part of wisdom begat the resolution that whenever he
could not get a dinner to suit his taste, he would endeavor to get a
taste to suit his dinner. He became circumspect, then hesitant, and
finally timorous—lest he give offence in quarters where it might hurt.
And when, after seventeen years of schooling in European decorum,
he returned to his native land in 1832, his sense of propriety was
shocked and outraged at what he saw of Jacksonian democracy in
high places or of the free-and-easy manners of a frontier society. To
his trusted friends he complained that Americans had obviously gone
"masking mad" during his absence, but in his public statements he
measured out his critical and patriotic sentiments guardedly: he com-
plimented his fellow countrymen on the great strides forward of
"progress" that he saw on every hand, and, as for Andrew Jackson,
he confessed to "rather liking the old cock of the walk." Within a
year, this erstwhile Federalist became known as "a Jackson man,"
and was probably not very much surprised when Old Hickory did
not overlook him at the next division of the spoils.

Unconcerned as he had been about arrangements with publishers,
or the exacting requirements of seeing his earlier writings through
the press, he began, while the last numbers of *The Sketch Book* were
being published, to attend to such details, either for himself or through
the competence of Brevoort, and to begin negotiations that were
obviously designed to entice John Murray to become his publisher.
He managed the matter so well that while Murray had refused *The
Sketch Book* in 1819, by May of the next year "the Prince of Booksellers" capitulated. For his part, Murray (said Irving) conducted
himself "in a fair, open and liberal spirit," while Irving was at great
pains to supply Murray with successive successes. At one point, when
Irving sensed a lukewarmness on Murray's part toward a new manuscript, he outfoxed him by suggesting a figure well above what he
expected, only to find Murray taking the bait. The reception of
Bracebridge Hall was a disappointment; yet he played his cards so
well that even *Tales of a Traveller* (the composition of which had
caused him no end of grief so that he knew it was a mishmash) got
him surprisingly good terms from Murray. "Your offer," he wrote to
Murray on March 25, 1824, "of twelve hundred guineas without
seeing the mss. is I confess a liberal one and made in your own
gentlemanlike manner, but I would rather you see the mss. and make
it fifteen hundred" (see also *Journal*, May 29, 1824). In the meantime
he had traveled on the Continent, formed countless new alliances
with great and little men and women, indulged in a variety of literary
undertakings, and learned the ins and outs of the publishing business
as it was conducted in Paris, as well as the complications brought on

by the non-existence of a satisfactory international copyright law. His letters directing his agents or publishers were businesslike and specific, so much so that when it is remembered how nonchalant he had been about the tiresome details of publishing his earlier works (possibly in emulation of Byron's affectations in this regard), he strikes one as following now the older Byron's advice to authors to practice "the good old gentlemanly vice of avarice."

The adroit dealings by which he maneuvered his literary products through various publishers until he made the mutually profitable arrangement with George P. Putnam is a long story, too long to be detailed here, but it betokens a lively interest in, and capacity for, business. Equally important is the care he exercised during 1848–1850 in giving his books a complete and meticulous overhauling for the "Author's Revised Edition" by which he wished the world to know him. Although he complained often and long about slaving at revisions and reading proof in a hot city, while foregoing the comforts of his Sunnyside retreat, he stuck with it to safeguard and enhance his "literary capital." Even after this long chore was completed, he kept touching up individual volumes. *Knickerbocker*, having by then already undergone three complete revisions, was hauled out again for toning-up here and there, and *The Sketch Book* was subjected to a similar refurbishing. A recently discovered copy of an 1854 issue (printed from the 1848 plates) contains extensive revisions on the printed pages and forty-one new interleaves in Irving's handwriting. The precise identification of this volume and the edition for which these alterations were intended awaits exhaustive collation with 1855 and 1857 impressions, but the evidence is enough to suggest that even while Irving was preoccupied with the five-volume *Washington*, he neglected no opportunity if so well-established a volume as *The Sketch Book* could be made to add another mite to his reputation and his income.

During his later years he sometimes allowed his real or fancied need for additional income to get the better of his aesthetic judgment. The compulsion to add "capital" led him to collect in volume form some of his earlier, more ephemeral periodical contributions that might better have been allowed to remain forgotten. It may also have blinded him to John Jacob Astor's motive in enlisting his pen to romanticizing Astoria. And there are other instances (related in detail by Stanley T. Williams in the second volume of his biography) that explain, though they do not entirely excuse, Cooper's saying that Irving always trimmed his sails to the prevailing winds: "What an instinct that man has for gold!" A more charitable man than Cooper might have observed that Irving's later potboiler writings represented simply the overanxious and perhaps ill-considered efforts of the oldest "pro" of the American writers' guild to sell what remained of his literary energy and ability to the best advantage in the popular market.

It may be doubted that when Irving wrote "Rip Van Winkle" and "The Legend of Sleepy Hollow" he was fully aware that he was inventing a new genre; but once it was done, he was not slow to realize what he had done or to understand the techniques of his storytelling art. Thenceforth, as he said, "I have preferred adopting a mode of sketches & short tales rather than long works, because I chose to take a line of writing peculiar to myself, rather than fall into the manner or school of any other writer. . . . I believe the works I have written will be oftener re-read than any novel of the size I could have written." And with true Irvingesque whimsicality he could point out that "if the tales I have furnished should prove to be bad, at least they will be found short."[1]

If in his stories about Rip and Ichabod, he wrote better than he knew, he was not slow to make an astute assessment of the short story's potentialities. By 1824 he recognized the sterility of the then current American novel as an art form, and said as much. In Cooper's case, for example, the format required that it be "In Two Volumes," and it did not matter much whether he strung together a series of short narratives or strung out a short narrative to make two volumes duodecimo. Hawthorne and Melville had not yet demonstrated what could be done in the genre by adapting it to the "romance," as they preferred to call their longer narratives. At any rate, by the end of 1824 Irving knew what he was about, and, possibly with an eye on Cooper, he said, "It is comparatively easy to swell a story to any size when you have once the scheme & the characters in your mind; the mere interest of the story too carries the reader on through pages & pages of careless writing and the author may often be dull for half a volume at a time, if he has some striking scene at the end of it, but in these shorter writings every page must have its merit. The author must be continually piquant—woe to him if he makes an awkward sentence or writes a stupid page; the critics are sure to pounce upon it. Yet if he succeed, the very variety & piquancy of his writings, nay their very brevity, makes them frequently recurred to—and when the mere interest of the story is exhausted, he begins to get credit for his touches of pathos or humour, his points of wit or turns of language. I give these as some of the reasons that have induced me to keep on thus far in the way I have opened for my-self. . . ."

It may be useless to conjecture whether or not he could have written a novel. Certainly he never did (though he started at least one), and there is reason for believing he did not possess the requirements for writing a good play—sustained concentration, searching analysis of character, strict construction of plot, and fine adjustment of numberless details into a continuous fabric of thought. *The Sketch Book* is precisely what the title implies—a collection of sketches, odds and ends, many of them good enough in themselves, but without cohesion, one with another. *Bracebridge Hall* is a collection of stories gleaned from various sources and held together by the mechanical device, as old as *The Arabian Nights,* of having them all related by members of a hunting party marooned in Bracebridge Hall. By the time he wrote *Tales of a Traveller,* he was encountering real difficulty managing his heterogeneous materials, and the result is a hodgepodge in four parts, none of which has any relationship to the others. Irving resented the severity of the critics who took the book apart, but he was fully aware that he had exploited the sketch-book vein to the limit. The result was another change of climate and scene—a trip to and residence in Spain, where once more, under the stimulus of romantic surroundings, he produced something akin to *The Sketch Book's* excellence. Among the productions of his middle and more creative period, *The Alhambra* comes near being a book, in the sense that it is all of a piece, so far at least as atmosphere and tone could make it so. Thereafter he wisely limited himself mainly to biography (interwoven with history) or to the literature of exploration and adventure, chiefly as associated with the western United States. But in any case, the materials for these later works came ready to hand, and except for that inimitable style that was Irving's, he did little more than transcribe what lay before him. When he tried for more, as he did in *Goldsmith,* it was his basic sympathy for the man, in so many ways like himself, that made it an engaging biography. *Washington,* his most ambitious undertaking, is better in details than in conception. It exhibits no great structural skill; the incidents crystallize more around the man than around principles. For the method of the philosophical historian or the critical biographer he had little aptitude; he was at his best when he grasped his subject by his sympathies rather than by rationalization from causes to effects. All in all, his first book, properly so-called, namely *Diedrich Knickerbocker's History of New York,* came nearest to meeting the Aristotelian requirements of unity—in inception, in organization, and in execution; but cold analysis reduces even it to what is basically an aggregation of tales told in chapters and books rather than a continuous story or history.

However readily Irving composed his first literary efforts, he began to encounter trouble about the time he wrote *The Sketch Book.* Congenitally a man of moods, he was given to feelings of indolence, indirection, ineffectuality, melancholy, self-depreciation, insecurity, enervation, sterility, and despair. For months he did little more than register the state of his personal thermometer ten times daily. This preoccupation with the moody state of his mind first, last, and all the time becomes positively torturous for the reader of his journals, and belies the reputation he had of being habitually and by nature the soul of gaiety and geniality. If he managed to show the world the brighter side of himself, it was because he instinctively and consciously withdrew from social intercourse when he felt the dark moods coming on. So he carefully watched himself and nursed his oversensitive disposition. Following the great success of *The Sketch Book* he confided to his friend Leslie, "Now you suppose I am all on the alert, and full of spirit and excitement. No such thing. I am just as good for nothing as ever I was; and, indeed, have been flurried and put out by these puffings. I feel something as I suppose you did when your picture met with success—anxious to do something better, and at a loss what to do."[2]

"What to do next" became from now on a haunting worry and the natural cause for many ill-conceived plans, misdirected efforts, or false starts. At the time he refused Scott's offer to turn editor, he confessed, "My whole course of life has been desultory, and I am unfitted for any periodically recurring task, or any stipulated labor of body or mind. I have no command of my talents such as they are, and have to watch the varyings of my mind as I would a weather cock. Practice and training may bring me more into rule; but at present I am as useless for regular service as one of my own country Indians or a Don Cossack. I must, therefore, keep on pretty much as I have begun—writing when I can, not when I would. I shall occasionally shift my residence and write whatever is suggested by objects before me, or whatever runs in my imagination, and hope to write better and more copiously by and by."[3] He probably never wrote better than he did just then. This much is certain: whenever he wrote "more copiously," he did not compose as well. Often he gave way to distractions, if only to avoid the ordeal of sitting at the table unable to do more than chew his pen; and so he spent as much time preparing to write as in writing. These hesitations and doubts and the variety of uncongenial works undertaken, always with little satisfaction to himself, give evidence of the uncertainty of mind that never ended but did subside somewhat after he was fairly launched on the routine work of his biographical and historical research in Spain—that is, after he turned from composition to compilation. Routine proved a good wall to which to retreat. Even so, writing remained for him hard, agonizing work, and he had to drive himself mercilessly. During his last illness, when he was given the fifth and last volume of *Washington,* just arrived from the printer, he said with obvious and heartfelt relief, "Thank Heaven! Henceforth I give up all tasking with the pen!" Under these circumstances, the dilettante or tyro would never have produced the stout twenty-seven volumes that comprise Irving's literary output; only Irving the professional could pull it off. And the wonder is, as Dr. Samuel Johnson might have said, not that he did it so well, but that he did it at all.

We need not quarrel with Irving for not attempting what he could not and *knew* he could not do well. It is enough if we are to appreciate his doing so well with so little. His success is owing largely to his husbanding his slender store of genius and measuring out carefully his slim stock-in-trade. This studied procedure bespeaks the craftsman who knows his business rather than the divine amateur who expects a miracle. He believed he could do his countrymen a greater service chronicling Hudson River legends and bringing to them a touch of merry England and romantic Spain than by overtaxing his talents and tiring his readers' patience with moral or philosophical disquisitions; he calculated correctly that as an intermediary between old-world culture and new-world rawness and as a romancer in the sphere of belles-lettres he would speak to better purpose than as politician or preacher. "I have attempted no lofty theme, nor sought to look wise and learned, which appears to be very much the fashion among our American writers at present. . . . I seek only to blow a flute accompaniment in the national concert, and leave others to play the fiddle and French horn."[4] This careful calculation of his own potential labels him less the amateur toying with esoteric aspirations beyond his reach than the canny professional gauging his grasp by his reach.

Notes

1. *Letters of Washington Irving to Henry Brevoort*, ed. George S. Hellman (Library ed., 2 vols. in 1, New York, 1918), pp. 398–400.

2. Pierre M. Irving, *The Life and Letters of Washington Irving* (New York, 1862–1864), 1, 415.

3. *Ibid.*, 1, 441–42.

4. *Ibid.*, 1, 415, 416.

Washington Irving and the Theatre
Walter A. Reichart[*]

When Washington Irving, famous on both sides of the Atlantic since the publication of "The Sketch Book" and "Bracebridge Hall," arrived on the continent in the summer of 1822, he continued to be fascinated by the theatre despite his limited knowledge of French

[*] Reprinted by permission from *Maske und Kothurn* 14 (1968): 341–50.

and German. The stage had been a passion in his early youth and his first immature efforts at writing, which lack literary merit, have some interest because of his enthusiastic preoccupation with the theatre. These "Letters of Jonathan Oldstyle, Gent." had originally appeared anonymously in nine issues of the New York "Morning Chronicle" (1802/03), and are amateurish essays that won contemporary popularity. Irving's literary success almost twenty years later brought unauthorized printings in book form in New York and London (1824) and at the same time a German translation of a selection in "Der Gesellschafter oder Blätter für Geist und Herz," followed by a German edition (Duncker und Humblot, Berlin 1824), despite Irving's complete disavowal of these youthful indiscretions.

Most of the essays dealt with the drama in New York, the splendor of the new Park Theatre, the ranting of the actors, and the vulgarity of the audience. Irving was more than an eager theatre-goer, he was a hanger-on at stage doors and in the green-rooms, as in London a score of years later.[1] He saw the favorites of the day, John Hodgkinson, George F. Cooke, Thomas A. Cooper, and Elizabeth Kemble Whitlock, the sister of the famous Mrs. Siddons. Irving became their friend and paid homage to them behind the scenes, but he was also their critic. Especially Hodgkinson, whose rotundity and exaggerated mannerisms offended good taste, became the object of Oldstyle's ridicule. Because of his friendship with Cooper, who became the manager of the Park Theatre in 1806, Irving was persuaded to write a prologue, some hundred lines of youthful doggerel, that Cooper spoke the opening night of September 9, 1807.[2]

Irving's first trip to Europe in 1804, made primarily for his health, interrupted his study of law and a preoccupation with the theatre, but aroused an interest in and enthusiasm for Europe which later made him an expatriate for many years. Despite the critical and turbulent times that Napoleon now dominated, Bordeaux seemed indifferent to political events and provided Irving with glimpses of great acting. In a long letter to one of his cronies in New York he wrote:

> "The Grand Theatre is a superb building. The outside, particularly the front, is a masterpiece of workmanship and bears a most majestic appearance. I have been twice at that theatre to see Lafon one of the most celebrated French tragedians, and a competitor of Talma's though the latter is generally reckoned superior. Lafon is a young man and is not a veteran, like Talma. He possesses a handsome and commanding figure, his motions are graceful and his countenance extremely expressive. His voice is well toned, but his lungs are rather weak. This occasions him to fall off sometimes in his latter scenes, when he becomes fatigued with violent exertion and his voice grows hoarse. He is however a noble fellow, and

made me regret severely my ignorance of the language, which prevented my enjoying the excellence of his performance."[3]

Irving left Bordeaux for Genoa on August 5, 1804, and missed the opportunity of witnessing performances of Talma, who appeared later in the month, but during Irving's first visit to Paris (May 24 to September 22, 1805) began his more intimate acquaintance with the French theatre. Records show that he probably saw Lafon in Voltaire's "Oedipe" and in a French version of "Philoctète." Irving frequented seven different theatres and saw seventeen performances which ran the range from opera and ballet to the popular entertainment of vaudeville, melodrama, and variété. An American friend "joked me about my going to Theatre Montansier before any of the other theatres—it being the most disreputable theatre in the city."[4] Not until 1821, when Irving was introduced by his friend, John Howard Payne, was a personal friendship established with Talma.

After four months of travel on the continent Irving eagerly sought England, the land of his forefathers. Fifteen years later as a distinguished author he was welcome in Murray's drawing room and at Holland House, where Moore, Campbell, and Rogers dazzled the self-effacing young American. Now he was a stranger in London with only a letter from Mrs. John Johnston of the Park Theatre to Miss De Camp at Covent Garden. Before Irving left London and sailed home he had seen about twenty-nine different plays, Shakespeare, Restoration dramas, and the popular melodramas of the day.[5] He met Charles Kemble as well as John Philip Kemble, the manager of Covent Garden Theatre, but all his enthusiasm was reserved for Mrs. Siddons, now fifty years old and yet the most famous performer on the English stage. He saw her in Otway's "Venice Preserved" and Rowe's "Fair Penitent," and wrote his brother:

"Were I to indulge without reserve in my praises of Mrs. Siddons, I am afraid you would think them hyperbolical. What a wonderful woman! The very first time I saw her performance I was struck with admiration. It was in the part of Calista. Her looks, her voice, her gestures, delighted me. She penetrated in a moment to my heart. She froze and melted it by turns; a glance of her eye, a start, an exclamation, thrilled through my whole frame. The more I see her, the more I admire her. I hardly breathe while she is on stage. She works up my feelings till I am like a mere child. And yet this woman is old, and has lost all elegance of figure; think then what must be her powers that she can delight and astonish even in the characters of Calista and Belvidera."[6]

The next ten years saw Irving in New York, where he passed the examinations for the bar but devoted his energies to establish himself as a man of letters. "Salmagundi" (1807/08), a series of light satirical essays on the foibles of New York, first published serially, was an instantaneous success. Soon the names of Washington Irving, William Irving, and James K. Paulding were linked with the anonymous satirical publication. About this time Irving met John Howard Payne, whose "Home, Sweet Home" in "Clari or The Maid of Milan" (1823) alone has given him a semblance of immortality, and formed a lifelong friendship that led many years later to literary collaboration in Europe. In 1809 Payne made his début in the role of Young Norval in John Home's "The Tragedy of Douglas or the Noble Shepherd," after having astonished his friends three years earlier, as a fourteen year old boy, with a comedy, "Julia or the Wanderer," performed at the Park Theatre in New York. Boy actors were something of a novelty and Payne, who was small for his age and looked even younger, became the rage. Master Payne, as he was regularly billed, came to be known as "the American Roscius." He played in Baltimore, Philadelphia, Richmond, Charleston, Washington, and Boston, where he became the first American to play the role of Hamlet. In 1813 he repeated his successes in England, established his contacts with the London stage (for which he and Washington Irving adapted popular French comedies ten years later), and even managed for a season Sadler's Wells, probably London's oldest theatre.

Only "A History of New York" (1809, and promptly reprinted with alterations in 1812) and the English reprint of "Salmagundi" (1811) identified Irving to a small group of discerning Englishmen when he reached England in 1815, but five years later "The Sketch Book" made him "the most fashionable fellow of the day"[7] in London and the first American man of letters, eagerly welcomed in England, France, and Germany. Payne had become sufficiently established as an adapter of popular French plays of the day, usually melodramas, to be sent by Elliston to Paris as an agent for the Drury Lane Theatre. It was a time when London Theatres were crowded and the managers had difficulty in satisfying the demands of an enthusiastic, if not discriminating audience. Innumerable hack-writers attempted to supply this demand for ". . . the theatre-writers sought not for a new way of art, but for that which, being familiar, could hardly fail to make an appeal . . . They wrote plays, as a cobbler makes shoes, for the purpose of bringing in a few pence or a few pounds, and consequently they sought in Paris, not for what was new and vital, but for what was old and sure to please."[8]

Washington Irving met Payne in Paris in April, 1821, listened eagerly to his friend, "full of dramatic projects, and some that are very feasible," but was not quite ready to try his own hand at writing for the stage.[9] He saw Talma in "Hamlet" and called with Payne upon the famous tragedian. Many years later he expanded the rough notes in his journal and published them as "Conversations with Talma."[10]

Almost two years passed—his literary reputation was enhanced by the publication of "Bracebridge Hall"—before Irving succumbed to the illusory hope of achieving distinction as a dramatist. After traveling widely on the continent Irving took up residence in Dresden in the autumn of 1822 and soon became part of the English colony, eagerly welcomed by court society and the literary aspirants of the "Dresdener Liederkreis." The theatre and the opera delighted Irving. Ludwig Tieck and Carl Maria von Weber were the dominant figures in the world of drama and music. Irving met them both and many lesser figures, but was gradually so completely captivated by the congenial atmosphere of an English drawing room that he neglected his growing concern for German literature.

His friendship with the Fosters of Bedford, England, who had been living in Dresden for two years, brought him under the influence of their cousin Barham Livius, an enthusiastic adapter of popular French comedies. Livius' "Maid or Wife or The Deceiver Deceived," a musical comedy, based on very pleasant little Parisian comedy by Mons. Dupin and successfully produced at the Drury Lane Theatre in 1821, had launched the embryo dramatist. The next year he wrote the music for J.R. Planché's "All in the Dark or, The Banks of the Elbe" and collaborated further in "Fair Gabrielle."[11] Now he aroused Irving's interest in amateur theatricals and in the next few months Fielding's burlesque, "The Tragedy of Tragedies or The Life and Death of Tom Thumb," Livius' own "Maid or Wife," Arthur Murphy's "Three Weeks after Marriage," and Mrs. Centlivre's "The Wonder, a Woman Keeps a Secret" were performed before appreciative audiences of friends. Irving altered and arranged the pieces to fit the available cast, searched a masquerade warehouse for suitable costumes, and played the leading male roles. He proudly proclaimed his success with a typical humorous flourish in a letter to Leslie: "We have been getting up private theatricals here at the house of an English lady. I have already enacted Sir Charles Rackett in "Three Weeks after Marriage," with great applause, and am on the point of playing Don Felix in "The Wonder." I had no idea of this fund of dramatic talent lurking within me; and I now console myself that if the worst comes to the worst, I can turn stroller, and pick up a decent maintenance among the barns in England."[12]

Soon Livius enlisted Irving's help in translating and adapting Weber's "Der Freischütz" and "Abu Hassan," but progress was slow because of the delightful distractions of Dresden society. Irving visited the theatre regularly. En route to Dresden he had already seen some trivial plays by Frau von Weissenthurn, Holbein, and others, but he had also heard "Der Freischütz" in Darmstadt and Munich, "Fidelio" in Vienna, and "The Barber of Seville" in Prague. Dresden afforded him the opportunity to see Shakespeare, to be sure in German translations and unfortunately in popular adaptations that did violence to the original. He witnessed twice within a week Schröder's prose version of "King Lear" with a conciliatory ending, he saw "Hamlet" in A. W. Schlegel's translation (which Irving attributed to Schiller), and "The Merchant of Venice" with Werdy as Shylock. Aside from the popular comedies of Schröder, Jünger, Houwald, Castelli, Iffland, and Hell, Irving saw "Die Piccolomini," "Wallensteins Tod," "Jery und Bätely," "Der Prinz von Homburg," and "Das Käthchen von Heilbronn."

When Irving returned to Paris in August, 1823, his passion for the stage tempted him to become a full-fledged collaborator of John Howard Payne. The apparent success in preparing private theatricals had encouraged unwarranted hopes of winning laurels in the more impressive and perhaps more lucrative field of the drama. Throughout the winter and spring of 1823 Irving's notations in the "Journals" reveal how he first helped Livius with the lyrics for "Der Freischütz" and gradually determined to adapt the work in its entirety. He also began a translation of Weber's earlier success, "Abu Hassan," a Singspiel based on a tale from the "Thousand and One Nights," for which he "finish[ed] the alterations" before leaving for Prague, ("Journal," May 18, 1823.) Payne, too, was busily engaged in adaptations, hoping to achieve another great success, as had been the case with the operetta, "Clari or The Maid of Milan." Irving's reputation in England and his friendship with Robert Elliston and Stephen Price, both managers of Drury Lane in the 1820's, and Charles Kemble, the famous actor and manager of Covent Garden, might strengthen Payne's foothold on the London stage. Irving was also inclined "to accept the proposition of Payne to assist him in his pursuits and divide the profits of their joint dramatic manufacture, with the understanding that his agency was to be kept secret," and characterized his collaboration in a letter to his brother as "a slight literary job which I hope will put some money in my pocket without costing much time or trouble, or committing my name."[13]

Irving's intensive and serious concern to make such adaptations of light French theatrical fare is well documented because Payne left for London in October and remained for almost two years, constantly negotiating with stage managers and reporting to his collaborator. He took with him "Azendai," "Richelieu," and "Married and Single," of which the last two, after constant altering and rewriting, were eventually performed in London.

Some extracts from Irving's letters (Payne Collection, Columbia University) reveal the tribulations of these amateur dramatists:

Paris, November 12, 1823

. . . Let me know, if Azendai is approved, about what time it will be wanted—I shall write songs for it as soon as I can get in the rhyming vein again. I believe I told you that I had rewritten Henry V—tho' somewhat hastily. It will now I think, make a very pleasing drama, with the assistance of a few songs—to make it a complete opera would be very difficult.

I wish you to ascertain whether Kemble has rec[d] the corrected copy of the Freyschütz from Livius & what he feels disposed to do in the matter. I wish Abu Hassan to be offered to Elliston, by Miller, as from Livius . . .

November 22[d], 1823

. . . Kemble has accepted Richelieu in as short a time as could be expected, considering that he had others to consult, who had to read a long play before they gave judg[men]t.

I don't care which theatre takes Azendai—nor do I care much if either of them takes it—I beg you will let it be understood I ask nothing as a favor, and by no means advise their accepting a piece, as extending a kind of patronage. I feel perfectly independent of the theatre—tho' I feel more and more that I have dramatic stuff within me.

November 26th, 1823

I yesterday forwarded by the Diligence the Ms of La Jeunesse and at the same time 'The mother's crime,' & 'Le contrabandier' directed to you, care of Miller . . .

Do not suffer yourself, under any circumstances, to make a sacrifice of any of the pieces; if the theatres make difficulties, withdraw the pieces at once—they'll accept them at some future time. Don't let them think they can beat you down & get bargains out of you.

December 17th, 1823

. . . I shall be satisfied with any bargain you may make; recollect only, that I do not wish my name, on any account, to appear in connexion with them. It would be quite injurious to my present plans . . .

I send you five Plays in which Leontine Fay performed, viz: La nouvelle Clari—La petite lampe merveilleuse—Le mariage enfantin—La petite folle—La petite soeur . . .

Jan. 31, 1824

. . . Richelieu and Rochester if tolerably performed will do you credit and operate favorably for you in future dealings. You must not hesitate to claim them as your production; though to satisfy scruple & obviate cavilling you may say they have been revised & occasionally touched up by a literary friend—I wish however, my name to be kept completely out of sight.

I am sorry to say I cannot afford to write any more for the

theatres. The experience has satisfied me that I never should in any wise be compensated for my time and trouble. I speak not with any reference to my talents; but to the market price my productions will command in other departments of literature.

So candid an admission of failure did not terminate Irving's participation in Payne's play production. He continued to search for suitable plays and encouraged Payne. "I cannot afford to work for the theatre with sufficient zeal to entitle me to any reward, but I may help you to an occasional hint or a coup de plume," he wrote on March 24, 1824, after having secured F. W. Ziegler's "Parteyenwuth oder die Kraft des Glaubens." Already in January Irving had begun reading this drama with real interest.

> The scene in England in 1651, during the time of the covenanters. I saw it acted at Prague & was very much struck with it— on reading it over I am still more pleased—a very striking and spirited play might be made from it; with strongly marked characters. There is a coldblooded, crafty, meagre, hypocritical, merciless Judge with his coadjutor, a gore-bellied, bullying, swashbuckler colonel of the covenanters, that makes two prominent, half comic, half fearful characters in the piece. Had I been encouraged by the success of Richelieu I could have made a powerful piece of this— but, as it is, I cannot afford to touch it.[14]

Actually Irving was tempted again to revise and adapt a play that delighted him because of its historical background. In a letter of October 4, 1824, he was still concerned with it, complaining about inaccuracies in matters of "English law and English manners" and continuing, "every thing relating to the trials is contrary to laws & custom. There are fine characters & fine situations & good dialogue in the play; but it must be remodelled entirely for the English stage; & will then I think have great success. It will require some thought & labour, but it is worth a little time and trouble." Irving was very much concerned with Payne's career as a dramatist because of his own constant participation in preparing the final draft of these adaptations. In January, 1825, Irving returned "The Spanish Husband," a play that was finally produced at Drury Lane, May 25, 1829, with the comments, "terribly slashed and transposed. I have thought it necessary to make great alterations," but remained enthusiastic about its future. ". . . if ten theatres were to send it back it would only prove to me that they wanted discernment. It is a play which I am convinced will succeed and will give you both profit and reputation" (Letter of June 22, 1825).

In such a manner Irving continued to dabble in theatricals, sending news of Parisian successes, texts of popular plays, and much advice about innumerable adaptations that Payne was processing in his workshop. Unfortunately the results were meager and Payne acknowledged his discouragement:

> I have had such a stormy time for the last three or four months, and have been working so hard, that the very sight of pens, ink and paper, make me uncomfortable. I am nearly at the end of my thousand octavo pages, have had one play damned,—the opera returned from three theatres 'as not likely to prove successful in representation,'—a melodrama accepted,—three others ordered, finished and sent back because the Managers had altered their plans,—two of Elliston's bills dishonoured,—a two act drama commanded by Covent Garden which is now in their hands . . . (Letter of June 10, 1825).

Irving's most successful efforts at collaboration with Payne were based on French dramatic trifles from the pen of Alexander Duval, whose "La Jeunesse de Henry V" and "La Jeunesse de Richelieu" furnished the material for Payne's "Charles II or the Merry Monarch," a comedy in three acts with some songs, and "Richelieu." Irving created the character of Captain Copp, whose "horrible, rough old song" shocked and delighted London audiences. Irving was present at the second performance at Covent Garden, May 28, 1824, and noted, "it succeeds very well, though the critics attack the language."[15]

"Richelieu" created more serious problems. After years of writing and rewriting by Irving and Payne, the London theatrical management altered the plot, renamed the villainous hero in deference to the French minister to England, a kinsman of Richelieu, and called the play "The French Libertine." Six performances completed its London run. And this was the play which carried a generally recognized dedication expressing gratitude to Irving, the silent partner, for "aid [that] has been repeated to such an extent in the present work, as to render it imperative upon me to offer you my thanks publicly, and to beg you will suffer me to dedicate it to one from whose pen it has received its highest value."

Irving's dramatic writings were experimental. His literary ambitions tempted him to try his hand at various genres. Scattered poems, fragments of novels like "Rosalie" and "Buckthorne" give evidence of a desire to be more than an essayist or story-teller. In his preoccupation with the drama he also worked independently of Payne and completed, "The Wild Huntsman" ("Der Freischütz") and "Abu Hassan," Weber's operatic successes. Little was known of these adaptations until George S. Hellman published limited editions of these works from extant manuscripts for the Boston Bibliophile Society in 1924. Irving had become an enthusiastic admirer of Weber's music, had heard the "Freischütz" five times while in Germany, and met the composer in Dresden. In his ill-fated attempt to succeed in a literary genre foreign to his talents, Irving was first encouraged by Livius, who was eager to be first upon the London stage with an English version. Allardyce Nicoll lists five adaptations and a few parodies,[16] and this particular text, like all the others, a trifling piece of translation and adaptation, has actually been credited to three writers, to James Robinson Planché, who in his "Recollections" speaks of it as "my version of that opera, produced at Covent Garden, 14th October, 1824, to Barham Livius, who published it over his name with appropriate acknowledgments for help received, and to Washington Irving, for whom the editor, George S. Hellman, claimed it in its entirety.

A comparison of the text, published in 1924 by Hellman from the original manuscript, with that printed by Livius exactly a hundred years earlier, reveals only minor differences. Essentially the same text, it is, therefore, difficult to attribute particular parts of the translation and adaptation to either. Livius and Irving worked closely together in Dresden and Paris. They conferred and consulted, they wrote and recast their text frequently, as Irving's entries in his journals indicate. Their partnership was a fair one, but even their joint efforts were inadequate. Livius knew German better and had more experience in translating, but Irving's literary training provided more poetic quality and literary style. Livius was more familiar with music and had written a successful musical comedy, but neither had much practical knowledge of the theatre or—what was even more essential at the time—had the friendly ear of London managers. Payne failed to place the opera with Kemble and by the time Livius had persuaded him, three other adaptations were on the boards in London. Irving's libretto attempted to make the play more palatable to British taste and British morals. The prefatory remarks to the printed version extol poetic justice:

> The hero of the German author is represented as of a feeble undecided character; half saint, half sinner; he is easily prevailed on to employ foul means to accomplish his purpose, and is timid only as to the process of procuring those means; he tampers with the devil in a sort of half-and-half manner, as if he would sell half his soul and retain the other half to be saved upon . . .
>
> Attempt has been made in the present Opera, to obviate this glaring defect, so far at least as was possible, in writing a drama under the trammels of music already composed. It has been endeavoured to describe the hero of the piece inflexible in virtue— firm in resisting temptation, and spurning all base and sinister means of obtaining success; his confidence in Providence remains unshaken, and his steadfastness and constancy meet with their merited reward.[17]

And so Irving and Livius added and renamed characters, introduced high-sounding phrases and self-righteous moralizing in order to free the hero from any reproach of soliciting help from the devil. They diluted still further what was already a thin operatic plot, but despite it all they helped to establish Carl Maria von Weber's fame in England.

Irving's second attempt at translation, his version of "Abu Hassan," based upon a popular tale from the "Arabian Nights Entertainments," in which the Caliph's boon companion plays a trick upon his master in order to fatten his own purse, was never performed. A new vogue had struck the London stage and equestrian feats became an applauded part of theatre performances. Planché with his "Cortez or the Conquest of Peru" had scored such a hit with the novelty of cavalry appearing in full gallop that Payne wrote Irving from London: "Nothing answers now but the horses. I could not speak of terms at a first interview . . . and they have no room for Abul Hassan this season, unless, as some one observed, horses could be put in it!!!"[18]

Still Irving could not free himself from the spell of the stage. He continued to toy with operatic plots, helped Livius write and revise the text of "Léocadie" by Scribe and Mélesville, and struck out for himself with a "plan for dramatic work on story of 'El Embozado' "[19] This story of the dual nature of man had come to Irving's attention during his Spanish studies that began in 1825. Busy as he was with the constant altering of "Richelieu" he quietly pursued his own theatrical ambitions. Charles Kemble visited him in Paris in September. They talked about the Theatre, about Payne's circumstances, and about Irving's own dramatic plants. Irving heard with apparent pleasure that "Kemble wanted me to write a play. Declined for the present—."[20] How revealing is Irving's temporary refusal! Vague hopes of a future stage success stirred him to new action. His journal entries tell the story:

Oct. 26: Conceived plan of Play—Cavalier—noted down a hint or two . . . got Clarendon's "History of the Rebellion and Civil Wars in England Begun in the Year 1641."
Oct. 27: Sketched a little at the first act . . .
Oct. 28: Retouched the first act—get on but slowly—no excitement . . .
Oct. 29: More excited—rewrote the part I had already written of 1ᵗ Act—
Oct. 30: Wrote at the Cavalier—altering & rewriting first act . . .
Oct. 31: Laboured today at the play but very little to my satisfaction . . .
Nov. 1: . . . tried to write this morning but the news of Mr. Williams' failure had incapacitated me . . .

Nov. 2: Forced myself to write a little at the Cavalier—but did not satisfy myself . . .

Constantly revising and rewriting, Irving never reached the second act, experiencing his usual difficulties in maintaining the mood and continuing a sustained effort. The news of his banker's failure, which threatened his own and his brother's financial security, forced him to take stock. He could no longer afford indulging himself. The critics' hostile reception of "The Tales of a Traveller" haunted him, a vague fear that he had exhausted his particular genre of literature made him discard his essays on American character, and his hopes as a playwright were gone. He found consolation and distraction in travel and society, but sought frantically a new field of endeavor. He had already looked wistfully toward Spain, a yet unexplored realm that beckoned to him, and had begun Spanish studies. Irving made some overtures to his friend, the American Minister at Madrid. Suddenly a new opportunity presented itself and he could turn his back upon the theatrical hack-work that was clearly onerous to him. In a letter to Payne, dated Bordeaux, February 7, 1826, he joyously proclaimed the news: "I am on the wing for Madrid! A letter from our Minister Mr. Everett has determined me to go on without delay; for the purpose of translating into English a very interesting work printing here. The Voyage of Columbus compiled from his own papers."[21]

Irving the historian of "Columbus," the writer of "The Conquest of Granada" and of "The Alhambra" was launched. The second half of his career as a writer was just beginning.

Notes

1. Stanley T. Williams, The Life of Washington Irving, New York 1935, 1, p. 37.

2. Unfortunately they were preserved and reprinted. See P. M. Irving, The Life and Letters of Washington Irving, New York 1862, 1, pp. 204–206.

3. Cited from the original in the Yale University collection in S. T. Williams, The Life, 1, p. 49. Peculiarities of Irving's spelling here and later are normalized.

4. S. T. Williams, Washington Irving's First Stay in Paris, American Literature, 2 (1930), pp. 15–20. Irving saw Talma, Lafon, and Mlle. Georges in Raynouard's tragedy "Les Templiers" at the Théâtre Français, but noted: "Talma fine figure— great powers[.] I do not admire French style of acting."

5. The Life and Letters, 1, p. 72.

6. Ibidem, 1, p. 158 f.

7. C. R. Leslie, Autobiographical Recollections, Boston 1860, p. 230.

8. Allardyce Nicoll, A History of Early Nineteenth Century Drama 1800–1850, Cambridge 1930, 1, p. 80 f.

9. This journal entry and the detailed account of calling upon Talma and wit-

nessing his performance of "Hamlet" are printed in: The Life and Letters, 2, pp. 41–43.

10. In: The Knickerbocker Gallery: A Testimonial to the Editor of The Knickerbocker Magazine from its Contributors, New York 1855, pp. 15–22.

11. Walter A. Reichart, Washington Irving's Friend and Collaborator: Barham John Livius, Esq., PMLA, 56 (1941), pp. 513–531.

12. C. R. Leslie, Autobiographical Recollections, Boston 1860, p. 252.

13. The Life and Letters, 2, p. 166 f.

14. Letter of 31 January, 1824. He had ordered this play and others from Treuttel et Würtz, inquired impatiently for it, and received it on 9 January 1824, as his journal entries show.

15. Letter to his brother, in: The Life and Letters, 2, p. 194.

16. A History of Early Nineteenth Century Drama 1800–1850, Cambridge 1930, 2, "Handlist of Plays".

17. The Freyschütz, by Barham Livius, Esq., London 1824, p. v–viii.

18. Quoted in: The Life and Letters, 2, p. 171.

19. Journal entry of 25 March 1825. A few loose sheets with a detailed outline of the contemplated scenes of the first act have survived in the journal ending with 4 November 1825.

20. Journal entry of 11 September 1825.

21. John Howard Payne Collection, Columbia University.

Irving: A Littérateur in Politics   Donna Hagensick°

Although Washington Irving is recognized primarily for his literary contributions, he also is remembered for his role in the politics of his time. Irving's political associations fall roughly into two periods: those in which he was involved before leaving for Europe in 1815; and the allegiances he developed from the time he accepted a diplomatic post in London in 1829 to the termination of his Spanish mission in 1846. Irving was associated with or sympathetic to four political parties during these periods: The Federalists and Republicans during the first; the Democrats and Whigs during the second. He was involved in little or no political activity of any consequence in Europe from 1815 until 1829, or after resigning his position as minister to Spain until his death in 1859.

Much has been made of the shifts in Irving's political affiliations. Many of his contemporaries and later critics[1] level either harsh attacks against this "chameleon" who could not decide where he belonged, or imply that he was politically naive and did not really know what

° Reprinted by permission of Kenneth Walter Cameron, holder of copyright, from Washington Irving Reconsidered: A Symposium, ed. Ralph M. Aderman (Hartford: Transcendental Books, 1969); 53–60.

he was doing. However, a careful study of Irving would seem to remove him both from the class of "turncoat" and political neophyte. The facets of Irving's thought and personality considered are political theories, biases and attitudes toward practical politics. Sometimes it is impossible to draw a fine distinction among these topics, but overall a nonchronological approach seems to provide a better background for distinguishing how these elements intermingled.

Irving was imbued with a variety of political biases. Some of these were tempered or altered through the years, but certain of them were sustained throughout his life. It becomes apparent, however, in tracing these political biases, that he held relatively few consistently strong convictions. On many issues he was temperamentally quite able to vacillate; sometimes because he was indifferent, other times because his desire to compromise was stronger than his belief. There are two basic ideas, however, which he continually held. These include ardent nationalism, or patriotism; and an inherent conservatism.

These political biases, however, do not represent an intellectual commitment to a political philosophy, since it also seems that Irving was singularly lacking as a contributor of political thought. He understood American politics, but he did not exert or was incapable of exerting an influence in the area of political theory. He sums himself up best, perhaps, in the introductory essay, "The Author," in *Bracebridge Hall:* "I am no politician. The more I have considered the study of politics, the more I have found it full of perplexity; and I have contented myself, as I have in my religion, with the faith in which I was brought up. . . ."[2] This statement, which shows Irving adopting a kind of non-thinking attitude toward politics, exemplifies an approach which was to cause him trouble in subsequent years.

The contention that Irving was completely immune to great ideas,[3] however, seems as extreme as the one that he "thought clearly and aggressively on questions of government."[4] The former implies that he was somehow politically moronic, which certainly was never true. Though void of original contributions, he understood the essence of the conservatism he advocated: ". . . his Federalism was no passive bending before the wind—indeed, the wind was blowing a gale the other way."[5] Irving cherished his beliefs throughout a period when the easier path would have led him to the camp of the opposition. The latter contention, on the other hand, tends to imbue the author with a more fundamental philosophy of government than he possessed. Irving's thoughts may have been clear and aggressive in certain respects, but they were largely one-sided. For example, in *A History of New York,* he satirized, but he offered no alternative solutions to the problems outlined beyond those proffered by his party—and these were considered unworkable by the majority of people. Indeed, his party was in its death throes. Irving, in this sense, was too greatly influenced and motivated by external considerations to apply much creative thought to the problems of conservatives.

This is, for example, demonstrated not only by his defense of Aaron Burr in 1807, but by his apparent inability to recognize that through personal feelings he had "aligned himself on this issue with such people as Andrew Jackson . . ."[6] at a time when he could have nothing but political antipathy for the man. Similarly, in later years, Irving would never understand the attacks from a man like James Fenimore Cooper, whose criticism rested largely on intellectual grounds.[7] In fact, when one examines Irving solely from an intellectual perspective, it is indeed difficult to account for the man's seemingly fantastic leaps from Federalism to Jacksonian democracy, from warm friendship with Martin Van Buren to his opposite, John Jacob Astor, from a literary career which left him considerable freedom to diplomatic posts which continually demanded time and attention. But Irving's thought processes apparently were not sufficiently deep to carry him beyond the formation of some relatively uncomplicated precepts which readily allowed the varied alliances and allegiances he entered.

Yet, in 1838, on the eve of his break with Van Buren, Irving outlined some of his political beliefs in a letter to Gouverneur Kemble: "As far as I know my own mind, I am thoroughly a republican, and attached . . . to the institutions of my country; but I am a republican without gall, and have no bitterness in my creed. I have no relish for puritans either in religion or politics, who are for pushing principles to an extreme. . . . Ours is a government of compromise. We have several great and distinct interests bound up together, which, if not separately consulted and severally accommodated, may harass and impair each other."[8] While representing a direct attack on Van Buren and a parting with him in politics, this letter, of course, is most valuable as it reflects Irving: compromise is essential to the effective operation of the government; political principles must be set aside in the interests of the country. What Irving is outlining is an operational rather than a theoretical approach to the problems of government. He is right, perhaps, insofar as a discussion of effective administration is concerned, but his statements do not reflect an intellectual commitment to a particular philosophy. This, at least in part it seems, accounts for his ability to make political shifts. An examination of Irving's political biases, however, is necessary to show how and why he made these changes.

The seeds of political conservatism were sown early in his youth. His father was a Federalist, and though some of Irving's brothers evidenced Republican leanings, the family was generally conservative in its outlook.[9] In some measure, Irving was a product of his culture:

the son of a merchant family with social aspirations; reared in New York City, the center of Federalist politics; and, educated in the law, however imperfectly, by Josiah Ogden Hoffman, a prominent Federalist.[10]

Irving emerged from this background with a distinctly Federalist ideology. Broadly this meant endorsing the political ideas of Alexander Hamilton, while opposing those of Thomas Jefferson. More specifically it meant favoring nationalism over sectionalism; commercialism over agrarianism; and, the rights of wealth and property over the rights of the common people or mob.

Whether Irving reached these early political convictions instinctively or through conscious reasoning,[11] is not, for our purposes, particularly material. Certainly his temperament, attitudes and tastes would cause him to gravitate toward the party which represented the aristocracy to which he longed to belong.[12] It seems unlikely, however, that Irving's Federalism was "more a matter of economics than of class"[13] because "class" and "economics" were essentially interchangeable terms at this time. The possession of property was what gave one both social and political status. Thus, Irving "thought of party distinctions in terms of class distinctions."[14]

In light of this, the contention that Irving would not be interested in the political aims of either party seems incredible.[15] He may have been a "lukewarm partisan" in terms of indulging in the practical side of politics, but he was openly aligned with the Federalists.[16] Irving's Federalist-oriented thinking may not have been deep, but it was realistic. He was displeased with Jeffersonian democracy throughout the decade for reasons not based on mere prejudice. In essence, he reflected the views of Hamilton: fear of the mob achieving political victory when it was ill-equipped to govern.[17]

The transition from Federalist to Burrite Republican was not a difficult one to make in the New York of 1802–3. Support of Aaron Burr would not necessarily mean that one was leaving the Federalists, but rather that one had discovered a new and more lethal way to attack Jefferson.[18] Irving was close to the New York politics connected with Burr, as well as to the Federalist group which supported Burr over Jefferson. Peter Irving's newspaper supported Burrite Republican policies;[19] the *Morning Chronicle* published the *Letters of Jonathan Oldstyle*. It is during this period that Burr and Irving first met. Thus, Irving's "political relations were those commonly known as Burrite."[20] Though one critic contends that Irving was not a Burrite,[21] it is likely that he is referring to the period of Burr's trial in 1807. This first shift in political alliances reflects little more than the tenor of the times; in New York there was a massive movement of Federalists to this faction of the Republican party. Irving "knew what was going on about him and was ahead of the average intelligent citizen, not

behind him, in his capacity to play a responsible and intelligent part
in the life of the body politic to which he belonged.''[22] Thus, he
gravitated into a movement which was an irritant rather than an asset
to Jefferson. It was a transitory move in which a Federalist had
nothing to lose, but potentially much to gain.

After this brief acquaintance with Republicanism, Irving left in
1804 on his first trip to Europe. The political implications of this
journey are two-fold: his Federalist opinions were solidified; and he
recognized the inherent differences between a monarchy and a republic. Irving reacted violently when he viewed France where "the
remains of the French Revolution were not calculated to make him
more democratic";[23] however it is interesting to note that he also
wrote, ". . . while Europe is wasting its strength in perpetual com-
motions, the United States, blest with profound peace and an excellent
government, is gaining daily accesses of wealth & power. . . ."[24]
Irving had not altered his essential political beliefs, but it is significant
that Jefferson was president of this noble country which was moving
up in the world. This first exposure to Europe offers one example of
Irving's nationalist-patriotic bias: one may argue politics at home, but
party differences are not material when representing the nation abroad.

It was during this early period, of course, that Irving the Federalist, sometime Burrite Republican, launched his career as a satirist.
First with *The Letters of Jonathan Oldstyle* (1802–3), then with
Salmagundi (1807), and finally with his finest contribution of political
satire, *A History of New York* (1809). The young writer's conservative
biases are sharply, strongly and succinctly expressed in these works.
While all, and certainly the last, have considerable literary merit,
each also tells us much about the shaping of their author's political
convictions. Though *Oldstyle* is not a political satire but rather one
of manners and customs, it is cited here because the criticisms leveled
against contemporary society, however valid, reflect a conservative
reaction toward the attitudes developing in early nineteenth century
America.

It is *Salmagundi,* however, which represents Irving's first major
assault on Jefferson, his administration, and his ideas of Republicanism.
References to the President are unmistakable and numerous. Irving
attacks Jefferson's red trousers repeatedly,[25] presumes the President's
loss of popularity (p. 35), and cites him as the head of a government
based on reason and philosophy in which he is the principal planner
and mover (p. 86). Irving establishes the idea that the government
is operated by a mobocracy (p. 80), then writes disparagingly of the
"voice of the sovereign people" (p. 82). The author's evident disgust
with the election process is captured through a humorous description
by Mustapha: "I almost shrink at the recollection of the scenes of
confusion . . . which I have witnessed during the last three days. I

have beheld this whole state given up to the tongue, and the pen; to . . . the babblers, and the slang-whangers. . . . I have seen liberty; I have seen equality; I have seen fraternity!—I have seen that great political puppet-show—AN ELECTION." (p. 131) The conservatism of the author is evident throughout the political allusions. But the principal importance of *Salmagundi*, it seems, is that it paves the way for the author's next work in which many of the same failings of democracy (from Irving's viewpoint) are attacked with greater perfection.

Thus, it is in *A History of New York* that Irving shows himself as a master of political satire. The book may be the archetype of Federalist literature,[26] through which the author "has successfully assumed the aristocratic viewpoint toward 'the swinish multitude' ";[27] however, regardless of his personal biases, as author, Irving seems determined to prove his literary merit. It appears unfair to categorize Irving as a figure who is unable to cope with the "ideas" of the early 1800's[28] when he seems to do just that so well in his *History*. Much of his satire reflects neither Federalist, nor Burrite, but is "the product of a keen understanding of larger issues."[29] Though this is accurate, the conservative biases of the author cannot be overlooked; in fact, the adroit handling of the political satire makes it more devastating.

The political satire of the work centers in Book IV. Governor Kieft, or William the Testy, is Jefferson. From beginning to end Kieft is portrayed with all of the foibles Irving saw in Jefferson. For example, after an account of William's intellectual achievements, Irving notes, "had he been a less learned man, it is possible he would have been a much greater governor."[30] William, like Jefferson, believes that thought and words are an adequate substitute for action. He enjoys issuing proclamations; his favorite word is economy; he has an explosive temper. He is a pacifist who opposes sufficient national defenses, but encourages farcical military preparations.[31]

The development of national political parties is humorously described in the pipe anecdote where the *Long Pipes* represent the aristocracy; the *Short Pipes* represent the lower orders; and the *Quids* represent third parties (p. 197). After expanding his description of the parties, Irving points out that a few do the thinking for many: "How many a patriotic member of congress have I seen who would never have known how to make up his mind on any question, and might have run a great risk of voting right by mere accident, had he not had others to think for him. . . ." (p. 198) All that political parties do are to enable people to "organize dissension and to oppose and hate one another more accurately" (p. 198).

Finally, William ends his administration in disgrace both abroad and at home. Though this ending is "obviously inapplicable either to the historical Kieft or the real Jefferson, it corresponds with

Federalist versions of the latter's administration, save that it under-states their bitterness."[32]

During the next few years, however, as the clouds of war loomed and then broke, Irving's Federalism was tempered as his partisanship declined in the interests of nationalism. In 1811, disgusted with politics, factions and battles,[33] he wrote, "I do not suffer party feelings to bias my mind."[34] In the years to follow, Irving became an ardent supporter of President Madison insofar as the conduct of the war was concerned. He reacted against those who spoke slightingly of Madison, and when he heard the President's name mentioned sneeringly was prompted to write, "It is not now a question about *Jimmy* Madi-son. . . . The pride and honor of the nation are wounded."[35] Thus, war inspired Irving to feel politically nationalistic.

At the close of the war in 1815, Irving sailed for Europe, where he was to remain for seventeen years. This period was essentially one of political dormancy. He enjoyed life abroad, but stayed out of politics in England and the Continent. Though his large correspon-dence kept him current in American affairs, he was politically divorced from the United States, where genuine participation in politics de-manded physical presence. In the *Sketch Book* (1820), as well as in *Bracebridge Hall* (1822), political allusions occur, but are neither startling nor controversial.[36]

During this interlude abroad, there is nothing to indicate that Irving altered his essential political views. The few references to politics in his writing would imply that he has remained static and, perhaps, indifferent to events at home.

Toward the end of his stay in Europe, however, Irving was reawakened politically. When Irving began his first diplomatic as-signment in 1829 as Secretary to Legation at London, he could be viewed either as Federalist (considering past associations and biases), or apolitical (considering his long absence from America). He emerged from the post in 1832 as a Democrat. The contention that Irving, after the years abroad, apparently came out a Jackson man coinci-dentally with his English appointment,[37] seems an inadequate expla-nation of the transition which occurred. Whether Irving had changed, in fact, is not as important a consideration as the vast changes in politics at home during his absence. Despite all that he had heard in those years abroad, it would be impossible for him to realize fully the implications of the new political alliances. But an examination of these changes is essential when considering what in Irving seems to be a shift from right to left, from Federalist to Jacksonian Democrat. This political transformation seems the most difficult to understand, yet is not wholly untenable. First, the Federalist party was dead, and had no effective replacement. Secondly, the Democrats, ostensibly evolving from Jefferson's party, were not really of it, but represented a new alignment of political factions. Finally, though the Whigs were developing during this period, they were not a viable force, and were in a continual process of flux as they attempted to produce a national coalition. That is, from the close of the War of 1812 until 1840, the United States in national elections was operating virtually as a one-party system.[38] Thus, there was no ready-made party for Irving to adopt; he, like others, made accommodations to what existed. For Irving, adrift in Europe all these years, it was, perhaps, an easier adjustment to make.

While Irving was in England, he was greatly influenced by Martin Van Buren, a New Yorker and family friend, and Louis McLane, a conservative Democrat who later broke with Jackson over the bank issue. Irving arrived home in 1832 a partisan, but he accepted Jacksonian democracy on his own terms—terms which distinctly reflected his personal biases.

The critical issue before the Jackson administration in 1832–1833 was the tariff and nullification. In essence, the South raised the doctrine of nullification–the right of a state to deny the constitutionality of acts of the federal government—because of the high protective tariffs adopted in 1828 and 1832. South Carolina forced the issue by declaring the tariffs invalid, thus threatening secession. Jackson declared the federal government supreme and countered by sending land and naval forces to Charleston.[39]

Irving supported Jackson without reservation.[40] He watched the Senate debates and was indignant about the actions of South Carolina's representatives.[41] Irving's total support of Jackson, however, reflects his nationalistic temperament more than his Democratic politics. Far more important than any party consideration was the threat of secession. To Irving, the Democrats and Jackson were on the "right" side.

Another major concern of the Democrats during this period was western expansion. Irving, shortly after his return, toured the West where he was deeply impressed by the possibilities for development. He soon produced his western trilogy: *Tour on the Prairies* (1835); *Astoria* (1836); and, *The Adventures of Captain Bonneville* (1837). Though these books are deemed largely responsible for subsequent western migrations, none of them highlights those topics which involved internal politics.[42] Thus, while Irving was supporting the administration because the books reflect sympathy for the western point-of-view, the works cannot be cited as having a particularly political orientation. Irving was on the hunt for literary material; the subsequent products of his pen happened to agree in tone with the proponents of western expansion.

A third issue of considerable prominence during Jackson's administration was his "war on the banks," or, more specifically, his sustained attack on the Bank of the United States. The President was displeased with the bank's monopolistic position, from which it controlled state banks, and through them, allegedly curtailed loans essential to western expansion. Ultimately Jackson has the government's deposits withdrawn from the bank in an effort to cripple it. Jackson's policy, in part, was blamed for the panic of 1837.[43]

Irving's initial position on the bank question probably bordered on indifference. However, he was drawn into the milieu when Jackson decided to withdraw federal deposits from the bank. McLane, as Secretary of the Treasury, was the only person empowered to make the withdrawals; he refused. Van Buren asked Irving to intercede. Irving, as intermediary, was in a role well-suited to his talents, but after a number of exchanges was unable either to effect a compromise or to convince McLane, who finally resigned, to follow the advice of the Vice-President. In addition, Irving soon wearied of the task because he disliked being in the middle with personal friends—Van Buren and McLane—on opposite sides.[44] Later, he expressed more conservative views on the bank,[45] perhaps in part, because he lost money in the panic of 1837; in part, because of the influence of John Jacob Astor.

These were not the only concerns of the Jackson administration, but they were among the most widely publicized and the most controversial issues of the period. Irving's support of other policies, or his occasional displeasure with some reflected no particular change in his attitudes. Thus, while it can be demonstrated that Irving generally supported Jackson's administration, it can equally be shown that he was not a zealot. Irving's disenchantment with Jacksonian democracy dates approximately from 1837–1838, following the election of his friend Van Buren to the presidency. Political reasons for the rift cannot be sharply defined. However, it seems a valid assumption that Irving was "temperamentally incapable of being a practical Democrat,"[46] and, if he had allowed it, Van Buren would have made increasing demands on him in this capacity. More critical, perhaps, was the development of the Whigs as a national party with which Irving was more nearly in basic agreement. Certainly his return to the Whigs in 1840, Irving's final political shift, represented, at least in part, a return to the Federalists.[47]

Though Irving held distinct political biases, this does not mean he enjoyed the role of practitioner. Indeed, "He loathed them [practical politics] through a long life. . . ;"[48] and, in *A History of New York* his dislikes for "American political customs"[49] foretell the lifelong prejudice he would hold. But dislike should not be equated with lack of knowledge. Irving was distinctly interested in the mechanics of politics; he understood them; he wanted to learn how to use politics, if necessary, to be successful.[50] His satire would have fallen short if he had not been aware of the practical side of political parties.

Only as a young man did Irving occasionally participate in political action, and for him these were traumatic experiences. As an activist in the New York gubernatorial campaign of 1807 he is sorely disillusioned, writing to a friend, "never were poor devils more intolerably beaten and discomfited than my forlorn brethren, the Federalists."[51] But it is not only defeat of which Irving is conscious. He went on to describe his actions: "My patriotism all at once blazed forth, and I determined to save my country! O, my friend, I have been in such holes and corners, such filthy nooks and filthy corners, sweep offices and oyster cellars! . . . Truly this serving of one's country is a nauseous piece of business. . . ."[52] When he was asked to run for Congress in 1834, he declined, "The more I see of political life here, the more I am disgusted with it. . . . I want no part or parcel of such warfare."[53] And, when he refused a cabinet post offered by Van Buren in 1838, Irving wrote, "I shrink from the harsh cares and turmoils of public and political life at Washington, and feel that I am too sensitive to endure the bitter personal hostility, and the slanders and misrepresentations of the press, which beset high station in this country."[54]

While Irving abhorred practical politics, he was not above seeking political jobs for himself and others when that seemed necessary. During the 1830's he often made requests for friends and relatives, and some of these were honored. But Irving should not be criticized for requesting political favors. This was the accepted practice of his day. By the 1830's he could expect to have some of his appeals met. This was true not because "he owed more to politics than most men,"[55] but because, if anything, in the context of his times the opposite was the case. He was America's first man of letters; he was generally liked at home; he was especially popular abroad. An administration which showed him favor would be criticized by few.

Through the years, Irving declined more offers for himself than he accepted. Political opinions and discussion, private advice to politicians, an observer of government and politics—these, not public participation, were Irving's delights. "He loved the game—let no one think otherwise!—but feared its dust and weariness."[56]

Irving, despite his antipathies, did, of course, serve in two major government positions. The first of these, as Secretary to Legation at London, was obtained for him through the joint efforts of friends and relatives, with Van Buren as the primary instigator.[57] Despite the political origins of the job, however, Irving claimed that he was not personally involved in gaining it: "As the office has been unsought by me, so in accepting it I shall have it clearly understood, that I commit myself to no set of men or measures. . . ."[58] For the duration of his stay in London, Irving carried out the spirit, if not the letter, of his vow. By the time he came home in 1832 he was reacquainted with his country's politics, but his political commitments were not of a practical nature.

The post he next accepted, this time from a Whig administration, was Minister to Spain. His appointment to this position was tinged with many political ramifications. The chronological sequence of events provides one interpretation: Irving cooled toward the Democrats in 1837–1838; he supported the Whig candidacy of Harrison in 1840; he was willing to accept some tangible reward for this support; President Tyler appointed him Minister in 1842. Surely this was playing politics. But when Irving learned of the appointment he expressed surprise.[59] In addition, Daniel Webster, then Secretary of State, thought Irving would be astonished.[60] If one agrees that the appointment was a logical outcome of actions on Irving's part, it is true that "on the point that he was bewildered by receiving a plum from the pudding which he had helped to bake, we may remain more skeptical."[61] But Webster apparently believed that Irving was anticipating no such plum from the administration. Too, Irving, who undoubtedly viewed his most recent political shift as a natural and rational one, would not necessarily expect to be rewarded for it. Whatever the circumstances, the appointment was welcomed. Irving was off to Spain for a four-year stay.

There are a number of conclusions which can be drawn about Irving's politics, but it is important when making this assessment to remember that he was essentially a literary figure, not a political one.

It has been demonstrated that Irving was a non-contributor of intellectual thought or theory in the area of government; yet, he was not lacking in political convictions, or a basic understanding of politics. His biases, however, were simple ones: nationalism-patriotism and conservatism. Originally, ardent nationalism was one of the reasons he was a Federalist; later, it enabled him to support Madison in the War of 1812; and, it allowed him to support Jackson in the nullification fight. Secondly, his inherent conservatism, exemplified in his early days as a Federalist, is demonstrated in Europe by the political and social attitudes expressed in his writing, as well as by his ultimate return to a conservative political party. In addition, though not a political bias, it seems that Irving recognized the necessity to transcend party lines in order to achieve specific goals. This is shown in his support of Burrite Republicans, as well as in his support of Jackson.

More important, Irving's principal ventures into public political life were his two diplomatic posts. Though political strength was needed to acquire them, Irving viewed such service as divorced from politics. Neither job demanded the traditional party loyalties characteristic of most positions within the United States; neither job demanded the internal practical politicking he so intensely disliked. He was able to fulfill these roles successfully because the demands placed on him required not party loyalty, but national loyalty. In this sense, though he, perhaps, was unaware of it, Irving founded a pattern for what was to become in successive decades the epitome of the American diplomat: in essence a fundamental understanding of American politics and institutions; and, an ability to transcend party considerations in the interests of nationalism, whether as diplomat or simply American abroad.

Notes

1. See, for example, Henry Seidel Canby, *Classic Americans*, New York, Harcourt Brace and Co., 1931, or Vernon L. Parrington, *The Romantic Revolution in America 1800–1860*, New York, Harcourt Brace and Co., 1927, vol. 2.

2. Washington Irving, *Bracebridge Hall*, New York, Thomas Y. Crowell and Co., 1892, p. 9.

3. Canby, p. 72.

4. Washington Irving, *A History of New York*, ed. by S. T. Williams and G. T. McDowell, New York, Harcourt Brace and Co., 1927, p. lxxi.

5. Pete Kyle McCarter, "Literary, Political and Social Theories of Washington Irving," unpublished Ph.D. dissertation, University of Wisconsin, Madison, 1939, p. 291.

6. *Ibid.*, pp. 279–80.

7. Parrington, p. 200.

8. Pierre M. Irving, *The Life and Letters of Washington Irving*, 4 vols., New York, G. P. Putnam, 1864, vol. 3, pp. 119–20.

9. S. T. Williams, *The Life of Washington Irving*, 2 vols., New York, Oxford University Press, 1935, vol. 1, pp. 38, 93.

10. *Ibid.*, pp. 24, 93. McCarter, pp. 254–56.

11. Williams, vol. 1, p. 93.

12. *Ibid.*

13. William L. Hedges, *Washington Irving: An American Study*, Baltimore, Johns Hopkins Press, 1965, p. 63.

14. McCarter, p. 258.

15. Canby, pp. 78–79.

16. Williams, vol. 1, p. 92.

17. McCarter, pp. 291–92.

18. Samuel H. Wandell and Meade Minnigerode, *Aaron Burr—A Biography*, New York, G. P. Putnam's Sons, 1925, vol. 2, pp. 204–12. (Jefferson and Burr, both Republicans, tied in the election of 1800. The Federalists then attempted to elect Burr over Jefferson to the presidency, though it seems clear that the intent of the electors was that Jefferson should be President and Burr Vice President. There was no distinct vote for the two offices at this time.)

19. Williams, vol. 1, p. 35.

20. Henry Adams, *A History of the United States of America*, New York, Antiquarian Press, Ltd., 1962, vol. 3, p. 210.

21. G. T. McDowell, "General Wilkinson in the Knickerbocker *History of New York*," *Modern Language Notes*, 41(June, 1926), pp. 353–59.

22. Edward Wagenknecht, *Washington Irving: Moderation Displayed*, New York, Oxford University Press, 1962, p. 106.

23. McCarter, p. 266.

24. McCarter, p. 269, quoting Irving's *Notes and Journal*, vol. 3, pp. 89–90.

25. Washington Irving, *Salmagundi*, Chicago and New York, Belford, Clarke and Co., (no date), pp. 15, 21, 22. (All references are taken from this edition.)

26. Canby, p. 87.

27. McCarter, p. 344.

28. Canby, p. 79.

29. *A History of New York*, Williams-McDowell edition, p. lxxi.

30. Washington Irving, *A History of New York*, ed. by Edwin T. Bowden, New Haven, College and University Press, 1964 (1812 text). All quotations are taken from this edition.

31. *A History of New York*, Williams-McDowell edition, p. lxv.

32. *Ibid.*, p. lxix.

33. Williams, vol. 1, p. 130.

34. Washington Irving, *Letters of Washington Irving to Henry Brevoort*, ed. by G. S. Hellman, New York, G. P. Putnam's Sons, 1918, p. 29.

35. Pierre Irving, vol. 1., p. 312.

36. See, for example, "English Writers on America" and "Rip Van Winkle" in the *Sketch Book;* "The Village Politician" and "English Country Gentlemen" in *Bracebridge Hall.*

37. Canby, p. 79.

38. Madison and Monroe were Jeffersonian Republicans; Jackson and Van Buren became Democrats but traced their party's lineage to the Republicans. Political strife occurred among factions within the party.

39. John D. Hicks, *The Federal Union*, Cambridge, Mass., Riverside Press, 1937, pp. 408–18.

40. Williams, vol. 2, p. 63.

41. Pierre Irving, vol. 3, pp. 48–49.

42. McCarter, pp. 446–47.

43. Hicks, pp. 422–424; 428–33.

44. Williams, vol. 2, pp. 61–63.

45. Pierre Irving, vol. 3, p. 123.

46. McCarter, p. 452.

47. Wagenknecht, p. 108.

48. Canby, p. 77.

49. *A History of New York*, Williams-McDowell edition, p. lxxii.

50. Williams, vol. 1, pp. 95–96.

51. Pierre Irving, vol. 1, pp. 186–87.

52. *Ibid.*

53. *Ibid.*, vol. 3, p. 64.

54. *Ibid.*, p. 127.

55. Canby, p. 77.

56. Williams, vol. 2, p. 68.

57. *Ibid.*, pp. 1–2.

58. Pierre Irving, vol. 2, p. 401.

59. Williams, vol. 2, p. 112.

60. *Ibid.*, pp. 111–12, quoting *Harper's Weekly*, 27 May 1871.

61. *Ibid.*, p. 112.

[Washington Irving and the Comic Imagination]

Lewis Leary*

Washington Irving has been called the father of American Humor, but he was not. Ebenezer Cook, for one, preceded him, Benjamin Franklin and William Byrd, John Trumbull, Philip Freneau, and many another local wit. But Irving had the better chance, greater exposure at a better time, and his influence may be thought to have been greater. By the time he died, on the eve of the American Civil War, he had had more imitators than any of these others. Some, like Charles Dickens in England, and Bret Harte in California, did better than he, though many others, like barnstorming Artemus Ward and Orpheus C. Kerr, probably had not known him very much at all. For Irving stood at the headwaters of an American stream which flowed finally in many directions. Though its sources may be found in the great wits of England, from Chaucer to Addison and Goldsmith, to Hazlitt and Lamb, it was quickened by fresh native springs. It has never quite lost the delicate tinctures which Irving added to it.

The doubleness of Washington Irving, which is the doubleness of humor, most especially of American humor, is first discovered when at nineteen he contributed a series of eight letters to a newspaper edited by an older brother. Almost one hundred years before, young Benjamin Franklin had done much the same thing in a series of letters which he pretended had been written by Silence Dogood, and part of the joke then was that Mistress Dogood was not silent at all, but a talkative and opinionated woman. Young Irving used a pseudonym somewhat more subtle, less universal, and more distinctively American. He signed himself Jonathan Oldstyle, Gent., joining the familiar Yankee name of Jonathan, the perspicacious country bumpkin who was a popular comic figure on the American stage, to that which suggested a dignified personage who was conservative and retrospective, suspicious of what was new, preferring rather the old style to which he was comfortably accustomed. Furthermore, Jonathan

* Reprinted from *The Comic Imagination in American Literature*, ed. Louis D. Rubin (New Brunswick: Rutgers University Press, 1973), 63–76. ©1973 by Rutgers University, The State University of New Jersey. Reprinted by permission of the Rutgers University Press.

Oldstyle was a Gent., one of the gentry, a gentleman, and that was part of Irving's joke, and it had local, and somewhat new, and very American connotations, for democracy seemed to say that, all men being created equal, all men had the right and responsibility to become just as equal as anybody else.

One assumes that, like Washington Irving himself, Jonathan Oldstyle was a member of the new, self-conscious, and perhaps spurious aristocracy of wealth which sprang up in the United States after the American Revolution. It was the pretentious new society which a few years later Fitz-Greene Halleck good-naturedly satirized in *Fanny* which in rollicking octosyllabics set forth the misfortunes of the pretty daughter of a local nouveau riche who sought a husband among the older, established New York families. It was the upstart, half-democratic, half-anglophile, money-making society that Fenimore Cooper would castigate in *Home As Found.*

As a member of the first generation of his family to be born in America, and as the youngest son of an immigrant merchant father who had become wealthy enough to allow him early leisure, Irving never could quite withstand temptations toward sly, but usually ever so gentle, observations on incongruities in the life-styles and intentions of longer-settled (usually Dutch) families of Manhattan, and of gadabout new society in New York or Ballston Spa, and, especially, of upstart Yankees from New England. Even when travel and fame had taught him to be something of an aristocrat himself, secure behind the decent and respected pseudonym of Geoffrey Crayon, Gent., and admired as the genial dean of American letters whose quiet home overlooking the Hudson River near Sleepy Hollow in Tarrytown became a Mecca for admiring visitors—even then, he could not utterly withstand quizzical temptations, though he had learned cautious control and had acquired a mask behind which only the gentle twinkle of his eyes could not be hidden. No wonder that Fenimore Cooper, more securely to the manor born, disliked him. Cooper's humor, what he had of it, was blunt and boisterous and bruising, with no deception of geniality.

Jonathan Oldstyle pretended great contempt for innovation. Modern manners, modern marriages, modern modes of dress were objects of his ridicule in the letters which he contributed in 1802 and 1803 to the New York *Morning Chronicle.* His strategy was burlesque exaggeration, in the manner of Hogarth or Addison, with just enough intrusion of verisimilitude to insure a chuckle of recognition. When, for example, a bridegroom named Squire Stylish struts gravely into a room, "his ivory-headed ebony cane in one hand, and gently swaying his three-cornered beaver with the other," he is attired in a splendidly mod "suit of scarlet velvet, . . . the skirts stiffened with a yard or two of buckram; a long pigtailed wig, well powdered, adorned his head; and stockings of deep blue silk rolled over his knees. . .; the flaps of his vest reached to his knee-buckles, and the ends of his cravat, tied with the most precise neatness, twisted through every button hole." Nor was his bride less splendidly arrayed; her gown "of flame-coloured brocade" was flared ridiculously outward, in giant circumference, by a prodigious hoop, and it was embroidered all over with poppies and roses and gigantic yellow sunflowers.

This technique of exaggeration through caricature was as old as Theophrastus, as modern and as popular as Addison and Sterne, and, when applied to native idiosyncracies and native exploits, was to become one of the hallmarks of boisterous American frontier humor and of the slapstick buffooneries of the burlesque stage. Jonathan Oldstyle was on the right path certainly, and Irving was to move forward briefly later, exploring new and native comic possibilities. But now he looked over his shoulder backwards. There was little distinctively American, for example, in his remarks on modern marriage: they were as old as Eden, yet may seem to beleaguered husbands anywhere to be as true today as they have been every yesterday. "No longer," observes Jonathan, "does the wife tuck the napkin under her husband's chin. . . . The wife now considers herself as totally independent—will advance her own opinions, without hesitation, though directly opposite to his."

Perhaps the country people in the gallery of an American theater, described by Jonathan as pelting apples, nuts, and gingerbread on the heads of people below like thunderbolts from a plebeian heaven, may be thought of as presenting a kind of postparadigm of patriots at the Battle of Bunker Hill, a quizzical acknowledgement of the power of common people. And we may be tempted to discover democratic disapproval in Jonathan's description of a sharp-faced little Frenchman in trim white coat and small cocked hat who shook his fist at the gallery like "an irritable little animal," and to find in him local reference to emigrés, barbers, wig makers, dancing masters, and aristocrats, who swarmed to America in escape from the French Revolution, forgetting that the bumbling, irascible little Frenchman was a stock figure of stage comedy in England—as American, one might say, as roast beef or Yorkshire pudding, at best an imported commodity.

Much of Irving's humor, now and later, was borrowed from abroad. Strategies for the publication of the *Salmagundi* papers, in which Irving at twenty-four collaborated, were appropriated from Oliver Goldsmith's equally errant periodical the *Bee*. Irving was to remain a lifelong captive to the charm of Goldsmith, "the artless benevolence that beams through his works," his "whimsical, yet amiable views of human nature," his "unforced humor, blending so happily with good feeling and good sense." The Englishman's "soft-tinted style," his spontaneity and quiet humor, became and remained a tempting model.

But now in 1807 the young men who in *Salmagundi* would "instruct the young, reform the old, correct the town, and castigate the age, . . . interfering in all matters either of a public or private nature," were pert young Manhattan blades, quick with quip. They pretended genuine native distaste for neighbors who would spoil "honest American taste" with foreign "slop and fricasseed sentiment." Yet the Anthony Evergreen, Gent., and the Will Wizard, Esq., who contributed to it bore names which just as well might have been chosen by writers for a London periodical, though their associates Pindar Cockloft and Launcelot Langstaff may in their names reflect a pruriency, perhaps native, certainly jejune, which might not have issued from coffee houses by the Thames.

The subjects to which these young New Yorkers addressed themselves were often local enough: "This town," remarked Launcelot Langstaff, is "remarkable for dogs and democrats." They were likely to look down their noses at their "queer, old rantipole city" and their whimsical new country which together supplied, they said, enough ridiculousness "to keep our risible muscles and pens going until doomsday." Theirs was an aristocratic pose: "Thank Heaven," one of them exploded in a tone not unlike that of H. L. Mencken more than a century later, "we are not, like the unhappy rulers of this enlightened land, accountable to the mob for our actions." They spoke with disdain, however, of the naïveté of visitors from England, and explained carefully how to identify a cockney among them. They laughed at young women who were too genteel to risk a walk with local gentlemen along the Battery which fronted New York harbor. They pretended enormous expectation for the New World: Noah, one insisted, had been born there, so that all the world besides was populated by migrating Americans. But their mode and their tone was mainly borrowed. Mustapha Rub-a-Dub Khan, an enlightened stranger from abroad, comments on peculiarities of people in their strange land much as Montesquieu's Persian and Goldsmith's Chinese philosophers had done.

But when two years later, at twenty-six, Washington Irving invented Diedrich Knickerbocker, a fresh new era in American literature and native humor began. *The History of New York from the Beginning of the World to the End of the Dutch Dynasty* as published in 1809 over the new pseudonym, is a boisterous comic epic which contrasts the braggadocio and limitless expectations of adventurers in the New World with the Homeric exploits of ancient Greek heroes, testing Old World ideals against the frontier requirements of the New. The wharfsides of Manhattan are compared to the "walls of Jericho, or the heaven-built battlements of Troy." Blundering Dutch heroes are measured against Achilles, the god of golden deeds. The mood is consistently mock-heroic as Diedrich Knickerbocker reveals "Many Surprising and Curious Matters," including "the Unutterable Ponderings of Walter the Doubter, the Disastrous Projects of William the Testy, and the Chivalric Achievements of Peter the Headstrong" in what he boasted was "the only Authentic History of the Times that Ever Hath Been Published."

Authentic it certainly was not, though much of it can be read as personalized political satire, directed, for the most part, against Thomas Jefferson and his threats of democratic innovation. But readers need know little of American politics to chuckle over its droll burlesque. Many of the Dutch in New York did not like it, and Irving was so mercilessly attacked that he seldom dared such unrestraint again. But reviewers in Boston found Knickerbocker's *History* the wittiest book that young America had yet produced. In London it was greeted as "an honest attempt . . . to found an American literature. . . . The umbilical cord is severed. America is at last independent." It even reached frontier western outposts, "going the rounds," reported a witness in Mackinac, from the commandant of the fort to the smallest Indian trader, contributing "to their merriment and pleasure."

And well it might, for its humor was robust and hearty. Hendrick Hudson, who had discovered the bay of Manhattan, was described as a "square, brawny old gentleman with a . . . mastiff mouth, and a broad copper nose which . . . acquired its fiery hue from the constant neighborhood of his tobacco pipe. His vessel, the *Half-Moon*, which "floated sideways, like a majestic goose," was, like the fair Dutch maidens who inspired its building, "full in the bows, with a pair of enormous catheads, a copper bottom, and withal a most prodigious poop!"

Old Governor Wouter Van Twiller was "exactly five feet six inches in height, and six feet five inches in circumference. . . . His legs, though exceeding short, were sturdy in proportion to the weight they had to sustain; so that when erect he had not a little the appearance of a robustious beer barrel standing on skids." The renowned Wouter was not often erect, however: he preferred to sit and snooze, "would absolutely shut his eyes for two hours at a time, that he might not be disturbed by external objects—and at such a time the internal commotion of his mind was evinced by certain regular guttural sounds, exuding through his nose in monstrous snoring, "which his admirers declared were merely the noise of conflict" in his powerful, ever-working mighty mind.

Like Jonathan Oldstyle, Diedrich Knickerbocker looked longingly back to better times long past. How superior were the "delectable orgies" of teatime feasting among the old Dutch settlers compared to the effetely fashionable "iced creams, jellies, or syllabubs; . . . the musty almonds, mouldy raisons, or sour oranges" daintily consumed in "the present age of refinement." In better, older times, the teatime company ate lustily until each member was glutted: properly armed with a sharp-tined fork, each would thrust dexterously at brown-fried slices of fat pork swimming in gravy, "in much the same manner," said Diedrich Knickerbocker, "as sailors harpoon porpoises at sea, or our Indians spear salmon in the lakes."

The white man's attitude toward the Indian was quizzically lampooned. Before white settlers came to the New World, the red man had "lived a most vagabond, disorderly, unrighteous life,—rambling from place to place and prodigally rioting upon the sumptuous luxuries of nature without tasking her generosity to yield them anything more; whereas it has most unquestionably been shown that heaven intended the earth should be plowed and sown and manured and laid out into cities and towns and farms and country seats and pleasure grounds and public gardens, all of which the Indians knew nothing about . . . they were careless stewards—therefore they had no right to the soil—therefore they deserve to be exterminated."

But the white man was benevolent, and did his best to ameliorate and improve the sad condition of these poor savages who were unable to ravage the land as effectively as the white man could. So the white man "introduced among them rum, gin, brandy, and other comforts of life—and it is astonishing to read how these poor savages learnt to estimate these blessings. . . . By these and a variety of other methods was the condition of these poor savages wonderfully improved; they acquired a thousand wants of which they had before been ignorant."

What voice is this that now speaks? There is in it certainly something of the bitter, transatlantic Irish wit of Jonathan Swift, but it anticipates also the caustic comic tone which Mark Twain more than half a century later would make a hallmark of American humor. Thus snuggled unobtrusively among the rich tomfooleries of Diedrich Knickerbocker's *History* appears an augury of that species of corrective comedy which catches the reader unawares: a stopper, Mark Twain might have called it, with a twist of inverted meaning that is derived, not through burlesque exaggeration like that which tells of Wouter Van Twiller's massive girth and prodigious snoring, but through understatement in mock seriousness which allows a speaker to pretend surprise when an audience finds his revelations comic.

If Washington Irving as Diedrich Knickerbocker can thus be said to have invented Mark Twain, he can also be said to be the articulate father of the burly, bluff burlesque, the extravagant mock gravity and massive irreverence of the American tall tale—as when he describes a sunbeam bouncing off the gigantic red nose of Anthony the Trumpeter, acquiring from that nose such heat that it plunged "hissing hot" into the Hudson River "to kill a massive sturgeon that was sporting beside the vessel" in which the doughty Antony rode. And Diedrich's humor can be broad and mirthfully vulgar: Peter Stuyvesant, harassed in a duel, falls backward, Diedrich explains, "on his seat of honor" to land unceremoniously on a "cushion softer than velvet, which providence, or Minerva, or St. Nicholas, or some kindly cow, had benevolently prepared for his reception."

But Diedrich Knickerbocker invented more than this. From his sacrilegious pages there emerges, for the first time in full, disreputable array, the American backwoodsman, but presented as a comic rather than an heroic character, much as he remained when Fenimore Cooper introduced him as Natty Bumppo a dozen years later in *The Pioneers*, before he dehumanized a fallible human character by remaking him in later Leatherstocking Tales into more of an intrepid symbol than a man. The backwoodsman portrayed by Diedrich Knickerbocker is fallible indeed, and very human. His name is Dirk Scuiler, and he deserves remembrance as the progenitor of a long and lusty lustrous line which includes, not only Leatherstocking himself and all his quick-eyed, stealthily treading, honest fictional offspring, but Huckleberry Finn's disreputable father also, and many of the valiant vagabonds who appear on horse or motorcycle, bravely rapacious, in filmed adventures today—the scout, the advance man, the skulker just beyond boundaries of approved polite behavior, but a man who overcomes mammoth and menacing hardships, finally to succeed.

Dirk Scuiler was "a kind of hanger-on . . . who seemed to belong to nobody and in a manner to be self-outlawed." He was a vagabond, a poacher, an interloper: "Every garrison and country village," explained Diedrich Knickerbocker, "has one or more scapegoats of this kind, whose life is a kind of enigma, whose existence is without motive, who comes from the Lord knows where, and lives the Lord knows how." Dirk lounged about Peter Stuyvesant's frontier fort, "depending on chance for a subsistence, getting drunk whenever he could get liquor and stealing whatever he could lay his hands on." Sometimes, because of his myriad misdemeanors, he would find it advisable to disappear from the fort, often for as much as a month at a time,

> skulking about the woods and swamps, with a long fowling piece on his shoulder, laying in ambush for game—or squatting himself down on the edge of a pond catching fish for hours together. . . . When he thought his crimes had been forgotten or forgiven, he would sneak back to the fort with a bundle of skins or a bunch of poultry, which perchance he had stolen, and exchange them for liquor, with which having well soaked his carcass, he would lay in the sun [in] luxurious indolence. . . . [Dirk] was the terror of all

the farmyards of the country, into which he made fearful inroads; and sometimes he would make his sudden appearance at the garrison at daybreak with the whole neighborhood at his heels, like a scoundrel thief or a fox detected in his maraudings and hunted to his hole.

But, though Dirk apparently showed "total indifference . . . to the world or its concerns" and was "a fellow of few words," he nonetheless kept his "eyes and ears . . . always open," so that in the course of his prowlings he discovered a plot among the enemies of the Dutch that would mean the downfall of the garrison. So he set out overland to warn Peter Stuyvesant in New Amsterdam, from which city Dirk had "formerly been obliged to abscond precipitately in consequence of misfortune in business—that is to say, having been detected in the act of sheep stealing." Surely, there again is the voice of Mark Twain, laconic in understatement. And foreshadowings of the mighty feats of woodsmen like Paul Bunyan are discovered as gallant Dirk, "after wandering many days in the woods, toiling through swamps, fording brooks, swimming various rivers and encountering a world of hardship that would have killed any other being but an Indian, a backwoodsman or a devil, . . . at length arrived, half famished and lank as a weasel," on the western bank of the Hudson River, "where he stole a canoe and paddled over to New Amsterdam . . . and in more words than he had ever spoken before gave an account of the disastrous affair."

Like Faulkner's Sam Fathers, Dirk is part Indian, which explained, said Diedrich, his unusual propensities and habits. His appearance suggested that of almost any doughty woodsman in later tales of American Western adventures: "a tall, lank fellow" was Dirk, "swift of foot and long-winded. He was generally equipped in a half Indian dress with belt, leggings and moccasons." And then Diedrich Knickerbocker uses a phrase which may have long been a commonplace in the spoken vernacular and which, since Irving first wrote it in 1809, has passed down through many generations of tellers of tall tales. "It is an old remark," he has Diedrich explain, "that persons of Indian mixture are half civilized, half savage and half devil—a third half being expressly provided for their particular convenience. It is for similar reasons," he goes on, "and probably with equal truth, that the backwoodsmen of Kentucky are styled half man, half horse and half alligator."

As Diedrich Knickerbocker, Irving had the core of the matter in him, inventing or bringing together several of the attitudes and tones and modes which later and longer persevering hands would more securely mold to familiar native patterns. Perhaps stung by the bitterness of the reaction among New York friends against the gay burlesque of Knickerbocker's *History,* Irving never allowed his boisterous alter ego to speak so boisterously again. Yet almost everything for which Irving is now most affectionately remembered is told in the perspicacious words of Diedrich Knickerbocker. When, however, ten years later fame on both sides of the Atlantic descended on Washington Irving, he wrote most often then, and thereafter, in a quieter manner as Geoffrey Crayon, Gent., a gentle man whose gentle pictures of English life in *The Sketch Book* charmed but did not disturb. "Wit, after all," Irving had learned, "is a mighty tart, pungent ingredient, and much too acid for most stomachs; but honest good humor is the oil and wine of a merry meeting."

As Geoffrey Crayon, he built and maintained the reputation of being a remarkably placid and agreeable writer, deft and delightful, but only an extension, said Melville, of Oliver Goldsmith. A few critics, even then, in 1819, recognized that he had "lost something," one of them said, "of that natural run of style" for which his earlier writings had been remarkable. He had "given up something of his direct, simple manner," the "words and phrases, which were strong, distinct and definite, for a genteel sort of language." His native, American speech, "sent abroad to be improved, . . . had lost too many of her home qualities." His writings now seemed to another contemporary to "resemble a family of sickly but pretty children,— tall, feeble, and delicately slender," lacking vigor.

And these critics were correct. Little of the younger Irving's robust comic verve survives in *The Sketch Book, Bracebridge Hall,* or *Tales of a Traveller,* the three collections which in the early 1820's made Geoffrey Crayon's name a familiar household word. Irving's aim now was quietly to amuse, "to keep," he said, "mankind in good humor with one another." Even in burlesque portraiture, his comic touch became less vibrant, containing few barbs which might sting or anger.

Only seldom does Geoffrey Crayon allow himself such extravagant exuberance as romps through the story of "The Bold Dragoon" in *Tales of a Traveller,* in which "an old soldier, and an Irishman to boot . . . blarnied the landlord, kissed the landlord's wife, tickled the landlord's daughter, chucked the barmaid under the chin," and then proceeded to outdrink a fat distiller. Retiring befuddled to his room, he found his furniture all dancing—"a long-backed brandy-legged chair, . . . studded all over in a coxcombical fashion with little brass nails," led "an easy chair of tarnished brocade . . . gallantly out in a ghostly minuet." A "three-legged stool danced a horn-pipe, though horribly puzzled by its supernumerary limb; while the amorous tongs seized the shovel round the waist and whirled it around in a German waltz." Everything in the room swirled and danced, except the "great clothes-press, which kept curtsying and

curtsying, in a corner, like a dowager . . . too corpulent to dance."
The bold dragoon, a true Irish gentleman, pitied her loneliness, and
asked her to join him in a jig. But he reached toward her with such
uncontrolled good will that she crashed down on top of him with a
din that awakened the whole household. Sobered by his experience,
the bold dragoon retired to rest. However funny, this is London
music-hall slapstick of a kind which would be adapted to American
vaudeville or burlesque.

But when Geoffrey Crayon called on Diedrich Knickerbocker for
assistance, as he does in each of these collections of sketches, then
the tales come robustly alive. The stories of "Dolph Heyliger" and
of "The Storm Ship" in *Bracebridge Hall* are both "drawn from the
MSS. of the late Diedrich Knickerbocker." "The Devil and Tom
Walker" in *Tales of a Traveller*, sometimes identified as Irving's third-
best story, was also reported to have been found among old Diedrich's
papers. The better tales of "Rip Van Winkle" and "The Legend of
Sleepy Hollow" are both identified as by the late Diedrich Knickerbocker, and which of these two is Irving's best still provides matter
for critical discussion. They represent the high points of his literary
career, when in his late thirties Irving did better than he was ever
to do again. In them, the comic spirit of Knickerbocker's *History* is
briefly joined to the genial descriptive vein which thereafter Irving
genially and repetitiously mined.

Blundering, affable Rip Van Winkle has survived for a century
and a half as a comic paradigm of the American male. He is "one
of the boys" who never grows up, a "kid with a dog," content to
roam the woodlands in search of game or to "fish all day without a
murmur, even though he should not be encouraged by a single
nibble." Rip is "a simple good-natured man . . . a kind neighbor
. . . an obedient hen-pecked husband . . . foremost at all country
frolics." When things went wrong at home, he retired to the village
tavern "to sit in the shade through a long summer's day, talking
listlessly over village gossip." His was a sleepy little village, nestled
charmingly at the foot of the Catskill mountains, a small enclave of
quiet rural contentment, surrounded and protected by the lush bounty
of nature. It was the small town of pre-Revolutionary America, and
when Rip returns to it after a sleep of twenty years, he finds it only
a little changed. Disputatious people rant in democratic jargon about
the rights of man, but the old tavern, though new-named, is there,
and Rip's son is there, a replica of his younger self. Human nature
blunders irrepressibly on.

More than the charm of Irving's graceful style insures long life
to Rip Van Winkle. Hart Crane called him America's "muse of
memory," its "guardian angel of a trip to the past" who reminds
readers of something that is familiar because it is not altogether gone.

Much has been made of Irving's deft transfer of Old-World legend to a New-World setting, of his use of familiar elements of transatlantic popular lore as he transports Valhalla to the hills overlooking the Hudson, but these borrowed elements provide background only for what becomes a native comic legend. Rip survives as Huck Finn survives who would not be civilized either.

One of the most outrageously comic lines in "Rip Van Winkle," and one which certifies the tale as American, is slipped in without emphasis toward the close of the action, when Rip asks his daughter what had become of his wife. Mark Twain himself could not have contrived a more disorderly or more effective joining of comedy and pathos than she, in her laconic reply that her mother, Rip's wife, had died: "She broke a blood-vessel in a fit of passion at a Yankee peddler."

Yankees from New England had always been fair game to Diedrich Knickerbocker. In the *History of New York* they had been described as a "pumpkin-eating . . . notion-peddling people." But in the psalm-singing, lank and bony schoolmaster, Ichabod Crane, in "The Legend of Sleepy Hollow," the Yankee is more ruthlessly caricatured in all his Jonathan-like angularity, his awkward persistence in attempting to better himself by marrying the lush and wealthy Katrina, and his superstitious New England, Cotton Mather-bred doubts and fears. So persistent has been the memory of Ichabod that when in Faulkner's *The Hamlet* Eula Varner, also lush and wealthy, is wooed by her schoolmaster, she breaks from his arms exclaiming, "You old Ichabod Crane, you!" For Irving's Ichabod lives on, the mirror image of Rip Van Winkle. He is the busy American who plans to flee with the fair Katrina and make his fortune in the frontier west, and who finally leaves the rural village to become in New York a lawyer and then a judge, the successful, soulless American whose monstrous peccadilloes would be revealed on larger scale by Theodore Dreiser, Sinclair Lewis, and John Dos Passos. In a broad sense, he is a Yankee Flem Snopes, as impotent and predatory and hauntingly comic as Faulkner's ugly paradigm of democratic upward mobility.

Some forty years later, Mark Twain would first reach a national audience with a comic tale called "The Dandy Frightening the Squatter," in which a backwoodsman gets the best of an Eastern intruder. But, again, Irving anticipated him, for in "The Legend of Sleepy Hollow" Brom Bones, "a burly, roaring, roystering" country man, broad shouldered, bluff, and "always ready for fun or frolic," outwits Ichabod who is also an intruder from the East. Brom has been called "a Catskill Mink Fink, a ring-tailed roarer from Kinderhook," the ancestor of many brawlers and braggarts who rip and roar in later American frontier humor, in tales told of Davy Crockett or Daniel Boone, in Mark Twain's writings, and in all the dime novels and films in which the country boy outslicks the city slicker. Brom is no Dirk Scuiler, no skulker on the outskirts of civilization. He is part of an emerging society, the guardian of its integrity against intrusion from without.

Perhaps we are tempted to discover too much meaning in "The Legend of Sleepy Hollow." Like "Rip Van Winkle," it is an imported tale, retailored to native requirements. But Irving's skill in caricature, in appetizing description of luscious food crowded onto Dutch tables, of dance and frolic and rich tomfoolery is genuinely his own. He never did as well again, though his sense of scene and comic character is briefly revealed in *A Tour on the Prairies;* mildly impious jibes at Yankee transcendentalism appear years later in "Mount-Joy," and "The Great Mississippi Bubble" sketches frontier life in a manner which looks timidly toward the lustier ironic realism of Mark Twain. However respectworthy these tentative reachings toward a native comic mode, Irving became increasingly a timid writer who seldom dared dangers of public disapproval. "Failure," said Melville, "is the test of greatness." Success such as Irving's, he said, is "proof that a man wisely knows his powers" and "knows them to be small." A younger Irving had opened doors which gave access to native varieties of the comic spirit. But he closed them quickly, after only brief glances. But he was there at the start, beginning more than he dared finish. Our gratitude to him must be great. Our understanding of his failures is inevitably sympathetic. For Washington Irving himself is perhaps the most representative comic figure of all, an early nineteenth-century J. Alfred Prufrock, who ventures only tentatively, then draws back, content to polish and to please. It was Melville again who warned that "there is no hope for us in these smooth, pleasing writers."

Irving's Use of the Gothic Mode   Donald A. Ringe°

Although Washington Irving has long been recognized as an important practitioner of the Gothic mode in America, relatively little attempt has yet been made to understand his use of Gothic material. To be sure, individual stories, like "The Legend of Sleepy Hollow," have been studied repeatedly; his Gothic tales have been classified as belonging to different types, such as "sportive" or "sombre"; and extended discussions of the subject have indicated the range and variety of his Gothic stories and the important function of Gothic

° Reprinted by permission from *Studies in the Literary Imagination* 7 (Spring 1974): 51–65.

material in those books, like *Tales of a Traveller,* where it bulks very large.[1] All of these studies, however, focus most sharply on the stories themselves. They make little attempt to understand the intellectual basis of these tales, and more important, they generally miss the point that Geoffrey Crayon, the ostensible author of the books in which Irving's most significant Gothic tales are imbedded, has his own views on the validity of Gothic material. These views, derived from the dominant philosophy in early nineteenth-century America, determine to a large extent the kind of Gothic tale Irving writes and the manner in which each of the stories is told.

At the time Irving was writing, Scottish "common sense" philosophy dominated American thought. Although, like other eighteenth-century philosophies, it was ultimately based upon the act of perception, the school had developed in reaction against the skepticism and idealism which philosophers like Hume and Berkeley had derived from the same beginning. Fundamentally realistic, it accepted the physical world as objectively real and ultimately knowable by human beings, who could perceive the world as it is—the objects themselves—through impressions and sensations. It tended to distrust the imagination, which could substitute isolated conceptions for realities, and it was especially wary of fiction, which could lead the mind away from sober truth.[2] Such a position necessarily had a strong negative influence on the Gothic mode, which relies for its effects on such non-material beings as ghosts and goblins. If not accepted as objectively real—and they were not—they must result from faulty perception, a diseased imagination, or out-and-out madness.[3] Hence, the writer of Gothic tales, which, despite the philosophy, continued to be written, was unable to present his ghosts and goblins as actual beings, but had rather to account for them by one or another of the means that "common sense" philosophy had suggested.

That Irving subscribed to the major tenets of this philosophy seems highly probable, for he had some knowledge of one of its major adherents, and he seems to reflect the same realistic position. Three times in his Notebook of 1810, Irving mentions the name of Dugald Stewart, a leading philosopher of the school,[4] and he hoped to meet the man himself at a dinner in Scotland in 1817.[5] More important, we find in the same Notebook a brief notation that looks very much like the "common sense" position: "Perception/We perceive external objects thro the medium of impressions and sensations." This statement appears in a section of the Notebook in which Irving has not only copied out brief quotations from some unidentified philosophic work, but has also discussed the effect of superstition and ignorance on belief in supernatural beings. Though he finds "something indiscribably [sic] charming & fanciful in the extravagance—the superstitions and the supernal illusions with which chimerical ignorance once clothed every subject," he knows very well how such beliefs came about. "The reason being too weak to pierce the mystery that envelopes every natural phenomenon, the imagination takes it up—and dresses it out in forms & colours of its own— Hence the singular fables of Fairies, sylphs & enchanters by which ignorant nations attempted to explain the prodigies of nature." As knowledge advances, however, "the clear light of philosophy" puts an end to such pleasant fancies.[6]

Yet another passage in the Notebook of 1810 further illustrates Irving's interest in the supernatural and its relation to contemporary philosophy. He recognizes that even the strongest mind will dwell with fondness "on the superstitions of the nursery," and he knows that "we often endeavour . . . to conjure up past scenes and deceive ourselves for a moment in the pleasing falacy [sic] of superstition we once felt. . . . "[7] The implications here are important. Even though the most rational minds may take pleasure in the fantasies of the unsophisticated, Irving clearly implies that the enlightened man does not mistake the illusion for the reality. He knows full well that he is entertaining only a momentary fancy and maintains his basic relation to the world of actuality. Irving undoubtedly saw himself as this type, for although, as he writes, he may almost lament the fading of the more pleasant fancies of the past, he remains in the final analysis fundamentally a realist. As the Notebook passages clearly indicate, he accepts the modern, rational view of reality and attributes to the minds of the ignorant and superstitious such beings as the ghosts, goblins, and fairies that make up the stock in trade of the Gothic writer.

The effect of this view is immediately apparent when we turn to Irving's works, for he makes his narrator, Geoffrey Crayon, profess essentially the same intellectual position. In *The Sketch Book* and *Bracebridge Hall*, Crayon takes a rationalistic view of supernatural phenomena, an attitude which prevents him from taking the Gothic mode completely seriously. A man of imagination and sensibility, Crayon is, of course, attracted to the stories of fairies, ghosts, and goblins that he has picked up during his travels, and, like Irving in his Notebook, he half regrets that the time is past when men could take pleasure in the fanciful creations of the mind. But however much he may lament the changes in popular belief that have banished such fancies from the minds of men, he knows very well that they were the "creations of ignorance and credulity," and he is "convinced that the true interests and solid happiness of man are promoted by the advancement of truth." Crayon is essentially a realist. He accepts the "true philosophy," in whose light, he believes, the creations of superstitious belief must vanish.[8] Hence, he reports supernatural phenomena as either deceptive appearance or the creation of a superstitious mind.

In *Bracebridge Hall*, for example, he explains how such apparitions can result from faulty perception. They are sometimes no more than optical illusions or the effect of deceptive light. Even a rational man like himself can be deceived. On entering a dusky passage in the Hall, he has thought that the full length portrait of a knight in armor, "thrown into strong relief by the dark paneling against which it hangs," was actually advancing towards him. To a superstitious mind, moreover, "predisposed by the strange and melancholy stories connected with family paintings," the light of the moon or a flickering candle may "set the old pictures on the walls in motion, sweeping in their robes and trains about the galleries." The mind perceives an uncertain image, and, having been led to expect a supernatural occurrence, readily perceives it. Old houses, moreover, with their dusky corners, faded pictures, and strange noises are particularly liable to "produce a state of mind favorable to superstitious fancies" (VI, 357–58). In Crayon's view, the apparitions reported to have been seen in them have no objective reality, but result from the imaginative creation of minds predisposed to their perception.

Such minds exist, he believes, largely among the common folk in isolated rural areas, "for the general diffusion of knowledge" in England "and the bustling intercourse kept up throughout the country" have spread such enlightened views that only in "a retired neighborhood" like Bracebridge Hall can belief in popular superstitions still be found. Even here they are fading away, and the people themselves are reluctant to reveal their beliefs to strangers—or, for that matter, to the gentry—lest they be laughed at. Yet the beliefs persist. The parson at Bracebridge Hall assures Crayon that some of his old parishioners still remember the barghost, which was said "to predict any impending misfortune by midnight shrieks and wailings" (VI, 359), and he tells a group assembled around the supper table that he knows of a number of common folk who have maintained a lonely vigil on St. Mark's Eve for three successive years in the belief that on the third night they would see enter the church a ghostly procession of those to die in the coming year. Some claim to have actually seen it, much to the perturbation of others in the village who fear such persons may have advance knowledge of their deaths (VI, 133–34).

The favorite ghost of the neighborhood, Crayon learns in *The Sketch Book*, appears to be that of a crusader whose effigy is carved on his tomb by the church altar. The good wives of the village have always viewed it with superstition, and the usual stories are told about him. Some say he walks at night because of a wrong left unredressed at his death or because of a hidden treasure "which kept the spirit in a state of trouble and restlessness." His picture in Bracebridge Hall is viewed with awe by the servants, who believe its eyes follow them as they walk about, and the porter's wife avers that in her youth she heard it said "that on Midsummer eve, when it was well known all kinds of ghosts, goblins, and fairies become visible and walk abroad, the crusader used to mount his horse, come down from his picture, ride about the house, down the avenue, and so to the church to visit the tomb." Some of the rustics often laugh at these tales, but when night comes on, many of the strongest disbelievers in ghosts would not venture alone on the path across the churchyard (II, 293–94).

Yet Crayon knows that the common folk are not the only ones affected by such tales. Even the more educated act at times in similar ways and for the same reasons. The parson himself, Crayon believes, is "somewhat tinctured with superstition, as men are very apt to be who live a recluse and studious life in a sequestered part of the country, and pore over black-letter tracts, so often filled with the marvelous and supernatural" (II, 293). A naturally credulous man, the parson spends so much of his time in searching out the super-natural tales he tells "that his mind has probably become infected by them," and though he "never openly professes his belief in ghosts," he cites "the opinions of the ancient philosophers" and "quotes from the fathers of the church" in defense of the supernatural (VI, 135–36). The mind of the parson has been predisposed to belief in ghosts by the antiquarian habits he has developed, and the more he studies the popular lore of his and other nations, the more he is likely to lend credence to the stories he uncovers—a mental process not unlike that of the common people who feed their superstition with the tales they constantly retell.

Master Simon, too, a relative of Squire Bracebridge, can become as unnerved as the common folk by what appears to be a strange occurrence. He has heard of the ghost of a hard riding earlier squire who is said to gallop "with hound and horn, over a wild moor a few miles distant from the Hall." Crayon is inclined to believe that this story has been set abroad by the present squire, who, though himself a disbeliever, does not want to see the popular superstitions die, but Master Simon hints that there may be truth in the tale. He has "heard odd sounds at night, very like a pack of hounds in cry," and once, when returning home rather late from a dinner, he had seen a galloping figure on that very moor. But, he goes on to say, "as he was riding rather fast at the time, and in a hurry to get home, he did not stop to ascertain what it was" (VI, 358–59). Though Master Simon is not depicted as a superstitious man, his actions on this occasion are little different from those of the rustics who fear to cross the churchyard, or the dairy maid who will not venture after dark near a wood where an old owl is hooting (VI, 304–05).

Crayon's irony is light in these passages, for he wants to poke only mild fun at the parson and Master Simon. They are not so different, after all, from other educated people who find themselves at least partially affected by tales of the supernatural. Whenever such stories are introduced into social gatherings, they are frequently met with smiles, but no matter how gay or enlightened the audience may be, if the tales are continued long, they will soon absorb the interest of the listeners. "There is," Crayon believes, "a degree of superstition lurking in every mind; and I doubt if any one can thoroughly examine all his secret notions and impulses without detecting it, hidden, perhaps, even from himself. It seems, in fact, to be a part of our nature, like instinct in animals, acting independently of our reason" (VI, 135). Crayon, indeed, detects it in himself, for after an evening of such stories, he finds he cannot sleep, so strong a hold do they take on his imagination. The room he sits in, hung with tapestries whose faded figures "look like unsubstantial shapes melting away from sight," fosters a state of mind which turns naturally to supernatural things (VI, 137).

As he gazes out of the window on the "quiet groves and shadowy lawns, silvered over, and imperfectly lighted by streaks of dewy moonshine," his mind is filled with fancies concerning spiritual beings, and he wonders if they do indeed exist. Though he knows that belief in the return of departed spirits "has been debased by the absurd superstitions of the vulgar," he sees it "in itself [as] awfully solemn and sublime," and because it is so prevalent in all times and places, it seems to him "to be one of those mysterious, and almost instinctive beliefs, to which, if left to ourselves, we should naturally incline." He wonders, then, if such belief can ever be eradicated, whatever "pride of reason and philosophy" may say, and he entertains, at least for the moment, the possibility of reunion with the dead he has loved (VI, 137–40). Crayon is, of course, under a kind of spell at this point, one generated by the stories he has heard, the room in which he sits, and the silvery landscape over which he gazes. In the full light of day, he will turn again to the disbelief in ghosts that more usually characterizes his thought.

The Gothic tales that Crayon includes in his books, moreover, are markedly influenced by his philosophic view. In accordance with his usual practice, Crayon tells none of the stories in his own voice, but merely reports what he has heard from others, sometimes as much as twice removed from himself. Thus, the actual narrator of "The Spectre Bridegroom" is a corpulent Swiss with "a pleasant twinkling eye" (II, 191) who tells the story in a Flemish inn. "The Legend of Sleepy Hollow," "Dolph Heyliger," and "Wolfert Webber" all come from the posthumous papers of Diedrich Knickerbocker, but the first is told by an old gentleman "with a sadly humorous face" at a meeting of the Corporation of the city of Manhattoes (II, 461), the latter two by John Josse Vandermoere, "a pleasant gossiping man, whose whole life was spent in hearing and telling the news of the province" of New York (VI, 392), and who is generally considered to be "one of the most authentic narrators in the province" (VII, 392). Finally, "Strange Stories by a Nervous Gentleman," the first section of *Tales of a Traveller*, is told by the same person who recounts "The Stout Gentleman" in *Bracebridge Hall*, but each story told at the hunting dinner has its own narrator.

Because Crayon himself assumes no responsibility for any of these tales, he is able to achieve through his narrators a wide variety of effects. Both "The Spectre Bridegroom" and "The Legend of Sleepy Hollow" are told by somewhat roguish men whose purpose is to make their audiences laugh. In their hands, therefore, the Gothic mode becomes a vehicle for humor, the Gothic terrors turned against the credulous characters and converted into material for comedy. "Dolph Heyliger" and "Wolfert Webber," on the other hand, are told by a man deeply interested in the past. Though he too has his humorous side, he creates in both the tales a Gothic tone that is not completely destroyed by their comic conclusions. In "Strange Stories by a Nervous Gentleman," moreover, the use of different narrators for each tale permits a considerable range of tone, from the rollicking mood of "The Bold Dragoon" to the somber horror of "The Adventure of the German Student." Whatever the effect achieved, however, each of the stories is firmly based in the realistic philosophy that Crayon professes, and illustrates well the function of the mind in the perception of Gothic terrors.

In "The Spectre Bridegroom" and "The Legend of Sleepy Hollow," for example, the Gothic terrors experienced by the Landshort household and Ichabod Crane are shown to derive ultimately from their superstitious natures. In each case, however, the imagination is stimulated by external events that create the proper conditions for the credulous mind to mistake what it perceives. When Herman von Starkenfaust arrives at the Landshort castle, the Baron von Landshort, a man who delights in supernatural tales, gives him no opportunity to announce the death of the expected bridegroom, the Count von Altenburg. Instead, the Baron mistakes him for his murdered friend and entertains him handsomely. Because of the awkwardness of his situation—made even more difficult by the feud between their families—Herman becomes increasingly dejected and melancholy as the evening progresses. His "unaccountable gloom" chills the gayety of the feast, the singing and laughter are stilled, and the company soon falls into its favorite pastime of telling "wild tales and supernatural legends" (II, 204). The story of the fair Leonora who was carried off by the goblin horseman gives Herman an idea on how to extricate himself. Announcing his own death and imminent burial in Wurtzburg cathedral, he thoroughly frightens his superstitious hosts and leaves them fully convinced for a time that they have been entertaining a spectre.

A similar mental process occurs in "The Legend of Sleepy Hollow." Much like the Landshort household, Ichabod Crane is a credulous man who frightens himself with the tales he reads in Cotton Mather, who listens with "fearful pleasure" to the stories of ghosts and goblins told by the old Dutch wives, and who tells in return the tales of witchcraft, omens, and portents that he has brought from his native Connecticut. But the pleasure he gains from such tales when he sits in a chimney corner is dearly bought on his homeward walks when his path is beset by frightening "phantoms of the mind" (II, 430–32). Ichabod Crane is already ripe for the scare of his life well before Brom Bones drives him from Sleepy Hollow. On the night of the party at the van Tassel farm, the usual stories of ghosts and goblins are told, but most especially that of the Headless Horseman of Sleepy Hollow. By the time Ichabod leaves, therefore, his mind is so deeply affected that he begins to see spectres and hear ghostly groans before he even arrives at the spot where Brom Bones awaits him. Small wonder, then, that when he sees the horse with its apparently headless rider, he immediately believes that it is the well-known spectre and flees in terror.

In both of these stories, the usual Gothic devices are converted by knowing characters into the kind of practical joke that reveals the credulity and superstitious fears of those taken in by them. They are thus completely consistent with the realistic views expressed by Crayon, who attributes to the minds of the ignorant and superstitious the perceptions they report of supernatural beings and occurrences. Other of Irving's stories, however, handle the Gothic mode in a somewhat different way. "Wolfert Webber" and "Dolph Heyliger," the tales told by John Josse Vandermoere, have about them an aura of the legendary that permits a more truly Gothic tone. Already an old man when Diedrich Knickerbocker hears the stories from him— and Knickerbocker himself writes them down many years later— Vandermoere is far removed from the present age, and he tells his tales of times more distant still. Indeed, imbedded in both "Dolph Heyliger" and "Wolfert Webber"—stories of the early eighteenth century—are tales that are set in an even earlier period: "The Storm-Ship," a supernatural tale of the days of Dutch rule in New York, and "The Adventure of the Black Fisherman," a story laid in a time many years before it is heard by Wolfert Webber.

Twice removed from Crayon himself and set in the distant past,

Vandermoere's stories may contain strong Gothic elements without doing violence to Crayon's avowed disbelief in ghosts and goblins. Yet at the same time, "Wolfert Webber" and "Dolph Heyliger" cannot be considered purely Gothic tales. Both have their humorous aspects, and both contain obvious references to the realistic philosophy that consistently appears in Crayon's treatment of the supernatural. Where these stories differ from "The Spectre Bridegroom" and "The Legend of Sleepy Hollow" is in the narrator's willingness to allow a Gothic mood to form before it is undercut by the usual humor. Of the two stories told by Vandermoere, "Wolfert Webber" is the more closely related to "The Spectre Bridegroom" and "The Legend of Sleepy Hollow," for the hero is rather credulous and his main Gothic adventure is turned at last into a hilarious rout. The story as a whole, however, is not so broadly humorous as the other two, and it contains some truly threatening elements, most especially the supposed pirate who, for a time, dominates the village inn, and the group of smugglers who provide a real element of danger in the story.

The Gothic elements are common ones. Wolfert Webber dreams a prophetic dream that a fabulous treasure lies concealed in his cabbage garden, a dream that unexpectedly comes true when the city runs a street through his land and Wolfert becomes rich by parceling it out in building lots. Moreover, when he looks for pirate gold, Wolfert's adventures involve him in a number of Gothic episodes: he blunders into a tomb where a human skull lies exposed; he later sees what appears to be the red-capped ghost of a drowned seaman enter the vault; and at the moment he thinks he has found the gold he seeks, he confronts the grinning visage of the red-capped sailor. What all these events actually mean is never fully explained in the story, the narrator merely providing a number of alternate interpretations. What is strongly suggested, however, is that Wolfert's path has crossed that of a group of smugglers, and the fears and terrors he undergoes are the result of a mind so filled with tales of ghosts and pirate gold that on the night of his great adventure, he converts the red-capped smugglers into a legion of ghosts and goblins. This explanation, however, is not allowed to dominate the story, which, despite its humor, still manages to maintain something of a Gothic tone.

"Dolph Heyliger," on the other hand, is for most of its length a more serious Gothic tale. The hero sees a real ghost in a haunted house; he dreams a prophetic dream that leads him to believe he is under a supernatural influence; he journeys from New York to Albany, where he sees a picture resembling the ghost in a house he is visiting; and the ghost eventually reveals to him in a dream the well in New York where a wonderful treasure lies hidden. Dolph himself is not a credulous character. He tries to persuade himself that the ghost is "a mere freak of the imagination, conjured up by the stories he had heard" (VI, 416), and he later attempts to explain it away as merely a dream (VI, 418–19). Indeed, he begins to doubt at one point "whether his mind was not affected, and whether all that was passing in his thoughts might not be mere feverish fantasy" (VI, 422–23). "Dolph Heyliger" thus appears to be a most unusual story, in that the character who has the series of strange experiences is just the kind who, well aware of the deceptive quality of the imagination, ought to be able to see through the supernatural phenomena to a realistic explanation.

Yet for all its supernatural events, "Dolph Heyliger" is not inconsistent with the realistic psychology that underlies Irving's Gothic tales. Unlike Ichabod Crane and Wolfert Webber, Dolph is a shrewd man who does not permit his imagination to run away with him. He takes things as they come and, despite his real fears, maintains his equanimity even under the most unusual circumstances. Far from being frightened by imaginary terrors, he refuses to permit even a real ghost to intimidate him! The ghost, on the other hand, may not be real at all. Dolph Heyliger is the sole authority for the strange events that occur, and he tells the story to a few old cronies at his private table only after many years have passed. By this time, Dolph is rich, the result, apparently, of the treasure he finds in the well. No one ever contests the supernatural parts of his story, but that should not be surprising. Dolph, the narrator informs us, "was noted for being the ablest drawer of the long-bow in the whole province" (VI, 469). The story may thus be merely a tall tale told by the shrewd Dolph Heyliger to conceal the source of his wealth.

"Dolph Heyliger" is not unique among Irving's Gothic tales. "Strange Stories by a Nervous Gentleman" contains three similar ones, but because they are integrated into a larger whole, they must be seen in relation to the overall meaning of the entire sequence. The stories are told by a group of men, marooned by a winter storm, after a hunting dinner. Four are told the first evening, after which the Nervous Gentleman, who presents the entire series, undergoes a disturbing experience with a mysterious portrait in his chamber. The following day, their host tells a long story to account for the strange picture, after which the guests are given the opportunity to test their own reactions to it. The sequence of stories thus has a purpose that goes beyond the individual tales that the guests tell. The point of the series concerns the reactions of the guests both to the stories themselves and to the suggestion that the portrait they see may have a disquieting effect upon them. Their response, it is clear, results from the growing influence of the various stories on their imaginations.

The first three tales are comic and are partly designed by the narrators to take in their audience. All resemble "Dolph Heyliger" in the way the main characters react to the supernatural. In "The Adventure of My Uncle," the protagonist is a shrewd old traveler not easily frightened by strange occurrences, and although he is chilled to the marrow by the eyes of a ghost that appears in his room, he refuses to be disturbed. He simply pulls the covers over his head and goes to sleep. Though he attempts to learn the reason for the ghost's appearance and the narrator leads the audience on to expect some disclosure, the story is finally left up in the air with no explanation given. "The Adventure of My Aunt" is quite the opposite. Alone in her room when she hears a suspicious noise and sees the eyes of the portrait of her dead husband move, she takes matters firmly in hand, refuses to panic, and, leading a band of her servants, drives out an intruder who is hiding behind the picture. In "The Bold Dragoon," finally, an Irish soldier tells an improbable tale of goblins and dancing furniture in his room to conceal a midnight adventure with the landlord's daughter. And much like Dolph Heyliger, he makes his story stick because of his obvious skill "with sword or shillelah" (VII, 53).

All of these stories are snares to catch the unwary, to lead the credulous on with a promise of Gothic terror that is left unfulfilled. As the narrator of the first tale remarks, all three have "a burlesque tendency" (VII, 54). He proposes, therefore, to tell a fourth which is a different thing entirely. "The Adventure of the German Student" recounts the experience of a young man in Paris during the French Revolution. With a melancholy temperament, a mind filled with German philosophy, and fear that some evil hangs over him, he is alone and unhappy. Haunted by a recurring dream of a beautiful young woman, he finally meets her one stormy night near the guillotine. Highly striking in appearance but simply dressed, she wears around her neck "a broad black band . . . clasped by diamonds" (VII, 59). The student takes her home and spends the night with her. Believing he has formed a permanent union, he leaves next morning to seek a better apartment. On returning to his room, however, he finds her dead and learns from the police that she had been guillotined the previous day. When the officer unclasps the band around her neck, her head rolls on the floor.

Starkly horrible in its suggestion of necrophilia, "The Adventure of the German Student" adds a new note to the sequence of stories and turns it in a new direction. Not that the story departs completely from the sportive tone of the tales that precede it. However much it may seem to be a truly Gothic tale, its tone is undercut by a humorous conclusion that dissolves the Gothic effect. In providing authentication for the tales he has just completed, the narrator informs his listeners that he has the story on the best authority: he heard it from the German student himself—in a madhouse in Paris! Yet if this revelation makes the reader smile, the explanation has a significance beyond the humor. If superstition or a diseased imagination can affect one's perception of reality, how much more powerful is out-and-out madness in distorting a person's vision.[9] Seen in these terms, the tale can be accepted, much like those by Brown or Poe, as the mental projection of a mad protagonist. Even this tale of horror, then, is consistent with the realistic philosophy that underlies all of Irving's Gothic stories.

"The Adventure of the German Student" has yet another significance that cannot be overlooked. Though added to the group as almost an afterthought on Irving's part,[10] the tale is actually the keystone of the series. Related to the earlier stories through the humorous undercutting at its conclusion, it helps to stimulate the Gothic adventures that are to follow. Throughout most of its length, this tale, like "Dolph Heyliger," closely resembles conventional stories of ghosts and goblins. Though the narrator's final words may deny the relation, the effect it has had on the listeners cannot be wholly erased. Thus, by the time the story is finished, the assembled company has become engrossed in the subject of ghosts. No matter how sportively the evening may have begun, the characters would have gone on telling such tales if the spell had not been broken by the "loud and long-drawn yawn" of one of their number who had fallen asleep (VII, 63). The company decides instead to disperse for the night. At this point, the host informs his guests that one of them will sleep in a haunted chamber, but none shall know in advance who it will be. The assignment of rooms will be left "to chance and the allotment of the housekeeper" (VII, 64).

Thus, the stage is set for the events of the evening to begin to have an effect on the company. When the Nervous Gentleman goes to his room, he smiles "at its resemblance in style to those eventful apartments described in the tales of the supper-table." He draws a chair to the hearth, stirs up the fire, and sits "looking into it, and musing upon the odd stories [he] had heard" (VII, 64). Overcome by fatigue and the wine he has drunk, he soon falls asleep. Restless, as he believes, because of the heavy dinner he has eaten, he has a frightening dream in which he feels oppressed by something evil. Struggling in his dream to throw it off, he starts awake. The light of a flaring candle falls on a hitherto unnoticed portrait which gives him a growing sense of unease. The eyes of the picture seem to charm him, and although he instinctively tries "to brush away the illusion," it is in vain (VII, 65). Only one picture of all those in the room has this effect upon him, and he notes: "it was some horror of the mind, some inscrutable antipathy awakened by this picture, which harrowed up my feelings" (VII, 66).

Despite his nervous condition, the narrator is a rational man who knows full well how events can influence the mind. "I tried to persuade myself that this was chimerical, that my brain was confused by the fumes of mine host's good cheer, and in some measure by the odd stories about paintings which had been told at supper." But although he determines "to shake off these vapors of the mind," he finds he cannot do it (VII, 66). When he goes to the window, he sees the picture reflected in a pane of glass; when he turns his back, he feels it looking over his shoulder; when he goes to bed, he finds he has full view of the portrait. Even when he puts out the light he has no peace. The fire on the hearth gives an uncertain light to the room, but the picture is left in darkness, and the chamber itself, to his "infected imagination," begins "to assume strange appearances." He cannot convince himself that he is tormented only by his "diseased imagination" (VII, 67), and realizing that a nervous agitation can only increase the longer it continues, he quits the room to sleep on a drawing room sofa.

When on the following morning his companions discover that he has not slept in his assigned room, the Nervous Gentleman becomes the butt of their laughter. Though protesting that he is not superstitious and asserting his lack of faith in "silly stories" of haunted rooms, he maintains nonetheless that he has "met with something . . . strange and inexplicable" in his chamber: a picture that has had a "most singular and incomprehensible" effect upon him (VII, 71). The merriment of his companions merely makes him affirm more insistently that he has indeed experienced an unusual phenomenon, and the host soon has to come to his rescue. He tells his guests that he does indeed possess a picture which has an unsettling effect on all who view it. In fact, he would have had it covered the preceding night "had not the nature of our conversation, and the whimsical talk about a haunted chamber, tempted me to let it remain, by way of experiment, to see whether a stranger totally unacquainted with its story, would be affected by it" (VII, 72). This announcement instantly stills the banter of his guests, all of whom become anxious to hear the story behind the mysterious portrait.

The host tells a long tale of a young Italian he had met and befriended in Venice. This young man who had studied to be a painter, suffered grievously at the hands of the world. Rejected by his wealthy father, he endured a long series of misfortunes culminating in his betrayal by a man he had trusted. In love with a girl named Bianca, the young Italian was forced to leave her to attend his ailing father, with whom he had become reconciled. In his absence, however, the friend married Bianca after first convincing her that her lover was dead. Infuriated by his friend's treachery, the young Italian killed him, only to be haunted by a pursuing figure. This might have been either "an illusion of the mind," resulting from his early education at the hands of some monks, or "a phantom really sent by Heaven to punish" him (VII, 113), but in either case it pursued him relentlessly. The young Italian was finally influenced by a deep religious experience to give himself up, and he left with his English friend a manuscript detailing the story of his life and the horrible portrait he had painted of the phantom that had pursued him.

At the end of this tale, of course, the whole company wants to see the mysterious picture, and the host agrees to let them on one condition. The guests must go into the chamber one at a time. He gives the appropriate instructions to his housekeeper, and when the guests return, they all have felt the influence of the portrait: "some affected in one way, some in another; some more, some less; but all agreeing that there was a certain something about the painting that had a very odd effect upon the feelings." The Nervous Gentleman is deeply impressed and quickly concludes that there must indeed be "certain mysteries in our nature, certain inscrutable impulses and influences, which warrant one in being superstitious. Who can account for so many persons of different characters being thus strangely affected by a mere painting?" The host, however, reveals to his nervous friend that none of his companions have seen the mysterious portrait. Because he saw that some of them were in a bantering mood, and not wishing the Italian's painting to be made fun of, he had instructed his housekeeper "to show them all to a different chamber!" (VII, 115).

Because "Strange Stories by a Nervous Gentleman" ends in this way, it can be read as simply an extended joke, the final revelation designed to subvert the Gothic mood that has gradually been developed. The immediate effect is, of course, comic, but the ultimate purpose is serious. All of Irving's Gothic tales, sportive though most of them may be, are fundamentally concerned with a problem of human perception, the reasons why people sometimes fail to perceive the world as it is, but see instead a world of Gothic terror. Most of those who fall prey to these self-engendered delusions are men whose minds are filled with superstition, much like the common folk whom Geoffrey Crayon describes in *The Sketch Book* and *Bracebridge Hall*. Others, however, are hardly men of this type. The guests at the hunting dinner in the Nervous Gentleman's tales are by no means credulous men like Ichabod Crane or Wolfert Webber. Rather, the very stories they tell clearly reveal their disbelief in ghosts and goblins, and their initial response to the Nervous Gentleman's experience with the mysterious picture is to laugh uproariously at his discomfort.

As Crayon observes in *Bracebridge Hall*, however, men like these are not immune from feeling Gothic effects, especially if they submit themselves, however lightheartedly, to the influence of supernatural tales. This is, of course, the point of the Nervous Gentleman's stories. All the guests eventually feel the effect of even the sportive stories that have been told, and the comic conclusion makes it especially plain that what happens to them when they view what they think is the mysterious picture bears no relation to reality. They have simply projected into the real world a mental state that derives from a chain of circumstances which began with the sportive tales and ended with the host's story of the young Italian. Their imaginations have led them to perceive what their reason would deny. But the comic conclusion serves yet another purpose. In revealing the purely mental basis of the Gothic experience, it returns the series of stories to the world of actuality from which it began. In effect, it affirms the reality of the world perceived through reason—the world of common sense and prosaic daylight, which, though less attractive perhaps than the world of fantasy, is nonetheless the one in which Irving's Gothic tales are always firmly anchored.

Notes

1. See especially Oral S. Coad, "The Gothic Element in American Literature before 1835." *JEGP*, 24 (1925), 83–85; John Clendenning, "Irving and the Gothic Tradition," *Bucknell Review*, 12, no. 2 (May 1964), 90–98; William L. Hedges, *Washington Irving: An American Study, 1802–1832* (Baltimore: Johns Hopkins Univ. Press, 1965), 195–212. I have omitted from this study stories like "Rip Van Winkle" which are not Gothic at all, but which ought to be read as folk tales.

2. For good discussions of "common sense" thought in America, see William Charvat, *The Origins of American Critical Thought, 1810–1835* (Philadelphia: Univ. of Pennsylvania Press, 1936), and Terence Martin, *The Instructed Vision: Scottish Common Sense Philosophy and the Origins of American Fiction,* Indiana University Humanities Series, No. 48 (Bloomington, Ind.: Indiana Univ. Press, 1961). A brief discussion of the problems caused by an ill-regulated imagination may be found in Dugald Stewart, *Elements of the Philosophy of the Human Mind* (London: William Tegg, 1854), 272–79.

3. A good illustration of the "common sense" view on the perception of apparitions may be found in Martin, pp. 146–47.

4. Barbara D. Simison, ed., "Washington Irving's Notebook of 1810," *Yale University Library Gazette,* 24, No. 1 (July 1949), 12, 81, 86. While writing this Notebook, Irving was preparing his biography of Thomas Campbell, who, Irving knew, had been associated with Dugald Stewart in Edinburgh. See Washington Irving, *Biographies and Miscellanies,* ed. Pierre M. Irving (New York: G. P. Putnam's Sons, 1866), p. 148.

5. Pierre [M.] Irving, *The Life and Letters of Washington Irving.* Hudson Edition (New York: G. P. Putnam's Sons, 1869). 1. 280–81. Stewart, however, did not attend the dinner.

6. "Irving's Notebook of 1810," pp. 88–90. The passages quoted in my text are on p. 90.

7. "Irving's Notebook of 1810," p. 91.

8. *The Works of Washington Irving.* Author's Revised Edition (New York: G. P.

Putnam, 1856), 6, 366. Documentation in my text is to volume and page numbers in this edition.

9. For the influence of madness in distorting perception, see Stewart, pp. 78, 183. The madman mistakes imagined objects for realities.

10. Although Irving had been working on "Strange Stories by a Nervous Gentleman" since February, 1824, and sent part of the manuscript to John Murray, his publisher, on 18 June 1824, he heard the story that became "The Adventure of the German Student" from Thomas Moore on June 17, wrote the story on June 23–24, and forwarded it to the publisher with instructions to insert it after "The Bold Dragoon." See Washington Irving, *Journals and Notebooks, vol. 3, 1819–1827*, ed. Walter A. Reichart (Madison, Wis.: Univ. of Wisconsin Press, 1970), 352–54; and *Memoirs, Journal, and Correspondence of Thomas Moore*, ed. Lord John Russell (London: Longman, Brown, Green and Longmans, 1853), 4, 208.

Washington Irving and the Genesis of the Fictional Sketch Jeffrey Rubin-Dorsky°

With the publication of *The Sketch Book* in 1819–1820, Washington Irving transformed the popular travel sketch into a form uniquely his own, the fictional sketch. At such a crucial juncture in his career, when he had taken the bold step of making literature his profession (an achievement of which no other American could yet boast), Irving needed both a critical and financial success. The "travel sketch," a prose composition dedicated to expressing the rapture of an observer in the presence of Old World treasures, had become a fixture of both English and American magazines and therefore possessed this commercial appeal. Moreover, since the travel sketch relied heavily on recognizable detail, Irving realized that if he appropriated the form he could capitalize on his considerable artistic talent and his sharp appreciation for the visual element in prose. Indeed, by making his new fictional form an intensely descriptive one he was able to endow it with an aesthetic appeal that went far beyond the rather crude explication of scene and setting of the typical travel sketch. At the same time, plagued by deep personal problems, Irving saw that as he adopted the form he could simultaneously adapt it to his own psychological purposes. Although the consecutive losses of loved ones and the failure of the family business traumatized him, they were also responsible for the personal resonance of his sketch, for the pieces that composed his famous miscellany were attempts at self-discovery and evaluation, taking for their substance his actual physical and emotional experiences as he wandered through England

° Reprinted from *Early American Literature* 21 (Winter 1986/87): 226–47. © The University of North Carolina Press. Reprinted by permission.

in the years 1815–1819. In order to achieve this end he fictionalized the form, primarily by developing a filtering persona known as Geoffrey Crayon, and by expressing his emotions within a narrative, as opposed to a documentary, framework.[1] The innovation of Crayon, whose "adventures" in and around London mirror his own, gained for Irving the great advantage of being able to examine and reflect upon these experiences while remaining detached enough to perceive their significance. Crayon, in other words, became a buffer between Irving and the world. Thus, the creation of a fictional traveler/persona solved an emotional need and concurrently led to the beginning of a new genre in American literature.

A brief illustration shows how much fullness and complexity Irving added to the standard travel sketch. In "London Antiques," Crayon sets out in search of "reliques of a 'foregone world' locked up in the heart of the city." Passing through a "gothic gateway of mouldering antiquity" and stepping into a building beyond, he pauses to loiter about the great hall where he kindles his imagination by meditating upon the possible "ancient usages of this edifice." When a line of "grey headed old men, clad in long black cloaks" files past him, each one staring at him with a pale face while uttering not a word, he convinces himself that he is lost in a "realm of shadows, existing in the very centre of substantial realities." Hoping to discover the truly magical, the quintessentially romantic, Crayon enters the inner recesses of this "most venerable and mysterious pile." The old grey men in black mantles—to Crayon the "pervading genii of the place"—are everywhere, leading him to believe that he has stumbled into a medieval college of magical sciences, with black-cloaked old men as "professors of the black art."

Irving builds gothic suspense as Crayon attempts to lose himself in the shadowy grandeurs of his own speculations. In a chamber hung round with all kinds of weird and "uncouth objects," including "strange idols and stuffed alligators," "bottled serpents and monsters," Crayon encounters a small, shriveled old man. "[H]is quaint physiognomy, his obsolete garb, and the hideous and sinister objects by which he [is] surrounded" persuade Crayon that he is the "Arch Mago" who rules over this "magical fraternity." However, this last discovery punctures Crayon's expectations about the "antiquated pile" and its inhabitants, for he learns that the building is none other than the Charter House, an "ancient asylum for superannuated tradesmen and decayed householders." The black-cloaked magi are "pensioners returning from morning service in the chapel"; the arch magician of curiosities is actually one John Hallum, a garrulous old man who has decorated the "final nestling place of his old age with reliques and rarities picked up in the course of his life." After all his peregrinations, suppositions, and reveries, Crayon winds up the dupe of his own desires for something divine hidden under the mundane, at once arcane and mystical, at the heart of old England (*Sketch Book* 192–96).

Irving's achievement here is significant in three ways. Commercially, though Crayon may start out by approximating the ordinary traveler, his quickly straying from the usual path of the Grand Tour assures Irving a New World audience hungry for unique views of the Old. Visually, he creates a vivid, evocative, highly stylized portrait of the Charter House, yet one that is far more descriptive than any number of subjectively rendered travel sketches. And emotionally, while Crayon opts for imaginative flight over reality-based perception, Irving indulges in the fiction but uses the comic deflation of his persona to pull himself away from it. Crayon's heightened desire to inhabit an ideal world imbued with poetic feeling and transcendent wonder contrasts sharply with Irving's sober recognition that at its best reality affords little more than the commonplace, a bit of old style "amidst the modern changes and innovations of London." Humor may not resolve this tension, but it does diffuse some of the anxiety; it also enhances the charm and thus the appeal of Irving's persona. The commercial, visual, and emotional aspects of the Irvingesque sketch, therefore, are its distinguishing features and explain the changes Irving wrought in the popular travel pieces of the day as he sought both literary recognition and psychological stability.

Although Irving described his efforts in the "Prospectus" to the first number of *The Sketch Book* as an "experiment" (300), it is not surprising that so supple a form had significant application for other nineteenth-century American authors concerned with "seeing" themselves properly against an alien background. The list of those who adopted, and in the process modified, the sketch for their own purposes is large, and includes Hawthorne, Melville, Mark Twain, Howells, and James. What is surprising, however, is that despite Irving's unquestioned success, and despite his opening up a rich vein that others were to mine, no one has analyzed how the sketch evolved as his individual means of literary expression. It is this peculiar void, both in Irving scholarship and in American cultural history, that the present study seeks to fill. Since Irving's great strengths were a flair for style and an instinctive sense for structure, along with a keen appreciation for the dominant taste of his audience, his literary self-reflections reveal almost no concern with the rudiments and exigencies of form. Neither was he given to analyzing his own influences and progression. Thus, it is necessary to play literary detective and piece these together, to examine, that is, via letters, journals, notebooks, and the relevant cultural evidence, Irving's creative talents and literary habits and the crises in his life that directly affected his sensibility in order to understand how he transformed his experience into a new fictional mode. Accordingly, each section below focuses on one of the three simultaneously occurring phases in the genesis of Irving's form.

1. The Vogue of "Sketching": The Commercial Aspect

On August 19, 1817, in the time of *The Sketch Book's* prenatal period, Irving wrote to his brother Peter of having met, at the publisher John Murray's, the author Isaac D'Israeli and an artist "just returned from Italy with an immense number of beautiful sketches of Italian scenery and architecture" (*Letters* 1:488). That Irving had met an artist carrying a portfolio filled with sketches was certainly not unusual; the continent had been opened up for travel after the Napoleonic Wars, and visitors from all nations, especially Americans, came in ever expanding numbers. Among them were a large number of painters, who sketched the ruins in the Campagna or medieval streets of Italy, or for that matter, throughout Europe (Baker 2, 24; Wright 20). But professional and even amateur artists were not the only ones to take pencil in hand; dabbling in the fine arts became somewhat of a vogue, and it was quite common to see travelers and tourists making sketches of the more famous monuments, or of a beautiful landscape, or of a peasant in a picturesque native costume, or even of the paintings that they had viewed in the museums and galleries. Even though Irving saw himself as an artist, he was still quite typical of the travelers of his time: on one page of his journal he records that he "stopped at a Gallery & sketched," called on some acquaintances, one of whom was finishing a "Landscape sketch," and drove out to the country to see some friends, where "Miss Lowenstern sketched my likeness in her Sketch Book" (*Journals and Notebooks* 3:180). This journal also shows that frequently when guests called on Irving they would bring the sketches they had made on their travels and the group would spend the evening looking them over and enjoying the memories of previous experiences. Many of the travelers assumed this practice with no prior conception or aesthetic interest in mind and simply interlaced drawings and sketches with the written accounts in their journals, as if the verbal descriptions alone were not enough to do justice to the particular scenes and delights they had witnessed. The more sophisticated among them, however, conceived of the sketch as a way of commemorating, or giving permanence to, the responses that the beauties and wonders of the Old World had elicited from them. It was not visual accuracy they sought, but a deeper understanding of their experience, an attempt to grasp imaginatively the world they were encountering for the first time.

Irving acknowledges this vogue of sketching—and makes good use of it in terms of the commercial attractiveness of his book—first of all by entitling it *The Sketch Book,* and furthermore when he writes in his introduction that while he has "witnessed many of the shifting scenes of life," he has not "studied them with the eye of a philosopher," but rather with the "sauntering gaze" of the "humble lovers of the picturesque" ("The Author's Account of Himself" 9). And like these travelers he has gotten up a few sketches "for the entertainment of [his] friends." Moreover, Irving knew that, as the *Quarterly Review* commented in 1829, "Authorship and traveling are all the fashion,"[2] and although most of these journals and travelogues were a tedious collection of accounts and reminiscences of the obvious highlights, the reading public had a large appetite for them. Even more significantly, he was also aware of, and using to his advantage, the fact that the proliferation of travel writing, coupled with the concomitant fad of sketching, had given rise to a new term, the "travel sketch," which was used rather loosely as a descriptive label for a brief piece of writing that sought to present mainly the author's dominant impressions of his travels, including his responses to the mandatory sights. Occasionally, in the hands of a more thoughtful writer, the travel sketch became an informative, intelligent vehicle through which descriptions of the manners, customs, and habits of a group were conveyed to a more discerning public—though no one except Irving transformed it into a new genre. In any case, the English periodicals seized upon the travel sketch, incorporating it as a way of expanding their contents. They also began to appear in American magazines and newspapers, many of which simply reprinted, without permission, articles that had appeared in the English journals, as Irving undoubtedly knew from his wide reading and his brief stint as editor of the *Analectic Magazine* (1812–1814). Most often these "sketches" bore only a vague resemblance to finished drawings; unlike Irving's work, there was nothing especially visual, nor anything that showed creative ability or aesthetic sensitivity, in these writings. Since travelers had little or no interest in even the most rudimentary requirements of literary composition, *sketch* became a handy term to adopt; moreover, the suggestiveness of the word—i.e., an unfinished production, the working-out of an idea rather than the idea itself—gave legitimacy to uneven, and indeed often slipshod, presentations.

By using the term *sketch* to categorize his literary composition, Irving traded on these common and current associations, although there was nothing careless about the writing, construction, or publication of *The Sketch Book.* The popular portrait of the elegant idler indulging in sentiment, dallying with pen and pencil, and dashing off *The Sketch Book* is quite incorrect. Despite Hazlitt's remarks that he was a "mere trifler—a *filligree* man—an English *litterateur* at second hand" (*Conversations* 87), Irving was extremely serious about his literary endeavor.[3] Yet it is also true that he remained hesitant and doubtful about reappearing in print and that he was unable to compose for long periods of time. He often maintained a defensive posture about his writing, referring, for example, to a series of highly detailed and nicely executed descriptions of a Greenwich pensioner as "scribbling" (*Letters* 1:450–52). Such a casual remark was meant to suggest that he had expended no real energy in the expression and was even less concerned about the outcome, neither of which was the case. Moreover, his assumed skepticism about authorship served as a screen between himself and his audience, shielding him from the hostile response he dreaded. That he was fearful of public disapproval and uncertain of his own ability to sustain creative energy may be seen from his comments in the "Prospectus," where he informed his readers that "his writings will partake of the fluctuations of his own thoughts and feelings" and that "he will not be able to give them that tranquil attention necessary to finished composition" (300). Irving's undercutting of his own efforts is only one aspect of a tendency toward self-mocking irony, a strain in his personality largely responsible for the comic effects in *The Sketch Book*, generally expressed through the perspective and mental processes of Geoffrey Crayon. And in this regard, we should notice how Irving's full title, *The Sketch Book of Geoffrey Crayon, Gent.*, dramatically calls attention to the observing sketcher while the conventional title "Sketches of . . .," however impressionistic the volume may have been, emphasizes the object or place being sketched.

Unlike Irving, most would-be travel writers had no literary talent to speak of, but the popularity of travel literature was so enormous, and the public expectation and demand so great, that it was incumbent upon these fledgling authors to include in their journals, letters, notes, memoranda, and accounts, however hasty and unpolished, some verbal "sketches" of their encounters with European culture. The extent to which this was true can be seen in the work of Zachariah Allen, an industrial traveler who, in *The Practical Tourist* (1832), said that "the principal design of the writer of the following pages was to examine the effects of the important improvements in machinery upon the state of society at the present time." Unlike the usual traveler in Europe, he had not come to "indulge exclusively in the pleasures afforded to taste and intellect, by the examination of splendid buildings, paintings, statues, and libraries." Rather, he chose to spend his time by "entering apartments filled with the smoke of furnaces, and resounding with the deafening noise of machinery, or by conversing with men devoted to the common handicraft labors of life." However, "in accommodation to the taste of general readers, sketches of scenery, habits, and manners have been introduced to vary and enliven the subjects of remark" (quoted in Spiller 190). And as late as 1839, Francis J. Grund's book, *Aristocracy in America, from the*

Sketch-Book of a German Nobleman, offering a contemporary portrait of Jacksonian democracy, would still play on the idea of a rambling traveler making occasional drawings.

Another aspect of this revitalized interest in the fine art of sketching was the formation in 1799 in London of the Sketching Society, an organization that considered drawing and sketching not simply as diversion, but rather as a serious pastime in which both the intellectual and emotional faculties were engaged in an aesthetic contemplation of the environment (Reynolds 92–95).[4] The society (which survived for over fifty years) also encouraged its members to sketch from their own imaginations scenes that were suggested to them from literature, especially "passages creating a generalized poetical image." As a result of this latter activity, the Sketching Society fostered the application of poetic feeling to painting, including landscape painting (Reynolds 44), and in this respect it functioned remarkably like Irving's writings that have provided the landscapes of the upper Hudson with permanent poetical associations. If we think specifically in terms of Irving's re-creation of the sketch as a fictional form, however, the existence of the Sketching Society bears witness to the currency of certain trends and ideas about visual representation that, if they did not directly affect his choice of form, at least resemble his artistic designs. It thus indicates in a subtle way the extent of Irving's awareness of important aesthetic shifts and developments of his time, as well as highlighting the role the visual arts played in the formulation of his literary strategies.

2. Irving and the Painters: The Visual Aspect

Irving's literary sketches call attention to object as well as to observer and therefore rely upon a strong visual rendering of the realistic details of scene and setting. For example, in "The Inn Kitchen," a brief sketch that prefaces the tale of "The Spectre Bridegroom," Crayon's evocative description of domestic harmony among a group of travelers invites the reader to share with them the warmth and comfort emanating from "a great burnished stove, that might have been mistaken for an altar, at which they were worshipping":

> It was covered with various kitchen vessels of resplendent brightness; among which steamed and hissed a huge copper tea kettle. A large lamp threw a strong mass of light upon the group, bringing out many odd features in strong relief. Its yellow rays partially illumined the spacious kitchen, dying duskily away into remote corners, except where they settled in mellow radiance on the broad side of a flitch of bacon, or were reflected back from well scoured utensils, that gleamed from the midst of obscurity. A strapping Flemish lass, with

long golden pendants in her ears, and a necklace with a golden heart suspended to it, was the presiding priestess of the temple. (*Sketch Book* 119)

Having concentrated the reader's attention on this glowing sanctuary from night's dark chill, Crayon then fixes his focus on the "corpulent old Swiss" storyteller "dressed in a tarnished green travelling jacket, with a broad belt round his waist, and a pair of overalls, with buttons from the hips to the ankles." "I wish my readers could imagine," Crayon says in conclusion, "the old fellow lolling in a huge arm chair, one arm akimbo, the other holding a curiously twisted tobacco pipe, formed of genuine *écume de mer*, decorated with silver chain and silken tassel—his head cocked on one side, and a whimsical cut of the eye occasionally, as he related the following story" (*Sketch Book* 120). Yet it is precisely because his imagination *is* aroused by the portrait of the playful narrator that Irving's reader eagerly awaits the tale to follow.

In a revealing way, moreover, Crayon's pictures are also metaphorical reflections of his psychological state. In the above passage, his likening the stove to an "altar" and the kitchen maid to a "priestess" suggests that for the solitary voyager the scene is one of communion (the inn kitchen becomes the "temple"), a gathering of souls to relieve weariness and boredom. Crayon's participation through the act of listening evinces his need for meaningful ritual at the same time that it momentarily alleviates his sense of isolation. The counterpart to this mood occurs when anxiety is too great to be transposed into comforting ceremony. For example, during the pilgrim's initial departure in "The Voyage," his reveries and speculations "on the tranquil bosom of a summer's sea" are interrupted by the sight of a wrecked ship, prompting self-reflexive meditations on the fate of the lost crew. The ravages of an ensuing storm, evoked in nightmarish images and onomatopoetic language—"a fearful sullen sound of rushing waves and broken surges"; "the whistling of the wind through the rigging . . . like funereal wailings"; "the straining and groaning of bulk heads . . . in the weltering sea" (14)—mirror the unsteady movements of Crayon's distraught mind, while his personification of death "raging round this floating prison" exposes his fear of discontinuity, his anxiety at having left behind the "settled life" of the known world.

This painterly quality of Irving's prose can be traced to a talent for drawing and sketching that manifested itself early on in his life and that he continued to develop throughout his career. In the notebooks and journals that Irving kept on his first European voyage he made some forty-odd sketches and drawings, which reveal his interest in the people he encountered and the romantic aspects of the landscape he traversed (*Journals and Notebooks* 1:45 plates following 346). Obviously most of them were made in haste, but a considerable number do bring the subject to life. When in Rome in 1805 Irving met the American painter Washington Allston, who had gone abroad in 1800 to study art, he considered staying on and training himself for a career in the fine arts (Duyckinck 2:18–20). Irving had, as he said, a "strong inclination" for drawing, and Allston, after looking over his portfolio of sketches, declared that Irving had considerable potential. Allston encouraged him in this proposed endeavor, but eventually Irving reconsidered and decided against the venture, not, however, before he had sharpened his critical vision under Allston's tutelage. His biographer believes that Irving made a judicious decision, for in respect to painting, his continued interest "never transcended intelligent appreciation" (Williams, *Life* 1:65). However, this sense of "appreciation"—in effect, the development of an aesthetic sensibility—was just the way in which Irving's prose sketches benefited from his involvement in the graphic arts (Pauly 491–92).[5] From Allston he learned how to concentrate his sight solely on one discrete object at a time because, as he later recalled it, "the mind can only take in a certain number of images and impressions directly; by multiplying the number you weaken each, and render the whole confused and vague" (Duyckinck 2:18). Coupled with a "talent not unlike Thackeray's" (Williams, *Life* 1:65), this guidance helped him rid his prose style of abstractions as it encouraged the development of a more visually oriented prose form.

Irving maintained his association with painters throughout his long stay in Europe from 1815 to 1832. Chief among them were Charles Robert Leslie, a young American artist and friend of Allston's, and Stuart Newton, nephew of the great American portrait painter, Gilbert Stuart. Leslie has testified to Irving's visual acumen and how he, as a painter, was able to profit from their friendship: "You opened to me a new range of observation in my own art, and a perception of the qualities and character of things which painters do not always imbibe from each other" (quoted in Williams, *Life* 1:169). The influence was mutually enriching: during the years when Irving first conceived of *The Sketch Book,* and while it was being completed, polished, and published, he conscientiously applied himself to a study of Leslie's art, which came to have an enormous hold over him. Leslie was primarily a genre painter, taking his scenes of human activity from everyday life and, even more, from literary sources. His work, therefore, has a "decided literary cast" to it (Prown 5). Irving sensed the possibilities in the fusion of the mediums—after all, what he had seen on his journeys was always an amalgam of the actual scene he encountered with the associations he brought to it from his vast literary heritage—and wondered whether he could create verbally what Leslie was accomplishing visually. It was about this time, late in 1818, that Irving first invented his fictional traveler—i.e., the "Geoffrey Crayon" persona—and decided to publish his sketches in clusters of three or four, each cluster a group portrait of England, with an occasional added view of America.

In identifying his work more and more with the visual arts, Irving turned to the verbal sketching techniques with which he had earlier experimented. In an 1818 notebook, he dashed off a typical pencil sketch of an old man's head accompanied by this laconic verbal description: "Old crown of hat without rim[—]purple plush vest[—]tarnished old leather breeches that reach below calves of the legs—worsted stocking & land shoes" (*Journals and Notebooks* 2:274). A crucial difference between these later verbal and visual activities and the earlier ones is that now Irving was consciously trying to fuse the mediums into a new form. Indeed, he had really come to view nature and human activity with a painter's eye, which means, if nothing else, with the intention of reproducing it. The reminiscence of William Preston, a traveling companion with whom he toured Scotland in 1817, points to the way Irving linked his talent for drawing and sketching to a kind of writing that would accommodate his acute visual sense:

> Irving decided that literature was to be his profession and the means of support. He had taken lessons in drawing, and had a decided turn for the art. He sketched very well, even in the estimation of Washington Allston, Leslie, and Stewart [*sic*] Newton, and it was perhaps some feeling of this kind that suggested to him the notion of his Sketch Book. He turned it [over] in his mind—spoke a good deal to me about it—occasionally asked me when he gave an account of anything that touched him, how would that do in print. We went to the Athenaeum together and on our return he jotted down what he saw or what had struck him. (36)

That Irving's prose easily translates to a visual medium is a measure of his success. He inspired painters to give artistic expression to his creations via original compositions; among these, of course, are the famous haunting visions of John Quidor. And because artists could easily visualize in their minds the scenes he was creating, his work has been more handsomely illustrated than that of any other writer in American literary history.

In fact, Irving's literary designs were brought into clearer focus by a set of illustrations that were made for a third edition of *Knickerbocker's History* that he was planning to bring out in 1818. Irving, in need of money and support, solicited drawings from Allston and Leslie, believing that a more elegant, illustrated edition would encourage a greater sale. He was delighted with the results, he informed

Allston, not simply because the designs were beautifully executed and would enhance the new edition, but more so because they provided him with a fresh impetus in relation to his own writing: "I dwell on these little sketches, because they give me quite a new train of ideas in respect to my work: and I only wish I had it now to write, as I am sure I should conceive the scenes in a much purer style; having these pic[tures] before me as corrections of the *grossierté* into which the sent[iment of?] a work of humour is apt to run" (*Letters* 1:479; original brackets). It is most likely that what Irving consciously meant here is that the contrast of Allston's carefully delineated pictures with the fulsome burlesque humor of *A History of New York* made him feel that his caricature had been too excessive in that earlier work. The robustness of spirit prevalent in *Knickerbocker's History* had already been quite muted by the loss of his beloved and the failure of the family business, so it is unlikely that he was directly inspired by these pictures to adopt the more genteel tones of *The Sketch Book*, though what he admires about the drawings—their "delicate humor," "graceful composition," and "rural air"—are qualities equally attributable to *The Sketch Book*. But there was a definite link between Allston's drawings and the visual sketches that he had already made in his notebooks, even though it is true that his own sketches result from a desire for "aesthetic sensitivity" rather than "artistic achievement" (Pauly 491). These associations confirmed the ideas he was currently entertaining on literary production. If his previous work could "present such pleasing images to imaginations like [Allston's] & Leslie's" (*Letters* 1:479), was he not now moving in the right direction in especially concentrating on his talent for visual prose in his new work? Though he probably would have liked to have rewritten the *History* to correct the "impurities," by August 1817, only three months after he wrote this letter to Allston, he had completed the drafts of nine sketches that were to appear in *The Sketch Book* (Williams, *Life* 1:168). And since that famous work was designed to express his sensory and emotional experience, he made a fortuitous choice in relying on visual detail to capture and present the essence of that experience.

3. The Sketch as a Personal Form: The Emotional Aspect

Irving's fictional sketches, then, besides being more painterly and precise than the ordinary travel sketch, also have an emotional depth below the artistic surface. In fact, beyond its development of narrative, the sketch is characterized by the moods and tones of personality, ostensibly Crayon's, but certainly reflective of Irving's. Whatever "happens" in the sketch, happens inside of Crayon; this internalizing process colors the sketch and turns what began seemingly as an objective observation into a subjective reverie (Hedges 145–46).[6] The most dynamic aspect of the form, this personal element is also the most difficult to trace to its origins. It is clear, however, that the emphasis on self, on the concern for the individual rather than the society, is one of the principles at the very heart of Romanticism. G. Harrison Orians has noted that one of the dominant characteristics of early nineteenth-century literature is "the return to the nature of individual man, paralleled by an assertion of the importance of personality" (166–67). The Irvingesque sketch takes its place as one of the romantic forms of literature that emerged after neoclassical values and traditions lost their hegemony. Two possible reasons for this connection therefore suggest themselves: Irving was either influenced by the Romantic movement or guided by a romanticist.

Regarding the former possibility, it is true that Irving was developing the fictional sketch during the very years that the gradual shift from the objective to the subjective mode in literature was occurring, when in general authors were beginning to turn from thoughtful observation of life to the sheer revelation of personality. For all that has been said about his romanticism, however, Irving was not consciously working in this revelatory vein; he did not, like the great Romantic writers, boldly project the self onto the world's surface, nor did he journey into the interior and display a self struggling through inner division into growth. In fact, like most American writers of this time, he retreated from this "extreme subjectivism"; moreover, the philosophical and ontological depths of Romanticism were beyond him. Yet, to the extent that external scenes and recreated experiences take on meaning only in their relation to Crayon—to the extent, that is, that the perspective has shifted from an emphasis on the recognized social world to a preoccupation with the individual's private perceptions—the sketch partakes of the new subjectivism of the early nineteenth century. Not a Shelley or a Wordsworth, Irving chose to pursue the self metaphorically as it was reflected in its surroundings.

If the currents of nineteenth-century Romanticism circling about Irving did not cause this shift in perspective—did not, in other words, lead to the creation of an alter ego named Geoffrey Crayon—then perhaps, as F. L. Pattee asserted, he was changed from an eighteenth-century classicist to a nineteenth-century romanticist through the reading of Walter Scott (7–9). Such a claim has validity: there is no doubt that from the reading of the Waverley novels, from the direct stimulus of Scott's personality, from the conversations Irving had with him on his visit to Abbotsford in 1817, and from his travels through the Scottish terrain near Edinburgh, Irving absorbed the ambience of romantic literature in which the older and more accomplished writer was already steeped. Scott, with his innumerable border tales and legendary stories, filled his mind with a "world of ideas, images, and impressions," Irving told his brother Peter in 1817 (*Letters* 1:501). Certainly Scott directed Irving to a wealth of legend and folklore, especially of German origin, and showed him the richness of anti-quarian material. From Scott, too, Irving borrowed elements of the gothic—spectral bridegrooms, demon lovers, pumpkin-headed ghosts—that appear in his works. Irving also shared with Scott an affinity for picturesque landscape, and surely in some of the areas of *The Sketch Book* Scott's love of romantic atmosphere can be detected. Yet all of these elements represent only the accoutrements of literary romanticism, the artifice of the quaint and the occult with which the standard popular literature of the day was draped. However, since Scott did not see literature as conditioned by the literary creator's personality, his influence was not responsible for the more subtle, more intriguing aspects of the sketch form. By adopting and yet adapting the travel sketch, and by developing the persona of Geoffrey Crayon, Irving moved beyond his mentor in his approach to fiction.[7]

To understand fully how Irving came to mold the sketch into a romantic form, one must measure the effects of his intimate emotional life at the time he was writing *The Sketch Book*. In 1817–1818, while he was in England, he suffered terrible anxiety and emotional strain over the collapse of the family business and the attendant threat of impoverishment. Although he was only a nominal partner in the firm, he believed that he shared in his brother's "notoriety" (Williams, *Life* 1:151). This "horrible ordeal of bankruptcy" cast a terrible gloom upon Irving, as he agonized to his brother William over the plight of their family: "My heart is torn every way by anxiety for my relatives. My own individual interests are nothing. The merest pittance would content me if I could crawl out from among these troubles and see my connections safe around me" (*Letters* 1:457). As much as he worried over this immediate situation and suffered from a deeply felt sense of shame, Irving was also thrown back to a previous period in his life when he had lost his betrothed, Matilda Hoffman, to an early death by consumption. When she died in April 1809, Irving suffered waves of despair; in 1817 he evinced the identical symptoms: sleeplessness, loss of appetite, extreme depression, nightmares, fits of nervousness. In both instances he took the same initial measure: "I shut myself up from society," he wrote in his most personally revealing letter, "—and would See no one" (*Letters* 1:743). In his psyche, the new and the old sorrows formed a continuous link; brooding upon one he brooded upon the other. In the midst of this distress, another calamity befell him: he was told of his mother's death on April 9, 1817. This great loss paralleled his former one; he now feared that all the human contact he had left, the protection of his brothers upon which he had always relied, would also be taken from him. In his isolation the images of failure, loss, and bereavement crowded into his mind. The world was again, as it had been in 1809, an alien place to him. While others rejoiced at the restoration of peace brought by the end of the Napoleonic Wars, his hopes had been "overwhelmed" (*Journals and Notebooks* 2:174).

The central entry in this notebook of 1817 shows quite vividly that the grief Irving suffered over the financial ruin of the business reawakened and deepened his former grief over his early loss.[8] In a passage apostrophizing Matilda Hoffman, Irving recollects their parting scene and recalls his misery: "Oh Matilda where was the soul-felt devotion—the buoyancy—the consciousness of worth & happiness that once seemed to lift me from the earth when our eyes interchanged silent but eloquent vows of affection . . . how lovely was then my life—How has it changed since—what scenes have I gone through since thou hast left me—what jarring collisions with the world—what heartless pleasures—what sordid pursuits—what gross associations—what rude struggles—. . . The romance of life is past" (*Journals and Notebooks* 2:185–86). The pain in this passage suggests the empty, dispirited years that passed between Matilda Hoffman's death and Irving's new tragedy; once again, he collided with life's mutability. Yet his biographer warns that "precisely what this event [Matilda Hoffman's death] meant to Irving, or what its influence was upon his writing, no one knows." "Attributions . . . of the influence of Matilda Hoffman upon his essays mean very little" (Williams, *Notes* 26).[9] We cannot say that the memory of Matilda Hoffman is solely responsible for the mood of reverie in *The Sketch Book* or the profound melancholy of "St. Mark's Eve" in *Bracebridge Hall*. As wise as these cautionary words are, however, they do not invalidate the notebook entries that indicate a definite effect upon Irving and precise connections between the two periods in his life. The importance of the link is that the death of Matilda Hoffman and the recurring crisis affected not individual passages and particular sketches, but the whole genesis of Irving's fictional sketch form.

What exactly happened to Irving emotionally in 1809, and how that crisis recurred in 1817, and even more, how that led him to an original form, are crucial questions that demand scrutiny and analysis. In particular, Irving twice exhibited a pattern of behavior with three distinct phases: seclusion, social detachment, and authorship. First, his distress was so great that he could find no comfort in either solitude or company. In both crises of his life he tried to shut himself away: in 1809 he sought the silence of a country seat at Kinderhook, just outside New York, but returned periodically to the city; in 1817 he retreated, first to Birmingham at the home of his sister, then to his room in London, yet in the city he found it necessary to roam the streets when he could bear the seclusion no more. In his confessional letter of 1823, he wrote of the earlier time:

> I cannot tell you what a horrid state of mind I was in for a long time—I seemed to care for nothing—the world was a blank to me—I abandoned all thoughts of the Law—I went into the country, but could not bear solitude yet could not enjoy society—There was a dismal horror continually in my mind that made me fear to be alone—I had often to get up in the night & seek the bedroom of my brother, as if the having a human being by me would relieve me from the frightful gloom of my own thoughts. (*Letters* 1:740)

This was certainly a change from the "fairy land" that the world had once been (*Letters* 1:738). Second, his change in character and attitude remained permanent; Irving was never able to assimilate himself into the world as he once had done. There would be no more melding into the dreamy surroundings of Sleepy Hollow or elsewhere. His estrangement was permanent: ". . . the despondency I had suffered for a long time in the course of this attachment, and the anguish that attended its catastrophe seemed to give a turn to my whole character, and threw some clouds into my disposition which have ever since hung about it" (*Letters* 1:740). Third, in each case, either as an attempt to tame moods of despair, or in the belief that solace was attainable there, Irving took up writing: "The idea suddenly came to return to my pen" (*Letters* 1:743). In 1809 he returned to *A History of New York* and reworked the original conception, and in 1817 he began the sketches that were to become *The Sketch Book.*

Grief implanted in Irving a strong recognition of the essential separateness of the world and the self; in addition, the self, conscious of its vulnerability, was forced to take refuge in its own repository of feelings. In time it came to regard those feelings as of paramount importance. People, places, and objects that had previously been part of a vast panoramic scene, capable of producing pleasant and soothing impressions, were now filtered through a consciousness that did not just record those impressions, but at the same time registered responses, because the troubled self had been bruised by disappointment, rebuff, and betrayal. The spellbinding regions of New York State and the wonders of the first European tour (1804–1805) had been viewed through the eyes of a very different Irving from the one who filled his sketchbook with the sights and sounds of old England. The "I" that emerged from the first emotional trauma and was reawakened in the second was not one to sing its own celebration; rather, it murmured the equivalent of "I must watch and protect myself." Although he was still attracted, although he still explored, pain had taught Irving to distrust the world.

When Irving sat down in 1817 to write of his experiences in

England, his stance was not that of the objective observer or the detached spectator. He was, moreover, too close to his recent calamities and the memory of his earlier misfortunes for personal emotions to become completely assimilated in the process of creation, the artistic result being a correlative of these emotions. It was more a matter of discovering a form through which these emotions could be sifted and thereby examined. And the vehicle Irving discovered for accomplishing this—the essence, in fact, of his form—was his persona, Geoffrey Crayon. Sometimes humorous, occasionally foolish, often sentimental, Crayon expresses Irving's desires and exhibits his anxieties, yet because he is the major device in a narrative strategy he permits his author to re-experience the emotional traumas and frustrated hopes of his recent past without becoming psychologically immobilized by them. The emphasis in Irving's sketches, therefore, is always on Crayon: the need for mystery and hidden meaning he brings to, and the frustrations, disappointments, and (occasionally) joys he extracts from his journeys into the dark recesses of the city or the rarely traversed areas of the country.

On one such peregrination about "the great metropolis" of London, described in "The Art of Book Making," Crayon discovers the reading room of the British Museum. Comparing himself to a "Knight errant" about to enter the "portal of [an] enchanted castle," and the black-clothed men he spies about the place to a "body of Magi, deeply engaged in the study of occult sciences," Crayon believes he has stumbled upon an "enchanted library." But the "pale, studious personages, poring intently over dusty volumes, rummaging among mouldy manuscripts, and taking copious notes of their contents," are nothing more than a group of modern authors principally occupied in manufacturing books by borrowing thoughts and sentiments— "classic lore, or 'pure English undefiled' "—from the literature of the past. Crayon's humor turns into revulsion at this instance of shabby pilfering. Subsequently, he falls asleep and dreams that these literary pretenders are metamorphosed into a "ragged, thread bare throng," garmented in leaves of ancient books and manuscripts. Outraged at the plunderers for their scandalous behavior, the nearby hanging portraits of eminent writers suddenly come alive and dispel the parasites. Crayon laughs out loud at these fleeing bookworms, and the laughter wakes him from his uneasy dream at the same time that it alerts the librarian, who thereupon dismisses *him* for failing to present the necessary identification for admission (*Sketch Book* 61–66). In effect, Crayon's imagination self-reflexively expresses Irving's doubts and anxieties about his literary practices, as it transforms, in a humorously exaggerated fashion, what he [Crayon] has seen in the reading room into what Irving fears: that the fictional sketches of his experiences, fleshed-out by his reworking of the moods, descriptions, and nuances of feeling of his favorite writers (in fact, he himself prefaces at least two-thirds of the sketches with an epigraph from one of these revered authors) were only another form of imitation, similar to the productions of the seedy rag-pickers Crayon had envisioned (Kasson 37).

Burdened by insecurity over his professional commitment to literature and troubled about the substantiality of the form he had developed, Irving worried that like the patchwork productions of the "scholars" in the British Museum reading room, his creations did not have a life and meaning of their own. He feared, too, that his process of composing was just one more instance of "book making" and that he was a mediocre copy of one of the long line of writers who had described the British scene. And as an American ostensibly commenting upon English manners and customs, Irving could not help but speculate whether he would be viewed as an imposter or a fraud by the British, and as an affected fool by the Americans. The conflict in this particular sketch, however, is resolved in the same way as many of the other personal problems Irving dealt with in *The Sketch Book*, through comedy and the good-natured mockery of his persona. The importance of Geoffrey Crayon here cannot be overstated: even though he has no "card of admission" to the British Museum reading room, as an original creation he gives to Irving, who heretofore felt that he had no legitimacy as a writer, admission to the world of professional authorship.

The sketch as Irving developed it, then, incorporated formal techniques by which the perceptions and responses of an unassertive, tentative observer could be tested against the landscape of the outside world. His speaker/persona alternatively seeks out and withdraws from a society that both fascinates him and threatens him—he desires both to see life and to maintain his distance from it (Hedges 148–49). The process, which is both narrative and psychological, is an intricate one: though it tends to reinforce Irving's sense of isolation, it also permits him the luxury of meditating on it under a fictional guise. Irving's form was so much a product of his personality—and so responsive to it—that the paradoxical desires of approach and withdrawal, and the variations in degree of separation and the emotions attendant upon it, make the relationship between observer and object a complex and intense one. Such an integral part of the Irvingesque sketch, the creation of a persona was an innovation that cleverly fulfilled his emotional needs while at the same time enhancing the commercial and artistic attractiveness of the new form.

Thus, what we have is a network of factors surrounding Irving's choice of the word *Sketch* to describe his fictional practices and his methods of distancing himself from his emotional experience in *The Sketch Book*. His talent for drawing, his keen powers of observation, his early and continued experiments in descriptive prose, and his long and mutually beneficial association with painters pointed to the possibilities of a form that relied heavily upon the creation of a strong visual sense in prose. By applying the terminology of one medium to another, he could transfer at least one of the essentials of crayon sketching—an imaginative grasp, understanding, and appreciation of the environment—to his own writing. The climate created by the sudden burst of travel in Europe after the Napoleonic Wars, including the accompanying travel writing and sketching (and the concurrent development of the travel sketch as a mainstay of the periodicals), suggested to him the means by which he could bring his endeavor for literary expression into line with public taste. The idea of a traveler making sketches also served a covert purpose, for it acted as an emotional camouflage behind which Irving could explore his own responses to a perplexing and often disturbing world. Through the multifaceted functioning of Crayon, Irving advanced his composition well beyond the usual travel pieces. In addition, by aligning his writings with a series of travel sketches he gained a considerable amount of maneuverability; as "travel sketches" were rambling, unstructured prose compositions, he could test his observations and experiment with a narrative technique without violating any strict generic rules. Moreover, the varied format permitted by a collection of fictional sketches enabled him to include within the contents of *The Sketch Book* several fully developed short stories, the most famous of which were, of course, "Rip Van Winkle" and "The Legend of Sleepy Hollow." All of this proved to be a shrewd calculation on Irving's part: having accurately gauged the intensity of the American passion for news and picturesque views of the Old World, especially from England, he assured himself a solid readership, while at the same time freeing himself from the burdens of a rigid form. The result was a work of undeniable originality, though the full achievement of *The Sketch Book* has yet to be revealed.[10]

When Irving made the decision to write about his travels in England, his goal was professional success. For him this meant not only popular acclaim and financial remuneration, but critical recognition as well. Yet because the events of the past few years had eroded his confidence, he needed a form that could accommodate his doubts about their meaning and the stability of his point of view. As he understood it, a hesitant nature puzzling over the complexities and ambiguities of experience need not drift into confusion or vagueness if the author is in control of his medium. Adapting the readily available travel sketch for this purpose proved to be the perfect choice: at the same time that it enabled him to hold in check his continued vacillation and unresolved anxiety, it gave him license to present these to the world as the tentative perceptions and troubled vagaries of mind of his authorial persona, Geoffrey Crayon. Thus by building on his strengths (especially his skill as a painter in prose) while exorcising his weaknesses, he at once solved personal, professional, and artistic problems. The fact that many other nineteenth-century writers found the form amenable to their literary purposes attests to its durability and suggests that a study of the sketch tradition in our literature would be a profitable undertaking. But no matter what direction such a study takes, it would necessarily have to commence with the work of Washington Irving, where the sketch received its first genuine fictional expression.

Notes

1. As a miscellany, *The Sketch Book* contains a variety of literary forms, including the sketch, the short story, and the essay. In this paper I am concerned only with how Irving created the fictional sketch, which centers on the consciousness and activities of Geoffrey Crayon.

2. Dulles also points to the fact that "every important American writer of the first half of the nineteenth century lived or traveled abroad except Thoreau and Poe." Of course, huge numbers of minor figures also crossed the ocean, and it would seem that most of them presented their impressions of Europe in letters, journal, or diary to a welcoming public.

3. Of all Irving's contemporary critics, Hazlitt was the most severe. Five years earlier, in *The Spirit of the Age*, he had written that Irving "gives us very good American copies of our British Essayists and Novelists . . . [His] writings are literary *anachronisms*"(405).

4. I am indebted to Pauly (491–92, n. 8) for this source, and for his ideas regarding the possible influence of the practices of this society on Irving.

5. When Pauly mentions Irving's sketches in this context, he is apparently referring to what he calls the "hasty," "awkward" drawings Irving made in his travel journals. Irving's prose "sketches," however, are more significant in this regard than his pencil sketches.

6. Pauly sees Crayon as a "vehicle for a sentimental-romantic point of view," which is a narrow and confining way of explaining the function of this persona, though he does observe that "as a tourist in England, Crayon is consistently more interested in the effect of his experience than in the experience itself" (492). In addition, while Addison also might be considered "subjective" in his observations, he always delivered his criticism from a culturally sanctioned position. As "Mr. Spectator," he made judgments that carried the authority of eighteenth-century English society. Crayon has no such identification and no such certainty.

7. It might also be argued that the British gothic writers, in particular Ann Radcliffe, influenced Irving in the direction of romanticism. Indeed, in "Irving and the Gothic Tradition" John Clendenning shows the extent to which Irving was familiar with gothic motifs, with their "emphasis on the subjective rather than the objective" (97). Yet, however much Irving may have appropriated the genre for his own purposes— which were either outright parody or what Clendenning calls the "sportive gothic" (where Irving employs gothic "machinery" in a lighthearted way, as in "Sleepy Hollow," to illustrate the results of the disassociation of imagination from life)—the gothic

tradition bears primarily upon Irving's short stories and does not explain the development of the sketch, which is essentially autobiographical in nature.

8. Aware of this depression, Richard Ellmann has approached "Rip Van Winkle" as a "parable" of Irving's life, that is, as "the presentation, with as much directness as possible, of the meaning of Irving's experience as a man in the world." What Ellmann says about "Rip" is true for all of Irving's best and most interesting work: it is a "sifting of his personal emotion" through a fictional medium and an assimilation of his experience into an artistic context that served both a literary and psychological need (27, col. 3).

9. But Williams adds that while the problem is "essentially insoluble, it is nevertheless important in a study of Irving's life and art."

10. The opening chapter in my forthcoming study, *Adrift in the Old World: The Psychological Pilgrimage of Washington Irving* (Univ. of Chicago Press, Fall 1987), details the development of the Crayonesque persona and, in coordination with this, highlights the anxiety, both personal and cultural, that Irving had to overcome to attain distinction as America's first successful author.

Works Cited

Baker, Paul R. *The Fortunate Pilgrims: Americans in Italy, 1800–1860.* Cambridge, Mass.: Harvard Univ. Press, 1964.

Clendenning, John. "Irving and the Gothic Tradition." *Bucknell Review* 12 (1964): 90–98.

Dulles, Foster Rhea. *Americans Abroad: Two Centuries of European Travel.* Ann Arbor: Univ. of Michigan Press, 1964.

Duyckinck, Evert A., and George Duyckinck. *The Cyclopaedia of American Literature.* Ed. M. Laird Simons. 2 vols. 1855; rpt. Philadelphia: T. Elwood Zell, 1875.

Ellmann, Richard. "Love in the Catskills." *New York Review of Books* 5 Feb. 1976: 27–28.

Grund, Francis J. *Aristocracy in America, from the Sketch-Book of a German Nobleman.* 1839; rpt. New York: Harper, 1959.

Hazlitt, William. *The Spirit of the Age: or Contemporary Portraits.* 2nd ed. London: Henry Colburn, 1825.

———. *Conversations of James Northcote, Esq. R.A.* Ed. Frank Swinnerton. 1830; rpt. London: Frederick Muller, 1949.

Hedges, William L. *Washington Irving: An American Study, 1802–1832.* Baltimore: Johns Hopkins Univ. Press, 1965.

Irving, Washington. *The Sketch Book of Geoffrey Crayon, Gent.* Ed. Haskell Springer. Boston: Twayne, 1978.

———. *Letters: Volume 1, 1802–1823.* Ed. Ralph M. Aderman, et al. Boston: Twayne, 1978.

———. *Journals and Notebooks: Volume 1, 1803–1806.* Ed. Nathalia Wright. Madison: Univ. of Wisconsin Press, 1969.

———. *Journals and Notebooks: Volume 2, 1807–1822.* Ed. Walter A. Reichart and Lillian Schlissel. Boston: Twayne, 1981.

———. *Journals and Notebooks: Volume 3, 1819–1827.* Ed. Walter A. Reichart. Madison: Univ. of Wisconsin Press, 1970.

———. "St. Mark's Eve." In *Bracebridge Hall*. Ed. Herbert F. Smith. Boston: Twayne, 1977. 81–87.

Kasson, Joy. *Artistic Voyagers: Europe and the American Imagination in the Works of Irving, Allston, Cole, Cooper, and Hawthorne*. Contributions in American Studies, Number 60. Westport, Conn.: Greenwood Press, 1982.

Orians, G. Harrison. "The Rise of Romanticism, 1805–1855." In *Transitions in American Literary History*. Ed. Harry Hayden Clark. Durham, N.C.: Duke Univ. Press, 1953. 163–244.

Pattee, Fred Lewis. *The Development of the American Short Story: An Historical Survey*. New York: Harper and Bros., 1923.

Pauly, Thomas H. "The Literary Sketch in Nineteenth Century America." *Texas Studies in Literature and Language* 17 (1975):489–503.

Preston, William C. *The Reminiscences of William C. Preston*. Ed. Minnie C. Yarborough. Chapel Hill: Univ. of North Carolina Press, 1933.

Prown, Jules David. "Washington Irving's Interest in Art and His Influence Upon American Painting." Master's thesis. Univ. of Delaware, 1956.

Reynolds, Graham, *A Concise History of Watercolors*. New York: Abrams, 1971.

Spiller, Robert E. *The American in England in the First Half Century of Independence*. New York: H. Holt and Co., 1926.

Williams, Stanley, ed. *Notes While Preparing "Sketch Book" &c., 1817*. By Washington Irving. New Haven: Yale Univ. Press, 1927.

———. *The Life of Washington Irving*. 2 vols. New York: Oxford Univ. Press, 1935.

Wright, Nathalia. *American Novelists in Italy. The Discoverers: Allston to James*. Philadelphia: Univ. of Pennsylvania Press, 1965.

The Author as Professional: Washington Irving's "Rambling Anecdotes" of the West

Wayne R. Kime[*]

By returning to New York City in May 1832, after a seventeen-year absence in Europe, Washington Irving realized a long-deferred intention. Even amid his successes as "Geoffrey Crayon," author of *The Sketch Book* (1819–1820), *Bracebridge Hall* (1822), and *Tales of a Traveller* (1824), and later under his own name as historian-producer of *The Life and Voyages of Christopher Columbus* (1828) and *A Chronicle of the Conquest of Granada* (1829), Irving had looked forward to coming home. He had formed a clear conception of the manner in which, once he resettled among his countrymen, he wished to pass his days. His "true course," he considered, was to continue

[*] This essay was written specifically for this volume and is published here for the first time by permission of the author.

devoting himself to the central interest of his lifetime, "my literary career."[1] Yet, afflicted by a lonely fear that the long stay in Europe was transforming him into a rootless wanderer, he felt the need to establish himself near the large Irving family among whom he had once been a familiar member. Thus, not long after his repatriation Irving began considering the purchase of a property that fronted the Hudson River near Tarrytown, a few miles north of New York City. He would renovate the old stone cottage on this plot of land, transforming it into a "snuggery" for himself and those family members who chose to reside with him there. He would fashion a mode of life modest yet elegant, rural yet within easy reach of the city, and affording comfortable conditions for writing. Of course, to realize these aims he would need to add substantially to his wealth; and this he intended to do through continued activity as a professional author.

During the five years that followed his return to the United States, Irving succeeded handily in fulfilling his wishes. His three books on the American West, *A Tour on the Prairies* (1835), *Astoria* (1836), and *The Adventures of Captain Bonneville* (1837), were issued concurrently with his purchase and renovation of "the Roost," later renamed "Sunnyside," the modest estate that became his permanent home. The sums he realized from these works were a major source of funds for improvements. In the letters he wrote during this period he often summarized his literary activities immediately before or after describing progress at the cottage. Home ownership and professional authorship were closely linked in his mind.

Irving's three western books are the productions of a professional writer in a broader sense of that term. They all exhibit a confident certainty of touch, an easy grace, and a resourcefulness that bespeak an artist at the height of his powers. Through his varied experience Irving had learned to gauge the potentialities of a given body of material and then to mold that material into an artistically and popularly satisfying product. Sensitive to the preferences of his audience, he was able to correlate these deftly with his personal inclinations. He knew his own tastes, had formed his individual habits, and had mastered his tools. The western volumes are thus characteristic products of his talent, revealing development and recombination of techniques he had employed in earlier writings.

During the summer of 1832 Irving began an extensive tour of the United States, a journey that gave impetus to his subsequent literary activity. Passing through his native state, near Buffalo he happened to meet Henry L. Ellsworth, a Connecticut gentleman who was one of three persons commissioned by the federal government to visit and inspect western lands set aside for emigrating Indian tribes.[2] Ellsworth invited Irving to accompany him on the official expedition. The opportunity to observe Osage and Pawnee Indians

in their native territory, perhaps to participate in a buffalo hunt—
in general, to experience the Far West at first hand and under military
escort—was not to be refused. Proceeding south to Cincinnati, Ohio,
and thence west as far as Independence, Missouri, the Ellsworth party
again turned south and traveled on horseback for eleven more days
before reaching its jumping-off place, Fort Gibson, the first military
installation in what is now Oklahoma. On the following day, 9 October,
the delegation with its escort set out westward into open country.
"I felt now completely launched in a savage life," Irving later reported
to his brother Peter, "and extremely excited and interested by this
wild country, and the wild scenes and people by which I was surrounded."[3] During his thirty-one-day absence from Fort Gibson the
author participated actively in the routines of the official party.
Meanwhile, as was his habit, he recorded his impressions in daily
journal entries, no doubt anticipating some future use. Continuing
his tour, Irving boarded a steamboat bound for New Orleans. At last,
after a four-month journey of more than three thousand miles, in
mid-December he arrived in Washington, D.C. He had amassed a
fund of new experiences, but the foray into Indian country seems to
have been the portion of his travels that most stimulated his imagination.

During his stay in the national capital Irving attempted to settle
into writing for publication, but he was unable to do so. The welter
of his recent memories refused to take shape amidst distractions from
social engagements and other interests. An added impediment was
the "fancied necessity,"[4] as he put it, of preparing a volume on a
specifically American topic to satisfy demanding admirers. Months
passed, and by the fall of 1833 Irving had reached the stage of mental
gestation that preceded his most satisfying periods of work. The
scenes and incidents of the western tour had begun to assume "a
proper tone and grouping in my mind, and to take a tinge from my
imagination," he wrote Peter, indicating that he was anticipating a
productive winter.[5] In this painterly way he reported progress on
the first of his western books, A Tour on the Prairies.

To satisfy at once the public's appetite for a work in which the
celebrated "Geoffrey Crayon" portrayed himself in an American
setting, Irving projected A Tour as the first of three short volumes,
each of which would develop a topic associated with a separate area
of his experience or reputation. The whole would be entitled The
Crayon Miscellany, as befitted a collection in which the persona of
"Geoffrey Crayon" was the sole unifying feature. By combining A
Tour with two other recognizably Irvingesque topics, accounts of
visits to the homes of Sir Walter Scott and Lord Byron and a series
of narratives relating half-legendary events in the wars between Spaniards and Moors, he would offer readers a sampler that recalled his

earlier writings about England and Spain and also portrayed scenes he had witnessed since his return to the United States. If none of the three projected volumes was very weighty by itself, the whole should give satisfaction. Individual titles would appeal to various tastes, and perceived weaknesses in one book would be offset by strengths in another.

In a preface specially prepared for the American edition of *A Tour*, issued in April 1835, Irving reintroduced himself to his countrymen, drawing upon certain of his best-remembered literary creations to illustrate passages in his own life history. To characterize the lonely apprehension he had felt upon first sailing from New York in 1815, he quoted a full paragraph on precisely that theme from "The Voyage," the sketch that follows "The Author's Account of Himself" in *The Sketch-Book*. To dramatize the doubts of continuing regard he had harbored on his return, he likened himself to Rip Van Winkle wandering confused and forgotten along village streets he had last seen twenty years before. "I passed through places that ought to be familiar to me," he wrote, "but all were changed. . . . As I passed on, I looked wistfully in every face: not one was known to me—not one!"[6] And he ended the preface by characterizing *A Tour* in a manner that recalled the corresponding passage in *The Sketch Book*. There, contrasting himself to more ambitious travelers whose portfolios boasted representations of all the chief scenes in a European traveler's standard itinerary, he confessed the modesty and miscellaneousness of the out-of-the-way sketches he had assembled. In *A Tour* he promised "nothing wonderful or adventurous," but only "a simple narrative of every day occurrences; such as happen to every one who travels the prairies"(9). By these allusive passages Irving assured his audience that *A Tour* was indeed a work "By the Author of *The Sketch Book*," as he had indicated on the title page.

The book's representation of western scenes yet visited by few persons was no doubt more "wonderful" to contemporary readers than the author modestly claimed. But to the appeal of novel subject matter, Irving added a complementary focus of interest, his own portrayed self. He seems to have judged that the mere description of these adventures in a style recognizably his own would be considered an asset to the book. Thus, the most casual reader would have noticed continuity between certain of his earlier practices and his performance in *A Tour*. Repeatedly, for example, he likens the prairie landscape to Spanish scenes he had described in *Granada* and *The Alhambra*. Or Indians, with their colorful costumes, nomadic habits, and superb horsemanship, he compares to Arabs or Tartars.

Beyond adopting mannerisms of style that are reminiscent of his earlier writings, Irving portrays himself explicitly in *A Tour*. He presents his adventures as a journey of initiation, the progressive engagement between a man of the eastern states and Europe, with civilized habits and tastes, and the personnel and customs of a wild and forbidding country. He records his developing ideas as, from day to day, he gradually builds up a budget of informed opinion about the West. Within this scheme he arranges an order of climax that culminates in an exhilarating buffalo hunt, an event made even more exciting by the presence of bloodthirsty Pawnees in the region. Once the hunt is over, realities dictate that the official party's experience of frontier life must come to an end. The fatigues of travel and hunting have left the horses gaunt and weak. The young rangers who have escorted the party, "unaccustomed to the life of the prairies" (110), are demoralized and famished for civilized amenities like bread. Nor is Irving, as he portrays himself, unwilling to turn back toward Fort Gibson. Wayworn and exhausted, on the return march he hails as a "palace of plenty" (121) a frontier farmhouse whose occupant serves up a simple meal of boiled beef and turnips. With mixed seriousness and humor the author thus concludes his narrative of interinvolvement between East and West, the civilized and the wild. Having passed a full month in this setting, he now understands it better; and he also perceives himself anew, as by nurture not a frontiersman but simply himself, a cultivated visitor from the East.

Although Irving designed *A Tour* to develop as a whole the conjoined themes of initiation and self-discovery, he does not advance this interpretation obtrusively. Rather, he directs primary attention to the activities of the official party from day to day. Relying closely upon his journal entries from the 1832 tour, on several occasions he even carries over the convention of specifying the month and date, journal style, when beginning the account of a new day. By this simple means he suggests the faithfulness of his text to actual experience. Meanwhile, from chapter to chapter he mediates between craftsmanly shaping of the narrative and an easy willingness to introduce a variety of material, seemingly just as it occurred or came to notice.

Irving clearly placed *variety* high among his criteria for material to include in *A Tour*, for a keynote of the volume is miscellaneousness. Writing chapters that average fewer than two thousand words apiece, he permitted himself little space for elaboration but instead arranged the work as a medley of briefly sketched western scenes and topics. Anecdotes, dialogue, prose panoramas, recounted folk beliefs, details of diet, genre scenes—he slides from topic to related topic with a light touch. *A Tour* is suggestive, not exhaustive; in it he offers readers a little of everything. Undertaken to satisfy the public's wish for a book about the West by "Geoffrey Crayon," it was well-calculated to whet the appetite for another.

In the summer of 1834, while still at work on the "light volumes" that became *The Crayon Miscellany*,[7] Irving was presented an opportunity to begin a more challenging project of authorship about the recent history of the American West. This opportunity came in the form of almost importunate invitations from John Jacob Astor, the wealthy merchant and fur magnate, to prepare for publication an account of a commercial venture in which the old gentleman took much pride. Between 1809 and 1813, only a few years after the splendid explorations of Lewis and Clark, Astor had organized and underwritten an attempt to establish an American fur trading depot on the Pacific coast, at the mouth of the Columbia River. Though unsuccessful ultimately, this experiment in empire building had been boldly conceived and, Astor believed, was too little known. He urged Irving to write a book on the subject.

The author quickly discerned the merits of the prospective project. Having felt a desultory interest in the fur trade since youth, he found the Astor topic attractive simply for the congeniality of its subject matter. Moreover, the facilities for research and writing were unparalleled. Astor was ready to make available journals, correspondence, account books, inventories—a wealth of unpublished information to support an authoritative relation of the enterprise. Moreover, several participants in the venture were still available for consultation, and the younger merchants and frontiersmen who regularly stopped in at Astor's home could also provide assistance. The range and extent of source material within easy reach was almost daunting. Even so, Irving's labors in the archives of Spain had taught him the value of a centralized research collection to which he would enjoy unlimited access.

Astor was willing to pay Irving generously, but the prospect of direct remuneration from a wealthy man held no attraction for the author. A professional he was, but not a hack nor yet a sycophant. He made clear that, should he write the book, he would do so as an independent speculation, looking for profit to the arrangements he made with publishers in England and the United States. At present, his real impediment was simple lack of time. Engaged as he was in completing *The Crayon Miscellany* and in other employments, he could not perform by himself the careful study and collation of sources that would be necessary to set the subject in order. Yet, once this yeoman work was complete, he was confident of his ability "to dress it up advantageously, and with little labor, for the press."[8] He therefore suggested that a research assistant be engaged; and not surprisingly, Astor agreed at once. Irving now corresponded with an eligible nephew, Pierre Munro Irving, who was living in Toledo, Ohio, and secured his agreement to perform the necessary research. *The Crayon Miscellany* was months from completion, but the author thus set preparations in motion for the book that would follow it. Meanwhile he was in the process of buying the land he had admired near Tarrytown.

On 29 October 1834 Irving addressed a second letter to his nephew, explaining his preliminary conception of the Astor work and further defining the contribution Pierre would make to it. His summary of the unwritten book's contents, organization, and appeal is a remarkable statement, for it demonstrates his experienced ability to assess fully the possibilities latent in a new literary project. "My present idea," he wrote, "is to call the work by the general name of *Astoria*—the name of the settlement made by Mr. Astor at the mouth of Columbia River." He continued:

> Under this head to give not merely a history of his great colonial and commercial enterprise, and of the fortunes of his colony, but a body of information concerning the whole region beyond the Rocky Mountains, on the borders of Columbia River, comprising the adventures, by sea and land, of traders, trappers, Indian warriors, hunters, &c.; their habits, characters, persons, costumes, &c.; descriptions of natural scenery, animals, plants, &c., &c. I think, in this way, a rich and varied work may be formed, both entertaining and instructive, and laying open scenes in the wild life of that adventurous region which would possess the charm of freshness and novelty.[9]

In the two years that intervened between the date of this letter and the publication of *Astoria*, in October 1836, the author's plan for his work remained unchanged.

Irving's references to *Astoria* in the letters he wrote during this period almost invariably included the word "rich," or some derivative, as had his summary statement to Pierre ("a rich and varied work"). Whereas in *A Tour* he was serving up a once-over-lightly, in *Astoria* he projected a feast of information, a book dense with lore of all sorts. In April 1835 he reported to Peter Irving that Pierre was busy with his duties and that, even though he himself had not yet "taken hold of the subject," he had "no doubt I shall be able to make of it a rich piece of mosaic." Two months later he informed the same correspondent that Pierre, an "excellent pioneer," was still at work. He had now "rough-cast several of the chapters" himself, he added, and he was confident that "I shall make a rich and taking work of it." Progress was steady and satisfying, and on October 8 Irving informed Peter that he had already completed a first draft. Much remained to be done, but "merely in the way of enriching it by personal anecdotes, &c." A note of pleased satisfaction is perceptible in his 16 February 1836 letter wherein he reports to Peter that he is administering to the book manuscript that "last handling . . .

which, like the touching and toning of a picture, gives the richest effects."[10]

The wide range of subject matter in *Astoria* is the result of Irving's early decision that its inclusiveness should be virtually unlimited. Perhaps the repeated ampersands in his statement to Pierre indicate this intention most clearly. The range of his planned coverage bears comparision with the hardly more comprehensive instructions written by Thomas Jefferson to Lewis and Clark as they prepared to explore and report on this same transmontane region.[11] Even though the variety of the published book's contents validates Irving's characterization of it as a collection of "rambling anecdotes,"[12] it fulfills his intention to create in *Astoria* a compendium of frontier lore.

Initially and above all, of course, he conceived the work as a history of the "great colonial and commercial enterprise" launched by John Jacob Astor. Whereas he had regarded *A Tour* as a "light" book and published it diffidently, he viewed *Astoria* as, like *Columbus* and *Granada*, a *"make weight"* for his reputation.[13] The narrator of *Astoria* is predominantly businesslike and serious, as befits recounting events of national import. The speaker is not "I," the portrayed author in his subjectivity, but "we," the magisterial historian. At times this narrator comments on the "casual discrepancies" (72) among his conflicting sources. Elsewhere, solicitous to ensure comprehension of the relationship between simultaneous occurrences at widely separated locations, he summarizes earlier developments, ranges backward and forward in time as necessary, and in general visibly organizes the work. Dignified and in control, he is Washington Irving—the name that appears on the title page—rather than "The Author of *The Sketch Book*."

The narrative scheme of *Astoria* follows the "grand scheme" (4) of John Jacob Astor, suggesting through its structure the magnitude of the projector's undertaking but also the forces that doomed it to failure. In the first two-thirds of the book Irving portrays in succession the activities of two parties of men, the partners and employees of Astor's Pacific Fur Company. The first group, aboard the ship *Tonquin*, proceeds from New York to the mouth of the Columbia River and establishes a trading settlement there. The second, under Wilson P. Hunt, journeys across the plains and Rocky Mountains toward the same destination. Through chapter 40 (of sixty-one), *Astoria* traces these two widely diverging and then converging itineraries. Although by its sheer hemispheric scope it reveals the daring of the project, by protraying two small parties so far removed from each other, it also suggests the manifold potentialities for miscalculation and misadventure.

The final twenty-one chapters depart from the earlier simple pattern, suggesting through accelerating shifts of scene the bad faith, cross purposes, and lack of communication that together brought down the undertaking. Once the sea and land parties meet at Astoria and pass together the winter of 1811–1812, they attempt to strengthen their foothold in the region and to communicate with Astor in New York. Meantime the capitalist dispatches a second ship with supplies for the new colony. But from this point the portrayed coordination of effort between the various groups breaks down. The returning Astorians require ten full months to reach St. Louis, and Astor eventually learns of their safety only by chancing to read of it in a Missouri newspaper.

Following the account of this temporarily inspiriting discovery by the projector, given in chapter 51, Irving details the rapid disintegration of Astor's scheme. The far-flung enterprise takes on an anarchic life of its own, and the author's careful narration brings into relief the very confusedness of the events themselves. Timely communication over thousands of miles is impossible, so that the persons responsible for various components of the venture must direct their individual courses according to the limited information they possess. War with England breaks out, and amidst the ensuing uncertainty the individuals in charge at Astoria, British sympathizers, determine to abandon the fort and dispose of its contents to representatives of the rival North West Company. When H.M.S. *Raccoon* eventually arrives at Astoria to take possession, the ship's commander is informed that the fort has already been placed in British hands through commercial traffic. Astoria is renamed Fort George, and the undertaking of John Jacob Astor is at an end.

The overall structure Irving devised for *Astoria* entailed one awkward constraint: namely, that his focus on events as they occurred among various sets of characters in several parts of the world precluded sustained attention to John Jacob Astor. Only at points where the focus could naturally return to New York, as when the entire plan was being formed, when news of its progress reached that city, and when additional ships were dispatched, could the book's protagonist receive more than passing attention. These occasions were few. However, Irving was able to turn the infrequency of Astor's appearances to advantage. Having enlisted sympathy for his central figure early in the book by emphasizing Astor's patriotic aims, Irving shifted the scene back to New York only four times in the entire book. Yet he did not permit the reader to lose sight of the capitalist, whom he mentioned occasionally as correspondent, issuer of instructions or warnings, recipient of news, or expresser of resolute hopes. The entire effort, the product of Astor's own imagination, is one with which he identified absolutely. "Were I on the spot," he is quoted as writing to Wilson P. Hunt in March 1813, "and had the management of affairs, I would defy them all [*i.e.*, the North West Company]; but as it is, every thing depends upon you and your friends about you"(309). Separated though he is from the action, the portrayed Astor regards himself as the comrade of all those who share his vision and determination.

Irving represented the absence of his protagonist from the scenes of activity that concerned him so deeply as contributing to the failure of the enterprise. He noted that Astor "battled resolutely against every difficulty and pursued his course in defiance of every loss"(355), but clearly the projector could not carry out his plan single-handed. Based in New York, he had to rely on the sagacity and good faith of his subordinate partners in the field, not all of whom shared his zeal, his steady good judgment, or even his orientation in favor of American interests. The shape Irving imposed on *Astoria* thus reflects his understanding of the conditions that shaped the events he portrayed; so that, as he wrote in his introduction, "the work, without any labored attempt at artificial construction, actually possesses much of that unity so much sought after in works of fiction, and considered so important to the interest of every history"(4).

Of course, the apparent inevitability in the design of *Astoria* is the result of thoughtful analysis that led to the very "artificial construction" Irving seems here almost to deprecate. At the outset of his work on the book he had surveyed the material before him, identified the major themes implicit in it, devised an approach that would body these forth, and engaged Pierre to trace a thread of continuity along which he could arrange the discursive material that would lend the work its "richness." He managed to combine the writing of serious history in the narrative segments with openness elsewhere to material of all kinds, including what he once described to Peter as "those apocryphal details which are so improbable, yet so picturesque and romantic."[14] Like no other of his historical writings, *Astoria* combines without confusion or disharmony features of earlier volumes reflecting the author's tastes and sensibility and his graver aspects in an impartial judge and commentator.

Astoria stands alone among Irving's writings in one additional regard, its vigorous advocacy of a specific federal policy. Early in the work he placed the entire action in an international context of exploration, commerce, and competition for empire. Here he drew a contrast between "the keen activity of private enterprize," as represented by Astor, and "the dull patronage of government"(14) that, in failing effectively to support the initiatives of its citizens, frustrated its own best interests. In subsequent chapters he showed that, although Astor had communicated his plans to the United States government and received encouragement and assurances from President Thomas Jefferson, federal assistance was too little and too late to prevent the loss of the outpost. At the close of *Astoria*, therefore,

Irving looked to the future and foresaw the possibility of renewed international tension over the question of sovereignty. American pioneers consider the West "a grand outlet of our empire" (356), he pointed out, and they will be impatient of British claims to the contrary. The lesson of history is plain: having once let slip its opportunity to assert control over that tract of country, the United States government should actively advance its own claim. *Astoria* is in this regard a thesis history, favoring an activist stance by the federal government in fostering private enterprise and thereby extending its geographical influence.

In June 1836 Irving wrote to his nephew Pierre that he was "printing my book and completing my cottage slowly, and hope the former will contribute toward defraying the accumulated expenses of the latter."[15] His speculation in authorship to produce *Astoria* was yielding handsome results. The publishing arrangements he had made with Richard Bentley of London and Messrs. Carey, Lea, and Blanchard of Philadelphia were more than satisfactory, and he had taken up residence at the Roost well before the book was offered for sale. John Jacob Astor was pleased with the final product, and the reviewers praised the book far beyond the author's hopes. "In fact," he wrote again to Pierre in December, "I have heard more talk about this work, considering the short time it has been launched, than about any other that I have published for some time past."[16]

Irving's involvement with the American West as a theme for literary treatment was to yield one more book, an outgrowth of *Astoria*. During the several months in 1835 and 1836 when he was seeking "collateral lights" (4) for that work, he gathered information from persons whose familiarity with the Rocky Mountain region and westward postdated the 1813 termination of the Astor venture. Among these individuals was a military man of wide experience, Captain Benjamin Bonneville. An officer in the United States Army, Bonneville had been granted leave from duty in 1831 in order to fulfill a longstanding wish to explore the Rocky Mountain region while pursuing a campaign of fur trapping and trading there. He had badly overstayed his eighteen months' leave, and despite his efforts to communicate with headquarters to explain the situation, he was given up for lost and his name dropped from the army rolls. Now, having reported to his commanding officer and turned over the journals and maps he had accumulated, he awaited reinstatement.

Within the next few months Irving met Captain Bonneville twice again, once in Washington, where he came upon his informant at work preparing an account of his adventures for publication, and later in New York. At the latter meeting, in March 1836, Bonneville was seeking without success to find a publisher for his book manuscript. Irving's attentions to *Astoria* were now nearing completion, and in the unsaleable manuscript of his acquaintance he saw the potential for a sequel. Whatever its deficiencies from the publishers' point of view, the work was a detailed account of Bonneville's peregrinations, already organized. Irving calculated that, if supplemented from additional sources, a rewritten narrative of the Captain's adventures might prove a creditable offering under his own name.

Other considerations suggested the wisdom of purchasing and reworking the Bonneville manuscript. By this time Irving was rather well versed in the history and character of the remote territory the captain had visited, so no extensive background study would be required. And much curious material relating to western localities remained to be placed before American and English readers. For example, the customs and colorful personnel of the great fur trading companies that had vied for dominance in the Rocky Mountains in recent decades were but little known. Finally, the continuing struggle for control of the fur trade highlighted the question broached in *Astoria,* whether the United States or Great Britain would ultimately enjoy the benefits of possession in that territory. Acting on all these inducements, Irving purchased the manuscript from Bonneville for $1,000. With "commendable prudence," as R. W. Emerson termed it in "The American Scholar," this celebrated portrayer of European scenes was adding once more to his "merchantable stock" in native subject matter.[17]

As he composed *The Adventures of Captain Bonneville,* Irving made the book stylistically his own, but he also drew attention throughout to the personality of its chief source and central character. Bonneville's tastes and opinions on many topics receive treatment. Irving portrayed him less as a practical man of business than as a person of ardent temperament, to whom the Rocky Mountains are a "region of romance."[18] True, Bonneville had secured financial backing from New York investors and did engage in fur trapping and trading, on the whole unsuccessfully, but the author utilized this mercantile component of the captain's activity as occasion to portray his contacts with more purely "business" types, independent trappers and representatives of the fur companies. He dwelt on Bonneville's pleasant character—his *bonhommie,* his sense of humor, his curiosity, his admiration of natural beauty, his eye for the eccentric. In fact, the portrayed Bonneville faintly resembles Irving's representation of himself in *A Tour.* Perhaps a perceived kinship of spirit accounts for the author's comment in his introduction that something in the appearance of Captain Bonneville had "prepossessed me in his favor"(5). At any rate, the captain's account of his own adventures proved easy for Irving to work with, for it was written from a point of view akin to his own. The book portrays a neophyte's initiation to the wilderness, as had *A Tour,* but with Bonneville in the central role.

The Rocky Mountain exploits of Captain Bonneville and his party provided Irving an ample fund of adventures—skirmishes with Indians, maneuverings against rival traders, explorations—and the Captain's genial sense of humor supplied additional opportunities. The scene in which an Indian chief adroitly constrains Bonneville and his men to reciprocate again and again for the single gift of a horse; the quasi-judicial proceedings in which an obviously unoffending dog is judged guilty by his Indian owners of absconding with a valuable fur, and summarily executed—these droll incidents, for example, derive from the captain's manuscript. Bonneville's lively imagination was attuned to moods other than the comic. Almost a full chapter is devoted to an autobiographical tale of love and revenge related to him by Kosato, a renegade Blackfoot Indian. Irving likened the principals of this story to "the novel-read heroes and heroines of sentimental civilization" (79).

Like A Tour and also Astoria, Bonneville is diverse in its contents. The catholicity of his central character's interests would have virtually dictated this feature to Irving, had he not embraced it as a point for emphasis. Thus, when Bonneville chances upon a colony of beaver, several pages of paraphrased observations on that species follow. When he and his party come across a natural wonder such as the Great Tar Spring, of supposedly medicinal powers, a speculative discussion ensues. An overall pattern of expository or descriptive passages interpolated at the initial mention of the persons, peoples, scenes, or phenomena they illustrate characterizes this book as it had the earlier two.

However, in contrast to the simple and distinct main lines of action in those works, Bonneville utterly lacks a similar frame of continuity. As a matter of historical fact, at the time Captain Bonneville entered the Rocky Mountain trading region, he had formed only the most rudimentary of plans. Thereafter he guided his party's course, and changed course, as events dictated, dividing his followers into subgroups, losing some, later reuniting with others, crossing and recrossing the same territory until, after more than two years had passed, he returned to civilization. As a result, even if it recounted the travels only of Captain Bonneville and the persons associated with him, this book would have resisted the shaping Irving had given A Tour and Astoria. But while preparing the work he had secured information from several persons besides Bonneville, individuals who had visited the Rocky Mountain region at approximately the same time as he. The information obtained from these other veterans enhanced the authoritativeness of the account, and yet the portrayal of their activities exacerbated the problem of continuity. Once, perhaps in frustration with the tendency of his story to fly out in all directions, Irving referred to the book as "our wanderings about the

Far West"(126). These were "rambling anecdotes" with a vengeance, for they traced no line of development. He entitled the book not *The Adventures of Captain Bonneville*, as it has since become known, but in a manner to acknowledge its discontinuous character. The first American edition was issued as *The Rocky Mountains: or Scenes, Incidents, and Adventures in the Far West.*

Notwithstanding the obstacles he faced in attempting to shape *Bonneville*, Irving appears to have enjoyed writing this book even more than he had the two earlier western volumes. In *A Tour* he had been constrained by his plan to produce a deft and suggestive work rather than an exhaustive one, and also by the modest character of the action. In *Astoria*, "enriched" and enlarged by miscellaneous information though it was, his performance as narrator was governed by the role he chose as judicious historian and by the complexity of the story he told. By contrast, in writing *Bonneville* he felt free to work up his material to whatever extent he wished, adopting whatever tone his topics seemed to require, and shaping passages with regard to their effectiveness in themselves rather than as interlinked segments of some developing whole. The very diffuseness of the book in effect released him from the need to attempt developing in it a single controlling theme. He could present it as a loose arrangement of scenes and anecdotes, many substantial enough for treatment along lines he had followed in the early 1820s, when he had confined himself to writing sketches and tales. In fact, the effects he achieved from chapter to chapter in *Bonneville* often recall those in earlier works such as *Bracebridge Hall* and *Tales of a Traveller*. At the same time, the completed work was "*all true*," as he emphasized in a letter, "being based on journals" and other forms of firsthand reportage.[19] It was written with verve and attention to literary effect, but it possessed solid credentials as an authentic historical source.

Irving underlined the historicity of *Bonneville* by summarizing the intervening fortunes of individuals who had figured in *Astoria* and now reappeared in the later cast of characters. He devoted attention of this sort not only to major figures but also to individuals of lower station like Edward Rose, the "designing vagabond" (*Bonneville*, 118) who had served as guide and interpreter to the Astorians traveling westward until he elected to remain behind among the Crow Indians. The most important instance of his representing *Bonneville* as a sequel to *Astoria* is his portrayal of Nathaniel P. Wyeth, a New England man whom he represented as inheriting the business acumen and enterprising spirit of John Jacob Astor. In an appendix he detailed the innovative scheme of Wyeth to combine fur trading and salmon fishing along the Pacific Coast as a single business, noting that through his efforts, the New Englander "had once more reared the American flag in the lost domains of Astoria; and had he been enabled to maintain the footing he had so gallantly effected, he might have regained for his country the opulent trade of the Columbia, of which our statesmen have negligently suffered us to be dispossessed"(274). The language here strikingly recalls that in the concluding pages of *Astoria* where Irving advanced the political thesis of the work. Yet he chose not to emphasize these views in *Bonneville*, expressing them most forcefully in an appendix.

By the time *Bonneville* was offered for sale, five years after Irving's return to the United States, he had situated himself in the style of life he had envisioned in 1832. He had induced his brother Peter to return from Europe and take up residence with him at the Roost, which he was busy improving, and he looked forward to future literary activity at a more relaxed pace. Never, except when in Spain between 1826 and 1829, had he written so much for publication as he had in the past three years. The stimuli of tempting new opportunities for authorship, enjoyment of the material that occupied him, and confidence that his efforts would pay financially had led him to continue writing about the West until by 1837 that broad subject ranked second in bulk only to Spain among those he had treated.

The western frontier had served Irving well as a professional author. Not only did the sums he realized from arrangements to issue *A Tour, Astoria,* and *Bonneville* compare favorably with what he had obtained from earlier writings, but his performance as an author on western themes demonstrated his literary professionalism in a fuller sense. His varied experience as an essayist, fictionist, sketch writer, historian, and author of semihistorical "legends" and "chronicles" guided his judgment as he evaluated his topics' possibilities for treatment and then set out to realize them. His authorship of the three books was, after all, remarkably sure-handed. The works are all distinctly his own, yet the differing achievements they represent manifest his versatility. Deft, evocative, and pleasant, *A Tour* suggests an elegant personal essay in narrative form. Consciously architectonic, predominantly sober, historiographically orthodox, *Astoria* sets forth its wide-ranging subject matter in a manner calculated to emphasize its national significance. Various, unhurried, humorous, *Bonneville* resembles a portfolio of piquant sketches assembled to illustrate a common topic. Each book draws upon skills Irving had developed at earlier stages in his career, so that together they constitute a reprise or recombination of his several styles.

Irving wrote the western books when he was between the ages of fifty and fifty-three and in a state of physical and mental vigor he never enjoyed so fully thereafter. Following two years of dabbling as star contributor to the *Knickerbocker Magazine*, between 1839 and 1841, he accepted an appointment as United States minister to Spain, a position he occupied between 1842 and 1846 and in which he accomplished little as a writer. Upon returning to the United States, he set himself to the heavy but remunerative labor of revising his works for republication in a collected edition issued between 1848 and 1850. He added a *Life of Mahomet* (1850) to the list of his published books before addressing himself singlemindedly to what he had come to regard as the "crowning effort" of his career,[20] the five-volume *Life of George Washington* (1855–1859), which he completed only months before his death. In short, during the two decades that followed the western books, Irving remained relatively active as a writer, but his later periods of productivity were fitful, not always personally satisfying, and toward the last, notable more for the courage with which he toiled than for the quality of the results.

Irving never in his career wrote so much, so well as when he produced his contributions to the literature of the American West. Once dismissed as apocryphal romanticized history or uninspired hackwork, in recent years *A Tour, Astoria*, and *Bonneville* have begun to receive recognition as among the most artistically satisfying of his writings. The current of opinion is thus returning these works to the status they enjoyed when they first appeared. A contemporary reviewer for the London *Spectator* judged *Astoria* "the *chef d'oeuvre* of Washington Irving," for example, and in the United States no less demanding a critic than Edgar Allan Poe declared the same work a "masterly" performance.[21] The western books were the work of a professional—America's first professional man of letters—writing at the height of his powers.

Notes

1. Irving to Peter Irving, Washington, 16 June 1832, in Washington Irving, *Letters*, Volume 2, 1823–1838, ed. Ralph M. Aderman, Herbert L. Kleinfield, and Jenifer S. Banks (Boston: Twayne Publishers, 1979), 705. Cited hereafter as *Letters*.

2. Ellsworth's journal of his expedition has been edited by Stanley T. Williams and Barbara Damon Simison as *Washington Irving on the Prairie, or a Narrative of a Tour of the Southwest in the Year 1832* (New York: American Book Company, 1937).

3. Irving to Peter Irving, Washington City, 18 December 1832, in *Letters*, 2, 735.

4. Irving to Peter Irving, New York, 28 October 1833, in *Letters*, 2, 780.

5. Irving to Peter Irving, New York, 28 October 1833, in *Letters*, 2, 780.

6. Irving, *The Crayon Miscellany*, ed. Dahlia Kirby Terrell (Boston: Twayne Publishers, 1979), 7. Parenthetical page references to *A Tour* in the text that follows refer to this edition.

7. Irving to Peter Irving, New York, 25 May 1835, in *Letters*, 2, 825.

8. Irving to Pierre M. Irving, New York, 15 September 1834, in *Letters*, 2, 798.

9. Irving to Pierre M. Irving, New York, 29 October 1834, in *Letters*, 2, 802.

10. Irving to Peter Irving, [n.p., 17 April 1835]; New York, 10 June 1835; n.p., 8 October 1835; n.p., 16 February 1836, in *Letters*, 2, 818, 832, 843, 856. See also

the letter cited in the preceding note and Irving to Peter Irving, n.p., 24 August 1835 and 26 September 1835, in *Letters*, 2, 839, 842.

11. Jefferson to Meriwether Lewis, Washington, June 1803; quoted in Meriwether Lewis and William Clark, *History of the Expedition . . . to the Sources of the Missouri, Thence Across the Rocky Mountains, and Down the River Columbia to the Pacific Ocean*, eds. Nicholas Biddle and Paul Allen (New York: Amsterdam Book Company, 1902), 1, xxxiv–xl.

12. Irving, *Astoria, or Anecdotes of an Enterprize Beyond the Rocky Mountains*, ed. Richard D. Rust (Boston: Twayne Publishers, 1976), 193. Parenthetical page references to *Astoria* in the text that follows refer to this edition.

13. Irving to Colonel Thomas Aspinwall, Seville, 4 April 1829, in *Letters*, 2, 396.

14. Irving to Peter Irving, New York, 8 July 1835, in *Letters*, 2, 835.

15. Irving to Pierre M. Irving, [n.p., late June 1836], in *Letters*, 2, 873.

16. Irving to Pierre M. Irving, Tarrytown, December 12, 1836, in *Letters*, 2, 884.

17. Emerson, "The American Scholar," in *The Collected Works of Ralph Waldo Emerson*, vol. 1, *Nature, Addresses, and Lectures*, ed. Robert E. Spiller and Alfred R. Ferguson (Cambridge, Mass.: Harvard University Press, 1971), 60. In the quoted passage Emerson appears to be alluding to Irving's western journey that led to *A Tour on the Prairies*.

18. Irving, *The Adventures of Captain Bonneville*, ed. Robert A. Rees and Alan Sandy (Boston: Twayne Publishers, 1977), 14. Parenthetical page references to *Bonneville* in the text that follows refer to this edition.

19. Irving to Colonel Thomas Aspinwall, New York, 9 February 1837, in *Letters*, 2, 897.

20. Irving, *The Life of George Washington*, ed. Allen Guttmann and James A. Sappenfield (Boston: Twayne Publishers, 1982), vols. 4 and 5, 292.

21. The *Spectator* review is quoted in Pierre M. Irving, *The Life and Letters of Washington Irving* (New York: George P. Putnam, 1863), 3, 92; Poe, "Astoria," *Southern Literary Messenger*, 3 (1837), 64.

Washington Irving, the Nineteenth-Century American Bachelor

Jenifer S. Banks°

The theme of growing up and accepting adult responsibility is central to a study of American literature; and relationships between men and women are a central element in this maturing, as such different critics as Leslie Fiedler and Judith Fetterley have shown. Washington Irving's "Rip Van Winkle" is often cited as a peculiarly American example of flight from this responsibility. Fetterley has

° This essay was written specifically for this volume and is published here for the first time by permission of the author.

noted that in fact Irving borrowed this story from German folklore and set it in an American scene; but among his most significant additions is the character of Dame Van Winkle, whom he presents as the cause of Rip Van Winkle's flight into the Catskill Mountains. She is an "obstacle to the achievement of the dream of pleasure. . . . Significantly, Irving's tale connects the image of woman with the birth of America as a nation and with the theme of growing up."[1] As the voice of duty and obligation, she most clearly exemplifies Irving's imaginative use of women as a focus of those elements in society he wished to escape. This image of the oppressive power of women and of men's flight from them—both literally and imaginatively—is just one manifestation of a larger and more pervasive issue concerning commitment present throughout Irving's life. Whether writing for publication or more personally in his correspondence, he reveals himself as a prototype of the American male struggling to reconcile the conflict between freedom and adult responsibility, independence and social obligation, fantasy and reality. Irving was clearly attracted to women; but whatever their surface appearance, most of his imaginative projections of women reflect some aspect of the repressiveness associated with Dame Van Winkle. Similarly, in real life, Irving's circumscribed relationships with women reflect his flight from commitment and adult responsibility. But if Irving was singularly ambivalent about women, his reactions to them also reflect many of the contradictions inherent in the attitudes dominating American society in the early nineteenth century. Through his images of women and his relationships with them, he reflects the contemporary struggle between the appeal of the old ordered and hierarchical society and the call of the new republican egalitarianism, between the security of established institutions and the independence of the new American Adam.

Irving's lifelong ambivalence toward women is manifested in both his personal letters and his published writings in an unresolved tension between fantasy and reality. There can be no doubt that Irving was a lady's man. Whether at nineteen boasting to his friend Amos Eaton that he could "never be in company with a fine girl half an hour without falling in love,"[2] or some forty years later in Madrid playing "the old beau to a young belle [Cuban singer Leocadia Zamora]," (6 December 1844, 3:843), or relishing the memory of how beautiful a certain lovely widow, Mrs. Ellis, had once appeared at a New York ball (10 February 1844, 2:679), he clearly enjoyed this concept of himself. He preferred, however, to remain an uncommitted observer, maintaining carefully circumscribed relationships with women—usually considerably younger than he or "safely" married. Irving's lifelong struggle between the appeal and the threat of women, between fantasy and his sense of reality, is reflected in his confidence to his close

friend, Prince Dmitri Ivanovitch Dolgorouki, "Heavens! what power
women would have over us if they knew how to Sustain the attractions
which nature had bestowed upon them, and which we are so ready
to assist by our imaginations" (22 January 1828, 2:265). The same
ambivalence is implicit in his persona Geoffrey Crayon's observation
in "Wives": "It is appalling to those who have not adventured into
the holy state, to see how soon the flame of romantic love burns out
. . . in matrimony. . . . Men are always doomed to be duped, not
so much by the arts of the sex, as by their own imaginations. They
are always wooing goddesses, and marrying mortals."[3] Even as he
grew fearful of being lonely in his old age, Irving's observations often
included a wistfulness tinged with a certain cynicism. Reviewing his
life in his late fifties, Irving confided to his niece Sarah Storrow,
"God knows I have no great idea of bachelor hood, and am not one
of the fraternity through choice—but providence has some how or
other thwarted the warm wishes of my heart and the tendencies of
my nature in those earlier seasons of life when tender and happy
unions are made; and has protected me in those more advanced
periods when matrimonial unions are apt to be unsuited or ungen-
ial. . . ." (12 December 1842, 3:437).

Some have argued that at twenty-five he was permanently scarred
by the tragic death of his first real love, Matilda Hoffman, and then
kept running away from that pain. But, in a fifteen-year retrospective
letter to Mrs. Amelia Foster, Irving revealed that his flight was based
on more complex motives than grief alone. His relationship with her
epitomizes the conflict between the ideals of social responsibility and
individual freedom that influenced his relationships throughout his
life. He described his possible child-bride, who was only seventeen
when she died, as "a timid, shy, silent little being" with a "mantling
modesty . . . intuitive rectitude of mind . . . native delicacy . . .
exquisite propriety in thought, word & action" which he idolized.
"I felt at times rebuked by her superior delicacy & purity and as if
I were a coarse unworthy being in comparison" (April–May 1823,
1:738–39). However, if the idealized Matilda seemed unattainable as
a paragon of virtue, the real-life Matilda forced him to face the harsh
reality of the financial liability of a wife. In the same letter he
explained that on his return from his European Grand Tour he had
tried to devote himself to the study of law under Josiah Ogden
Hoffman, who had promised him a partnership in his firm and his
daughter in marriage if he could succeed in the profession. Irving
had recognized that law "in America is the path to honour and
preferment—to every thing that is distinguished in public life" (1:739),
but he confessed that he had been unable to surmount his "insuperable
repugnance" to it. "I had gone on blindly, like a boy in Love, but
now I began to open my eyes and be miserable. I had nothing in

purse nor in expectation. . . . I was in a wretched state of doubt and self distrust . . . [and] was secretly writing, hoping it would give me reputation and gain me Some public appointment" (1:739–40). Thus he faced apparently irreconcilable choices: marriage and the financial responsibilities of a dutiful husband, or freedom to write. Before he could "qualify" as a husband, Matilda died, and Irving described himself as drifting through New York society "without aim or object, at the mercy of every breeze; my heart wanted anchorage" (1:741). Because he could not escape from his own sense of unworthiness and inadequacy nor from the social pressure to succeed in some "useful and honourable application," Irving fled to England and Europe (1:742).

Irving spent almost half of his adult life in England and Europe, and his correspondence reveals that his long absences from home reflect his particular accommodations to the conflicting ideals in America of his day. His expatriation was determined in part by his pursuit of the middle-class dream of social advancement and financial security, in part by his more idiosyncratic pursuit of freedom, in part by his desire to serve as a literary and a political ambassador for America, and in part to avoid routine jobs. His decision to become a *professional* writer rather than to commit himself to a respected profession was a compromise he made with his society's materialistic definition of the self-made man and success.

Both the evolution and the content of *The Sketch Book* represent the coming together of fact and fiction in Irving's life, and they reflect his struggle with the conflicts among financial security, social status, and freedom. Irving initially submitted to family pressure and tried to help his brother Peter with the family business in Liverpool. He hated it; but because he was not immune to the value system that accorded a certain status to wealth and business acumen, he was devastated when they had to declare bankruptcy. "This was vile and sordid and humiliated me to the dust. . . . I felt cast down—abased—I had lost my *cast*—. . . I shut myself up from society—and would See no one." Feeling totally bereft of any social status, he then determined to avoid all financially secure but restrictive jobs by trying to "reinstate [himself] in the world's thoughts" through his writing. He therefore rejected both a lucrative clerkship in the navy that his brother William secured for him in America and an editorship that Walter Scott offered him in Edinburgh. In this way he produced *The Sketch Book* (April–May 1823, 1:742–43).

The popularity of both *The Sketch Book* and *Bracebridge Hall* confirms how successfully Irving catered to the dominant taste of his day. Through the persona of Crayon, a self-described wanderer and explorer since childhood, he appealed both to the American ideal of the individual who makes his own way alone and to the current interest in the romance of the past. But, even though Irving was writing for the market, the biographical facts reveal he was also pursuing his own conflicting ideals—a certain status in and freedom from society. Perhaps unintentionally Irving drew attention to the strong escapist dimension behind his apparently heroic decision to commit himself to being an author. In the "Preface" to the revised edition of *The Sketch Book* he recalled his real-life letter rejecting Scott's offer of the editorship: "My whole course of life has been desultory and I am unfitted for any periodically recurring task, or any stipulated labour of body or mind. . . . I shall occasionally shift my residence, and trust to the excitement of various scenes & objects to furnish me with materials" (20 November 1819, 1:570). In fiction he celebrated this free spirit in "The Author's Account of Himself" by immersing Crayon in the romance of the past and in "the charms of storied and poetical association" of Europe. He longed "to escape . . . from the commonplace realities of the present, and lose [himself] among the shadowy grandeurs of the past."[4] The autobiographical parallel with Rip Van Winkle becomes clearer.

In many ways Irving's life reflected that of the American male whom Fiedler described as "on the run—anywhere—to avoid 'civilization' which is to say the confrontation of a man and a woman which leads to the fall to sex, marriage and responsibility."[5] Irving's desire to escape civilization was based on a complex of related motives that incorporated but were larger than the fear of "confronting" a woman. She was an important part but only a part of the whole "civilization" that threatened him. He was often "on the run," ironically not like Huck Finn "lightin' out for the territory" but rather retreating into British and European society, and into history and myth. He thus avoided sustained involvement not only with American, British, and European women, but with American "civilization" and indeed with each "civilization" he visited. As Fetterley has argued, " 'Rip Van Winkle' is the . . . inevitable consequence of the massive suppressions required by Franklin's code of success." Each work represents a different kind of American success story. "If Franklin's book is a testament to how lucky it is to be an American, 'Rip Van Winkle' is perhaps the first registering of a disillusionment with America as idea and fact. . . ." (2).

But even thousands of miles away from home the free spirit is not totally free, and Irving, unlike Rip Van Winkle, was not able thus to "lose himself" in the past and slough off the influence of contemporary American thought and attitudes. His resistance to changes taking place in American thought is reflected in his conservative reaction to the contemporary reconsiderations of women's role in society. It is well-known that as a result of both the political and industrial revolutions in America, the role and status of women in the new republic came under considerable scrutiny in the late eighteenth and early nineteenth centuries. As Linda Kerber has argued, theoretically the republic depended on the virtue, intelligence, and responsibility of all of its citizens. Theoretically this was a step toward greater equality as the model republican woman became a figure of competence and independence, of self-confidence and rationality.[6] Irving seemed threatened by this movement toward women's independence and equality and the changes in the status quo that this philosophy implied. In his fiction as in his life, he reduced women to two basic and essentially adolescent classes: his positive category included figures of nurturing, sustaining supporters of men or figures of passive innocence and virtue; his negative category included the aggressor, the seductress and the albatross threatening or draining men. Despite their English subjects and their surface of sentimental fantasy, his essays on women in *The Sketch Book* and *Bracebridge Hall* reflect Irving's particular reactions to the changes and confusions in contemporary American thought and the cautionary tone of much contemporary American popular literature. Through Crayon, Irving explored several variations on the theme of women's latent power, and below the reassuring surface his images reveal his sense of inadequacy when faced with women's superior strength and powers of endurance.

The tension between Irving's idealized image of women and his sense of the reality of their power is evident in *The Sketch Book.* "The Widow and Her Son" presented an idealized version of the enduring strength of the republican mother. Since her husband died of grief at the young man's fate, only she survived to nurse her dying son. Crayon argued that she was sustained by a mother's love for her son which "transcends all other affections of the heart. It is neither to be chilled by selfishness—nor daunted by danger—nor weakened by worthlessness—nor stifled by ingratitude. . . . And if misfortune overtake him [her son] will be the dearer to her from misfortune" (87). Indeed, she was the only survivor since her husband had died of grief at their son's fatal illness. Ironically, in real life Irving dared not test his fantasy. When the family business in Liverpool went bankrupt, he expressed relief that his mother had died without learning of the financial disaster.

Similarly, "The Wife" reflects Irving's ambivalent feelings about the idealized republican wife. On the surface it romanticized the comfort a man can take from his supportive wife. Crayon assured Leslie, "Those disasters which break down the spirits of a man, and prostrate him in the dust, seem to call forth all the energies of the softer sex, and give such intrepidity and elevation to their character, that at times it approaches to sublimity" (22). The dominant images, however, are of Leslie's feelings of inadequacy as a provider and of

Mary's towering resilience as she fulfills Crayon's promise. Their happiness depends on her strength of will. In real life Irving explained to Mrs. Foster that after the bankruptcy of the family business in Liverpool he felt he could not marry because he was "involved in ruin. It was not for a man broken down in the world to drag down any woman to his paltry circumstances, and I was too proud to tolerate the idea of ever mending my circumstances by matrimony" (April–May 1823, 1:737). But his motivation may have been influenced by more than financial concerns. If the idealized portraits of mothers and wives seem to offer appealing images of acceptance and support, they also project an awesome and inherently claustrophobic power. As Rip Van Winkle learned, to succumb to them is to submit to an ultimately stifling society.

Kerber has shown that to counter this threat of women's domination both radicals and conservatives used popular literature to warn women against trusting their own emotions and instinct (206, 235). Similarly, Joyce Warren has illustrated that whatever the theoretical base for the new republican society, the rising "cult of the individual" was male-dominated as women's sense of independence was subverted by pressure to establish their social status through marriage and their virtuous reputation through devotion to the well-being of the male. Despite the efforts of women's rights advocates such as Lucy Stone, Susan B. Anthony, and Elizabeth Cady Stanton, the "cult of the lady" emphasized "submissiveness, piety, purity and domesticity."[7]

Irving also imitated current didactic literature as he appealed to domestic responsibility, religion, and even nature to shore up the status quo. On the issue of women the tone of *Bracebridge Hall* is rather more dogmatic than the more sentimental *The Sketch Book*. The ultra-conservative Crayon presented his ideal couched in terms of female submission and self-control precluding any maturing or self-development. In "Wives" he argued that it is the woman's responsibility to sustain romantic love in a marriage by maintaining the girlish charms that originally made her so attractive—"the chariness of herself and her conduct," "the same niceness and reserve in her person and habits," "a freshness and virgin delicacy"; she must "protect herself from that dangerous familiarity, that thorough acquaintance with every weakness and imperfection incident to matrimony" (46–47). Just as Irving had seriously considered marriage only with Matilda Hoffman and Emily Foster, both considerably younger than he, so Crayon's image of marriage is far from a union of equals. The distinct roles of husband and wife are clear, sanctioned not only by tradition but also by the church. He closed his "musings" by citing Jeremy Taylor's sermon on the wedding ring: for the man love and duty, for the woman reverence and obedience. "He provides, and she dispenses; he gives commandments, and she rules by them;

he rules her by authority, and she rules him by love; she ought by all means to please him, and he must by no means displease her" (47).

Conservatives were particularly opposed to romantic fiction which offered models of women who dared to trust their own feelings and instincts to break out of the traditional boundaries. Irving supported his advocacy of women's social submissiveness by focusing on the laws of nature to justify their present position. Through Crayon he countered his fear of women's hidden superior strength with more sentimental but evocative images of their vulnerability. In "The Broken Heart" he emphasized that while the conventions of society kept them economically dependent on men, the laws of nature held them emotionally dependent on men. A woman's *raison d'être* is the love of a man. This was her basic attraction. "Man is the creature of interest and ambition. His nature leads him forth into the struggle and bustle of the world. . . . But a woman's whole life is a history of the affections. The heart is her world . . . and if unhappy in her love, her heart is like some fortress that has been captured, and sacked, and abandoned, and left desolate." Without love "the great charm of existence is at an end" (56–57).

Irving wrote for a living, so his appeal to the majority through popular themes is to be expected, but his private life and correspondence reveal that he held to the conservative position for years after the publication of *The Sketch Book* and *Bracebridge Hall*. This is reflected within his own immediately personal circle in his reaction to Mary Shelley, the poet's widow. During the period 1823 to 1830 she showed sustained interest in Irving; he responded with disgust and determined evasion. This may have been because in general he resisted aggressive women or, as Ralph Aderman has suggested, "because he was unwilling to associate with someone whose unconventional behavior had provoked scandal and gossip."[8] Several years later Irving drew on the ladies of the Spanish court to vividly emphasize real-life warnings to the women of his family of the price women paid when they dared to venture beyond the natural, if proscriptive, roles of dutiful mother and wife. He particularly condemned the Infanta Luisa Carlota, the young queen's aunt, for participating in the public arena. Irving saw her as a woman of "strong passions and restless ambition" whose scheming nature and disappointment at her failure to marry her son to the queen first "mortified her pride and exasperated her temper" so that her looks began to fade and she suffered "a kind of fever of the mind" which "acting upon an extremely full, plethoric habit, hurried her out of existence" at thirty-nine. From Irving's perspective her arrogance was duly punished as she lay in state, "in a Gala dress, . . . the face livid and bloated with disease," reduced to the gaze and contempt of the "unmannered populace" (9 February 1844, 3:675). He had also condemned the Queen Regent for violating all natural laws because as a widow of the King she had abused her regal position and her woman's role by plotting both in Spain and in France to undermine the Spanish constitution. As a mother she indulged in even more unnatural behavior by establishing a "scandalous connexion" with one of the royal bodyguards and thus neglecting "her sacred duties to her legitimate children" (2 September 1842, 3:309). On her return Irving interpreted her aging physical appearance and her subdued spirit as signs of decline due to her unnatural behavior. While he explicitly used these women to moralize on royal grandeur and morality, he also exploited them to warn his women readers against any show of independence they might be contemplating.

Irving was often attacked as unpatriotic because of his lengthy absences abroad, and throughout his life he confessed that he longed for the "storied and poetical association" found in Britain and Europe but missing from America. However, as an expatriate author and politician he served his country as it strove to distinguish itself from its European and British heritage. His ambivalent reactions to the seduction of the old established European cultures and the appeal of the fresh young Republic are most often and vividly reflected in his contrasting portraits of European and American women. As a young man he responded most obviously to their sensuality and sexuality. At twenty-one Irving was clearly fascinated and repelled by the various forms of "immodesty" he saw in European women. In a representative letter to his friend Beebee his fascination emerges in his long and detailed descriptions, and his revulsion in the extravagance of his language. Every elaboration to his contemporaries on the sensual attractions in Europe is accompanied by refrain-like assurances of superior American morality and his attempts to keep his American morals "as untainted as possible from foreign profligacy." Delighted by the performance of French female dancers, he indulged in a detailed description of their "flesh colored habit that is fitted exactly to the shape and looks like the skin . . . their figures are perfectly visible" through the muslin dresses which, flying up, "discovers their whole person. . . ." But he assured Beebee, "my american notions of delicacy & propriety are not sufficiently conquerd for me to view this shameless exposure of their persons without sentiments bordering on disgust." His particular contempt was held for the married women who were "often *themselves the assailants*, . . . [throwing] out a lure with the most consummate address" (18 September 1804, 1:78–80).

As the more mature Irving recognized the conflict between his fantasies and the realities of Europe, he recorded the immorality he saw with resigned disappointment. He had once been deeply enough moved by a young bride in a tableau of Murillo's *Virgin of the Assumption* to describe it as "more like a vision of Something Spiritual and celestial than a representation of any thing merely mortal; or rather it was woman . . . approaching to the Angelic nature" (22 January 1828, 2:265). Fourteen years later he saw the same lady with her daughters, flaunting her younger lover at the theatre. Disappointed, he mused, "Time dispells charms and illusions. . . . She may have the customs of a depraved country and licentious state of society to excuse her; but I can never think of her again in the halo of feminine purity and loveliness that surrounded the Virgin of Murillo" (18 October 1842, 3:357).

While Irving was threatened by the open intrigue of the Europeans, he felt secure, if bored, with the unworldly American ladies who, in their apparent simplicity, seemed harmless. Social bias, which ridiculed the "Learned Lady," and social practice, which limited female education, discouraged women from much public display of independent thought. As a petulant twenty-four-year-old, Irving wrote from Richmond, Virginia, to Mary Fairlie mocking the fashion for reading romances and complaining about the "novel-read damsels. . .[,] the tender hearted fair ones [who] think you absolutely at their command—they conclude that you must of course be fond of moonlight walks—and rides at day break and red hot strolls in the middle of the day . . . and 'Melting hot—hissing hot' tea parties—and what is worse they expect you to talk sentiment. . . ." He had gone to Richmond to observe the trial of Aaron Burr, and he praised the ladies for their support of Burr, for their "compassion" which "results from that merciful—that heavenly disposition implanted in the female bosom, which ever inclines in favour of the accused & the unfortunate" (7 July 1807, 1:244–45). Even while he joked that their unworldliness "exalted" them ever higher in his estimation, he celebrated the laws of nature that had made women all feeling and very little thought and thus powerless.

Even in his maturity Irving rarely recognized women for their intellect. In his descriptions of the American and European women he met in the social scene in Madrid, he repeated the same accolades, reflecting admiration for only the most superficial qualities: affable, engaging, sensitive, graceful, and conversable. His references to women's intellect were always brief, almost asides. He valued one of his closest friends, Mrs. O'Shea, because she was "of good understanding and the kindest and most amiable manners" (12 March 1844, 3:692). When he first met Madame Calderón, he barely acknowledged her "lively" book, *Life in Mexico*, emphasizing rather William H. Prescott's *Conquest of Mexico*, in which he had been "deeply interested and highly pleased" (7 January 1844, 3:645). He subsequently came to appreciate her as much for her "very good humor" and "good spirits" as for her intelligence (13 April 1844, 3:720). In his letters to his sister and nieces describing Spanish politics, he was equally condescending, assuming their interests were restricted to the romance and excitement of the events. He promised to pursue themes from Spanish history for his sister Catharine Paris "as it will be carrying on a living historical romance for her gratification. . . ." (26 November 1842, 3:414). He was patronizing even to his beloved niece, Sarah Storrow: "I do not wonder that you are . . . disposed to think hardly of Espartero for the measures he has taken to suppress the insurrection: you would not have a womans feelings if you did not. But you must not believe all that you read in the newspapers. . . . I will endeavor in some future letter to give you a key to the mysteries of Spanish politics. . . ." (5 January 1843, 3:446). His highest praise went to those women who exercised their abilities to maintain their homes, their families, or Irving himself. He respected the Duchess of Berwick primarily because she had been able to restore her husband's "immense wealth" after his estates had been ruined by poor management (16 March 1844, 3:695). His dearest friend in Spain was his "fair neighbor and countrywoman," Madame Albuquerque, whose strongest appeal for him was that she acted "the part of a niece towards" him (19 January 1844, 3:649). She helped him organize his apartments, arrange official dinner parties, and let him accompany her with her children on rides to the country.

Jeffrey Rubin-Dorsky has noted that during his earlier stay in Spain the idea of an earthly paradise had become central in Irving's thinking and writing, but such an Eden had eluded him until he found the Alhambra. Irving rejoiced, "Behold for once a day-dream realized."[9] Never again did he find what Rubin-Dorsky defined as a paradise "commensurate with his capacity for wonder," an ideal retreat in a timeless place like this where historical fact, mystery, and myth are accepted as equally valid and essentially interchangeable by its inhabitants.[10] It was the ideal retreat that demanded nothing from him. From the balcony of the Hall of Ambassadors he used a pocket telescope to observe both nature and an alameda, or public walk, immediately below. Irving recalled, "It was a moving picture of Spanish life and character, which I delighted to study. . . . I was thus in a manner, an invisible observer, and, without quitting my solitude, could throw myself in an instant into the midst of society,— a rare advantage to one of somewhat shy and quiet habits, and fond, like myself, of observing the drama of life without becoming an actor in the scene" (Alhambra, 71). Significantly, this is a paradise with virtually no women, certainly none making any demands on him. He could fantasize about "the white arm of some mysterious princess beckoning from the gallery, or some dark eye sparkling through the lattice" (Alhambra, 32–33), or he could observe the colorful squatters like the little old Cockle-queen. Mostly he allowed himself to be attended by Tia Antonia, the custodian of the Alhambra, and plump Dolores, his particular servant.

Only at Sunnyside did he reach anything like this domestic security. Having voluntarily undertaken the support of several family members there, he had created a home for himself and accepted the responsibilities of a family man without the inconvenience of a wife. Sometimes he chafed under the financial obligation of this arrangement, but mostly he relished the idea of himself as *père de famille*. Just as Rip Van Winkle returned from his dream, so did Irving. Although he could never fully escape the social and political pressures of the day, he could retreat to his "little paradise on earth" (5 November 1842, 3:370). While in Madrid, chafing to be at Sunnyside, he had come to appreciate that he had maintained a distanced posture which had influenced most aspects of his life. He confided in Sarah Storrow, "Indeed I have been for so much of my life a mere looker on in the game of society that it has become habitual to me. . . ." He acknowledged that in his youth his "imagination was always in the advance, picturing out the future and building castles in the air, now memory comes in the place of imagination" to cast a soft light over the past (28 March 1845, 3:924). He ended his life at Sunnyside, absorbed by the past of his and America's mythic hero, George Washington, and "spoiled . . . by living continually in the bosom of a family surrounded by affectionate beings who cherished" him (29 May 1842, 3:303). Surely this was what he had been preparing himself for all of his life: surrounded by women, unwilling to let go totally of the public world and free to escape into the past whenever he chose.

Notes

1. Judith Fetterley, *The Resisting Reader: A Feminist Approach to American Fiction* (Bloomington: Indiana University Press, 1978), 3.

2. Washington Irving, *Letters*, ed. Ralph M. Aderman, Herbert L. Kleinfield, and Jenifer S. Banks (Boston: Twayne Publishers, vol. 1, 1978; vol. 2, 1979; vols. 3 and 4, 1982), 15 December 1802, 1:6. Subsequent references are given in the text with the date of each letter followed by the volume and page number.

3. Washington Irving, *Bracebridge Hall, or The Humourists: A Medley by Geoffrey Crayon, Gent.*, ed. Herbert F. Smith (Boston: Twayne Publishers, 1977), 43–44, 46.

4. Washington Irving, *The Sketch Book of Geoffrey Crayon, Gent.*, ed. Haskell Springer (Boston: Twayne Publishers, 1978), 9.

5. Leslie A. Fiedler, *Love and Death in the American Novel* (Cleveland: World Publishing Co., 1960), xx–xxi.

6. Linda K. Kerber, *Women of the Republic: Intellect and Ideology in Revolutionary America* (Chapel Hill: University of North Carolina Press, 1980), 189, 231.

7. Joyce M. Warren, *The American Narcissus* (New Brunswick: Rutgers University Press, 1984), 6–11.

8. Ralph M. Aderman, "Mary Shelley and Washington Irving Once More," *Keats-Shelley Journal*, 31 (1982), 24–28.

9. Washington Irving, *The Alhambra*, ed. William T. Lenehan and Andrew B. Myers (Boston: Twayne Publishers, 1983), 7.

10. Jeffrey Rubin-Dorsky, "*The Alhambra:* Washington Irving's House of Fiction," *Studies in American Fiction*, 2 (Autumn 1983), 179.

INDEX

Entries listed in capital letters are the names of characters from the writings of Irving and other authors mentioned in the text.